Legal Terminology and Transcription

Dorothy Adams
Professor Emeritus, Department of Business
Colby-Sawyer College
New London, New Hampshire

Margaret A. Kurtz, Ed.D.
Professor, Department of Business
Colby-Sawyer College
New London, New Hampshire

Series 90 shorthand written by
Jerome P. Edelman

GLENCOE

Macmillan/McGraw-Hill

Lake Forest, Illinois Columbus, Ohio
Mission Hills, California Peoria, Illinois

SPONSORING EDITOR: Barbara N. Oakley
DESIGN SUPERVISOR: Karen T. Mino
PRODUCTION SUPERVISOR: Frank Bellantoni
INTERIOR DESIGN: A Good Thing, Inc.
COVER ILLUSTRATOR: Manny Leite

Library of Congress Cataloging in Publication Data

Adams, Dorothy, date
Legal terminology and transcription.
Includes bibliographical references.
1. Legal secretaries—United States—
Handbooks, manuals, etc. 2. Law—United States—
Terms and phrases. I. Kurtz, Margaret A., joint
author. II. Title.
KF319.A3 340'.1'4 79-28733
ISBN 0-07-000330-0

Legal Terminology and Transcription

Imprint 1991

Send all inquiries to: Glencoe Division, Macmillan/McGraw-Hill, 936 Eastwind Drive, Westerville, Ohio 43081.

6 7 8 9 10 11 12 13 14 15 RRD-C 00 99 98 97 96 95 94 93 92 91

Preface

Legal Terminology and Transcription is designed to prepare students for interesting secretarial positions within the legal profession. The ability to take a lawyer's dictation and transcribe it accurately requires the mastery of a specialized vocabulary and a knowledge of points of style that are distinctly legal in character. With its wide coverage, this skill-building text develops the student's competence through a variety of instructional materials.

ORGANIZATION

Legal Terminology and Transcription consists of seven units containing ten lessons each. Each unit presents an actual case and includes all types of interrelated communications concerned with that case. Memos, letters, court papers, and other legal documents from different law firms have been included. The material selected provides practice in terms used in the following types of cases: tax evasion, divorce, insurance (auto negligence), drug smuggling, probate, corporations, and equity (lease violation).

Each lesson is divided into three parts. "Building Your Legal Vocabulary" helps the student toward a mastery of legal terminology through word studies that provide definitions of terms encountered in the dictation material. Exercises aid in constructing fluent outlines by a study of shortcuts and word beginnings and endings.

"Building Your Legal Transcription Skill" gives transcription aids in the form of guides to punctuation, capitalization, number usage, Latin and French words and phrases that are commonly used, legal collocations or expressions that have come to have specific legal meanings, and correct methods of typing citations.

"Building Your Legal Dictation Proficiency" provides the connected matter for dictation practice along with previews of the material. In this part the student will practice dictation given by five different lawyers in the fictitious firm of Greenberg, O'Brien, Mason & McCann.

SPECIAL FEATURES

As laws differ from state to state and change from time to time, so may the ways of handling cases vary according to the particular time or place in which they occur. In addition, government agencies change and a lawyer may be in the position of dealing with one bureau initially and with a different bureau as the situation develops. However, the basic issues that necessitate the services of attorneys as well as the terms used by attorneys remain fairly constant.

Legal forms and wording as well as styles for typing documents will also vary throughout the nation, and the legal secretary must always be guided by local practice. *A Uniform System of Citation,* published by the Harvard Law Review Association, was used in this text as a general guide. However, some of the contributors have used other citators and several different styles are represented. The legal secretary should be familiar with the variety of acceptable styles, remembering at the same time that a single consistent style should be followed in each case.

ACKNOWLEDGMENTS

We wish to thank the lawyers who supplied the case material that made this book possible. We are also indebted to Sister Jeannette Vezeau, C.S.C., for the use of her unpublished doctoral thesis, "A Study of Legal Terminology Pertinent to the Educational Preparation of the Legal Secretary," (Boston University, 1969); to Marjorie Keaton of the M. J. Neeley School of Business of Texas Christian University, who acted as consultant on many points of legal style; to F. Graham McSwiney, attorney, who reviewed the complete text; and to Gwendolyn Alexis, attorney, who acted as consultant regarding the styles of citations.

Dorothy Adams

Margaret A. Kurtz

Contents

UNIT

I Tax Evasion

John and Doris Harper, Petitioners
v.
Commissioner of Internal Revenue, Respondent

Criminal actions or lawsuits are those in which the government of the nation or of a state is the plaintiff who charges the defendant of violating a law and thus committing a crime against the people.

Civil actions or suits are those in which the plaintiff brings suit against the defendant to secure compensation for a private wrong or loss or to obtain a court order for the defendant to do or not to do a thing.

This case concerns federal prosecution in a criminal action in which John and Doris Harper were charged with evasion of income taxes over a period of 12 years. Such cases are tried in a tax court of the United States.

In order to recover a fine imposed as a result of this suit, the United States subsequently instituted a civil action against the defendants.

The attorney for the defendants is James E. McCann, Esq.

Lesson 1

BUILDING YOUR LEGAL VOCABULARY

Shortcuts Shortcuts for 50 frequently used words are introduced in the first five lessons. To increase your speed and fluency, practice these common words until writing them becomes automatic.

accident 

administer 

affidavit 

alimony 

allow 

amend 

appeal 

arbitrate 

criminal 

indict 

Word Study

 **attorney** A legal agent qualified to act for a person bringing suit or a defendant in legal proceedings.

 **cocounsel** One of the two or more legal advisers or attorneys assigned to a case.

 **counsel** A legal adviser or attorney.

 **internal revenue** Relating to income tax or federal taxation.

 **retainer** A fee paid in advance to a lawyer for advice or services to be rendered.

 **trial** A formal examination of evidence before a court of law to determine the facts, apply pertinent law to those facts, and thus reach a determination on the legal issues.

BUILDING YOUR LEGAL TRANSCRIPTION SKILL

Transcription Aid

Transcription Aids introduced in the first 63 lessons cover important rules for punctuation, number usage, capitalization, the compounding of words, and the use of the possessive case. For quick reference, consult the Index of Transcription Aids in the back of this text.

Comma or Semicolon in Compound Sentences

☐ Use a semicolon between the two independent clauses of a compound sentence when the coordinating conjunction is not expressed.

> I am enclosing a photocopy of the letter from the Regional Commissioner; the original, I believe, is in Mr. Harper's possession.

☐ Use a comma before the coordinating conjunction in a compound sentence, but substitute a semicolon if either or both clauses are subdivided by commas unless no misreading is likely to occur.

> I would appreciate an immediate reply to this letter, but in the meantime I will attempt to contact the Regional Office at Boston.

> As you realize, this is not the first case of this type in which I have been involved; and I must consider that the possibility of a criminal trial is great at this time.

Typing Citations

Citations are references to laws or other cases that support claims in a current case. The attorney will dictate the necessary citation to the legal secretary. Although it is the attorney's responsibility to dictate the citation correctly, it is the secretary's responsibility to transcribe it accurately and exactly as it has been dictated and to abbreviate correctly. The importance of typing a citation correctly cannot be stressed enough, since it refers to the authority for the statement of law. The citation must be clear enough so that the reader can find the work cited. An experienced secretary will verify the citation by looking up each case cited to see that all quotations are correct and that names are spelled correctly.

Although general rules for typing citations and citing statutory material, reports, books, periodicals, newspapers, and legal encyclopedias will be briefly covered in succeeding lessons, every legal secretary should have these four books for ready reference:

U.S. Government Printing Office Style Manual, rev. ed., U.S. Government Printing Office, Washington, 1973.

How to Use Shepard's Citations, Shepard's Citations, McGraw-Hill Book Company, Colorado Springs, CO, 1971.

A Uniform System of Citation, Harvard Law Review Association, Gannet House, Cambridge, MA.

Price & Bitner, *Effective Legal Research*, 4th ed., Little, Brown & Co., Waltham, MA, 1970.

BUILDING YOUR LEGAL DICTATION PROFICIENCY

Preview

accountant 

compensation 

imminent 

net worth 

real estate 

Register of Deeds 

remuneration 

thereon 

Reading and Writing Practice

1. MR. JOHN HARPER, RFD 2, CONCORD, MA 01742

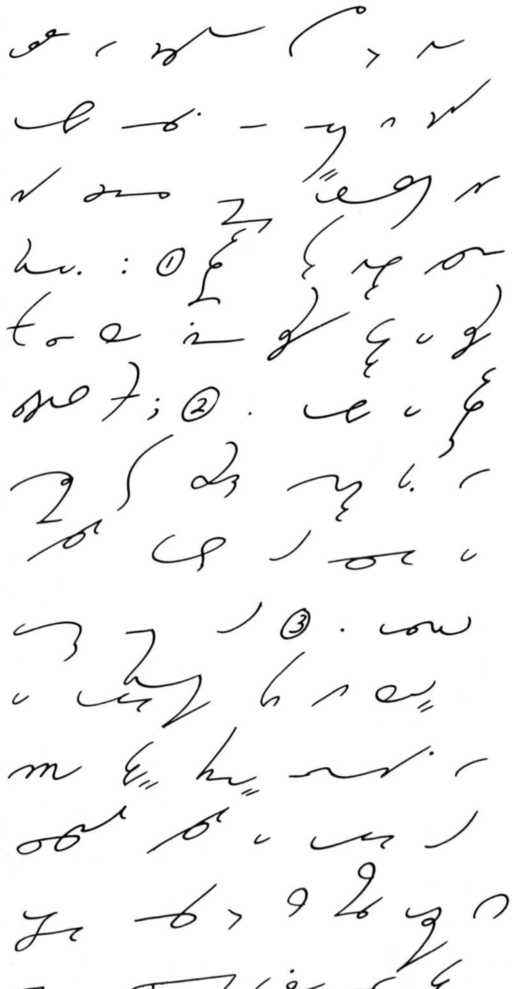

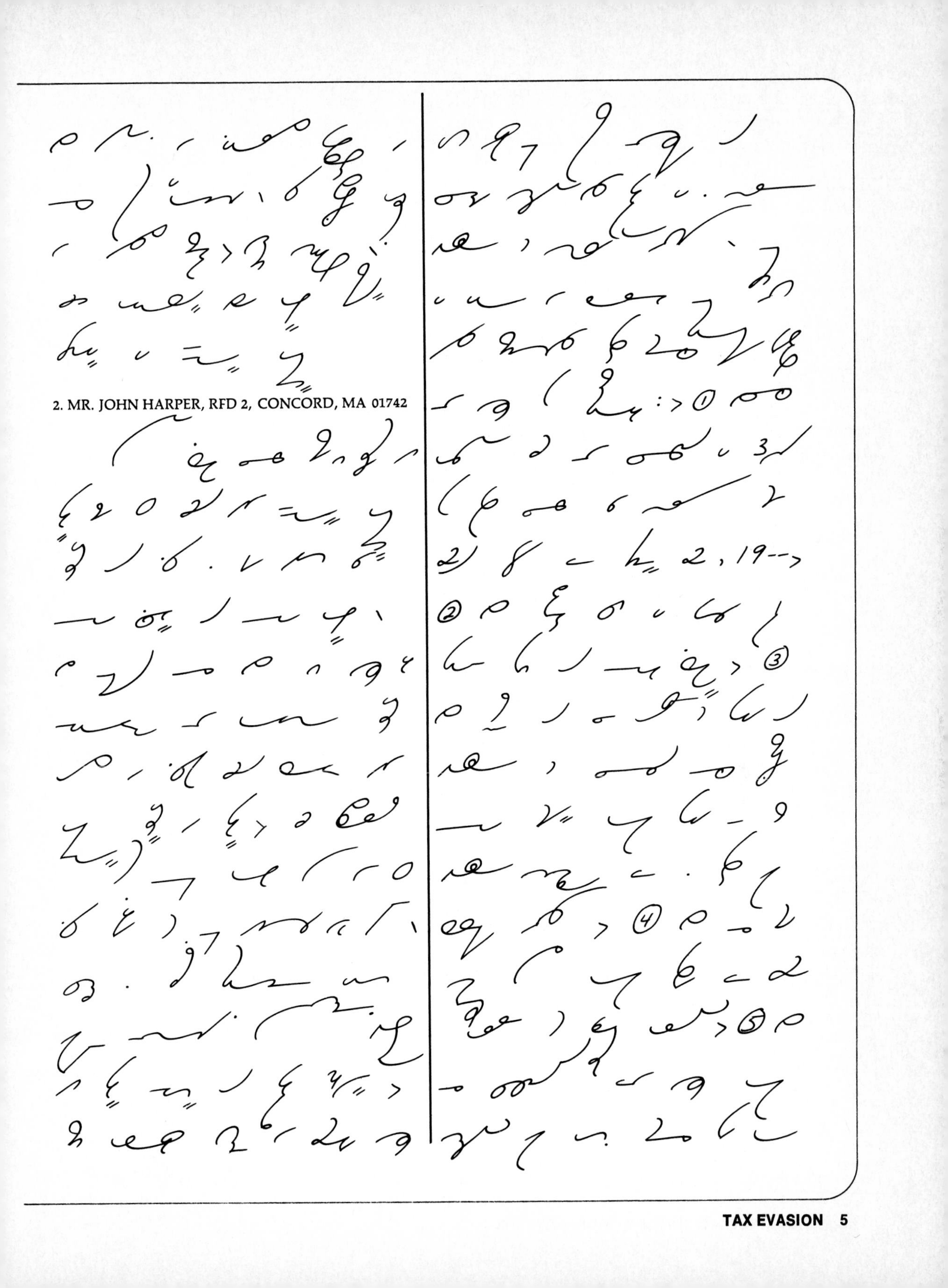

2. MR. JOHN HARPER, RFD 2, CONCORD, MA 01742

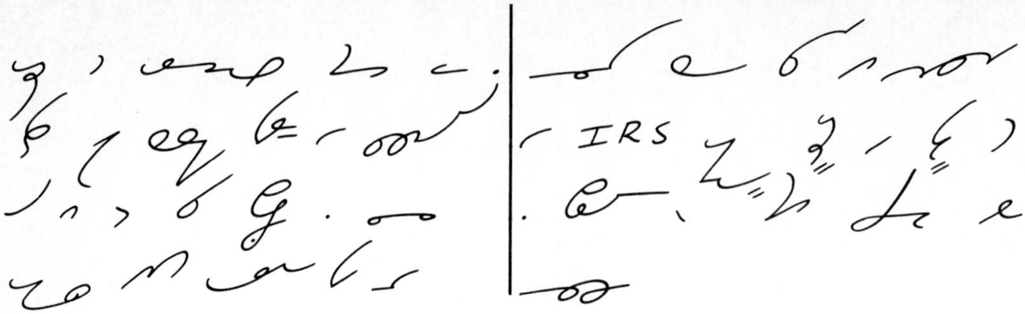

Lesson 2

BUILDING YOUR LEGAL VOCABULARY

Shortcuts

bankrupt	corporate
beneficiary	court
bureau	covenant
certificate	declaration
complaint	defendant

Word Study

defense Denial, answer, or pleas by the defendant; an argument in support or justification.

disposition A final settlement or verdict; final sentence or dismissal.

civil Relating to the state or to citizens.

contingent Possible but not certain to happen; dependent on something else.

criminal Relating to an offense punishable by law.

defendant A person required to make answer in a legal action of suit.

felony A serious crime punishable by death or by imprisonment in a state or federal prison for more than one year.

BUILDING YOUR LEGAL TRANSCRIPTION SKILL

Transcription Aid

Restrictive and Nonrestrictive Clauses

☐ A *restrictive* (or essential) adjective clause is one that is necessary to identify, define, or in some way restrict the meaning of the noun it modifies; therefore, it should not be set off by commas. (Such clauses properly begin with *that* or *who*, but occasionally the dictator will prefer to use *which*; the secretary must be alert to the idea that is intended.) If the clause is not necessary to the meaning of the sentence, it is *nonrestrictive* (or nonessential) and should be set off by commas.

Please send me a doctor's certificate that outlines the extent of your disability. (Restrictive.)

Enclosed is a computation of what the Department considers to be your civil liability for tax, which is entirely separate from any criminal phase. (Nonrestrictive.)

Restrictive and Nonrestrictive Appositives

☐ If the appositive identifies the noun with which it is in apposition, do not use commas. Nonrestrictive (or nonessential) appositives are set off by commas.

The defendant, Frank Smith, made several statements about the matter. (Only one defendant; therefore, appositive is nonrestrictive.)

The defendant Frank Smith made several statements about the matter. (More than one defendant; therefore, *Frank Smith* identifies which defendant.)

Legal Collocations Certain collocations or expressions have come to have specific legal meanings. Five such expressions are presented in every other lesson. Increase your understanding of legal terminology by learning their meanings.

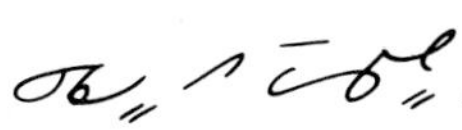

Answer to Interrogatories A legal document that answers a series of formal written questions made by a party to a suit.

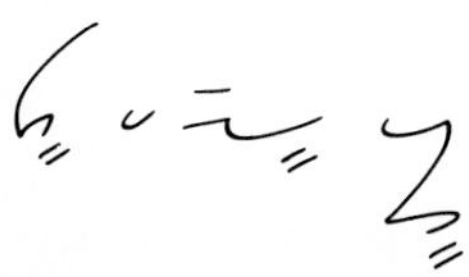

Bureau of Internal Revenue The federal government bureau that collects taxes on income.

civil action A proceeding in court by which one demands or enforces one's private right, as distinguished from a criminal prosecution for an offense against the public.

joint and several Together and separate.

power of attorney A legal instrument authorizing another to act as one's agent or attorney.

BUILDING YOUR LEGAL DICTATION PROFICIENCY

Preview

commissioner	regional
contingent	retained
diabetes	taxpayers
enforcement	ulcer
herewith	wheelchair
internal revenue	wherein
pending	Xerox

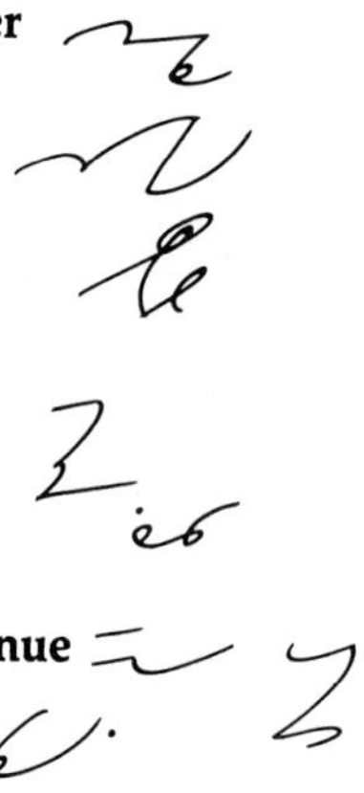

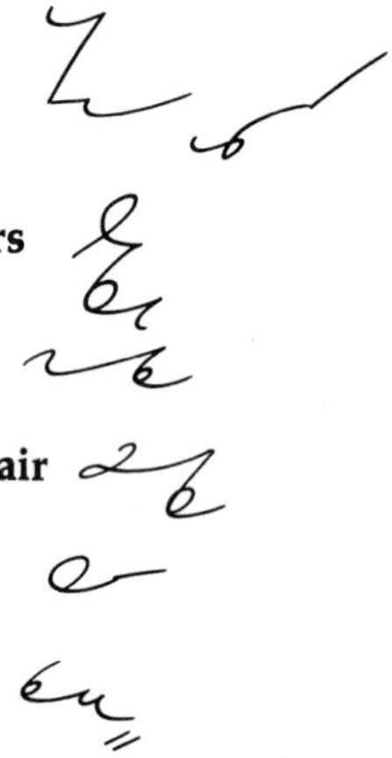

Reading and Writing Practice

3. CONTINGENT FEE STATEMENT

Boston, Massachusetts

This is to certify that I have not entered into a contingent or partially[1] contingent fee agreement for the representation of John Harper and Doris Harper before the Treasury[2] Department in the matter of income taxes under the terms of a Power of Attorney filed with the Treasury[3] Department herewith.

James E. McCann (68)

4. U.S. TREASURY DEPARTMENT, INTERNAL REVENUE SERVICE, OFFICE OF THE REGIONAL COUNSEL, ROOM 1005D, 90 CHURCH STREET, NEW YORK, NY 10000

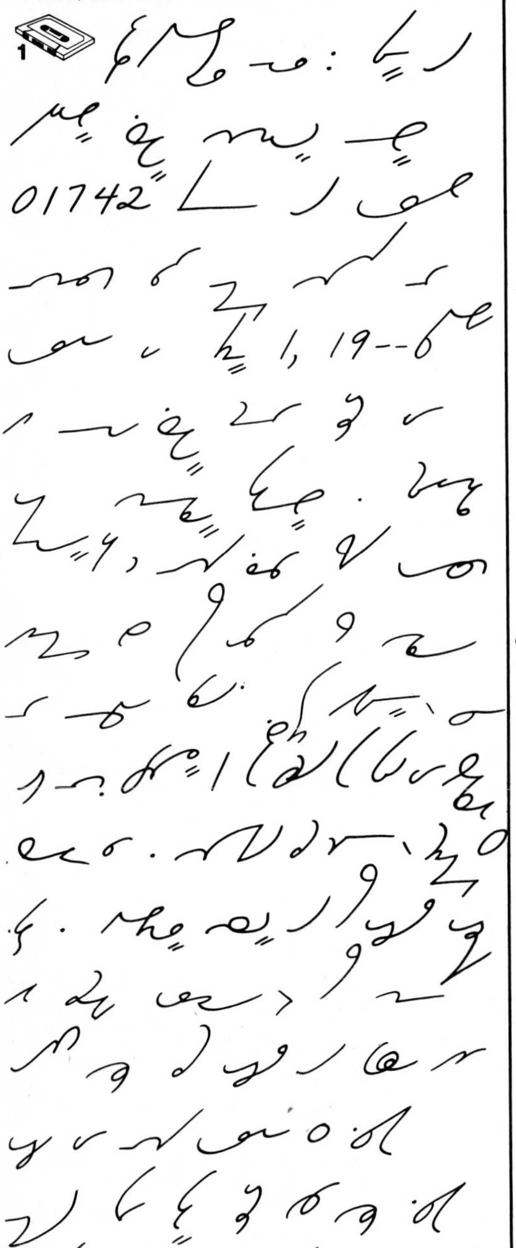

5. SIDNEY MOREY, ESQ., ASSISTANT REGIONAL COUNSEL, ENFORCEMENT, INTERNAL REVENUE SERVICE, 90 CHURCH STREET, NEW YORK, NY 10000 YOUR REFERENCE, CC: NYC: RC-E, AS-NYC 805135, NYC 805136

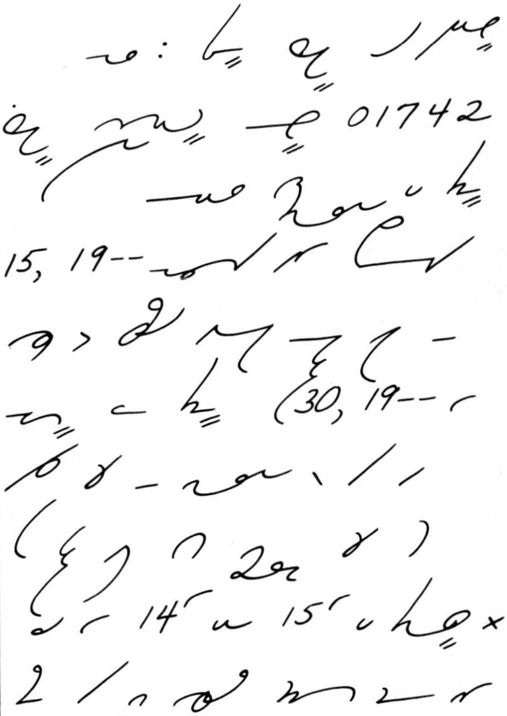

6. MEMORANDUM

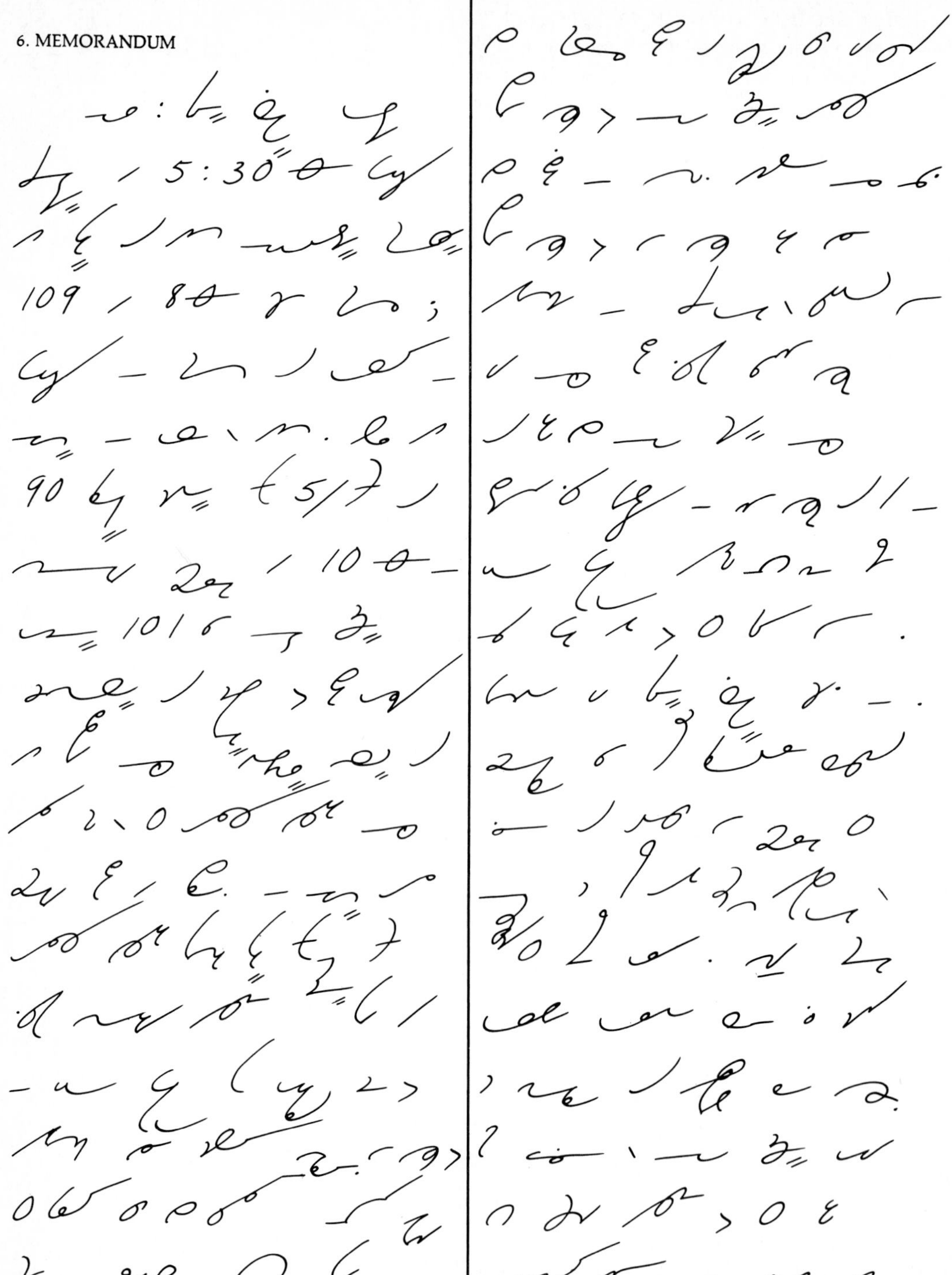

7. MR. JOHN HARPER, RFD 2, CONCORD, MA 01742

1

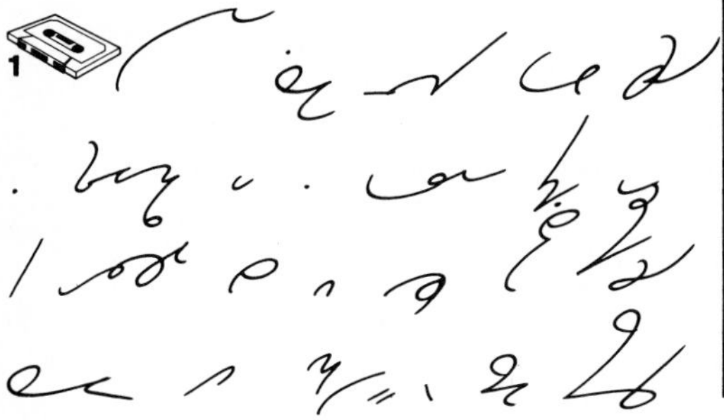

Lesson 3

BUILDING YOUR LEGAL VOCABULARY

Shortcuts

employ 

estate 

evidence 

execute 

guarantee 

guardian 

incorporate 

judicial 

jurisdiction 

landlord 

Word Study

 **computation** Reckoning, calculation.

 **indictment** A written statement filed by a grand jury charging a person with committing a crime.

interrogating Questioning formally and systematically.

misdemeanor A misdeed or a crime less serious than a felony, not punishable by death or by imprisonment in a state or federal prison.

penalties Punishment for crime.

prejudice Preconceived judgment or opinion.

prosecution The process of pursuing formal charges against an offender to final judgment.

violation Breaking or disregarding a law.

BUILDING YOUR LEGAL TRANSCRIPTION SKILL

Transcription Aid

Interrupting Elements

☐ Use commas to set off nonessential interrupting elements within a sentence, such as simple parenthetical expressions, and in direct address.

The Government, I can see, naturally feels that they have a good case.

This letter, Mr. Harper, is in the nature of a report to you of the conference that I had in Washington yesterday, the 15th of December.

Clauses and Phrases Within Dependent Clauses

☐ If the interrupting clause or phrase within a dependent clause is essential to the meaning, no commas should be used. When the element is nonrestrictive, place a comma before and after the phrase or clause.

The witness stated that when he arrived at the scene of the accident the situation was as you described it.

The attorney remarked that, while he doubted its accuracy, this report was filed on March 8.

Latin and French Words and Phrases

Certain Latin and French words and phrases are presented in alternate lessons. Their selection was largely determined by their frequency of use or by their usefulness in expressing accepted legal concepts. By learning their spellings and meanings, you will increase your ability to transcribe with understanding.

non sui juris *(non sōō'i jur'is)* Without the capacity to manage own affairs.

per curiam *(per kur'e am)* By the court, rather than by a single judge.

supersedeas *(su'per seed'e as)* A writ commanding a stay of legal proceedings; an order forbidding enforcement of a judgment that is being reviewed by a court of appeal.

BUILDING YOUR LEGAL DICTATION PROFICIENCY

Preview

counsel

defense

enforcement

expenditures

Justice Department

law

liability

proceeding

proposition

regional

termination

thereof

thereupon

whatsoever

Reading and Writing Practice

8. MR. JOHN HARPER, RFD 2, CONCORD, MA 01742

1

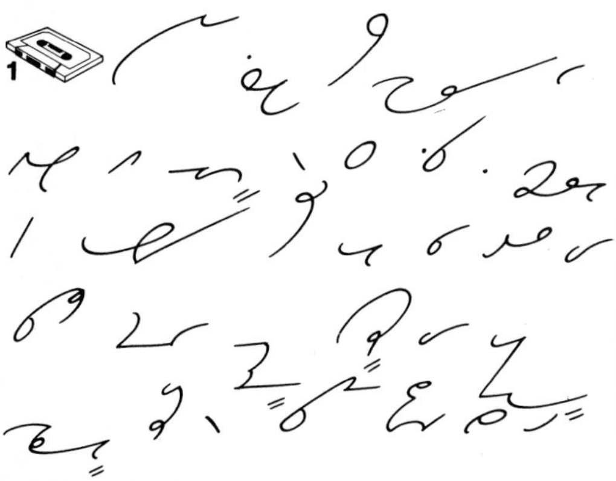

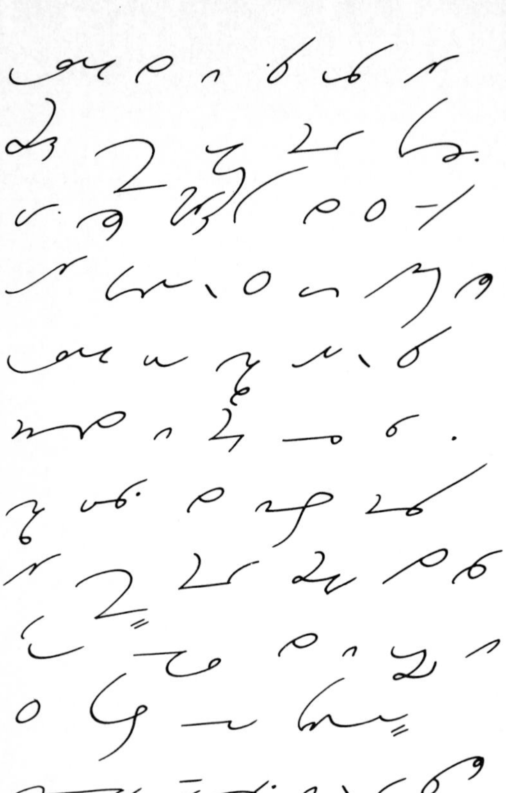

9. MR. JOHN HARPER, RFD 2, CONCORD, MA 01742

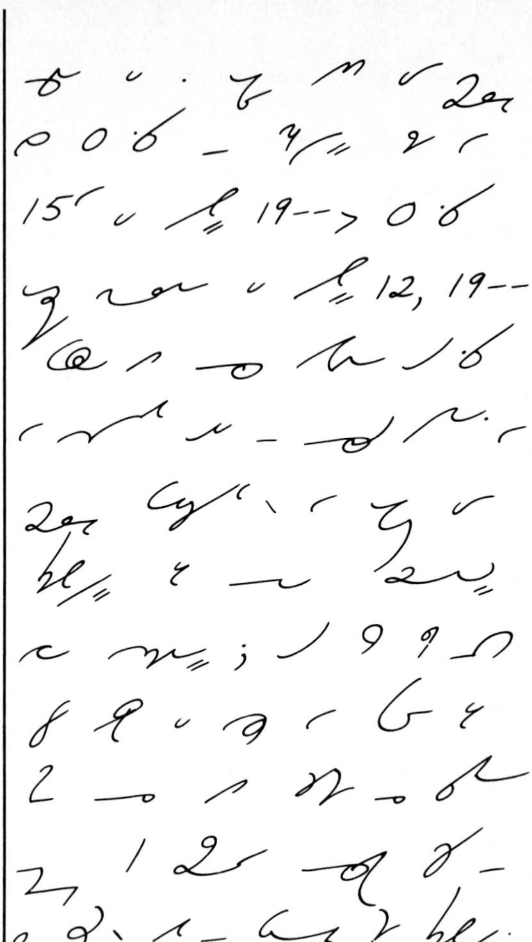

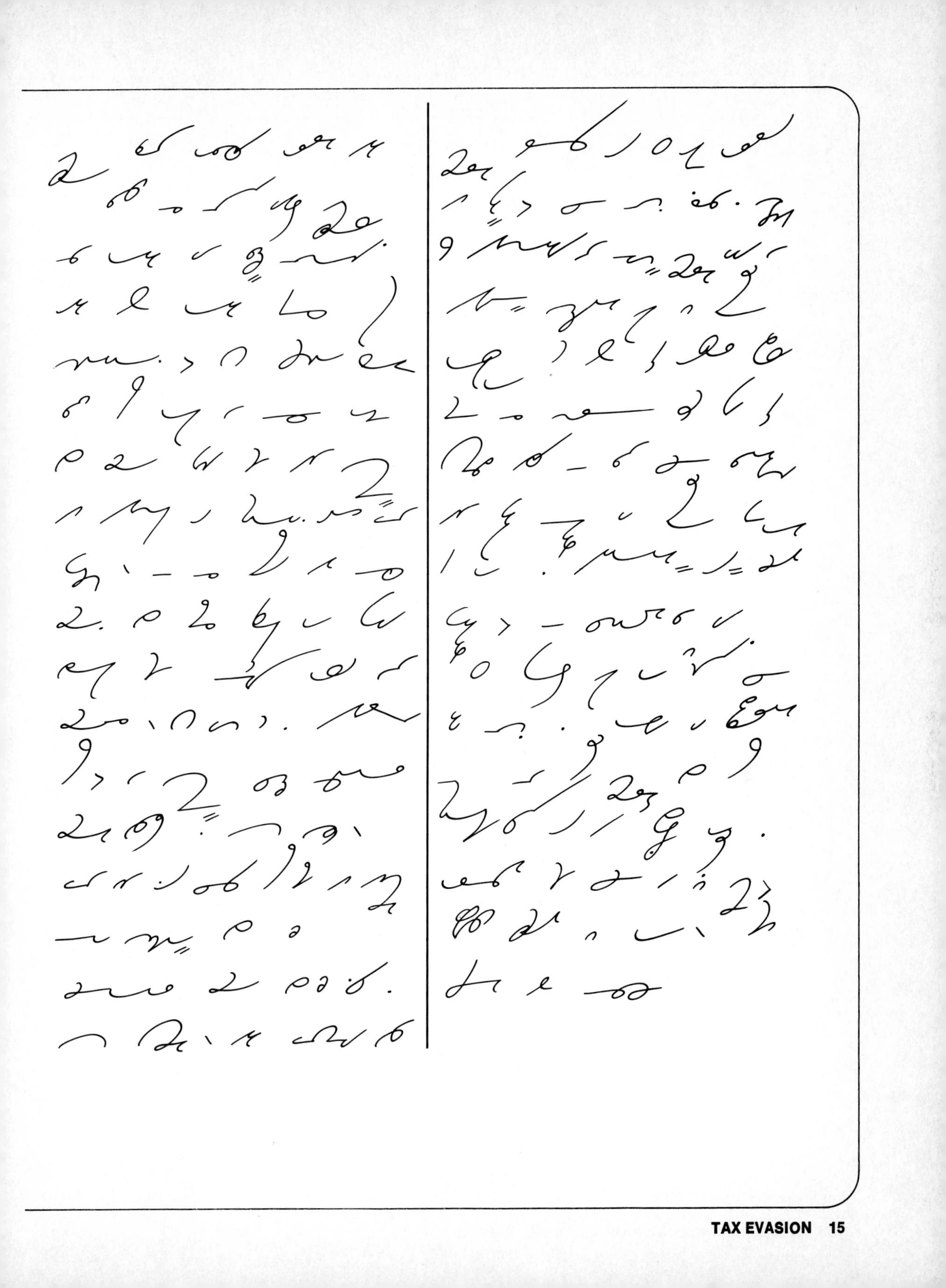

Lesson 4

BUILDING YOUR LEGAL VOCABULARY

Shortcuts

immigrate

insure
insurance

legal

legislate

litigate

mortgage

negligence

negotiate

notice

plaintiff

Word Study

a.k.a. or a/k/a Also known as.

alleges Affirms or asserts without proof or before proving.

fraudulently By deceit or trickery.

out-of-pocket expenses Expenses requiring an actual outlay of cash.

petition A formal written request to a court requesting action.

petitioners Persons making a written request to a court requesting action.

plaintiff The complaining party; the person who brings civil court action.

pursuant to In accordance with, according to, in carrying out.

respondent One who answers in various legal proceedings; the defendant in an action.

BUILDING YOUR LEGAL TRANSCRIPTION SKILL

Transcription Aid

Punctuation of a Series

☐ Use a comma between the items in a series and before the conjunction that connects the last two items. Use a semicolon to separate members of a series when the phrases or clauses themselves contain commas.

I left Chelmsford at 5:30 a.m., proceeded to Boston, and took Northeast Flight 109 at 8 a.m.

The petitioner, John Harper, is 75 years old; his health has been failing; and communications between counsel and said petitioner have been impaired, thus preventing the maximum preparation of a Stipulation of Facts with counsel for the Government.

☐ When several citations are listed one after the other, use a semicolon to separate the cases instead of writing the cases on separate lines.

The defendant intends to file with this Honorable Court a Motion for Continuance, in the light of the decisions of the Supreme Court of the United States in *Marchetti vs. United States*, 36 U.S.L.W. 4143 (January 29, 1968); *Grosso vs. United States*, 36 U.S.L.W. 4150 (January 29, 1968); and *Haynes vs. United States*, 36 U.S.L.W. 4164 January 29, 1968).

Legal Collocations

chattel mortgage A pledge of personal property as security for a debt or obligation.

community property Property owned jointly by husband and wife.

criminal action Criminal prosecution; the legal process against one accused of a crime.

income tax return A form prepared for the Bureau of Internal Revenue reporting the amount of tax due for any accounting period of 12 months.

motion to vacate A written or oral application to a court to nullify.

BUILDING YOUR LEGAL DICTATION PROFICIENCY

Preview

arbitrarily 

civil 

certificates 

collector 

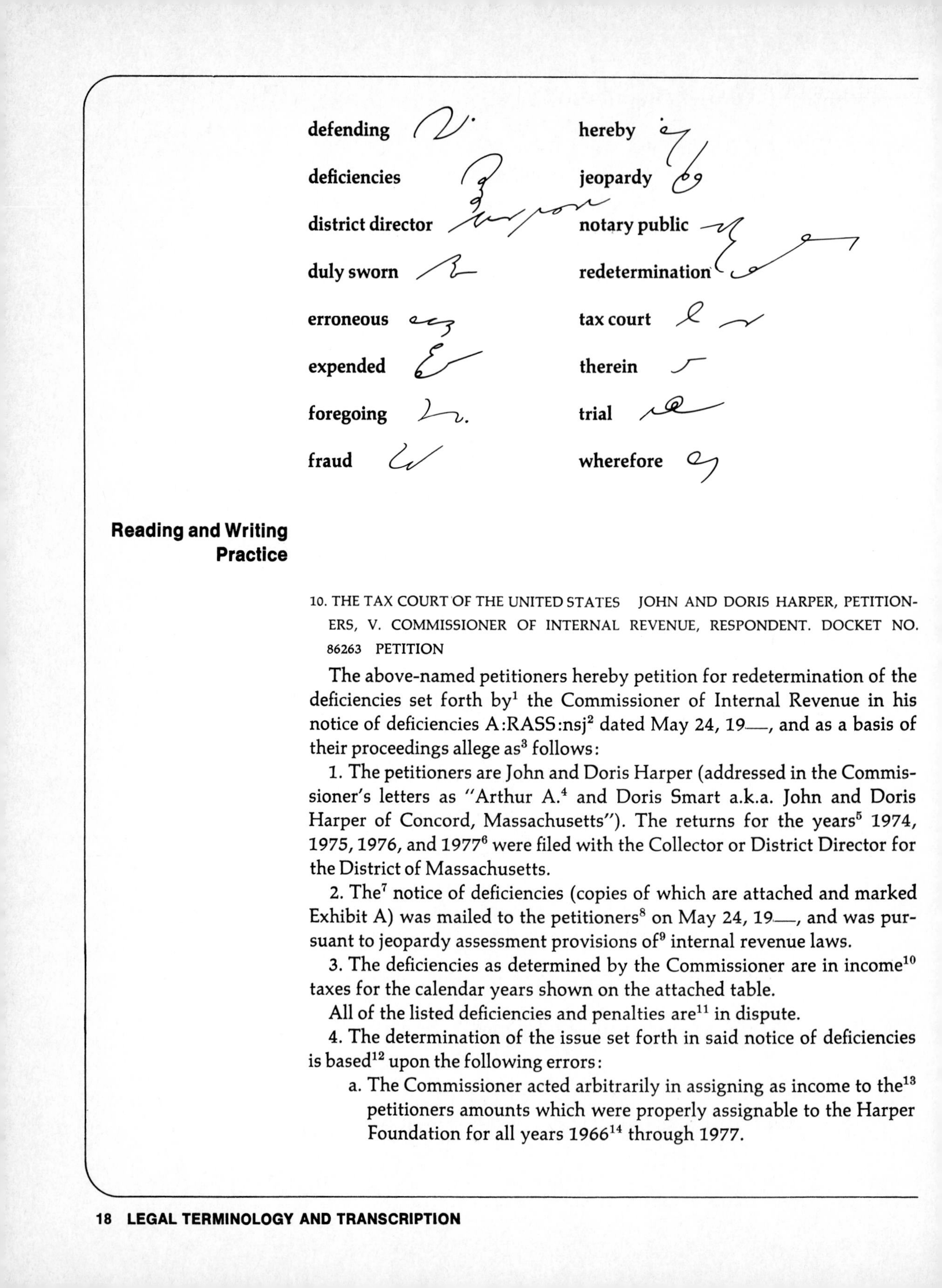

defending	**hereby**
deficiencies	**jeopardy**
district director	**notary public**
duly sworn	**redetermination**
erroneous	**tax court**
expended	**therein**
foregoing	**trial**
fraud	**wherefore**

Reading and Writing Practice

10. THE TAX COURT OF THE UNITED STATES JOHN AND DORIS HARPER, PETITIONERS, V. COMMISSIONER OF INTERNAL REVENUE, RESPONDENT. DOCKET NO. 86263 PETITION

The above-named petitioners hereby petition for redetermination of the deficiencies set forth by[1] the Commissioner of Internal Revenue in his notice of deficiencies A:RASS:nsj[2] dated May 24, 19—, and as a basis of their proceedings allege as[3] follows:

1. The petitioners are John and Doris Harper (addressed in the Commissioner's letters as "Arthur A.[4] and Doris Smart a.k.a. John and Doris Harper of Concord, Massachusetts"). The returns for the years[5] 1974, 1975, 1976, and 1977[6] were filed with the Collector or District Director for the District of Massachusetts.

2. The[7] notice of deficiencies (copies of which are attached and marked Exhibit A) was mailed to the petitioners[8] on May 24, 19—, and was pursuant to jeopardy assessment provisions of[9] internal revenue laws.

3. The deficiencies as determined by the Commissioner are in income[10] taxes for the calendar years shown on the attached table.

All of the listed deficiencies and penalties are[11] in dispute.

4. The determination of the issue set forth in said notice of deficiencies is based[12] upon the following errors:

   a. The Commissioner acted arbitrarily in assigning as income to the[13] petitioners amounts which were properly assignable to the Harper Foundation for all years 1966[14] through 1977.

The petitioners at no time acted fraudulently or[15] in any manner with intent to evade tax.

b. There were no returns required to be filed by the petitioners for[16] the years 1966 through 1973.

c. The certificates for all years are[17] erroneous.

5. The facts upon which the petitioners rely as a basis for this proceeding are as[18] follows:

a. The petitioners had insufficient income for the years 1966 through[19] 1973 to be required to file an income tax return.

b. The amounts sought to be charged to the[20] petitioners as income were in fact amounts received by the Harper Foundation and not the petitioners'[21] income for all years 1966 through 1977.

WHEREFORE, the petitioners[22] pray that the Court may hear the proceeding and determine that:

There are no deficiencies in tax or penalties[23] due from the petitioners, John and Doris Harper nor from Arthur A. Smart nor Doris Smart for the years[24] 1966, 1967, 1968, 1969,[25] 1970, 1971, 1972, 1973,[26] 1974, 1975, 1976, and[27] 1977.

____
Counsel for the Petitioners
Boston, Massachusetts

STATE OF MASSACHUSETTS)[28]
COUNTY OF ESSEX) ss.

JOHN HARPER AND DORIS HARPER, being duly sworn, say that they are the petitioners[29] above named; that they have read the foregoing petition or had the same read to them and are familiar with the[30] statements contained therein; that the statements are true except those stated to be upon information and beliefs;[31] and that these they believe to be true.

____
John Harper

____
Doris Harper

Subscribed and sworn to before me this __________ day[32] of August 19__.

____
John Jones, Notary Public
My commission expires April 5, 19__.[33] (664)

11. MR. JOHN HARPER, RFD 2, CONCORD, MA 01742

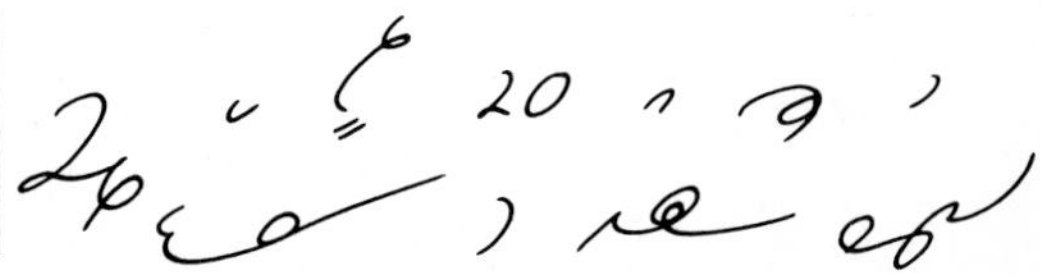

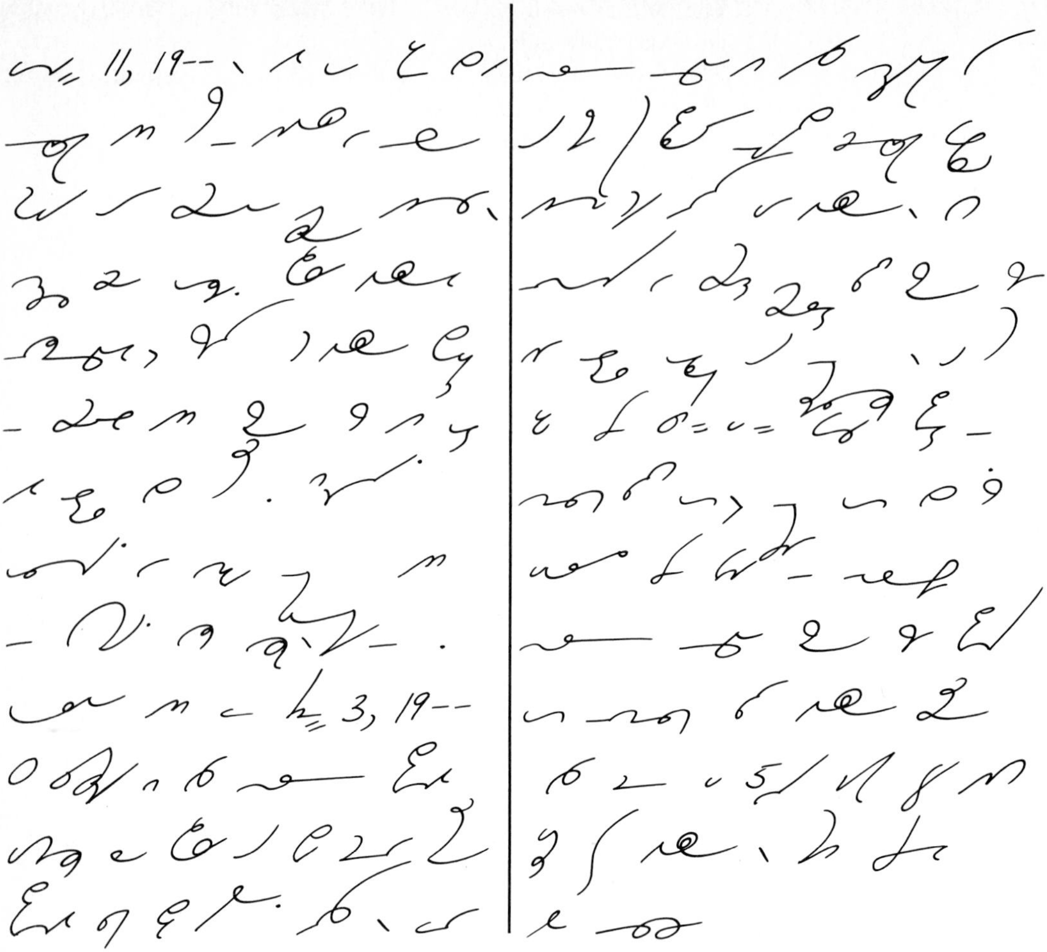

Lesson 5

BUILDING YOUR LEGAL VOCABULARY

Shortcuts

property		shall	
prosecute		statute	

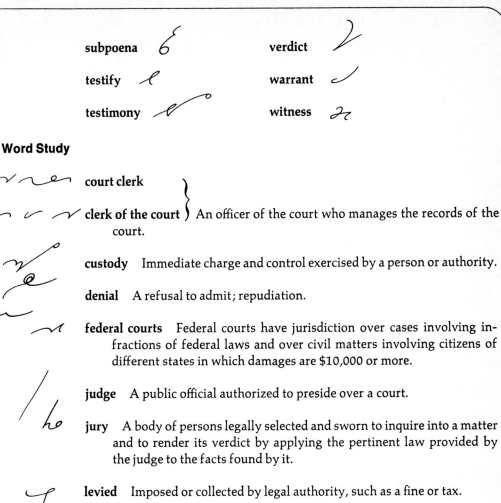

subpoena	**verdict**
testify	**warrant**
testimony	**witness**

Word Study

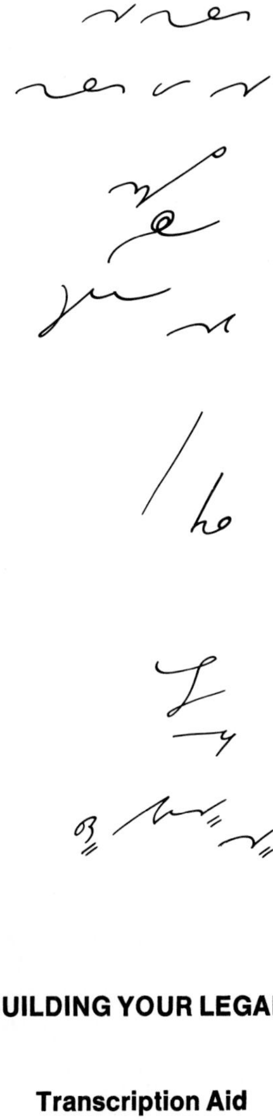

court clerk
clerk of the court An officer of the court who manages the records of the court.

custody Immediate charge and control exercised by a person or authority.

denial A refusal to admit; repudiation.

federal courts Federal courts have jurisdiction over cases involving infractions of federal laws and over civil matters involving citizens of different states in which damages are $10,000 or more.

judge A public official authorized to preside over a court.

jury A body of persons legally selected and sworn to inquire into a matter and to render its verdict by applying the pertinent law provided by the judge to the facts found by it.

levied Imposed or collected by legal authority, such as a fine or tax.

motion An application made to a court or judge to obtain an order, ruling, or direction.

U.S. District Court A court having authority over a district which may include all of the state or only part of it.

BUILDING YOUR LEGAL TRANSCRIPTION SKILL

Transcription Aid

Introductory Expressions

☐ Use a comma after a dependent introductory clause when it precedes the independent clause, and use a comma after an introductory participial phrase.

If nothing is done about it prior to December 27, the Judge will be powerless to reduce the fine imposed.

Having just received a telephone call from the Clerk of the Federal District Court, I am writing to inform you that the Judge denied the motion to vacate or reduce the fine.

Latin and French Words and Phrases

ad quod damnum *(ad kwod dam'num)* To what damage; what injury. (Used to describe the plaintiff's money loss or the damages that he claims for land seized for public use.)

in camera *(in kam'ra)* In a judge's chambers; in a private hearing.

amicus curiae *(a mē'kus kū'rēī)* Friend of the court; an individual not party to the action who states some matter of law for the assistance of the court.

BUILDING YOUR LEGAL DICTATION PROFICIENCY

Preview

automatically	imposed
chambers	interim
clerk	marshal
confinement	physically
courtroom	powerless
foundation	sentence
hearing	withstanding

Reading and Writing Practice

12. MR. JOHN HARPER, RFD 2, CONCORD, MA 01742

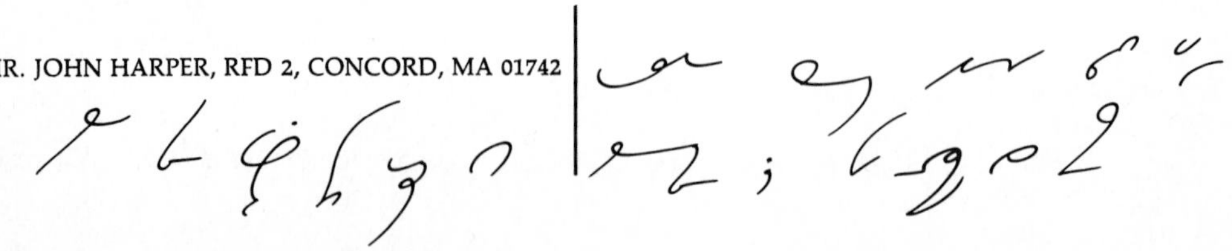

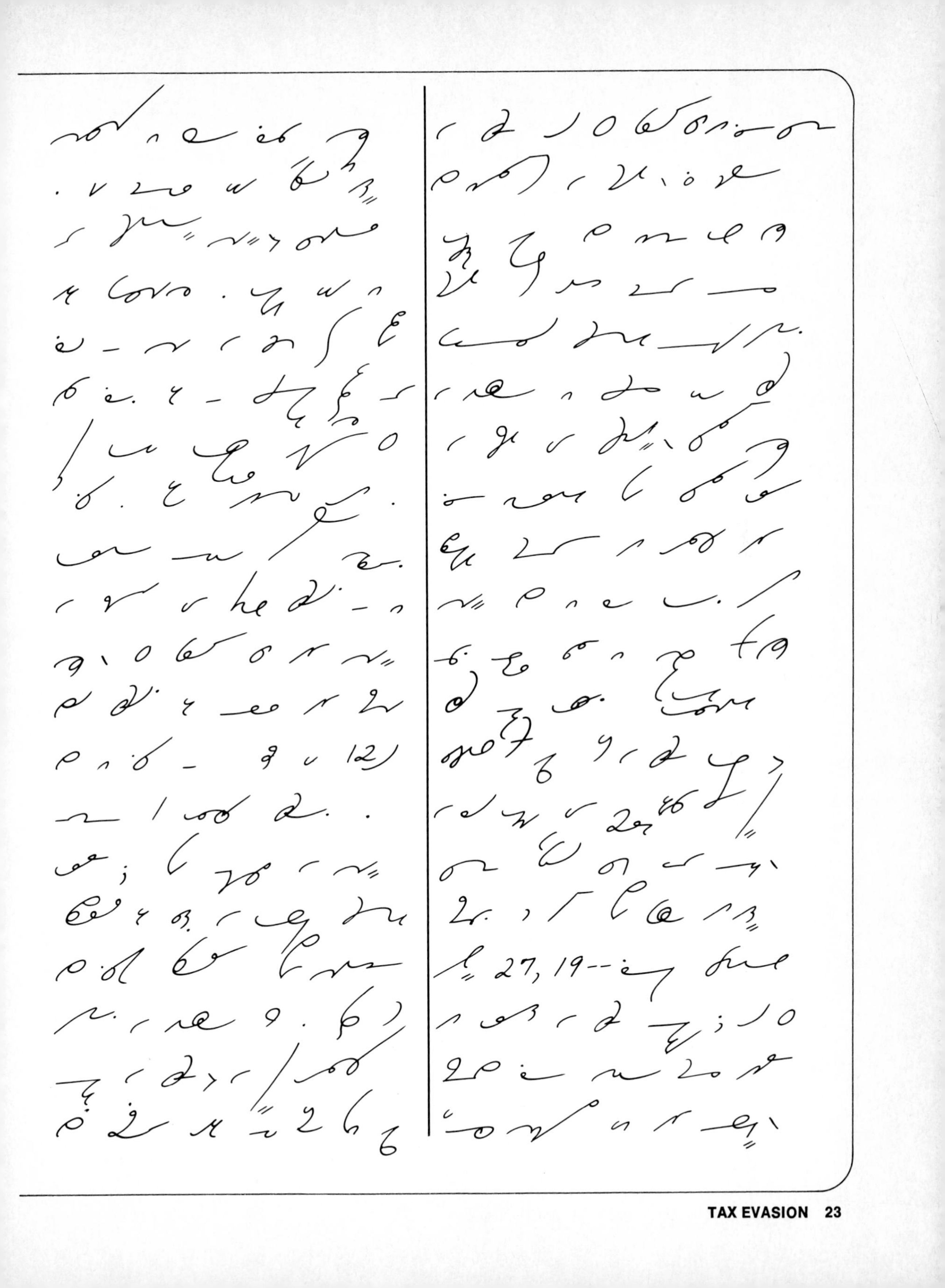

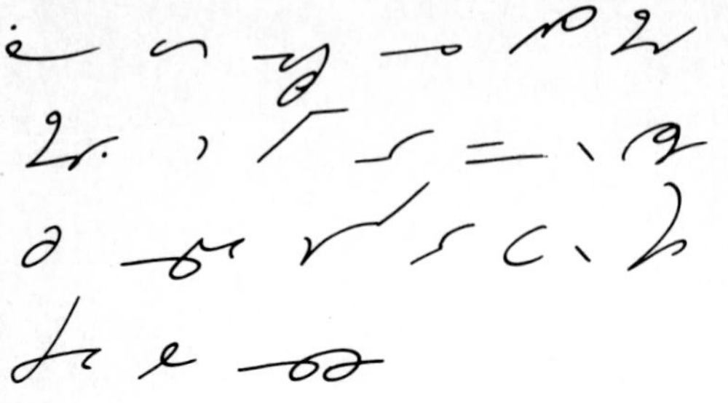

13. MR. JOHN HARPER, RFD 2, CONCORD, MA 01742

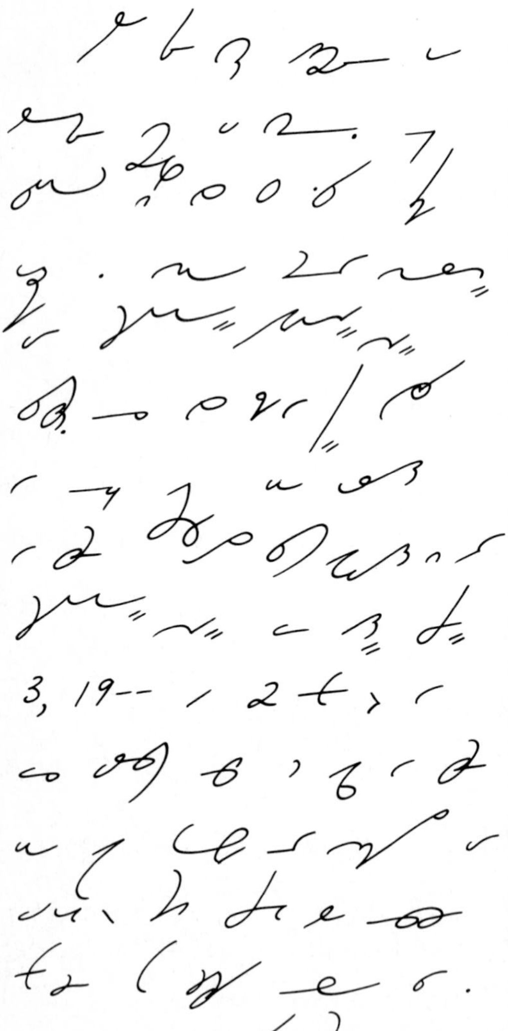

14. MR. JOHN HARPER, 125 MAIN STREET, DANBURY, CT 06810

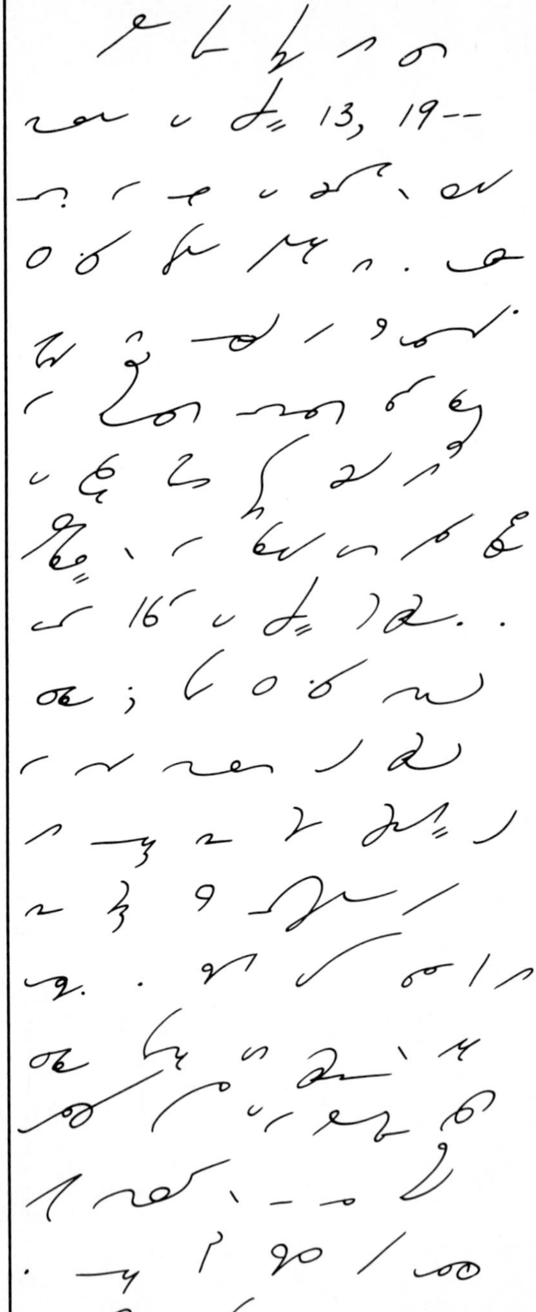

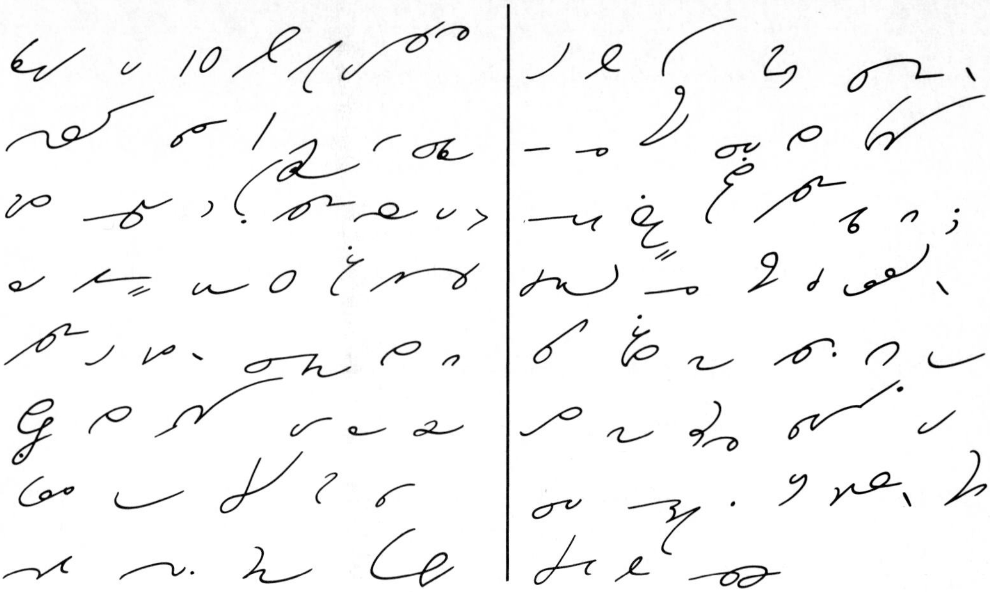

Lesson 6

BUILDING YOUR LEGAL VOCABULARY

Intersections The principle of intersecting often provides fluent shortcuts for expressions that recur frequently. The following may serve as patterns.

abstract of title

board of directors

caveat emptor

caveat venditor

eminent domain

grand jury

habeus corpus

last will and testament

promissory note

vice-versa

Word Study

adversary One who opposes or resists.

arguments Facts or statements offered as proof or evidence.

calendared Entered on a list of cases to be tried in court.

continuance Adjourning of court proceedings to a future day.

court of appeals A court to which appeals are made on points of law resulting from the judgment of another court.

docket A list of cases awaiting action in a court.

ex parte motions Motions made on behalf of one party and heard by the Court without the opposing party or the opposing party's representative present.

indisposition Slight illness.

stipulate To agree to definitely; to specify something as being a condition of agreement.

BUILDING YOUR LEGAL TRANSCRIPTION SKILL

Transcription Aid

Commas to Show Omission of Words

☐ Use a comma to show the omission of an important word or words that can be understood from the context.

A payment of $1,000 of the attorney's fee is due before the trial;
the remainder, to be secured by a note signed by you and Mrs. Harper.

Commas With Contrasted Expressions

☐ Use the comma to set off contrasting expressions. When such words qualify or contrast a common element in the sentence, be sure to include the full intervening expression and not just a part of it.

The witness may state only the facts, not hearsay evidence.

The doctor's certificate must indicate that your indisposition originates from a physical, not a mental, cause.

Legal Collocations

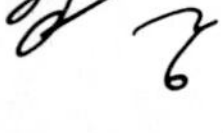
certified copy A copy declared to be true by the officer who has custody of the original.

referee in bankruptcy An officer appointed by the court with authority to hold a legal hearing and determine bankruptcy cases.

summary proceeding A short and simple proceeding in which many formalities are dispensed with.

tax sale A sale of property for the purpose of paying back taxes.

writ of attachment An order in writing issued under seal by a court commanding the sheriff to seize the property identified in the document and to hold it in custody pending court action.

BUILDING YOUR LEGAL DICTATION PROFICIENCY

Preview

condemnation	herein
confinement	institution
correctional	motion
District Court	petitioners
extension	proceedings
federal	virus

Reading and Writing Practice

15. TAX COURT OF THE UNITED STATES JOHN AND DORIS HARPER, PETITIONERS, V. COMMISSIONER OF INTERNAL REVENUE, RESPONDENT. DOCKET NO. 86263 MOTION FOR EXTENSION OF TIME WITHIN WHICH TO FILE REPLY

Petitioners move for an extension of time from March 6, 19—, to July 18,[1] 19—, within which to file their reply on the following grounds:

1. Confinement in Federal[2] Correctional Institution at Danbury, Connecticut, resulted in illness of John Harper.
2. The[3] condition of said John Harper has made it impossible to prepare a reply, but it is believed such a reply[4] can be made within the extension of time herein requested.

WHEREFORE, it is prayed that this motion be granted.[5]

Counsel for Petitioners
James E. McCann
74 State Street
Boston, MA 02100[6]

16. JOHN AND DORIS HARPER, PETITIONERS, V. COMMISSIONER OF INTERNAL REVENUE, RESPONDENT. DOCKET NO. 86263 TRIAL ON: OCTOBER 22, 19— TRIAL AT: COURT OF APPEALS COURTROOM UNITED STATES COURTHOUSE, BOSTON, MASSACHUSETTS NOTICE SETTING CASE FOR TRIAL

TAKE NOTICE that the above-entitled case is set for trial before a Division of the Tax Court of the[7] United States as indicated above.

The calendar for that Session will be called at 10 a.m. on the date[8] indicated, and you will be expected to answer the call at that time and be prepared when the case is reached for[9] trial. Failure to appear will be taken as cause for dismissal in accordance with Rule 27(b)(3)[10] of the Court's Rules of Practice.

You are expected to be familiar with the Court's Rules of Practice in all other[11] respects.

Your attention is called particularly to Rule 31(b), which requires that the parties stipulate[12] facts and evidence to the fullest possible extent prior to the call of the calendar. You should[13] confer with your adversary promptly in order to comply with that rule.

Clerk of the Court.

Ex parte motions[14] for continuance of trial, filed 30 days or less prior to the first day of the Session, will be calendared[15] for hearing at calendar call at the Session unless the Court, in its discretion, directs otherwise in[16] exceptional circumstances.

To: James E. McCann, Esq.
74 State Street
Boston, MA 02100[17]

(342)

17. CHARLES SANDERS, CLERK, U.S. DISTRICT COURT, FEDERAL BUILDING, BOSTON, MA 02100

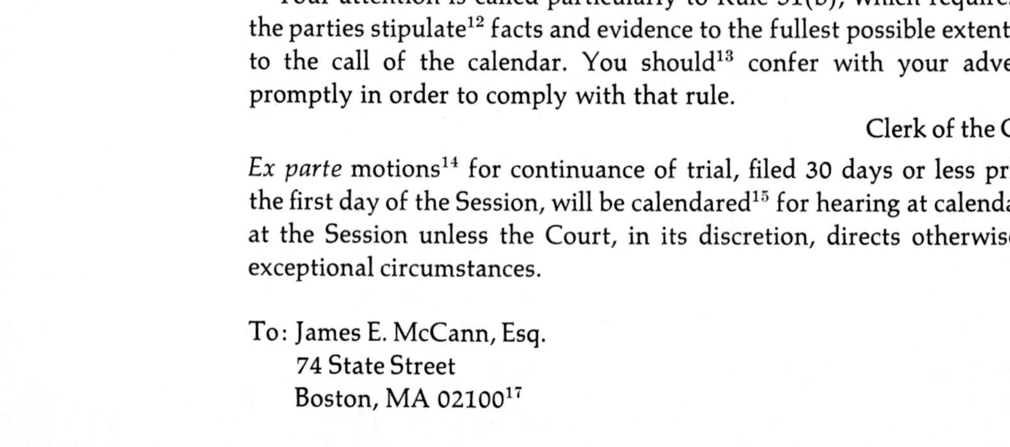

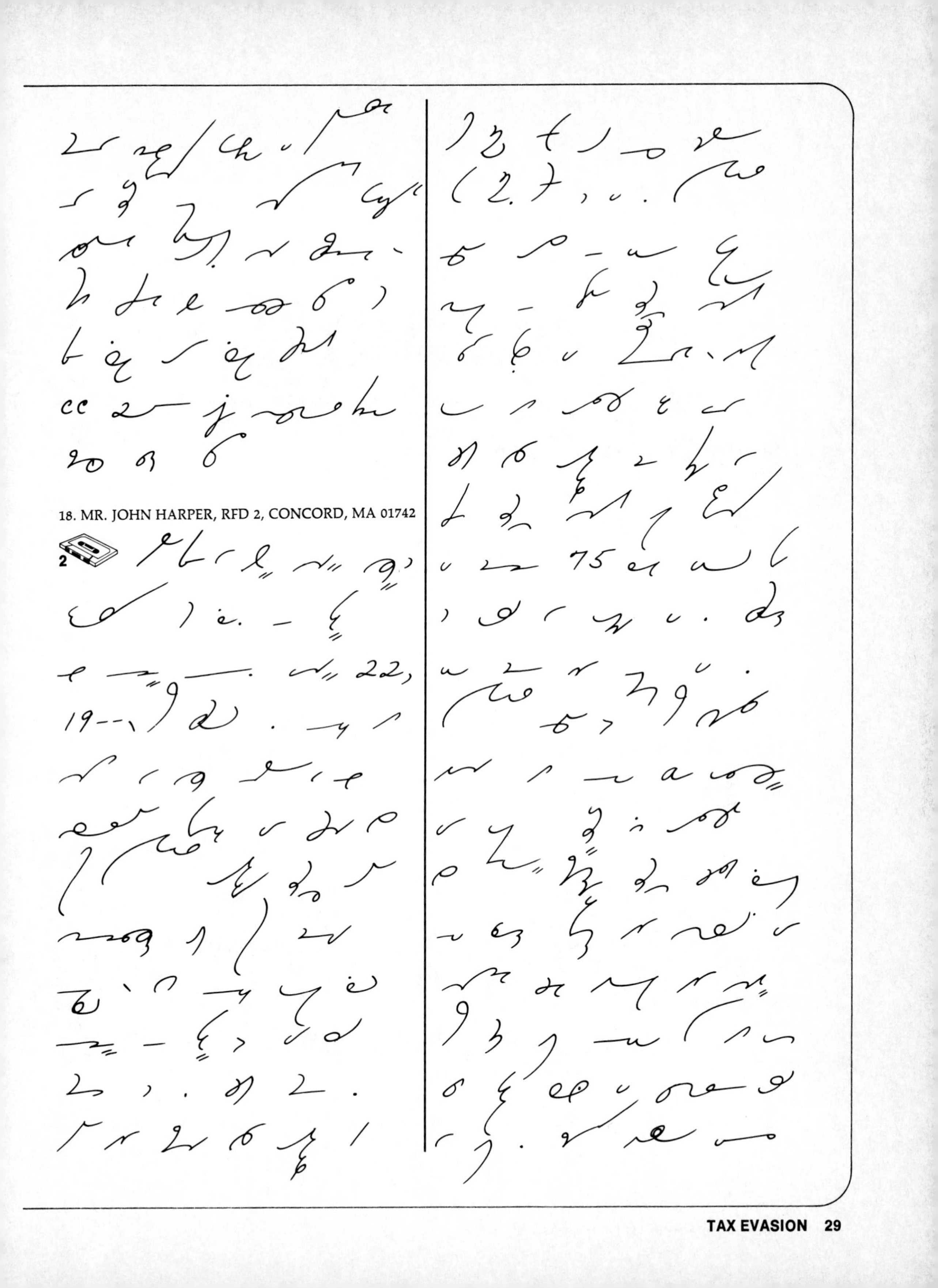

18. MR. JOHN HARPER, RFD 2, CONCORD, MA 01742

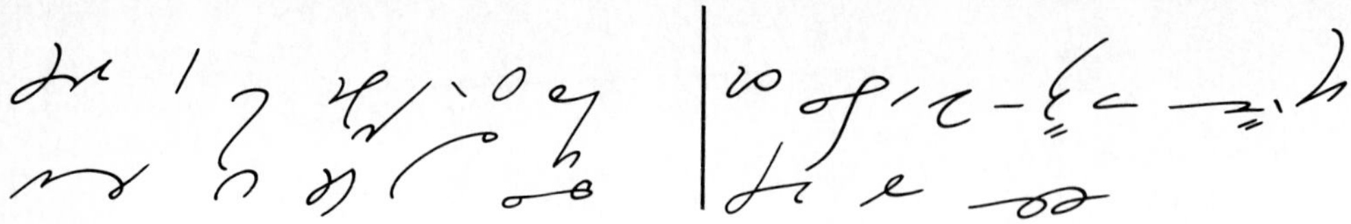

Lesson 7

BUILDING YOUR LEGAL VOCABULARY

Frequent Phrases

Outlines for frequent recurring phrases may be constructed by modifying key words or by omitting a word that common sense would supply. The following may serve as patterns for constructing others.

attorney-at-law 

attorney for the defendant 

attorney for the plaintiff 

being duly sworn 

being first duly sworn 

bill of exchange 

bill of sale 

cease and desist 

court of equity 

court of law 

defense attorney 

husband and wife 

in witness whereof 

know all men by these presents 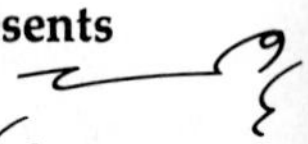

party of the first part 

prosecuting attorney 

Word Study

 **amendment** The process of correcting or changing by parliamentary or constitutional procedure.

 **circuit court** A court in which jurisdiction is limited by geographical divisions; U.S. Circuit Court of Appeals.

culminated Brought to the highest or a decisive point.

d.b.a. or d/b/a Doing business as.

district attorney The prosecuting officer of a judicial district, sometimes called the DA.

eviction The act of forcing from property by legal proceedings.

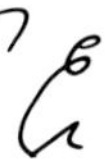

exhibits Documents or material objects produced and identified in court or before an examiner for use as evidence.

foreclosure A legal proceeding that takes away the mortgagor's right to get back his property that he has given as security on a loan.

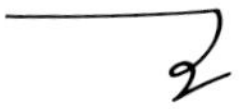

manifest Obvious; apparent.

plaintiff The complaining party; the person who brings civil court action.

stipulation An agreement between attorneys concerning the conduct of legal proceedings.

BUILDING YOUR LEGAL TRANSCRIPTION SKILL

Transcription Aid

Commas in Geographic Expressions and Dates

☐ Use a comma before and after the name of a state following the name of a city within a sentence.

This letter is to confirm our telephone conversation regarding the communication I received from the Regional Counsel of the Internal Revenue Service in Boston, Massachusetts, concerning the Stipulation of Facts.

☐ Use the comma before and after the year following the day of the month within a sentence.

The petitioner's counsel has been unable to contact him since Monday, November 16, 19—, until after 5 p.m. on November 18, 19—.

Latin and French Words and Phrases

bona fide *(bōn'a fīd)* With or made in good faith; authentic.

causa mortis *(kau'sa mor'tis)* By reason of death; in contemplation of imminent death.

habeas corpus *(hā'be as kor'pus)* A writ directing a person having custody of another to produce that person in court.

BUILDING YOUR LEGAL DICTATION PROFICIENCY

Preview

certify

continuance

injustice

judgment

marshal

notice of appeal

thereafter

whereas

Reading and Writing Practice

2

19. UNITED STATES DISTRICT COURT FOR THE DISTRICT OF MASSACHUSETTS UNITED STATES OF AMERICA, PLAINTIFF, V. JOHN HARPER, D.B.A. HARPER FOUNDATION AND HARPER FOUNDATION, DEFENDANTS. CIVIL ACTION NO. 279. MOTION

Come now the defendants in the above action and request the following:

1. That whereas the defendants through[1] accident, mistake, or misfortune, did not file a timely notice of appeal from the judgment in the above-captioned[2] case,

2. And whereas there are manifest errors of law contained in the opinion,

3. And whereas it has been[3] the intention of the defendants to appeal the decision from the date of the opinion,

4. And whereas[4] manifest injustice will result to the defendants if said appeal is not allowed to be entered,

Now, therefore,[5] the defendants request that they be allowed to enter a notice of appeal and to appeal the decision[6] to the Circuit Court of Appeals for the First District.

Respectfully submitted,

____

Attorney for the Defendants[7]
James E. McCann
74 State Street
Boston, MA 02100

I certify that I[8] have this day handed a copy of the foregoing motion to the United States District Attorney.
June 25,[9] 19__

20. TAX COURT OF THE UNITED STATES JOHN AND DORIS HARPER, PETITIONERS, V. COMMISSIONER OF INTERNAL REVENUE, RESPONDENT. DOCKET NO. 86263 MOTION FOR EXTENSION OF TIME WITHIN WHICH TO FILE REPLY TO AMENDMENT TO ANSWER

Petitioners move for an extension of time from August 15, 19__,[10] to October 15, 19__, within which to file their reply to Amendment[11] to Answer, and from August 23, 19__, to some date after October 15,[12] 19__, for hearing on the following grounds:

As a result of the Government's foreclosure,[13] referred to in the last request for extension, records are still in such condition that it has been impossible[14] to marshal the information for a reply. It is therefore requested that an additional extension[15] be granted to file said reply.

WHEREFORE, it is prayed that this motion be granted.

____

Counsel for Petitioners[16]
James E. McCann
74 State Street
Boston, MA 02100

21. TAX COURT OF THE UNITED STATES JOHN AND DORIS HARPER, PETITIONERS, V. COMMISSIONER OF INTERNAL REVENUE, RESPONDENT. DOCKET NO. 86263 MOTION FOR CONTINUANCE

Petitioner John Harper[17] moves the Court for an order continuing the trial of this case until the next term at Boston, Massachusetts,[18] on the ground that additional time is necessary to properly prepare the petitioner's case.

1. This[19] is a complicated case, and counsel for petitioner and for respondent have just recently stipulated[20] to many facts (most at respondent's and request) certain exhibits in said stipulations were not even[21] furnished to counsel for petitioner until November 17, 19__, and then only after[22] a special trip to Boston.

2. Petitioner's counsel has been unable to contact the petitioner since[23] Monday, November 16, 19__, until after 5 p.m. on November 17, 19__,[24] and this does not afford proper time to cover the many items required to prepare the case properly.[25]

3. The long history of this case has culminated with the petitioner being constructively evicted[26] from his residence after the Government

sold all assets to satisfy a fine, and thereafter bank[27] foreclosure proceedings completed the eviction.

Counsel for Petitioners
James E. McCann
74 State[28] Street
Boston, MA 02100 (569)

22. TREASURY DEPARTMENT, INTERNAL REVENUE SERVICE, OFFICE OF REGIONAL COUNSEL, 80 FEDERAL STREET, BOSTON, MA 02100

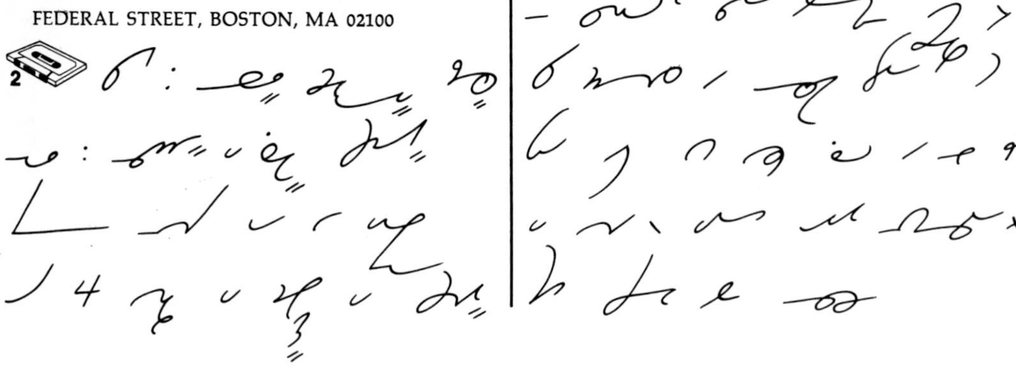

Lesson 8

BUILDING YOUR LEGAL VOCABULARY

Word Beginnings *Em-* and *im-* followed by a consonant are expressed by ___ ; when attached to a vowel, by ___ .

employees	**immigration**
empirical	**emergency**
imprisonment	**immaterial**

Word Study

appeal A legal proceeding by which a case is brought from a lower court to a court of appeals for a review of the lower court's application of the law to the facts as found by that lower court.

brief Attorney's condensed statement of the client's case.

revoked Annulled, rescinded, recalled.

situs The place where something exists or originates.

testimony Oral evidence of fact or truth, such as that given under oath before a court.

BUILDING YOUR LEGAL TRANSCRIPTION SKILL

Transcription Aid In this and the next six lessons you will review points concerned with handling quotations correctly.

Fragmentary Quotations

☐ When only a word or phrase of a quotation is used in a sentence, it is not introduced by a comma. The first word is not capitalized unless it is a proper noun or proper adjective. Use quotation marks to enclose only the exact words quoted.

> The testimony also brought out that his wife "has been involuntarily made a joint petitioner in this matter."

Unusual Meanings

☐ When a word or phrase is used in a somewhat different or specialized sense from its ordinary meaning, it is enclosed in quotation marks. This occurs frequently when a well-known idea is carried over into an unusual context to help in clarification.

> Mr. McCann stated that the Government had used a "shotgun" approach in the case against John Harper.

Legal Collocations

change of venue The removal of a case for trial from one county to another.

corporate charter The instrument that determines what the corporation is authorized to do by the state in which it is incorporated.

moving papers Papers made the basis of a motion in court proceedings.

real estate Landed property, including all interests in lands that are held for life.

 **tax lien** A charge upon property for the satisfaction of unpaid state or municipal taxes.

BUILDING YOUR LEGAL DICTATION PROFICIENCY

Preview

assignable 

fraudulently 

hybrid 

jeopardy 

legally 

mortgaging 

net worth 

penalties 

statement of facts 

taxable 

taxpayers 

transcript 

Reading and Writing Practice

23. TAX COURT OF THE UNITED STATES JOHN AND DORIS HARPER, PETITIONERS, V. COMMISSIONER OF INTERNAL REVENUE, RESPONDENT. DOCKET NO. 86263 BRIEF FOR THE TAXPAYERS

NATURE OF THE TAX

The taxes in controversy are income taxes and penalties for the calendar years[1] 1966, 1967, 1968, 1969,[2] 1970, 1971, 1972, 1973,[3] 1974, 1975, 1976,[4] and 1977, totaling $50,050.47.

NOW[5] APPEAL COMES BEFORE THE COURT

The said deficiencies were proposed in Commissioner's letter mailed to the petitioners[6] on May 24, 19—, pursuant to jeopardy assessment provisions of[7] the Internal Revenue laws. The taxpayers appealed from this determination on August 18, 19—,[8] and assigned the following errors:

1. The Commissioner acted arbitrarily in[9] assigning as income to the petitioners amounts that were properly assignable to the Harper Foundation[10] for all years 1966 through 1977.

2. The petitioners at no[11] time acted fraudulently and in any manner with intent to evade taxes.

3. There were no returns required[12] to be filed by petitioners for the years 1966 through 1977.[13]

4. The deficiencies for all years are erroneous.

STATEMENT OF FACTS

The facts upon which the taxpayers rely[14] in support of their appeal are as follows:

1. The petitioners had insufficient income for the years[15] 1966 through 1973 to be required to file an income tax return.[16]

2. The amount sought to be charged to the petitioners as income were in fact amounts received by the Harper Foundation[17] and were not the petitioners' income for all years 1966 through 1977.[18]

3. The Harper Foundation was legally chartered under the laws of the Commonwealth of Massachusetts.[19]

4. The charter of the said Harper Foundation, organized under the laws of the Commonwealth of[20] Massachusetts, has never been revoked and is still in effect.

5. The Harper Foundation possessed a tax-exempt[21] status by letter of the Commissioner of Internal Revenue.

6. Mrs. Doris Harper, through loans, was[22] able to purchase real estate. (See joint exhibit (AA) Transcript, p. 92.)

7. The real estate purchased[23] by Mrs. Harper served as a source for securing amounts of money by ways of mortgaging the real estate to[24] finance further purchases of real estate and was a source of funds for living expenses as well as a source[25] of funds to the Foundation at various times.

8. Taxpayer Doris Harper filed income tax returns in her[26] own name for the taxable years 1974, 1975, 1976,[27] and 1977. (See Transcript, p. 100.)

ARGUMENT

In support of its[28] appeal, taxpayers present the following argument:

1. Petitioners at all times, during the years here involved,[29] objectively and subjectively conducted the affairs of the Harper Foundation as a true Foundation,[30] and all contributions were received by or for the Foundation to carry on the avowed objectives of[31] the Foundation which were set out in its charter, which was never revoked. The Government agents had no right to[32] proceed as they did in this case by mixing up concepts of determining petitioners' income by using[33] a hybrid net worth method. The attempt involved ignoring the existence of a Foundation recognized by[34] the Commonwealth of Massachusetts and by the very examining Government itself which had granted it an[35] exemption certificate. Something cannot "be" and "not be" at the same time. It is submitted that this method[36] in and of itself is so erroneous as to be fatal to the Government's case. The testimony brought[37] out that the situs of the Foundation was in the remote area of the Berkshires and that it was necessary[38] for the petitioners to remain at the Foundation headquarters at all times, and consequently the value[39] of the benefits of meals and lodgings furnished to them by the Foundation did not constitute taxable income.[40] This last was the concept of the petitioners and is urged by them on two grounds.

a. for the fact of it, and[41]

b. as a basis for negating any mental state constituting a fraudulent income. (837)

(Continued in Lesson 9.)

Lesson 9

BUILDING YOUR LEGAL VOCABULARY

Word Beginnings *In-* and *en-* followed by a consonant are expressed by — ; when attached to vowels, by .

indebtedness

inequity

indictment

innocent

encumbrance

inheritance

Word Study

chattel A tangible, movable article of personal property.

complaint A formal allegation against a party.

corporate Formed into an association endowed by law with the rights and liabilities of an individual.

jurisdiction The authority to interpret and apply the law.

levy A collection by legal authority, such as a fine or tax.

mortgage A temporary and conditional pledge of property to a creditor as security against a debt.

negating Denying the existence or truth of; saying no.

BUILDING YOUR LEGAL TRANSCRIPTION SKILL

Transcription Aid **Introducing Quotations**

☐ Complete direct quotations within a sentence begin with a capital. Short quotations are introduced by a comma; long quotations, by a colon.

Federal Rules Civil Procedure 9 (B) states, "Circumstances instituting fraud shall be stated with particularity."

Emphasis in Quotations

☐ When a dictator wishes to emphasize part of the quotation, the emphasis is shown by underscoring and must be indicated by such expressions as *Italics ours* or *Italics supplied* in brackets at the end of the quotation.

> In 13 Am. Jur., sec. 45, p. 192, we find: "A bona fide attempt to organize a corporation under a valid existing statute authorizing the creation of a corporation such as that attempted to be created will result in the creation of a corporation *de facto . . . the existence of which can be called into question only by the state in a direct proceeding for that purpose.*" [Italics supplied.]

Latin and French Words and Phrases

ex parte *(ex par'tē)* One-sided; related to only one of two or more persons or parties.

de facto *(dē fak'tō)* In fact; actually, but often without legal status.

de jure *(dē ju'rā)* By right; by a lawful title.

BUILDING YOUR LEGAL DICTATION PROFICIENCY

Preview

appeal 

arbitrarily 

assessment 

charitable 

collaterally 

dismissal 

duly 

execution 

involuntarily 

legitimate 

pleadings 

shotgun 

Reading and Writing Practice

24. BRIEF FOR THE TAXPAYERS *(Continued from Lesson 8.)*

Petitioner Doris Harper has been involuntarily made a joint petitioner in this matter by virtue[1] of the jeopardy assessment procedure which was instituted by the Government in its "shotgun" approach[2] to get John Harper. By loans and mortgages Mrs. Harper had acquired real estate and money which eventually[3] led to her filing her own individual returns for the years 1974,[4] 1975, 1976, and 1977. The Government[5] ignored these, but arbitrarily includes her as a petitioner in its efforts to tax John Harper.[6] It is submitted that Doris Harper is not a proper party in this action and at the very least the Court[7] should order her name dropped from these proceedings.

2. The taxpayers, in support of their appeal, rely upon the[8] following propositions of law:

a. Meals and lodging furnished for the convenience of the employer are excluded[9] from gross income (Internal Revenue Code Section 119).

b. The petitioner Doris Harper[10] has a right to have her own tax liability determined separately on the basis of separate returns[11] which she filed. It is her election that should prevail. (Internal Revenue Code Section 6013).

WHEREFORE,[12] the taxpayers respectfully pray that this court may determine and sustain their appeal.

Respectfully[13] submitted,

James E. McCann
Attorney for the Petitioners
74 State Street
Boston, MA[14] 02100

25. IN THE UNITED STATES DISTRICT COURT FOR THE DISTRICT OF MASSACHUSETTS UNITED STATES OF AMERICA, PLAINTIFF, V. JOHN HARPER, D.B.A. HARPER FOUNDATION AND HARPER FOUNDATION, DEFENDANTS. CIVIL ACTION NO. 2791 MEMORANDUM

I. STATEMENT OF THE CASE

A. PLEADINGS

1. COMPLAINT

This action was instituted by a complaint brought[15] by the United States of America against the defendants, John Harper, d.b.a. the Harper Foundation,[16] and the Harper Foundation to recover a fine imposed on the defendant John Harper, as a result of[17] Criminal Action No. 5631 in the *United States of America* v. *Arthur A. Smart,*[18] *a.k.a. John Harper.*

2. ATTACHMENT

The goods and chattels of John Harper and the Harper Foundation, located[19] in the buildings of Doris Harper in Chesterfield, Massachusetts, were attached by the plaintiff on December[20] 29, 19__.

3. ANSWER

The defendant John Harper in his answer denied that[21] he did business as "the Harper Foundation" and alleged that the Harper Foundation had corporate existence[22] under the laws of the Commonwealth of Massachusetts, either *de jure, de facto,* or both, and prayed that the complaint[23] be dismissed as to him.

The defendant the Harper Foundation in its answer states that it believes that the[24] defendant John Harper is indebted to the United States of America as alleged and is within[25] the jurisdiction of this Court but denies that the Foundation is properly joined as a defendant.

By way[26] of further answer, it alleges it is a charitable corporation duly organized and having a charter[27] and existing under the laws of the sovereign Commonwealth of Massachusetts, that it is not indebted to[28] the United States, and that this is an attempt to collaterally attach its corporate charter, and it[29] prays for a dismissal of this action and for costs.

B. TRIAL

A trial by the Court in this case was held at[30] Boston, Massachusetts, on September 21, 22, and 26, 19__. The[31] defendants moved for dismissal at the conclusion of the trial.

II. ISSUES

A. What is the United States of[32] America seeking by the instant action?

B. Is the Harper Foundation a legitimate charitable[33] corporation under the laws of the Commonwealth of Massachusetts?

C. Is the personal property[34] of the Harper Foundation subject to levy and execution to satisfy debts of the defendant? (699)

(Continued in Lesson 10.)

Lesson 10

BUILDING YOUR LEGAL VOCABULARY

Word Beginnings *Un-* followed by a consonant is expressed by  ; when attached to a vowel, by  .

unmolested 

unascertainable 

uncontested 

unalterable 

unwarranted 

unethical 

Word Study

corporation A company or an association chartered as an individual.

equitable Just, fair, and right.

jurisprudence The law in general; the science of law.

particularity The detailed statement of particulars in a pleading, affidavit, or the like.

pleading Formal document filed in a court, including initial complaint, defendant's answers to the complaint, and all motions made by either party thereafter.

BUILDING YOUR LEGAL TRANSCRIPTION SKILL

Transcription Aid

Long Quotations

☐ Lengthy quotations in legal documents are usually single spaced and may be handled in either of the following ways:

1. Type opening quotation marks for each paragraph, but use the closing marks after the last paragraph only. If quotations occur within such material, change double quotation marks to single marks (apostrophe) to conform to the rule that quotations within quotations are indicated by single quotation marks.
2. Reset the left margin five spaces to the right and indent paragraphs ten spaces from the original margin. In this style, no quotation marks are necessary, unless quotations occur within the material.

Typing Citations

In citing cases, both *vs.* and *v.* are used to indicate *versus*. However, *v.* is the preferred form.

BUILDING YOUR LEGAL DICTATION PROFICIENCY

Preview

alleges 

bona fide 

de facto 

de jure 

fraud 

judgment 

levy  **validity** 

nonexistence  **warranting** 

Reading and Writing Practice

26. MEMORANDUM *(Continued from Lesson 9.)*

III. CONTENTION OF DEFENDANTS

A. The pleadings are such that it cannot be determined what the United States[1] of America is seeking by the action other than to secure a judgment for an amount for which it[2] already has a judgment; i.e., fines and costs assessed in the criminal action against John Harper.

B. The Harper[3] Foundation is a *de jure* corporation under the laws of the Commonwealth of Massachusetts.

C. The personal[4] property of the Harper Foundation is not subject to levy and execution to satisfy[5] the debts of the defendant John Harper.

IV. ARGUMENT

A. WHAT IS THE NATURE OF THE ACTION?

The plaintiff in[6] its complaints alleges that it already has a judgment against the defendant John Harper but attempts to proceed[7] to turn the action into one in the nature of an equitable action formerly known as a "Bill to Reach[8] and Apply."

It is the contention of the defendants that on the basis of the complaints *alone,* the actions[9] should be dismissed since they fail to state a cause of action warranting any relief by this Court.

B. THE HARPER[10] FOUNDATION IS A *DE JURE* CORPORATION UNDER THE LAWS OF MASSACHUSETTS.

The corporate charter and minute[11] book are in evidence. This is sufficient to establish the validity of the existence of the Harper[12] Foundation as a *de jure* corporation. The evidence requires a finding that if the Court finds that the[13] Foundation was not a *de jure* corporation, it was at very least a corporation *de facto.*

In 13[14] Am. Jur., sec.* 45, p. 192, we find:

"A bona fide attempt to organize a corporation[15] under a valid existing statute authorizing the creation of a corporation such as that[16] attempted to be created will result in the creation of a corporation *de facto . . . the existence*[17] *of which can be called into question only by the state in a direct proceeding for that purpose.*" [Italics[18] supplied.] See also *Con-*

*The symbol § may be used instead of *sec.*

solidated Elec. Corporation v. Panhandle Eastern Pipeline Co.[19] 189 F.2d 777.

The United States in its evidence would justify the finding[20] of nonexistence of corporation solely and exclusively on the grounds of fraud. Nowhere in the complaint[21] is there any mention of fraud. Where United States has placed all reliance for its contention on fraud, it was[22] bound to have made this charge clearly and specifically in its complaint.

"Circumstances instituting fraud shall[23] be stated with particularity." Federal Rules Civil Procedure 9 (B).

C. PERSONAL PROPERTY[24] OF FOUNDATION NOT SUBJECT TO LEVY AND EXECUTION FOR JOHN HARPER'S DEBTS.

The plaintiff has failed to prove that[25] the personal property under attachment is that of John Harper. It is a fundamental principle[26] that the property of a corporation is not available for the satisfaction of a corporate officer's[27] personal debt.

V. CONCLUSION

A. The Harper Foundation was either a *de jure* or a *de facto*[28] corporation.

B. The United States of America in this case is not entitled to a judgment, since it[29] already has a judgment against the defendant John Harper in its criminal action.

C. The action should be[30] dismissed as to the defendants, John Harper and the Harper Foundation; the attachments on the property dissolved;[31] and the Harper Foundation awarded its costs.

Respectfully submitted,

GREENBERG, O'BRIEN, MASON & MCCANN[32]

____

By James E. McCann,
Attorney for the Defendants (649)

UNIT

2 Divorce

Susan Andrew, Libelant
v.
Frank Andrew, Libelee

This is a case concerning domestic relations in which the wife is suing the husband for divorce and is seeking custody of the minor children as well as separate maintenance and a fair distribution of the husband's assets.

The attorney for Susan Andrew is Kevin O'Brien, Esq.

The attorney for Frank Andrew is Alice E. Bates.

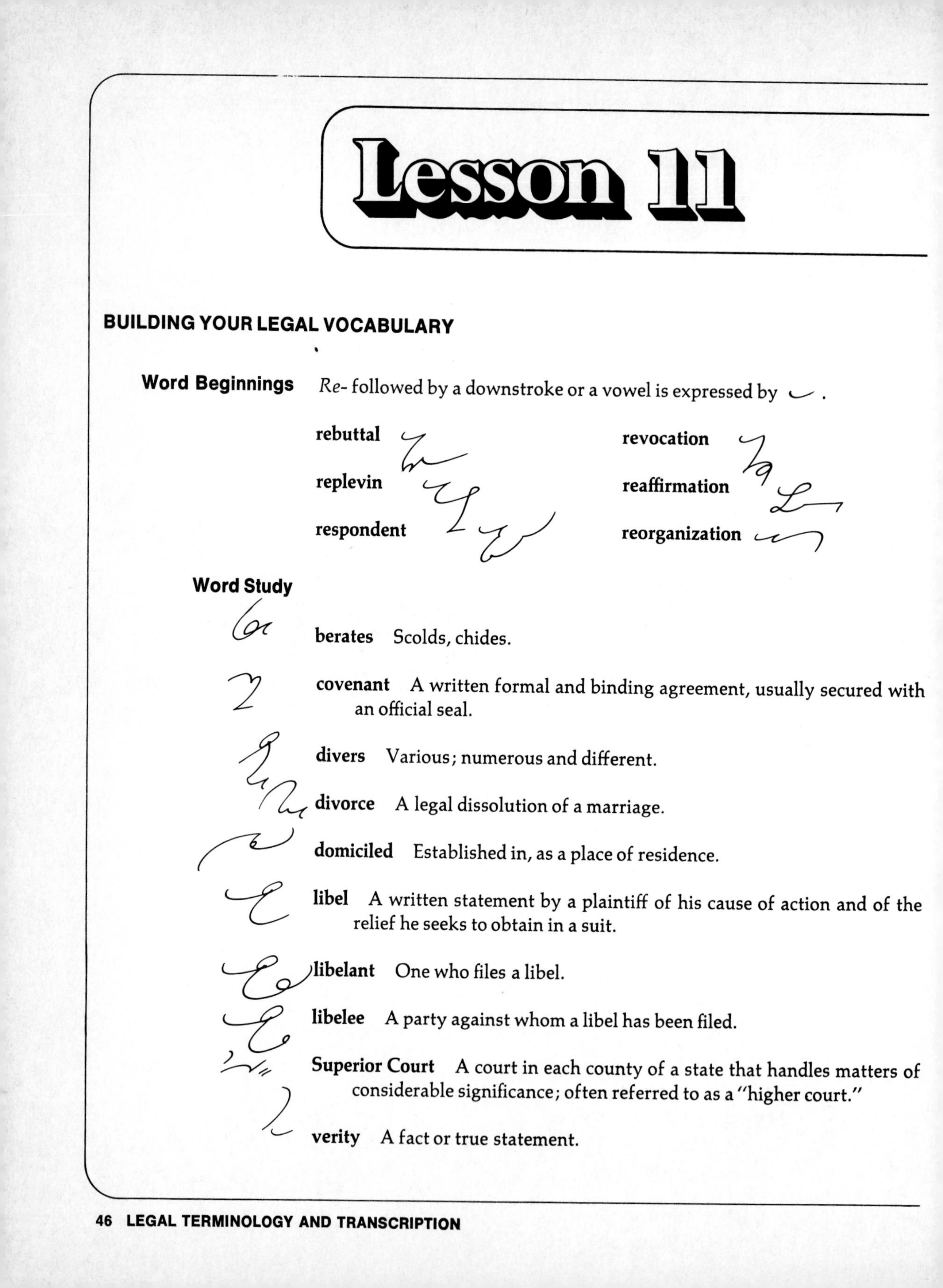

Lesson 11

BUILDING YOUR LEGAL VOCABULARY

Word Beginnings *Re-* followed by a downstroke or a vowel is expressed by .

rebuttal	**revocation**
replevin	**reaffirmation**
respondent	**reorganization**

Word Study

berates Scolds, chides.

covenant A written formal and binding agreement, usually secured with an official seal.

divers Various; numerous and different.

divorce A legal dissolution of a marriage.

domiciled Established in, as a place of residence.

libel A written statement by a plaintiff of his cause of action and of the relief he seeks to obtain in a suit.

libelant One who files a libel.

libelee A party against whom a libel has been filed.

Superior Court A court in each county of a state that handles matters of considerable significance; often referred to as a "higher court."

verity A fact or true statement.

BUILDING YOUR LEGAL TRANSCRIPTION SKILL

Transcription Aid **Relation of Quotation Marks to Other Punctuation**

□ Commas and periods are always typed inside the closing quotation mark. Colons and semicolons are always typed after the quotation mark.

> The Libel for Divorce specifically stated, "The libelant is without any funds whatsoever."
>
> The papers were clearly marked "Rush"; however, they were not sent by airmail.

□ Question marks and exclamation points are typed outside the closing quotation mark if the entire sentence is in the form of a question or exclamation.

> Does the will answer my question, "What is to become of the lake property"?

□ Question or exclamation marks are typed inside the quotation mark if the quoted material is a question or an exclamation.

> The will answers my original question, "What is to become of the lake property?"

Typing Citations In typing cases, underscore case names. The *v.* or *vs.* may or may not be underscored, depending on the preference of the attorney.

Carter v. Bergeron   Carter v. Bergeron   Carter vs. Bergeron

BUILDING YOUR LEGAL DICTATION PROFICIENCY

Preview

abused
associates
behaved
Buick
conduct
disagreeable
distraught
domestic
dutiful
erratic
faithful
injure
intolerance
jealous
justification
marital

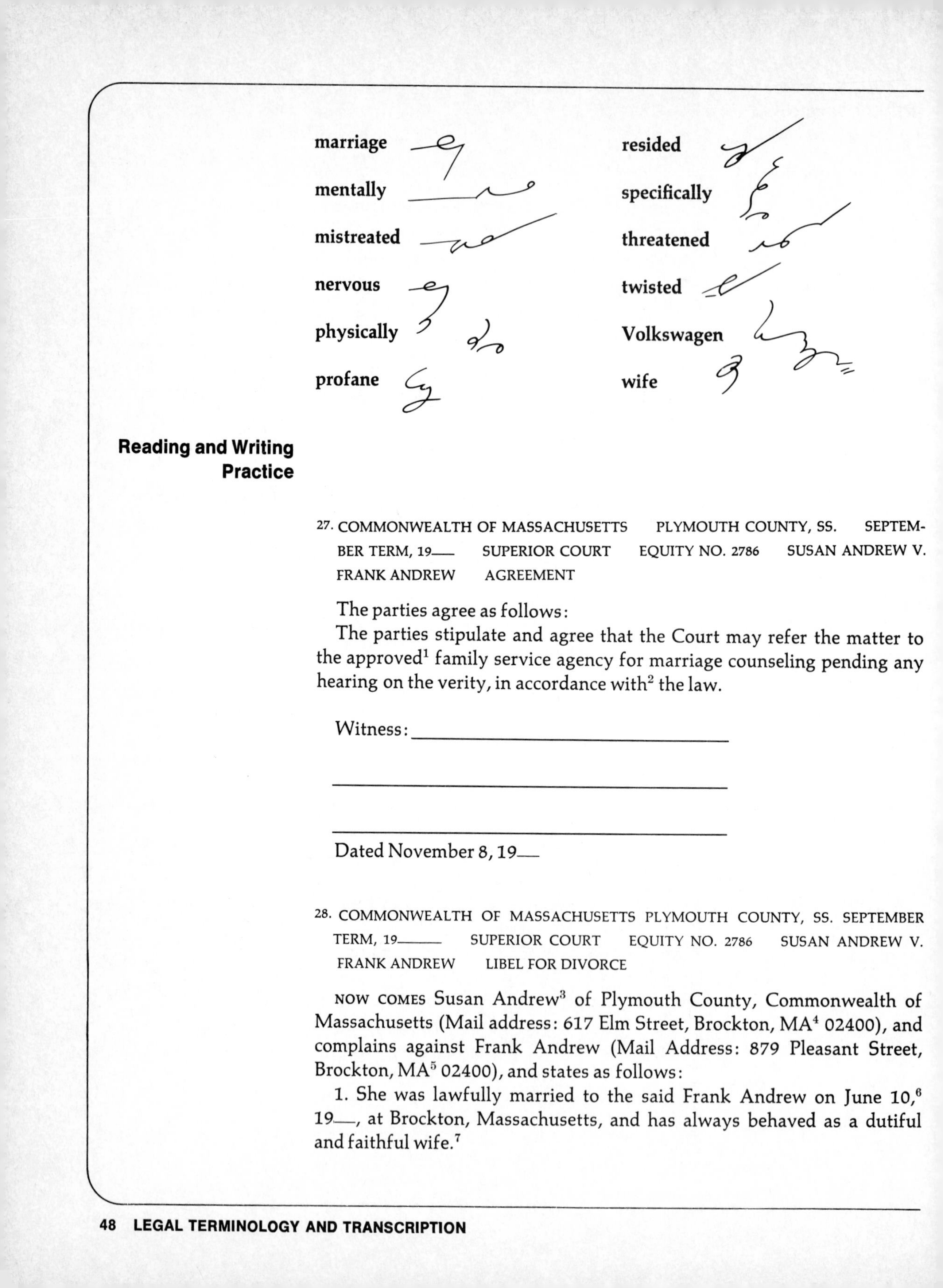

marriage

mentally

mistreated

nervous

physically

profane

resided

specifically

threatened

twisted

Volkswagen

wife

Reading and Writing Practice

27. COMMONWEALTH OF MASSACHUSETTS PLYMOUTH COUNTY, SS. SEPTEMBER TERM, 19___ SUPERIOR COURT EQUITY NO. 2786 SUSAN ANDREW V. FRANK ANDREW AGREEMENT

The parties agree as follows:

The parties stipulate and agree that the Court may refer the matter to the approved[1] family service agency for marriage counseling pending any hearing on the verity, in accordance with[2] the law.

Witness: ______________________________

____

____

Dated November 8, 19___

28. COMMONWEALTH OF MASSACHUSETTS PLYMOUTH COUNTY, SS. SEPTEMBER TERM, 19_____ SUPERIOR COURT EQUITY NO. 2786 SUSAN ANDREW V. FRANK ANDREW LIBEL FOR DIVORCE

NOW COMES Susan Andrew[3] of Plymouth County, Commonwealth of Massachusetts (Mail address: 617 Elm Street, Brockton, MA[4] 02400), and complains against Frank Andrew (Mail Address: 879 Pleasant Street, Brockton, MA[5] 02400), and states as follows:

1. She was lawfully married to the said Frank Andrew on June 10,[6] 19___, at Brockton, Massachusetts, and has always behaved as a dutiful and faithful wife.[7]

2. Since their marriage and continuously until the present time, the parties have resided and been domiciled[8] in said Brockton.

3. There are three children born of this marriage: namely, Susan Andrew, aged 6; John Andrew, aged 5;[9] and Charles Andrew, aged 4.

4. (a) Wholly regardless of his marriage covenants and duties, the libelee[10] does so treat and has so treated the libelant as seriously to injure her health and endanger her reason,[11] in that said libelee has behaved in an erratic manner, has exhibited intolerance of the[12] libelant, has been withdrawn, has failed and refused to discuss in a reasonable manner with the libelant their[13] mutual domestic affairs and financial and other matters usually discussed by husband and wife, has[14] frequently embarrassed the libelant with his erratic conduct towards the libelant, has frequently exhibited[15] an extremely jealous attitude of the libelant and refuses to allow her to carry on[16] a normal life, has refused to provide a normal social life for the libelant, resents the libelant's friends,[17] is disagreeable to them and complains constantly to the libelant about the fact that she associates with[18] them, constantly berates the libelant, complains about her methods of bringing up the children and uses profane[19] language towards the libelant in front of said children, frequently embarrasses libelant in the presence of[20] others, and has generally conducted himself in such a fashion as to disturb marital happiness and[21] make living with him intolerable. As a result of said conduct, the libelant has been made nervous and distraught[22] and has suffered both physically and mentally.

(b) Wholly regardless of his marriage covenants and[23] duties, the libelee has been guilty of extreme cruelty toward the libelant, in that at divers times and[24] places since their marriage and while residing in Massachusetts, he has generally mistreated her, struck her,[25] threatened her with bodily harm, and physically abused her; that specifically, on or about April 9, 19—,[26] without justification, libelee twisted her arm and threw her across the room with[27] sufficient force to cause her considerable pain and that on or about September 14, 19—,[28] again without justification, he struck her severely on the back of the head, with sufficient force to cause her[29] considerable pain.

5. The parties are owners of the real estate at which they now reside, being located[30] at Brockton, Massachusetts, subject to a mortgage in favor of the Brockton Federal Savings and Loan[31] Association in the amount of $20,000; the libelee has two cars registered in his name, one[32] a 19— Buick and the other a 19— Volkswagen; the libelee[33] has several life insurance policies and one or more savings accounts or checking accounts, the size[34] and location of which are unknown to the libelant; whereas the libelant is without any funds whatsoever[35] and without sufficient funds with which to pay her legal costs and attorney's fees. (715)

(Continued in Lesson 12.)

Lesson 12

BUILDING YOUR LEGAL VOCABULARY

Word Beginnings *De-* and *di-* are expressed by  except before , , or an upstroke.

deposition 

directors 

deputy 

detention 

devisee 

decree 

Word Study

 **decree** A decision or sentence made by order of a court.

 **encumber** To place a burden upon; to make land subject to a liability, e.g., by mortgage.

 **justice of the peace** A local official empowered to do some or all of the following, depending on the jurisdiction: administer justice in minor cases, commit for trial, administer oaths, and perform marriages.

 **relief** Legal remedy; object of a legal action.

BUILDING YOUR LEGAL TRANSCRIPTION SKILL

Transcription Aid **Quoting Telegrams**

☐ When typing a short quoted telegram, place the opening quotation mark before the date and before each new paragraph. Place the closing quotation mark after the typed signature.

"November 20, 19—. David L. Greenberg, Esq., 123 Commonwealth Avenue, Boston, Massachusetts.
"Have not received copy for your article, 'The Legal Secretary,' due last Friday. Jack Davidson, Editor"

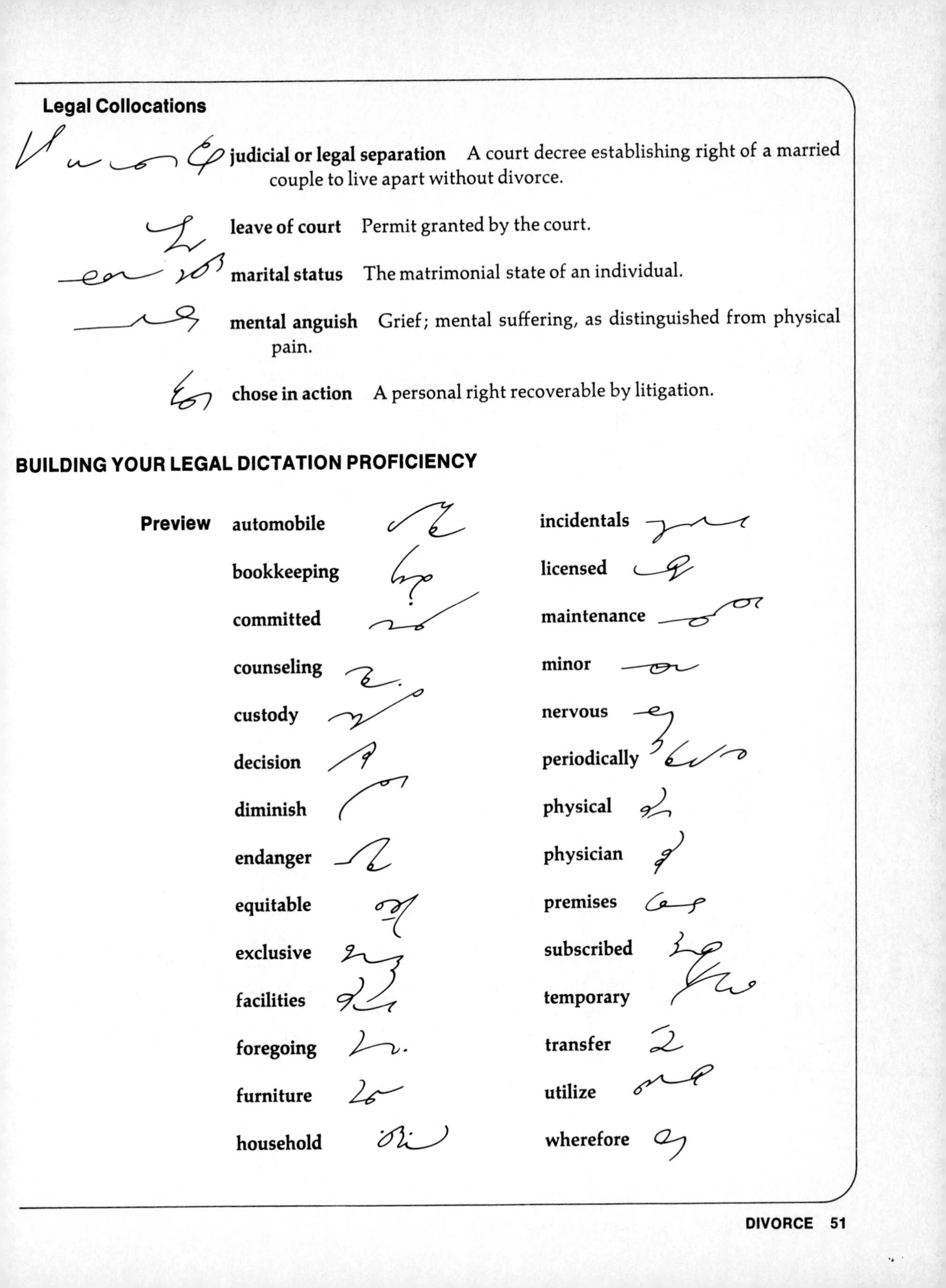

Legal Collocations

judicial or legal separation A court decree establishing right of a married couple to live apart without divorce.

leave of court Permit granted by the court.

marital status The matrimonial state of an individual.

mental anguish Grief; mental suffering, as distinguished from physical pain.

chose in action A personal right recoverable by litigation.

BUILDING YOUR LEGAL DICTATION PROFICIENCY

Preview

automobile
bookkeeping
committed
counseling
custody
decision
diminish
endanger
equitable
exclusive
facilities
foregoing
furniture
household
incidentals
licensed
maintenance
minor
nervous
periodically
physical
physician
premises
subscribed
temporary
transfer
utilize
wherefore

Reading and Writing Practice

29. LIBEL FOR DIVORCE *(Continued from Lesson 11.)*

WHEREFORE, your libelant prays as follows:

a. That a divorce from the bonds of matrimony between herself and[1] the libelee be decreed.

b. That the care, custody, and education of the said minor children be[2] committed to her.

c. That the libelee be ordered to pay to her, periodically, a reasonable amount[3] for her support and maintenance and for the support, maintenance, and education of the said minor children.[4]

d. That an equitable distribution of the libelee's assets be decreed to her.

e. That the libelee[5] be ordered to pay the libelant's costs and counsel fees.

f. And for such other and further relief as may be[6] just.

FURTHER, pending a decision on the merits and until further order of this Court, the libelant prays[7] for the following temporary relief:

g. That the care, custody, and education of the said minor[8] children be committed to her.

h. That she be given temporary exclusive use of the residence of[9] the parties and the household furniture therein.

i. That the libelee be ordered to pay to her, periodically,[10] a reasonable amount for her support and maintenance and for the support, maintenance, and education[11] of the said children.

j. That she be given use of the 19__ Volkswagen automobile.[12]

k. That the libelee be ordered not to transfer, encumber, or diminish said assets, except for[13] normal and reasonable use, pending a hearing on the merits and equitable distribution of said assets[14] to the libelant.

l. And for such other and further relief as may be just.

____
Susan Andrew

COMMONWEALTH OF[15] MASSACHUSETTS)
PLYMOUTH COUNTY) ss.

Personally appeared the above-named Susan Andrew and made oath that the foregoing[16] statements by her subscribed are true.

Before me,____________________________Justice of the Peace

30. DOCTOR'S STATEMENT

TO WHOM IT MAY CONCERN:[17]

I, ROBERT L. AUSTIN, M.D., a registered and licensed physician practicing in Brockton, Massachusetts,[18] have attended and treated Susan Andrew of Brockton, Massachusetts 02400.

Mrs. Andrew has[19] told me about the conduct of her husband, Frank Andrew, and about her physical and nervous symptoms which she had while[20] living with him. In my opinion, the conduct of Frank Andrew as described to me by Mrs. Andrew was such[21] as to seriously endanger her reason.

Robert L. Austin, M.D.
9 West Church Street
Brockton,[22] MA 02400 (447)

31. ALICE E. BATES, ESQ., 54 FRANKLIN STREET, BOSTON, MA 02100

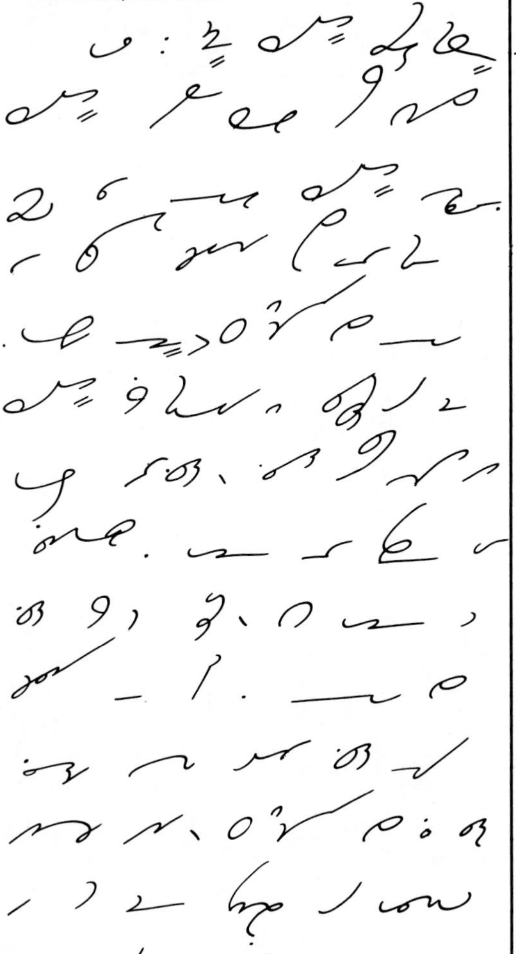

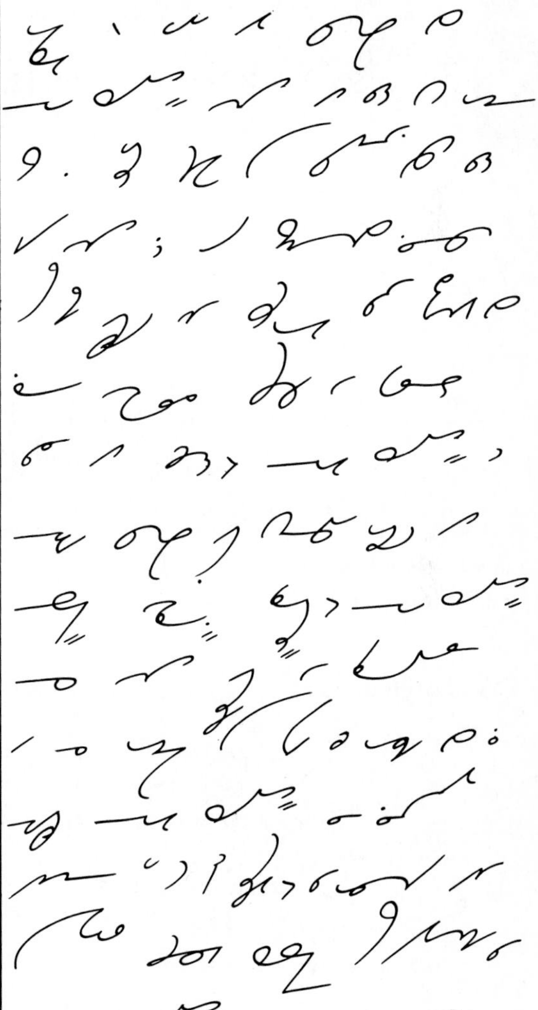

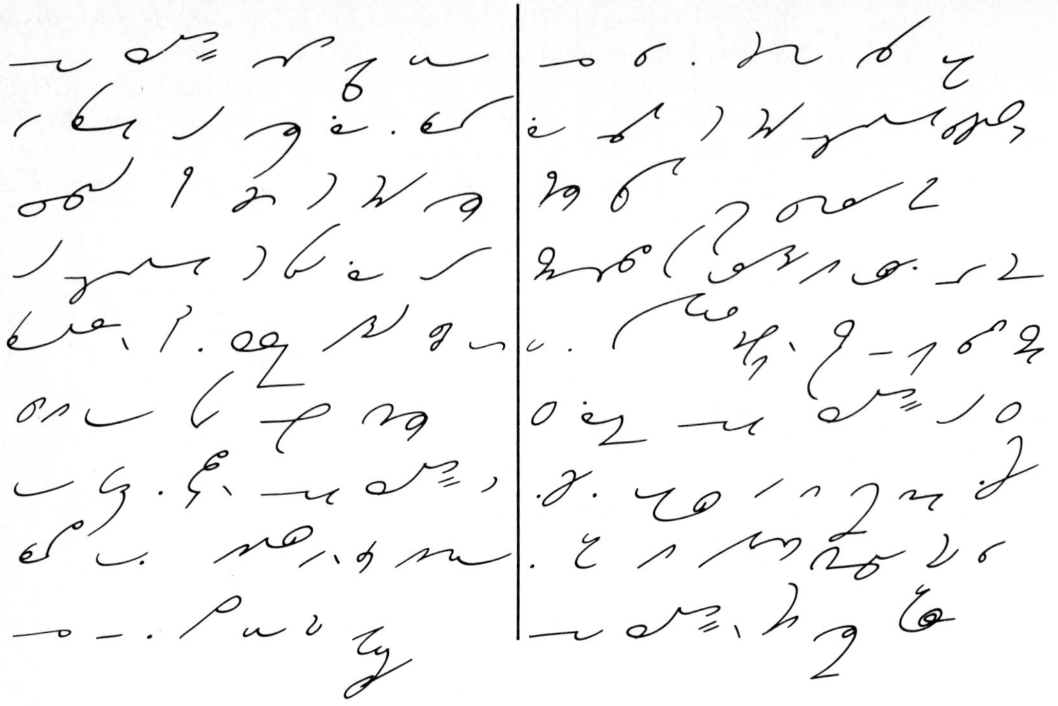

Lesson 13

BUILDING YOUR LEGAL VOCABULARY

Word Beginnings *Dis-* and *des-* are expressed by .

desertion		dissolution	
destitute		dismissal	
discontinuance		discretionary	

Word Study

 **agreement** A contract or a bargain.

equity Equal and impartial justice; a financial interest in property.

irreconcilable So different that opposing views cannot be brought together.

witness *(n.)* One who gives evidence.
(v.) To testify or give evidence; to be present at or have personal knowledge of.

BUILDING YOUR LEGAL TRANSCRIPTION SKILL

Transcription Aid

Indicating Source of Quotation

- ☐ When a quoted sentence is interrupted to give the source, type a comma inside the quotation mark that closes the first portion and a comma before the quotation mark that indicated the continuation.

  "Were you present," asked the lawyer, "when the accident occurred at the intersection of Division and Pearl Streets?"

- ☐ When an expression indicating the source follows the material quoted, it is separated from the quotation by a comma. If, however, a question mark or explanation point closes the quotation, no comma is used.

  "Were you present at the intersection of Division and Pearl Streets when the accident occurred?" the lawyer asked.

Latin and French Words and Phrases

de novo *(dā nō'vō)* Anew; afresh; a second time.

feme sole *(fem sōl)* An unmarried woman; a single woman (unmarried, widowed, divorced).

in loco parentis *(in lō'ko pa ren'tis)* In place of a parent.

BUILDING YOUR LEGAL DICTATION PROFICIENCY

Preview

aforesaid 

diminish 

electricity 

groceries 

hereto 

household 

insurance	**prescribed**
libelant	**referral**
libelee	**residence**
minor	**scheduled**
miscellaneous	**stipulate**
misunderstanding	**temporary**
mortgage	**thereto**
physician	**visitation**

Reading and Writing Practice

32. COMMONWEALTH OF MASSACHUSETTS PLYMOUTH COUNTY, SS. SEPTEMBER TERM, 19____ SUPERIOR COURT EQUITY NO. 2786 SUSAN ANDREW V. FRANK ANDREW TEMPORARY STIPULATION

Pending a hearing on the merits, or further order of the Court, the parties hereto stipulate and agree as[1] follows:

1. The care and custody of the three minor children, Susan Andrew, John Andrew, and Charles Andrew, be[2] awarded to libelant.

2. Libelee shall have reasonable rights of visitation with said children at reasonable[3] times and places. Said visits may take place either at the home of the libelant or away from said home, as the[4] parties may agree. Libelee agrees to give libelant reasonable notice of his intention to visit the[5] children.

3. Libelee agrees to assume and pay all reasonable household expenses, including mortgage payments,[6] real estate taxes, water assessment, house insurance, electricity and telephone bills, heating bills, bills[7] for necessary repairs to real estate, Blue Cross or other medical insurance on the family, and any other[8] medical and dental expenses prescribed by a physician or dentist and not covered by the aforesaid insurance,[9] liability insurance on the personal automobile of the libelant and the reasonable[10] repair bills to said automobile, clothing bills for the family, and the monthly milk bill. In addition,[11] libelee agrees to pay the libelant One Hundred Dollars ($100) per week for the support of the minor children, said payment[12] to be made directly to the libelant.

4. Libelant is to have temporary use of the residence[13] of the parties and

the household furniture therein, excepting that libelee shall have the right to make reasonable[14] use of a basement office, located in said residence, for business purposes only.

5. Libelant[15] shall be given temporary use of a 19— Volkswagen automobile.

6.[16] Libelee agrees not to transfer, encumber, or diminish any of his assets, except for normal and reasonable[17] use.

Susan Andrew, Libelant	Attorney for Libelant
Frank Andrew, Libelee	Attorney for Libelee[18] (360)

33. ALICE E. BATES, ESQ., 54 FRANKLIN STREET, BOSTON, MA 02100

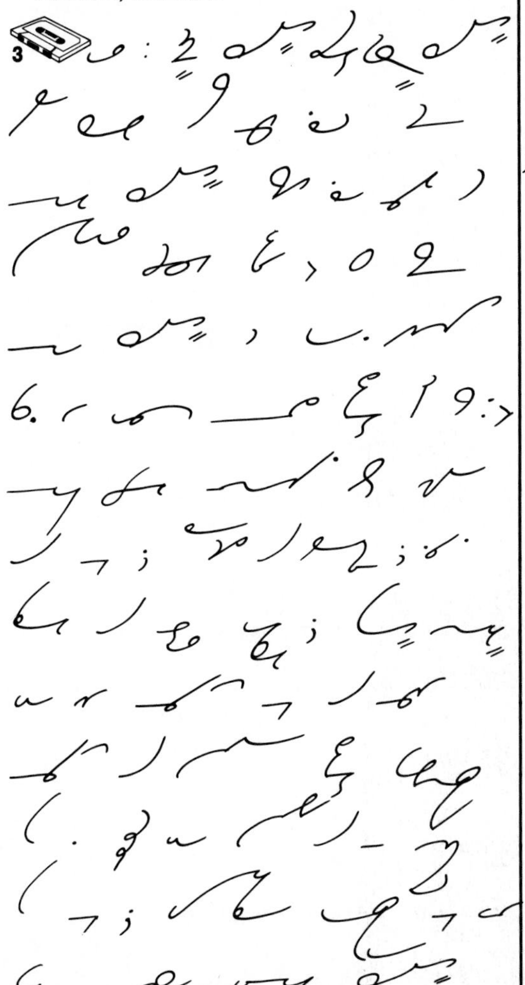

34. THOMAS N. BELL, ESQ., CLERK OF SUPREME COURT, PEMBERTON SQUARE, BOSTON, MA 02100

35. ALICE E. BATES, ESQ., 54 FRANKLIN STREET, BOSTON, MA 02100

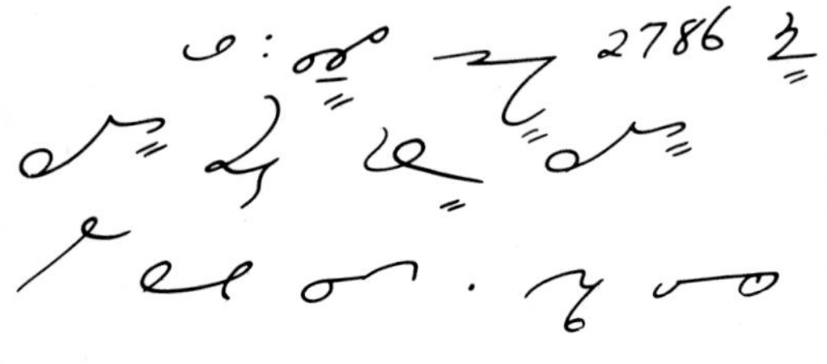

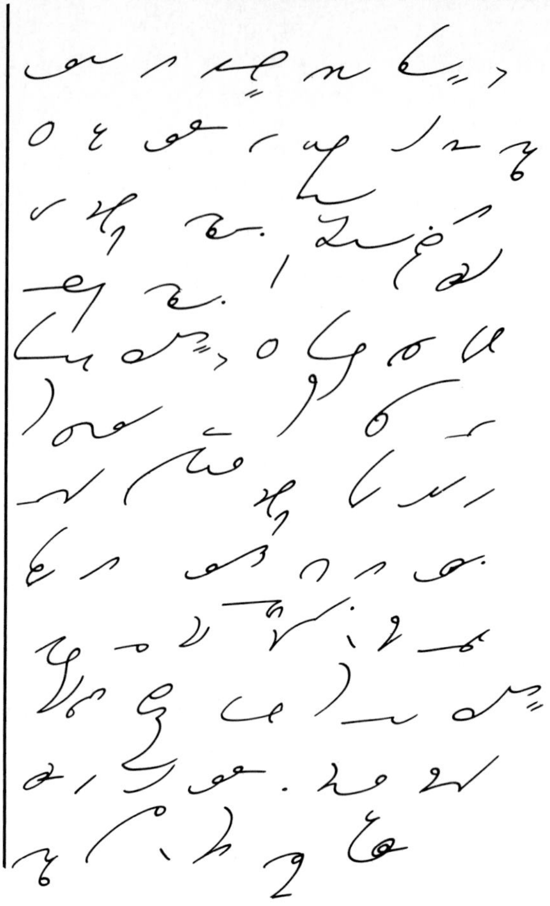

Lesson 14

BUILDING YOUR LEGAL VOCABULARY

Word Beginnings *Mis-* is expressed by  .

misappropriation 

misconduct 

misrepresentations 

misstatements 

mistrial  misusage 

Word Study

aggrieved Injured in some way by the actions of another.

deposition Testimony under oath.

grievous Very serious.

re With regard to.

BUILDING YOUR LEGAL TRANSCRIPTION SKILL

Transcription Aid

Quotation Marks With Reference Expressions

☐ Use quotation marks to enclose words or phrases in the following instances:

1. Words or phrases following such expressions as *entitled, signed, marked,* or *labeled.*

   The document entitled "Temporary Stipulations" set forth the points agreed upon by the libelant and the libelee.

2. The definition of a word or expression when the term itself is underscored.

   The term *custody* may be defined as "immediate charge and control exercised by a person or an authority."

3. Words or phrases following such expressions as *called, so-called,* and *known* as when emphasis is desired or when such expressions are misnomers, slang, or words used in a sense that is different from the usual meaning.

   Numerous so-called "relatives" appeared when the will could not be found.

Legal Collocations

intrinsic value The true, inherent, or essential value of a thing.

null and void Binding no one; having no legal effect.

privileged communication A confidence communicated to counsel that may not be divulged—even in court.

public notice A notice given to the public either by posting the notice in a public place or publishing it in a newspaper.

seised of, seized of In legal possession of; having ownership of real property, the ownership carrying with it the right of possession of the land, rights of way, minerals, buildings, and the like.

BUILDING YOUR LEGAL DICTATION PROFICIENCY

Preview

above-captioned	outstanding
clients	pertinent
disposition	proceeding
divorce	status
financial	support
homestead	uncontested
insurance	verifying
justified	visitation

Reading and Writing Practice

36. ALICE E. BATES, ESQ., 54 FRANKLIN STREET, BOSTON, MA 02100

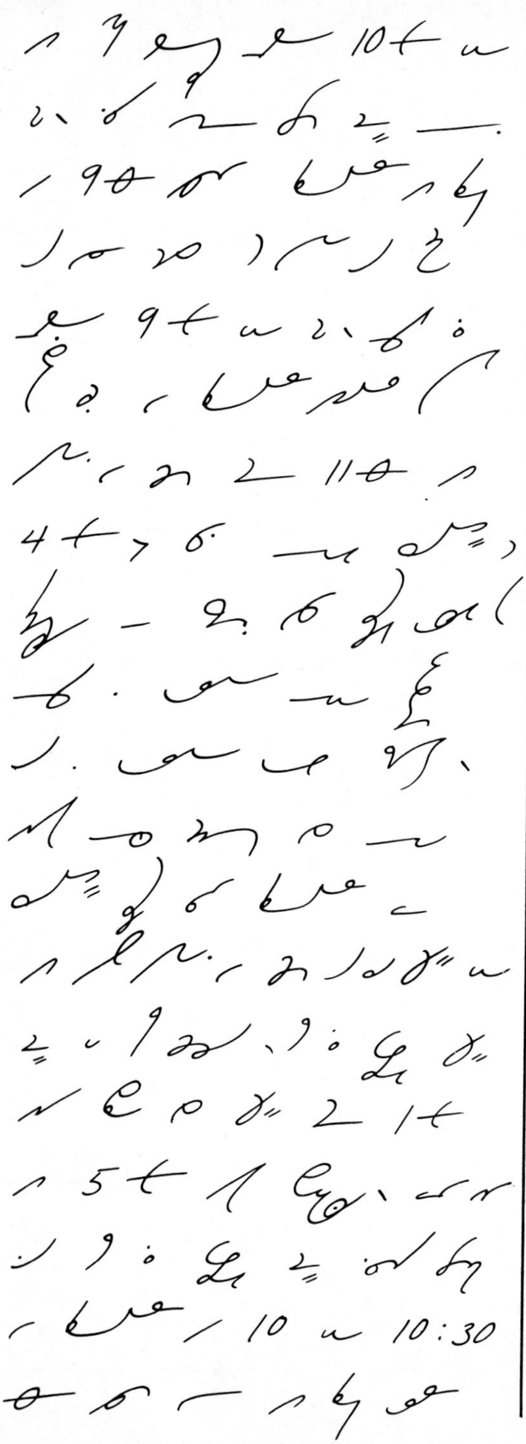

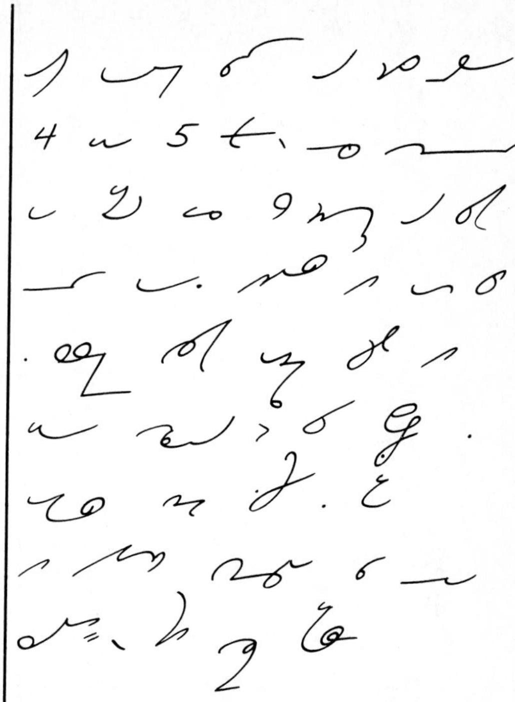

37. ALICE E. BATES, ESQ., 54 FRANKLIN STREET, BOSTON, MA 02100

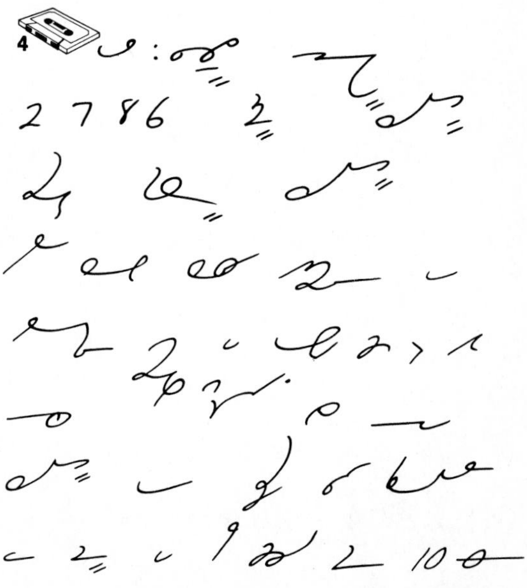

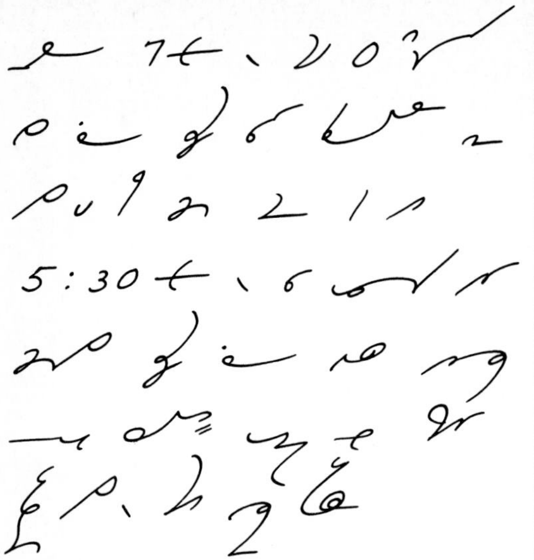

38. ALICE E. BATES, ESQ., 54 FRANKLIN STREET, BOSTON, MA 02100

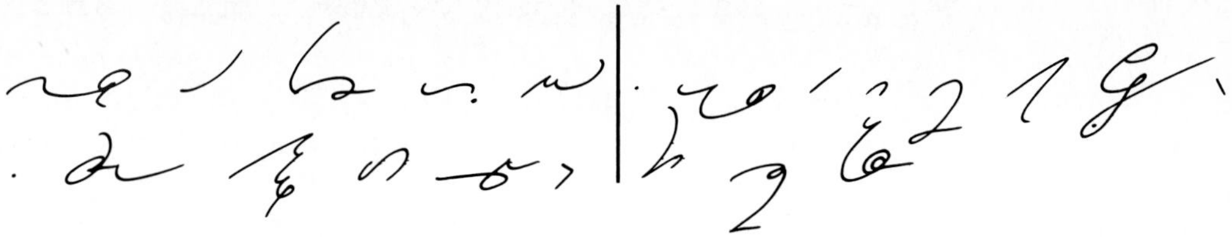

Lesson 15

BUILDING YOUR LEGAL VOCABULARY

Word Beginnings *Con-* attached to a consonant is expressed by  ; attached to a vowel, by  .

consignee 
contingency 
conspiracy 
controversies 
confiscation 
connived 

Word Study

 **alimony** An allowance for support made under court order to a divorced person by the former spouse, out of the former spouse's income or estate.

 **incur** To become liable or subject to.

 **insinuate** To cause doubt or suspicion.

 **tenuous** Flimsy; having little substance or strength.

BUILDING YOUR LEGAL TRANSCRIPTION SKILL

Transcription Aid **Semicolons With Transitional Expressions**

☐ Use a semicolon to separate independent clauses that are joined by

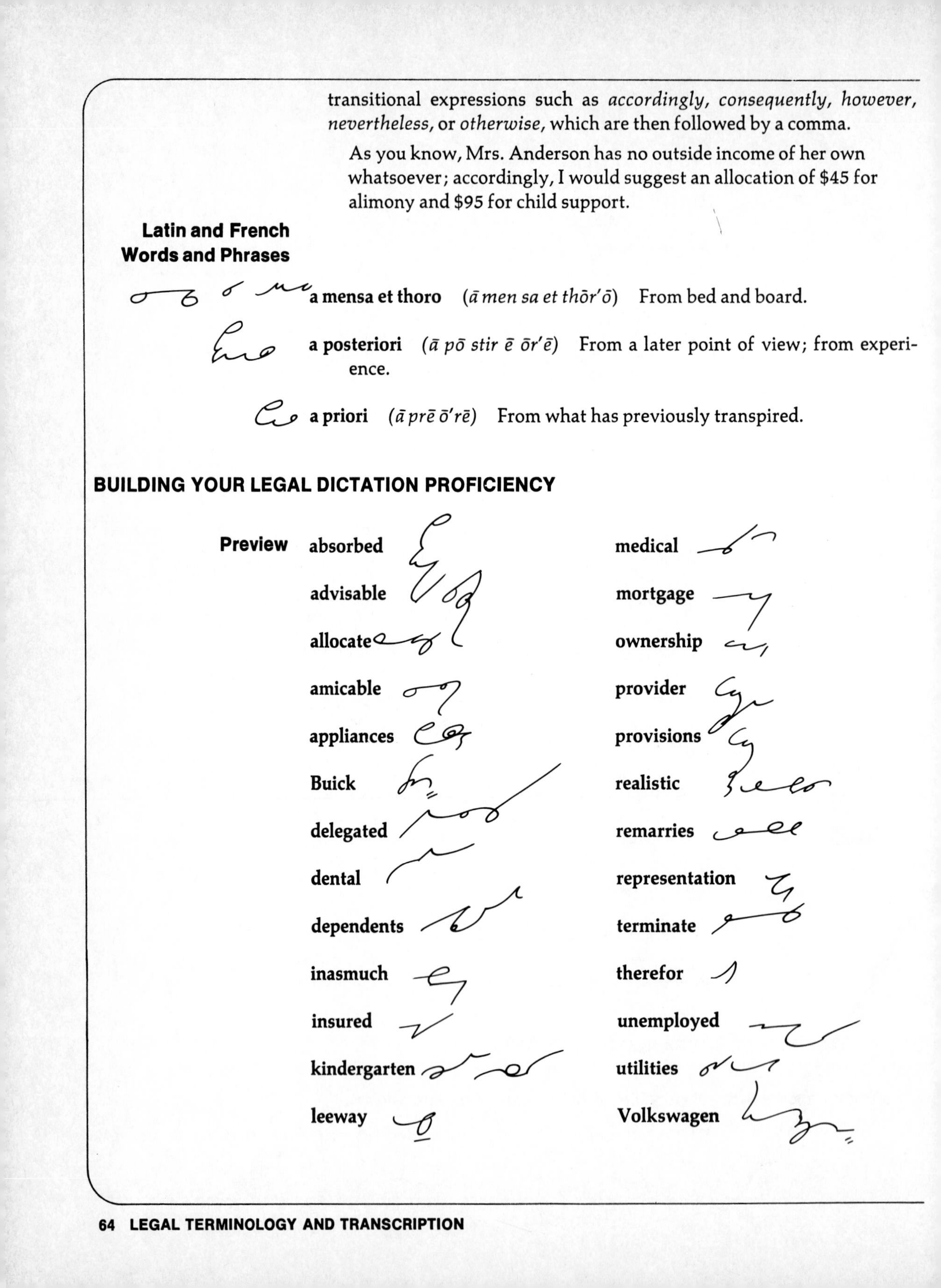

transitional expressions such as *accordingly, consequently, however, nevertheless,* or *otherwise,* which are then followed by a comma.

As you know, Mrs. Anderson has no outside income of her own whatsoever; accordingly, I would suggest an allocation of $45 for alimony and $95 for child support.

Latin and French Words and Phrases

a mensa et thoro (*ā men sa et thōr′ō*) From bed and board.

a posteriori (*ā pō stir ē ōr′ē*) From a later point of view; from experience.

a priori (*ā prē ō′rē*) From what has previously transpired.

BUILDING YOUR LEGAL DICTATION PROFICIENCY

Preview

absorbed
advisable
allocate
amicable
appliances
Buick
delegated
dental
dependents
inasmuch
insured
kindergarten
leeway
medical
mortgage
ownership
provider
provisions
realistic
remarries
representation
terminate
therefor
unemployed
utilities
Volkswagen

Reading and Writing Practice

39. ALICE E. BATES, ESQ., 54 FRANKLIN STREET, BOSTON, MA 02100

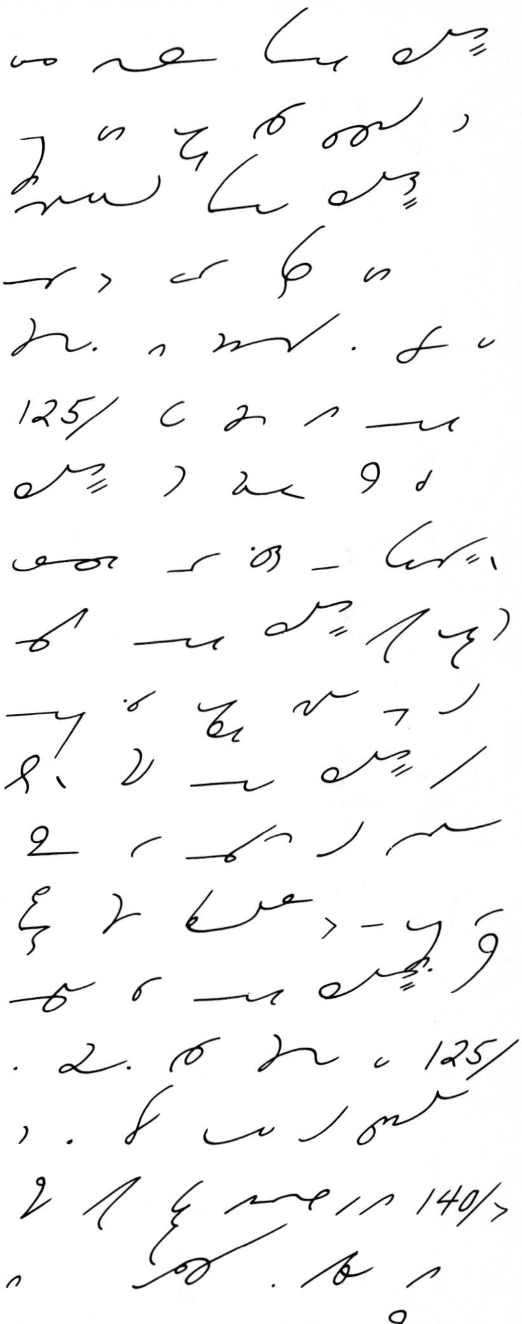

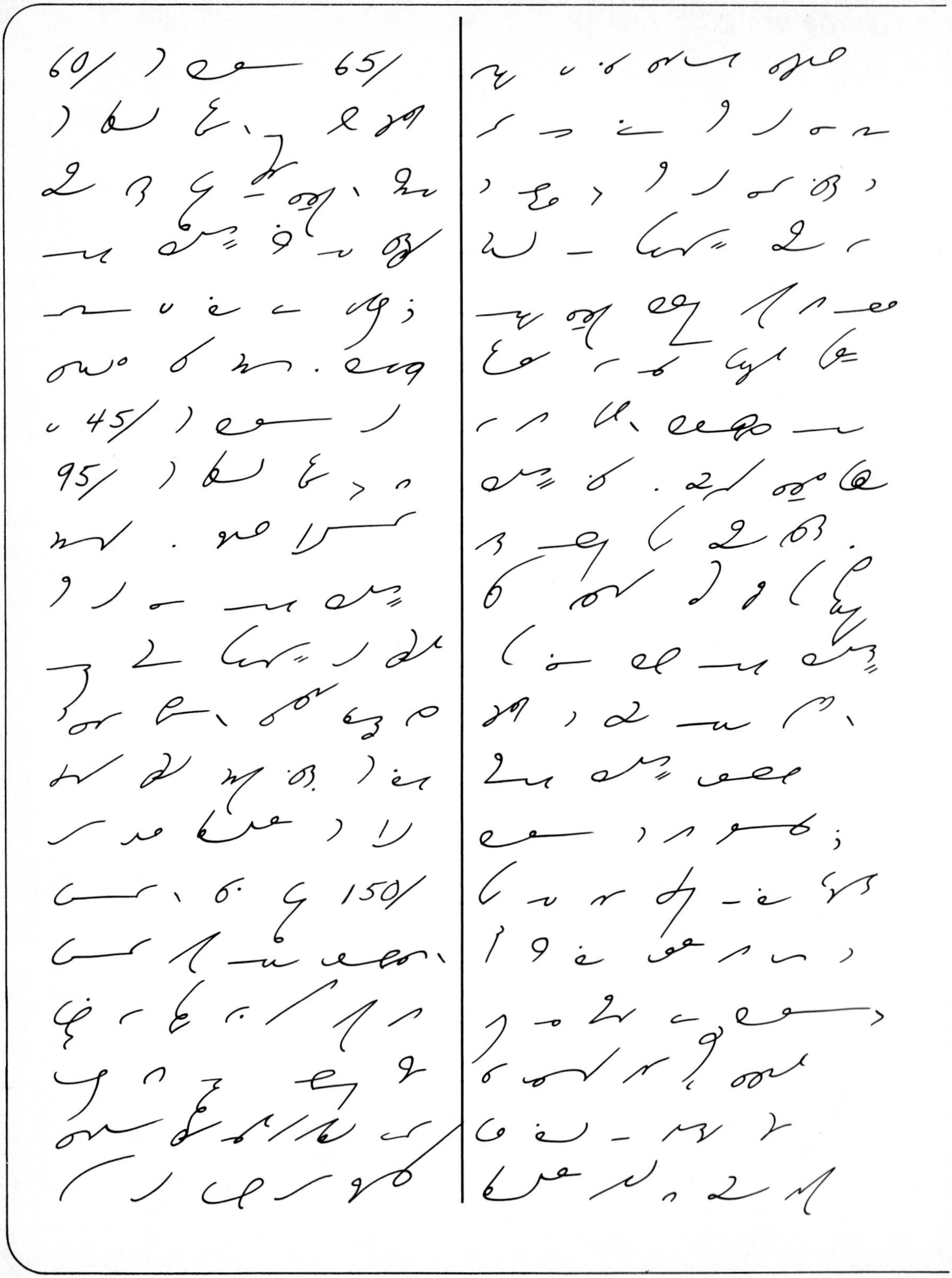

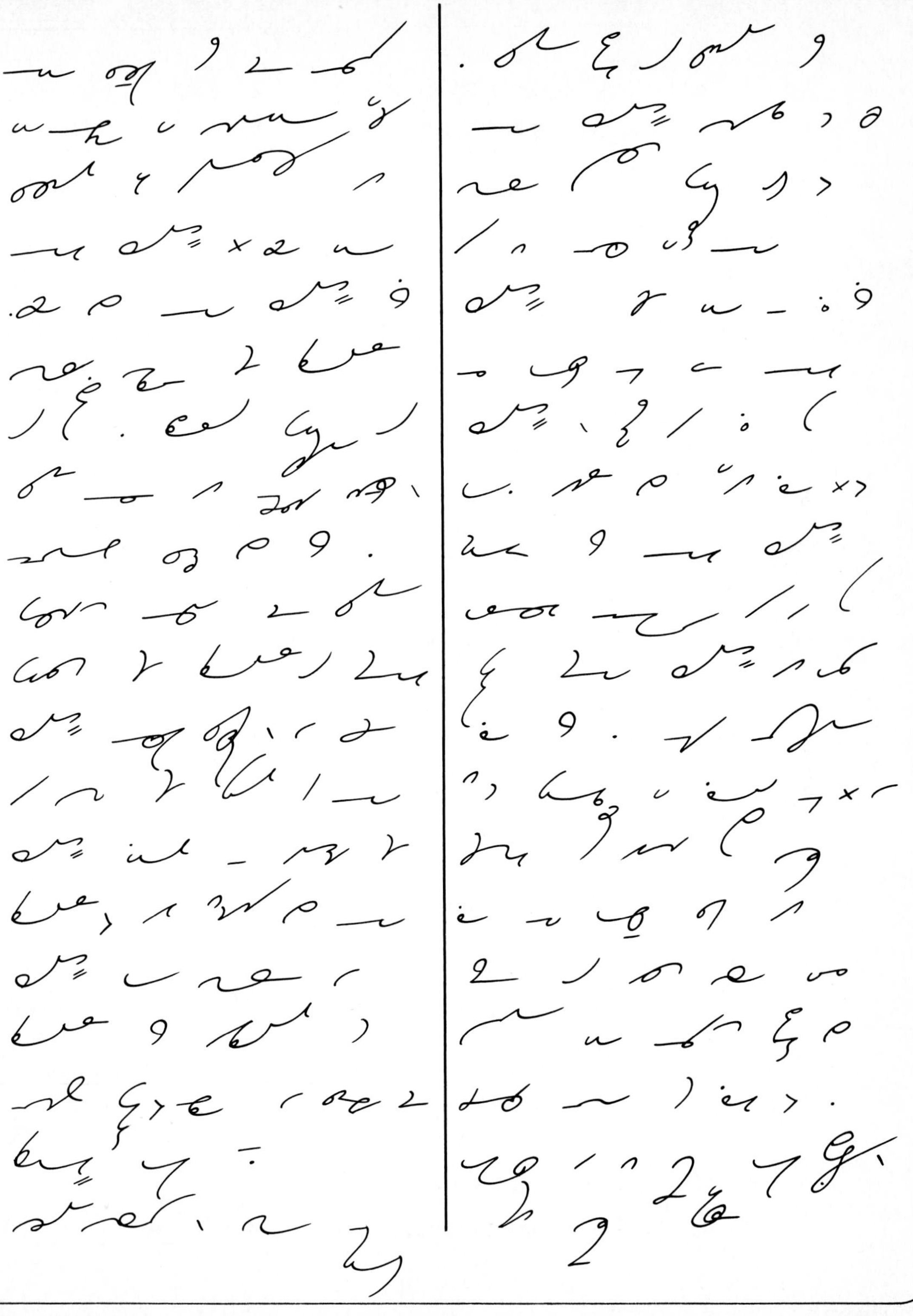

Lesson 16

BUILDING YOUR LEGAL VOCABULARY

Word Beginnings *Com-* attached to a consonant is expressed by  ; attached to a vowel, by  .

compensation 

competitors 

comptroller 

incompetent 

communal 

commodity 

Word Study

 **alienate** Withdraw affection.

 **counterproposal** An alternate proposal made by one who has just refused a proposal.

 **designated** That which is indicated and pointed out.

 **grounds for** Reasons for; basis of an action.

BUILDING YOUR LEGAL TRANSCRIPTION SKILL

Transcription Aid **Colons With Enumerations or Lists**

☐ Use the colon to introduce an enumeration of items or a list after expressions such as *the following, as follows, thus,* and *these.*

> The visitation hours were set as follows: from 3 p.m. to 6 p.m. two days a week, from 10 a.m. to 6 p.m. on Sundays, and from 10 a.m. to 6 p.m. on certain holidays by special agreement.

Colons With Explanatory Clauses

☐ Use the colon to introduce an independent clause that explains, il-

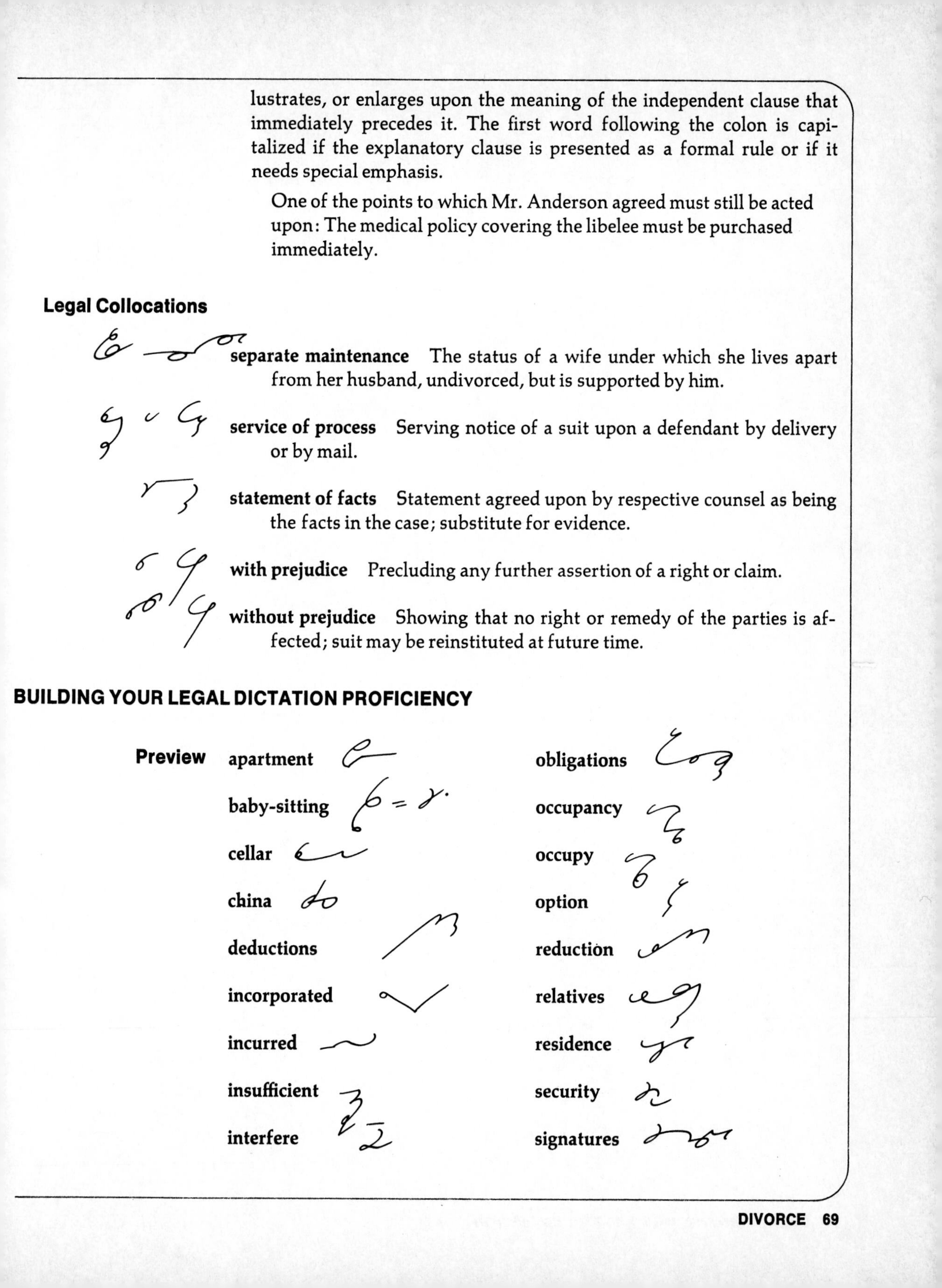

lustrates, or enlarges upon the meaning of the independent clause that immediately precedes it. The first word following the colon is capitalized if the explanatory clause is presented as a formal rule or if it needs special emphasis.

> One of the points to which Mr. Anderson agreed must still be acted upon: The medical policy covering the libelee must be purchased immediately.

Legal Collocations

separate maintenance The status of a wife under which she lives apart from her husband, undivorced, but is supported by him.

service of process Serving notice of a suit upon a defendant by delivery or by mail.

statement of facts Statement agreed upon by respective counsel as being the facts in the case; substitute for evidence.

with prejudice Precluding any further assertion of a right or claim.

without prejudice Showing that no right or remedy of the parties is affected; suit may be reinstituted at future time.

BUILDING YOUR LEGAL DICTATION PROFICIENCY

Preview

apartment
baby-sitting
cellar
china
deductions
incorporated
incurred
insufficient
interfere
obligations
occupancy
occupy
option
reduction
relatives
residence
security
signatures

silverware

swing

transportation

undue

unmarried

withdrawals

Reading and Writing Practice

40. ALICE E. BATES, ESQ., 54 FRANKLIN STREET, BOSTON, MA 02100

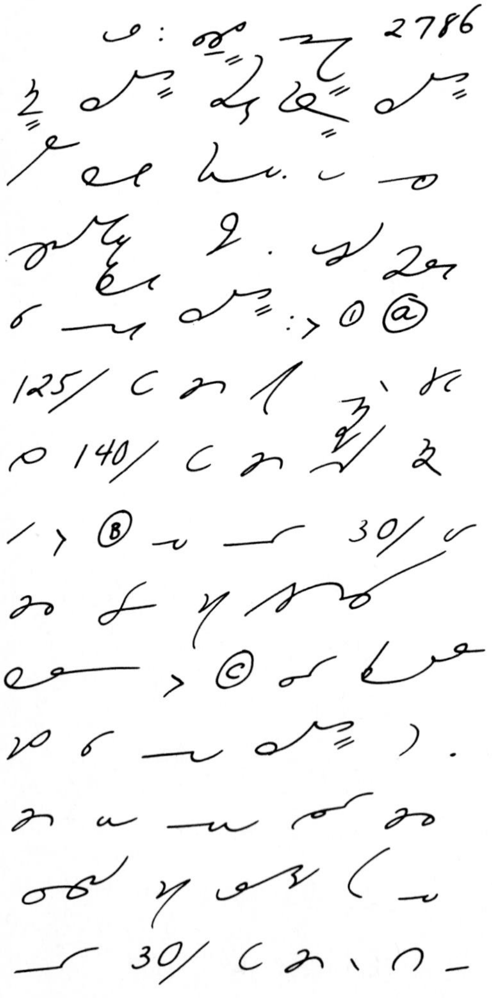

Lesson 17

BUILDING YOUR LEGAL VOCABULARY

Word Beginnings *Sub-* is expressed by  or .

subcontractor  subrogation 

sublease  subsidiary 

suborn  subversive 

Word Study

 **anguish** Pain and suffering.

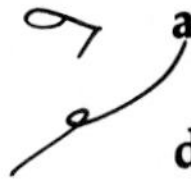 **deemed** Believed; judged.

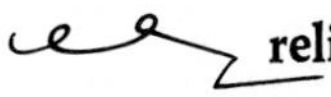 **relinquishment** The giving up of rights.

BUILDING YOUR LEGAL TRANSCRIPTION SKILL

Transcription Aid In this and the next ten lessons the specialized rules for capitalization that are most frequently encountered in a legal office will be summarized and illustrated.

Capitalization: Laws, Acts, and Bills

☐ Capitalize the official titles of laws, acts, and bills and also the generally accepted title; otherwise, use lower case in making a reference.

Social Security Act the National Labor Relations Act the Civil Rights Bill Atomic Energy Act

Capitalization: Courts

☐ Capitalize the formal title of a court and the word *Court* when it refers specifically to a judge or other presiding official.

There are 11 United States Courts of Appeal.

The Court sustained the objection made by the defendant's lawyer.

Latin and French Words and Phrases

capias *(ka'pē es)* A writ commanding the officer to arrest the person named in it or to seize his property.

inter virum et uxorem *(inter vir'um et ux ōr'em)* Between husband and wife.

a vinculo matrimonii *(ā vin'ku lō mā tri mō'ni ī)* Absolute divorce.

BUILDING YOUR LEGAL DICTATION PROFICIENCY

Preview

herein 

hospitalization 

maintenance 

obligated 

option 

remarry 

restriction 

specifically 

visitation 

withdraws 

Reading and Writing Practice

41. COMMONWEALTH OF MASSACHUSETTS PLYMOUTH COUNTY, SS. SEPTEMBER TERM, 19— SUPERIOR COURT EQUITY NO. 2786 SUSAN ANDREW V. FRANK ANDREW TEMPORARY STIPULATION

Now come the parties to the above-captioned Libel for Divorce and stipulate that this matter may be heard as[1] uncontested; and Frank Andrew, libelee, hereby specifically withdraws any contest of the action; and the[2] parties further stipulate that if, at the hearing, the Honorable Court finds cause for divorce in favor of Susan[3] Andrew, libelant, the following provisions, if deemed just, may be made part of the decree rendered:

I.[4] Custody, Support, and Alimony.

A. Susan Andrew, libelant, shall have the care and custody of the three minor[5] children of the parties:

Susan Andrew, born May 11, 19—; John Andrew, born[6] March 16, 19—; Charles Andrew, born September 30, 19—.

Frank[7] Andrew, libelee, shall have reasonable rights of visitation, which rights are more specifically set forth herein.[8]

B. Libelee shall have the right to have the children two (2) days a week from after school until 5 p.m. and[9] on each Sunday from 10 a.m. to 6 p.m. With regard to the weekday visits, he is to give libelant[10] at least two (2) days' notice unless otherwise agreed. Visitation periods, other than indicated above, may[11] be arranged by mutual consent of the parties. All visits, both weekdays and Sundays, are to take place away from[12] the residence of the libelant. If the libelant is to be away from her residence for a week or more,[13] then the libelee shall have the option of having the children with him during such period. The libelee[14] is to have the children for one (1) month during the summer upon reasonable notice to the libelant, with the[15] understanding that during such period, the children shall not live at the residence of the libelant.

C.[16] The parties hereby state that they realize it is to the mutual advantage of all, and of special advantage[17] of the children, that the libelant remain in Massachusetts so that the libelee be given a[18] reasonable opportunity to visit with the children. However, it is specifically agreed that there[19] shall be no restriction on the libelant's right to move except that should she, whether single or remarried, move[20] outside of New England or New York State, the libelee will no longer be obligated to continue to[21] support said children or to pay alimony to the libelant. (432)

(Continued in Lesson 18.)

42. *(Continued from Lesson 16.)*

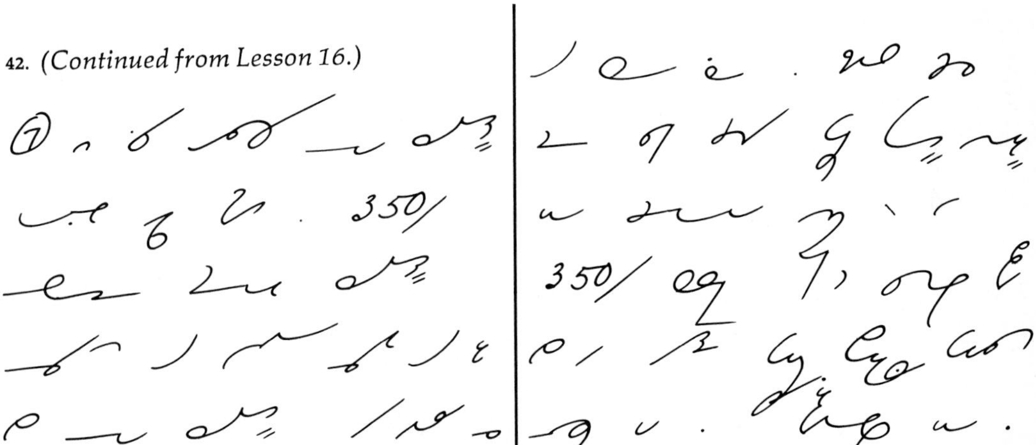

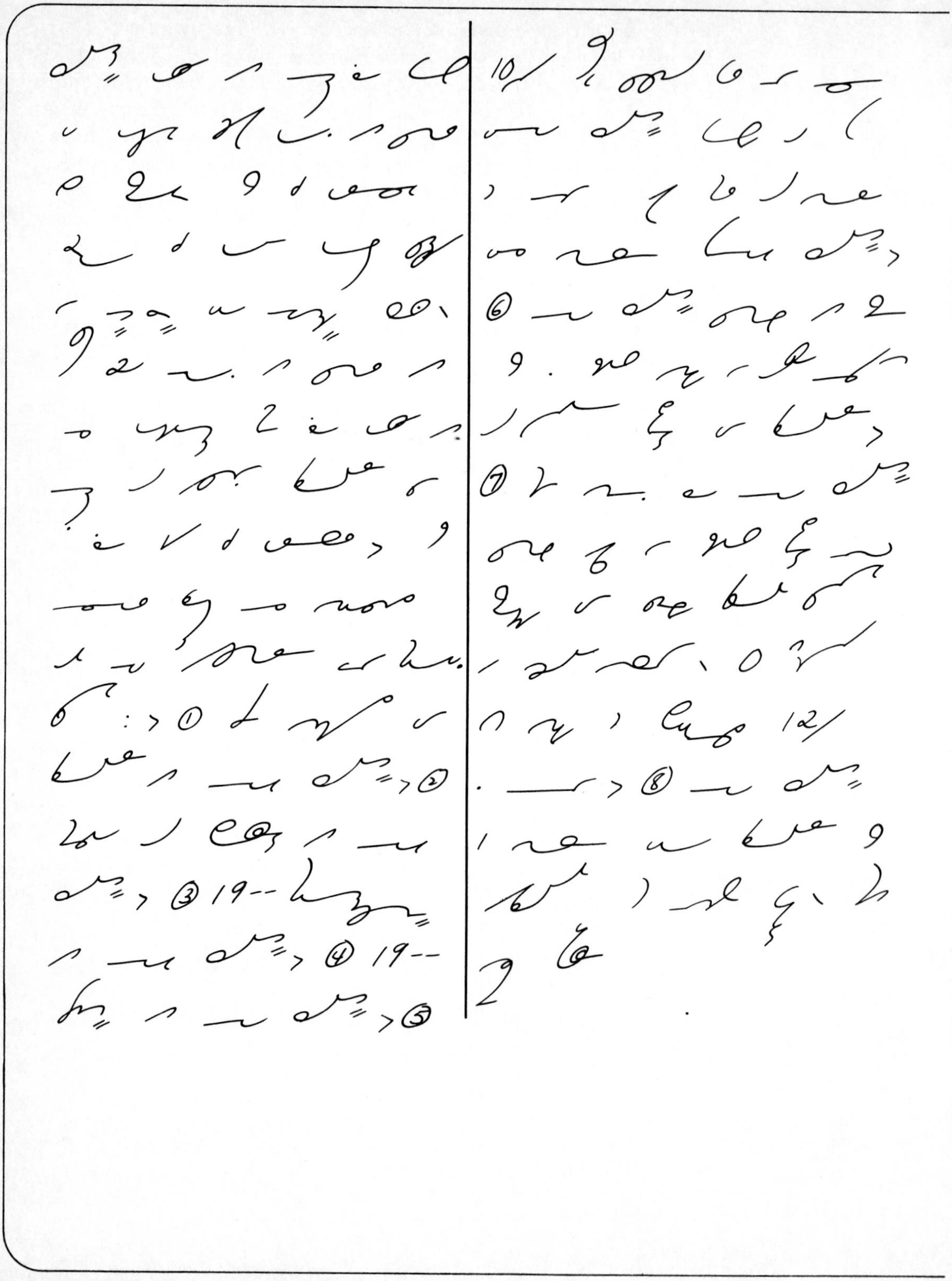

Lesson 18

BUILDING YOUR LEGAL VOCABULARY

Word Beginnings *Al-* is expressed by  .

alteration		**alterable**	
altercation		**alderman**	
alternative		**altered**	

Word Study

 **minor** A person not of legal age.

 **residence** The place in which one lives.

 **terminate** To end.

BUILDING YOUR LEGAL TRANSCRIPTION SKILL

Transcription Aid **Capitalization of Personal Titles**

☐ Capitalize titles of respect that precede personal names. Do not capitalize such titles when they follow a person's name or are used in place of the name. (An exception is made for high-ranking national or international officials and dignitaries. An exception is also made in formal minutes of meetings and in rules and bylaws.)

General Eisenhower Professor Robert Martin Dr. John Thompson, chairman of the Board of Health Mr. Kent Foster, president of Foster's, Inc.

Capitalization of Court Officials

☐ Capitalize titles of court officials such as *Judge, Justice, Magistrate,* and the like, when they stand alone and are used instead of a proper name; otherwise use lower case. Always capitalize *Chief Justice.*

The Judge ordered the courtroom cleared.

Legal Collocations

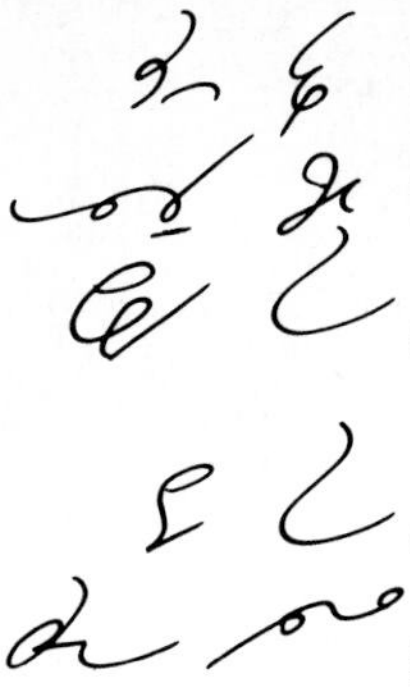

physical possession Taking hold of property; exercising control over it.

liquid assets Property that is readily convertible into cash.

appraised value The value of goods or property determined by a person given authority to set its value.

assessed value The value of property as determined for tax purposes.

final decree A decree granted by the court to dissolve or terminate a valid marriage or to set forth the end results in equity proceedings (where relief is not available through money damages or criminal punishment).

BUILDING YOUR LEGAL DICTATION PROFICIENCY

Preview

diagnosis 

hereafter 

incurred 

insofar 

kindergarten 

medical 

physical 

prescriptions 

remarriage 

surgical 

Reading and Writing Practice

43. STIPULATION *(Continued from Lesson 17.)*

D. The libelee agrees to pay the libelant One Hundred and Forty Dollars ($140) a week. Thirty-five Dollars ($35) of[1] such $140 is considered by the parties to be alimony; One Hundred and Five Dollars ($105)[2] is considered by the parties to be payments made for the care, maintenance, and support of the said minor children.[3] Upon remarriage, such payments shall be modified as hereafter provided.

E. On any occasion when[4] the said minor children stay with the libelee for a period of a week or more, the libelee's payments[5] for support of such minor children are to be reduced by no more than Thirty Dollars ($30) per week.

F. During the[6] school year 19__-19__, the libelee agrees to pay the extra[7] expenses incurred as a result of the youngest child, Charles's, attendance in kindergarten.

G. The libelee[8] assumes and agrees to pay and be solely responsible for the entire medical and dental expenses[9] for such minor children.

H. If and when the libelant returns to work and her net pay is greater than Thirty-five Dollars ($35)[10] a week, after making reasonable and appropriate deductions for baby-sitting expense,[11] transportation costs, and any other reasonable expenses incurred by her in order to work, there shall then be no[12] further payment of alimony made to the libelant by the libelee. At this time, however, the sum paid[13] for support of all such minor children shall be increased to a full total amount of One Hundred and Fifty Dollars ($150);[14] and such increased support for the minor children shall continue to be paid by the libelee to the libelant[15] for such children's benefit.

I. Insofar as it is legally possible, the obligations of[16] the libelee to make alimony payments to the libelant shall not cease at the end of three (3) years from the date[17] of decree but shall continue thereafter until such time as the libelant remarries.

J. In the event of the libelant's remarriage, all alimony payments shall terminate permanently. Upon this termination[18] the sum paid for the support of the minor children shall be increased to One Hundred and Fifty Dollars ($150), which[19] shall then be paid to the libelant as support for the minor children and which shall then continue regardless[20] of the libelant's remarriage.

K. The libelee agrees to obtain and pay for a medical insurance[21] policy on the libelant which will cover her health, accident, sickness, and major medical expenses. This[22] coverage will be of a kind comparable to Mutual of Omaha's hospital and surgical insurance[23] and will also cover, as presently indicated in such Mutual of Omaha's policy, doctor's[24] expenses for home care, medical diagnosis, physical examinations, X-ray examinations,[25] and laboratory examinations (with the usual Ten Dollars ($10) deduction on account of said[26] expenses); and such expenses are to be covered whether at home, in a hospital, or at a doctor's office.[27] In addition, the libelee agrees to be responsible for an amount equal to the difference between[28] what he has to pay for such medical insurance coverage on a yearly basis and the sum of Two Hundred[29] and Fifty Dollars ($250). This difference shall be available to be applied for the payment of the libelant's[30] reasonable dental needs, medical prescriptions, or such other medical expense not covered by the medical payment[31] policy herein provided. All such payments are agreed by the parties to be additional alimony.[32] The provisions of the paragraph shall terminate upon the libelant's remarriage. (657)

(Continued in Lesson 19.)

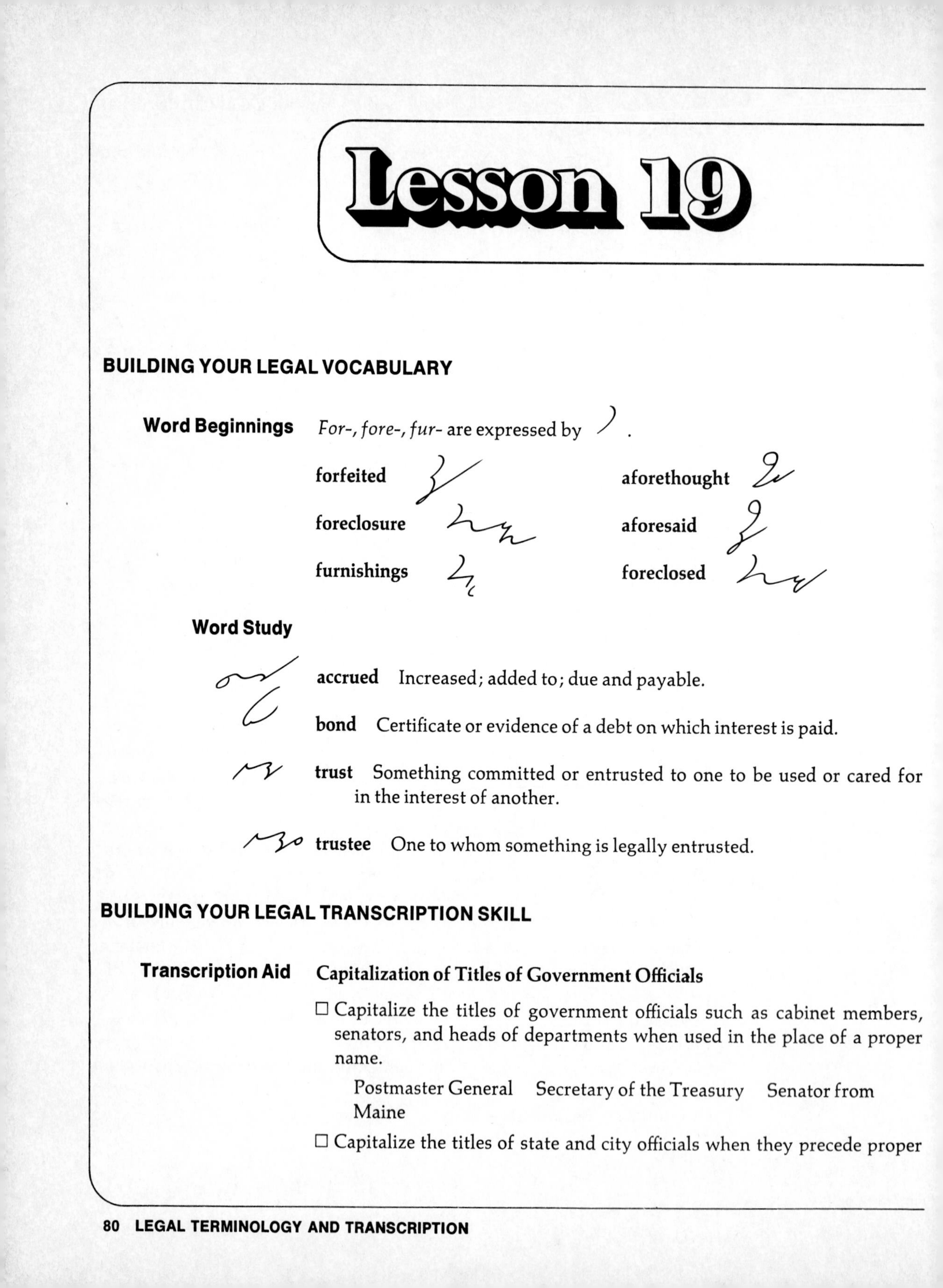

Lesson 19

BUILDING YOUR LEGAL VOCABULARY

Word Beginnings *For-, fore-, fur-* are expressed by .

forfeited	**aforethought**
foreclosure	**aforesaid**
furnishings	**foreclosed**

Word Study

accrued Increased; added to; due and payable.

bond Certificate or evidence of a debt on which interest is paid.

trust Something committed or entrusted to one to be used or cared for in the interest of another.

trustee One to whom something is legally entrusted.

BUILDING YOUR LEGAL TRANSCRIPTION SKILL

Transcription Aid **Capitalization of Titles of Government Officials**

☐ Capitalize the titles of government officials such as cabinet members, senators, and heads of departments when used in the place of a proper name.

Postmaster General Secretary of the Treasury Senator from Maine

☐ Capitalize the titles of state and city officials when they precede proper names or when they are used in place of proper names; otherwise, use lower case.

the City Manager   Mayor Goodwin   the District Attorney
Governor Fox

"Ex-" and "-elect"

☐ Do not capitalize *ex-* and *-elect* when joined to titles.

ex-Governor Brown   the President-elect

Latin and French Words and Phrases

 **dossier** *(dos'yā)* A bundle of papers containing a detailed report or detailed information.

 **per diem** *(per dē'em)* By the day.

 **sic** *(sik)* In such manner; thus. (Used in brackets)

BUILDING YOUR LEGAL DICTATION PROFICIENCY

Preview

initiate 
obligations 
premises 
redemption 
security 
signatures 
unencumbered 
withdrawal 

Reading and Writing Practice

44. STIPULATION *(Continued from Lesson 18.)*

II. Property, Allocation, and Use.

A. The following savings accounts and savings bonds presently held in[1] the name of the libelee for the benefit of the minor children shall, after the decree, be held in the[2] names of both the libelant and the libelee as trustees:

Brockton Federal Savings and Loan Association Account 1297
$2,260.60
Brockton Federal Savings[3] and Loan Association Account 1385
$1,784.60[4]

Brockton Federal Savings and Loan Association Account 1284
$2,765.31[5]

Total $6,810.51 (subject to deductions[6] as provided hereafter)

Various United States Savings Bonds in total face amount of $2,900.[7] Signatures of both trustees shall be required for withdrawal or redemption until each child[8] reaches the age of twenty-five (25). When the first child reaches the age of twenty-five (25), the then assets of the trust shall[9] be divided into three (3) equal parts; each child shall then receive his share, and thereafter as each child attains the[10] age of twenty-five (25), he shall receive full title and accrued income of his trust share of such accounts and bonds free[11] of such trust. It is understood that such savings accounts are presently subject to a security obligation[12] or a loan made against such accounts by the libelee, and the libelee agrees within sixty (60) days of the[13] decree of divorce to pay in full the amount of any loan or obligation so that such savings accounts will be[14] completely unencumbered. All deposits made in such savings accounts from November 1, 19—,[15] shall be returned to the libelee free of any claims of the trust, or of the libelant; but any interest[16] which has accrued on such deposits shall not be paid to him. The amount of such deposits made from November[17] 1, 19—, may be used by the libelee to repay in full or in part any loans or[18] obligations of the libelee for which such savings accounts are being held as security.

B. It is[19] understood and agreed that the following savings accounts are held in the name of Frank Andrew, libelee, and that the[20] libelee has been paying income tax on such accounts, but the actual passbooks are presently being held[21] by the libelee's mother; and the parties agree these accounts may be considered as assets of the[22] libelee's mother rather than assets of the libelee insofar as this Libel for Divorce is concerned.

Boston[23] Savings Bank $5,884.24

First National Bank of Boston[24] $6,253.72

National Commercial Bank & Trust Co.[25] $2,187.60

Citizens National Bank $369.41[26]

Total $14,694.97

C. The libelant is[27] presently occupying the family home known as "Larchview" in Brockton, Massachusetts (hereafter for[28] convenience referred to as the "premises"). So long as she continues to occupy such premises, the libelee[29] agrees to assume and pay the mortgage, the heating expense, the expense of reasonable repairs, and all bills[30] and charges in reasonable amount for water, insurance, and taxes with regard to such premises. The libelee[31] specifically does not agree to pay any expense for repairs to any furniture, fixtures, and equipment[32] which are not considered a part of the realty.

D. The libelant is to have the occupancy of such[33] premises in Brockton, which is jointly owned by the parties and agrees not to allow anyone except her relatives[34] to remain in the premises for any undue period of time. Upon her remarriage the right of[35] occupancy shall terminate.

E. Should the libelant cease to occupy the premises in Brockton and find[36] suitable rental for herself elsewhere (as provided in paragraph I. C. hereof), then the libelee shall pay,[37] as additional support, but not as alimony, an amount equal to the reasonable extra expenses[38] of such new rental, together with any cost of heating such premises. This additional support amount shall[39] terminate upon the libelant's remarriage. Should the libelant move within ten (10) miles of Brockton, the libelee[40] agrees to pay the reasonable costs of moving—limited to one move only.

F. If the libelant remarries,[41] or should she find other living quarters and move from the premises while still single, then the premises shall[42] be sold within a reasonable time. Until the premises are sold, however, the libelant move within ten (10) miles of Brockton, the libelee[40] agrees that although such a sale is to be managed exclusively by[44] the libelee, no sale shall occur without the libelant's prior consent. In any event, however, the[45] libelee shall have the right to initiate a sale of the premises. The libelant agrees to cooperate[46] with the libelee in such sale, providing she is given adequate notice thereof and is able to make[47] suitable and adequate arrangements for other housing. (950)

(Continued in Lesson 20.)

Lesson 20

BUILDING YOUR LEGAL VOCABULARY

Word Beginnings *Per-* and *pur-* are expressed by .

perjury 

perpetuities 

perpetrate 

pursuant

purview 

purported 

Word Study

 **discharge** To release; dismissal from an obligation.

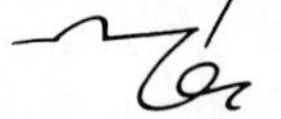 **encumbrance** Any indebtedness against a piece of real property.

 **Sections** Subdivisions of constitutions and laws.

 **signatories** Signers of a document.

BUILDING YOUR LEGAL TRANSCRIPTION SKILL

Transcription Aid

Capitalization of the Word "Government"

☐ Capitalize the word *government* when used as a proper noun or proper adjective referring to the government of a particular nation with the force of an official name.

The Government's agents made the arrest.

Capitalization of the Names of Governmental Bodies

☐ Capitalize the names of governmental bodies used as proper names or proper adjectives.

the House States' rights the New Hampshire Legislature the Ninety-second Congress

Typing Citations

Statutory Material

Statutory material is material enacted, created, or regulated by laws decreed by the legislative branch of a government. It includes legislation passed by the states as well as by the United States Congress. Other than the United States Constitution, examples of statutory material include slip laws (the first published form of a federal law in pamphlet form), Statutes at Large (the permanent published form of federal statutory law), the United States Code (positive laws of the United States), treatises, and supplements to the preceding editions.

☐ Cite statutory material by article, section, and clause (if given). In citing a state constitution, use the date only of those no longer in force.

37 U.S.C. Sec. 109 56 Stat. 363 (1942)

BUILDING YOUR LEGAL DICTATION PROFICIENCY

Preview appliances  apportioned 

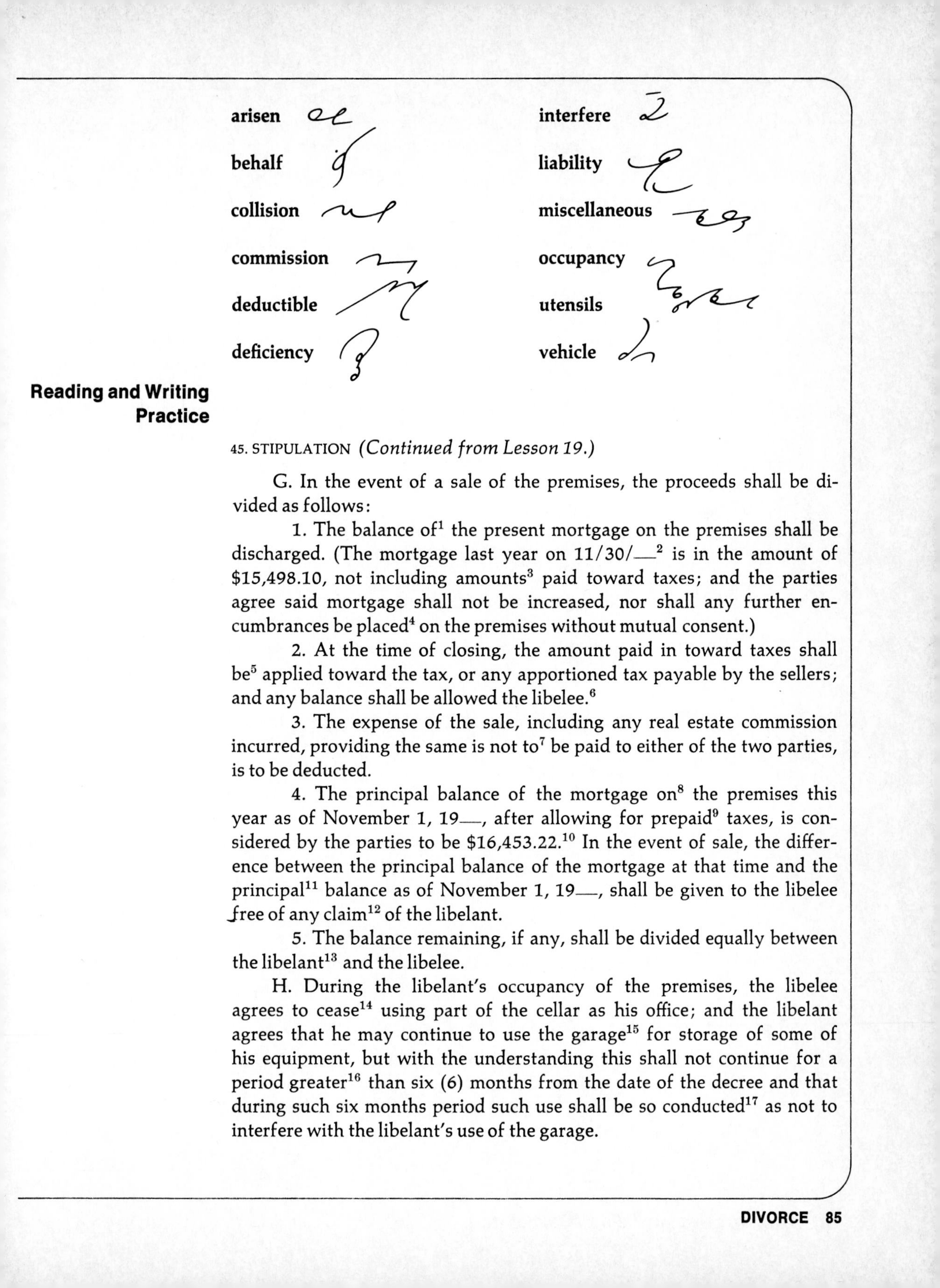

arisen	interfere
behalf	liability
collision	miscellaneous
commission	occupancy
deductible	utensils
deficiency	vehicle

Reading and Writing Practice

45. STIPULATION *(Continued from Lesson 19.)*

G. In the event of a sale of the premises, the proceeds shall be divided as follows:

1. The balance of[1] the present mortgage on the premises shall be discharged. (The mortgage last year on 11/30/—[2] is in the amount of $15,498.10, not including amounts[3] paid toward taxes; and the parties agree said mortgage shall not be increased, nor shall any further encumbrances be placed[4] on the premises without mutual consent.)

2. At the time of closing, the amount paid in toward taxes shall be[5] applied toward the tax, or any apportioned tax payable by the sellers; and any balance shall be allowed the libelee.[6]

3. The expense of the sale, including any real estate commission incurred, providing the same is not to[7] be paid to either of the two parties, is to be deducted.

4. The principal balance of the mortgage on[8] the premises this year as of November 1, 19—, after allowing for prepaid[9] taxes, is considered by the parties to be $16,453.22.[10] In the event of sale, the difference between the principal balance of the mortgage at that time and the principal[11] balance as of November 1, 19—, shall be given to the libelee free of any claim[12] of the libelant.

5. The balance remaining, if any, shall be divided equally between the libelant[13] and the libelee.

H. During the libelant's occupancy of the premises, the libelee agrees to cease[14] using part of the cellar as his office; and the libelant agrees that he may continue to use the garage[15] for storage of some of his equipment, but with the understanding this shall not continue for a period greater[16] than six (6) months from the date of the decree and that during such six months period such use shall be so conducted[17] as not to interfere with the libelant's use of the garage.

I. The furniture and appliances presently[18] located in the home shall become the property of the libelant free and clear of any claim by, or[19] on behalf of, the libelee, excepting the office equipment.

J. The 19__ Buick[20] presently owned by the libelee shall be his property, discharged and free and clear of any claim by the libelant;[21] the 19__ Volkswagen presently owned by the libelee shall become the property of[22] the libelant, discharged and made free and clear of any claim of the libelee. The libelant agrees to carry[23] insurance on any vehicle owned by her providing $50,000/$100,000[24] liability coverage, and collision coverage with $100 deductible. The premium[25] for such insurance shall be paid from the amount designated as her alimony. The libelee agrees to pay[26] for reasonable major repairs in excess of the amount of Twenty-five Dollars ($25) for any single repair bill incurred[27] by libelant for either her present or any subsequent motor vehicle she acquires, subject to his[28] approval of such repairs being made given in advance. The obligation to pay for repairs shall terminate[29] upon the libelant's remarriage, or upon her becoming employed as previously provided herein.[30]

K. The libelant is presently in possession of items of china, silverware, and other household[31] utensils formerly the property of the libelee's mother. The libelant agrees to return to the[32] libelee any such items which she may not use in the future, so that the libelee may, in turn, give them to his[33] mother.

III. Taxes

A. The libelee shall claim the minor children as dependents for income tax purposes,[34] and the libelant shall assert no opposing claim.

B. Any tax liability incurred by the libelant[35] as a result of alimony payments made to her, or the allocation of alimony payments, shall[36] be paid by the libelee.

C. The parties agree to file a joint return covering income taxes for the year[37] 19__. Thereafter they shall file separate income tax returns. The libelee agrees that if there shall be a deficiency assessment on any joint returns previously filed by the parties, to assume, pay,[38] and be solely responsible for said assessment.

IV. Miscellaneous

Except as herein provided, the[39] libelant and libelee do hereby mutually remise, release, and discharge each other from any and all claims,[40] demands, debts, suits, actions, or obligations whatsoever which have arisen, or may arise between them as[41] to events occurring prior to this stipulation.

In the presence of ______________________

Alice E. Bates,[42] Attorney for Frank Andrew, Libelee

Kevin O'Brien, Attorney for Susan Andrew, Libelant (858)

UNIT

3 Insurance

Auto Negligence

Jane Cox
v.
Thomas A. Pope et al.

This is a case concerning a lawsuit instituted by the plaintiff, Jane Cox, to collect damages for bodily injury caused by negligence on the part of the defendant, Thomas A. Pope, in the handling of an automobile.

While suit is initially brought against Thomas A. Pope, owner of Pope's Garage, and his wife, the two companies with which the plaintiff and the defendant are insured become involved in the suit. The plaintiff's car is insured by the National Insurance Company and that of the defendant is insured by the U.S. Casualty Company.

The attorney for Jane Cox is Roger L. Mason, Esq.

The attorney for the National Insurance Company is Henry I. Slater, Esq.

The attorney for Thomas A. Pope and Frances Pope and for the U.S. Casualty Company is Ann M. Larson.

Lesson 21

BUILDING YOUR LEGAL VOCABULARY

Word Beginnings *Ex-* is expressed by  or .

excise 

excludability 

exhibits 

exemptions 

exonerate 

expropriation 

Word Study

 **assured** Guaranteed, made secure or certain.

 **expediently** In a manner suitable for achieving a particular end.

 **expedite** To facilitate or quicken the progress of.

 **negotiations** The action or process of bargaining regarding terms or conditions.

 **prognosis** The prospect of recovery; forecast.

 **tolerance** A relative capacity to endure or adapt.

BUILDING YOUR LEGAL TRANSCRIPTION SKILL

Transcription Aid **Capitalization of Compound Titles**

☐ Capitalize *acting* and *under* when they form a part of a capitalized title.

Acting Secretary of Health, Education, and Welfare

Under Secretary of State

☐ Do not capitalize titles of the rank of assistant or deputy unless they precede proper names.

The new deputy sheriff the assistant attorney general

Deputy Sheriff Lee

Typing Citations In citing cases with abbreviations of two or more letters, omit spacing. Consider the ampersand (&) and numbers as letters.

Howe v. Howe, 87 N.H. 338, 341

Adolphus v. *Zebelman,* 486 F.2d 1323

BUILDING YOUR LEGAL DICTATION PROFICIENCY

Preview

accident 

authorized 

confirmation 

evaluating 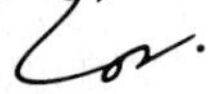

fracture 

garage 

hospitalization 

hospitalized 

inflict 

injuries 

momentarily 

negligence 

negotiated 

permanence 

settlement 

sustained 

tragedy 

vehicle 

Reading and Writing Practice

46. AUTHORIZATION TO FURNISH MEDICAL INFORMATION

TO WHOM IT MAY CONCERN:

You are hereby authorized to furnish to my attorneys, Greenberg, O'Brien, Mason[1] & McCann, 74 State Street, Boston, MA 02100, any medical information or records they[2] may request in connection with my hospitalization or treatment rendered as a result of my[3] accident of December 20, 19—.

____

Jane Cox (72)

47. MR. FRED J. COX, MAPLE LANE, WESTON, MA 02193

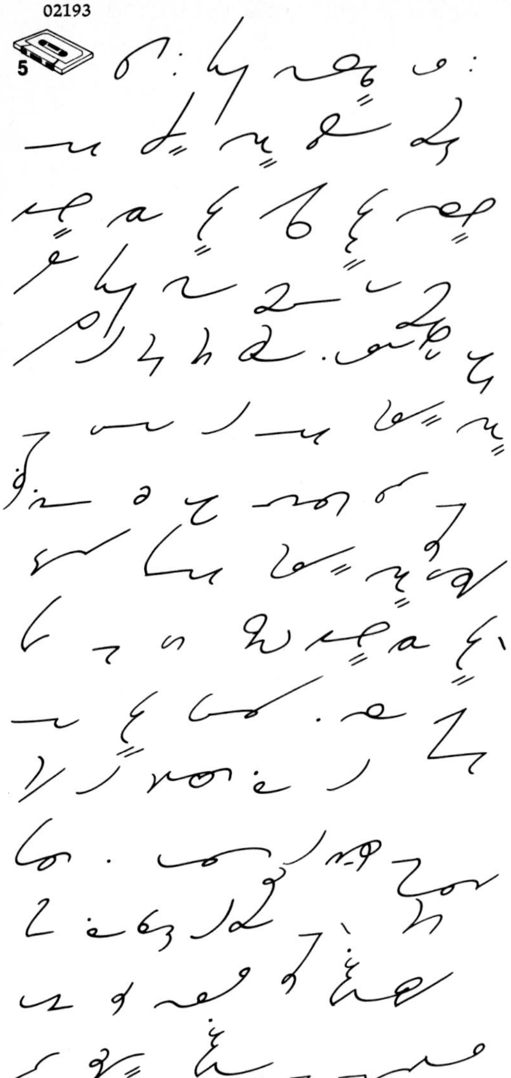

48. U.S. CASUALTY COMPANY, 1750 STATE STREET, BOSTON, MA 02100 ATTENTION GEORGE CLANCY

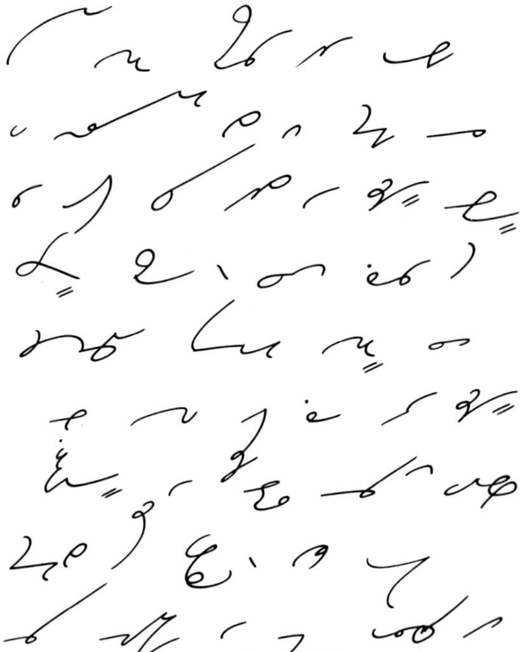

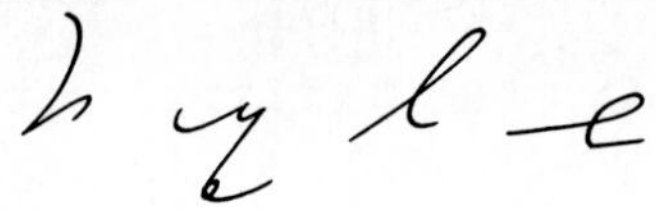

49. COLE FURNITURE COMPANY, INC., 12 SOUTH MAIN STREET, WESTON, MA 02193

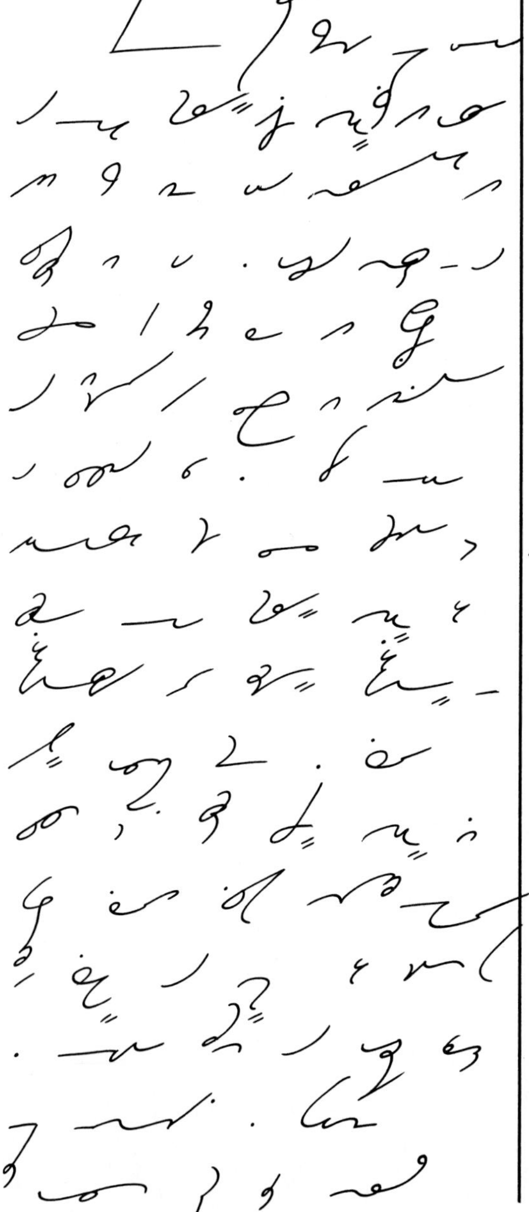

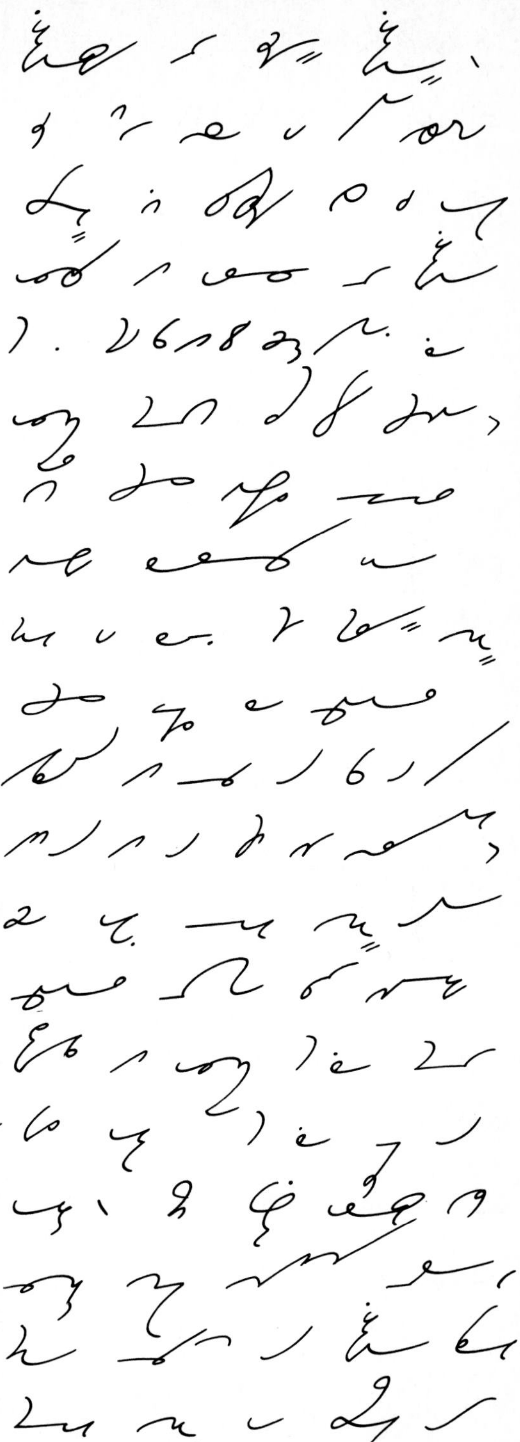

50. DR. O. R. BANKS, 5 SOUTH STATE STREET, WESTON, MA 02193

5

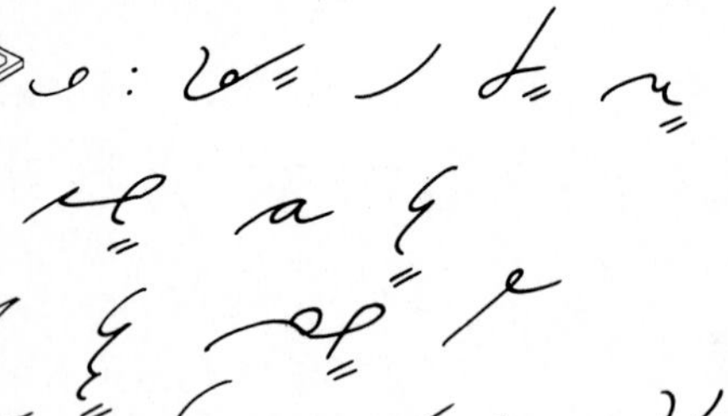

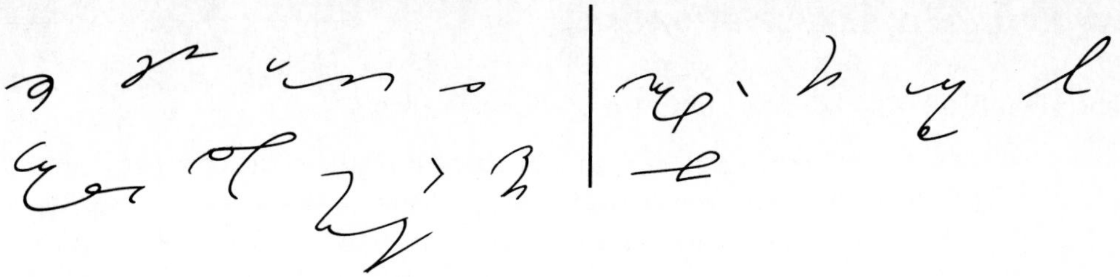

Lesson 22

BUILDING YOUR LEGAL VOCABULARY

Word Beginnings *Ul-* is expressed by before or blends of these.

ulterior

ultimatum

adultery

culminate

adulteration

consultant

Word Study

ad damnum The technical name of that clause of the writ or declaration which contains a statement of the plaintiff's money loss or the damages which he claims.

assert To state or declare.

comminuted Reduced to minute particles; crushed.

indemnify To secure against loss, hurt, or damage; to make good.

wantonly Recklessly; heedlessly; maliciously.

writ A written court order commanding a person to do or to refrain from doing a specified act.

BUILDING YOUR LEGAL TRANSCRIPTION SKILL

Transcription Aid

Capitalization of Common-Noun Elements

☐ Capitalize a common-noun element of the name of an organization, an individual, or a country when used alone as a short form for the proper name if the full name has been mentioned or is generally understood.

the Republic (of France) the National Institutes of Health—the Institutes General Dwight D. Eisenhower—the General the American Bar Association—the Association

Capitalization of Proper Adjectives

☐ Capitalize the proper adjective derived from the name of an individual associated with a law, a court, a bill, or a patented process or apparatus, and so forth, but do not capitalize the word it modifies.

the Harrison narcotic bill a Kelly clamp the Nelson process

☐ Do not capitalize words that were originally proper names but that have become common adjectives through use.

roman type india ink manila envelope venetian blinds

Legal Collocations

accord and satisfaction An agreement to compromise or settle; the adjustment of a disagreement as to what is due and the payment of the agreed amount, which is frequently less than that which might be legally enforced.

bill of particulars A statement of the facts and claims on which an action or claim is based.

contributory negligence Negligence on the plaintiff's part that is at least in part a cause of the plaintiff's injuries or damage.

declaratory judgment The Court's declaration or opinion of the rights of contesting parties, without ordering anything to be done.

joinder of issue The act by which the parties to a cause arrive at that point in their pleadings at which one asserts a fact to be so and the other denies it.

BUILDING YOUR LEGAL DICTATION PROFICIENCY

Preview amputation  assured 

derivative 

fracturing 

hospitalization 

initiated 

necessitating 

negligently 

pedestrian 

sustained 

Reading and Writing Practice

51. COMMONWEALTH OF MASSACHUSETTS MIDDLESEX, SS. APRIL TERM, 19— SUPERIOR COURT JANE COX V. NATIONAL INSURANCE CO., U.S. CASUALTY CO., AND THOMAS A. POPE AND FRANCES POPE, D.B.A. POPE'S GARAGE ANSWER OF NATIONAL INSURANCE COMPANY

For its answer to the Petition for Declaratory Judgment, the National Insurance Company states[1] as follows:

1. It admits the allegations of fact contained in paragraphs numbered 1, 5, 7, 9, 10,[2] 11, and 12 of said petition.

2. It admits the allegations of fact contained in paragraph numbered[3] 6 of said petition with the exception that it denies that any notice which was given was "timely." By[4] this denial, this Defendant does not intend to admit that any notice was required, it being the position[5] of this Defendant that its policy affords no coverage in any event.

3. It denies the allegations[6] of fact contained in paragraphs numbered 8, 13, 14, 15, and 17 of said petition.

4.[7] It is without information or belief or information sufficient to form a belief with respect to[8] the allegations set forth in paragraphs numbered 2, 3, 4, 16, and 18 of said petition and therefore[9] neither admits nor denies the same but leaves the Plaintiff to her proof.

Further answering said petition,[10] Defendant states as follows:

1. That Part I of said policy provides in part as follows:

"Exclusions

"This[11] policy does not apply under Part I:

* * *

"(g) to an owned automobile while used in the automobile[12] business, but this exclusion does not apply to the named insured, a resident of the same household as the named[13] insured or such resident is a partner, or any partner, agent or employee of the named insured, such resident[14] or partnership";

2. That under Part I of said policy "automobile business" is defined[15] as follows: " 'automobile business' means business or occupation of

selling,[16] repairing, servicing, storing, and parking automobiles";

This Defendant is informed and believes[17] and therefore alleges that at the time of the accident giving rise to Plaintiff's injuries the motor vehicle[18] described in its policy was on premises of the Defendants, Thomas A. Pope and Frances Pope, for[19] the purpose of servicing and repairs and was being used in the automobile business within the meaning[20] of said policy.

WHEREFORE, this Defendant prays that this Court enter a Declaratory Judgment whereby it[21] is adjusted and decreed that this Defendant is under no obligation to defend the action brought by[22] the Plaintiff herein against Thomas A. Pope and Frances Pope or to pay any judgment obtained therein; that it be[23] awarded its costs; and that it be granted such other further relief as may be just and equitable.

National Insurance[24] Company

____

By H. I. Slater
Its attorney

CERTIFICATE OF MAILING

I hereby certify that[25] on the 2d day of August 19__, I mailed a copy of the foregoing Answer to Roger[26] L. Mason, attorney for the Plaintiff; Larson, Lord & Vorhees, attorneys for the U.S. Casualty[27] Company; and the attorneys of record for the Defendants Thomas A. Pope and Frances Pope.

____

H. I. Slater[28] (560)

52. NATIONAL INSURANCE COMPANY, CLAIMS DEPARTMENT, 848 TREMONT STREET, BOSTON, MA 02100

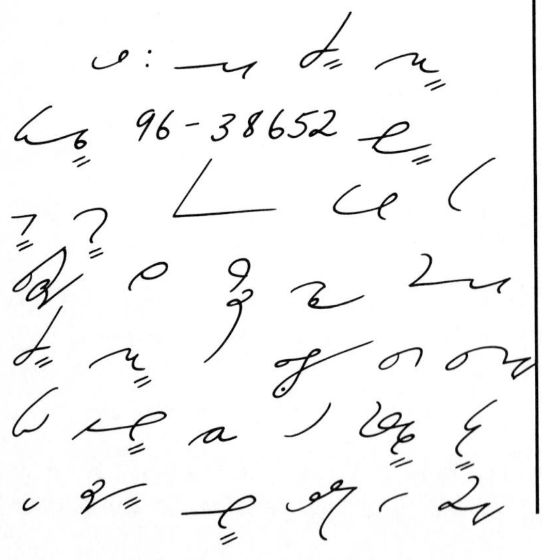

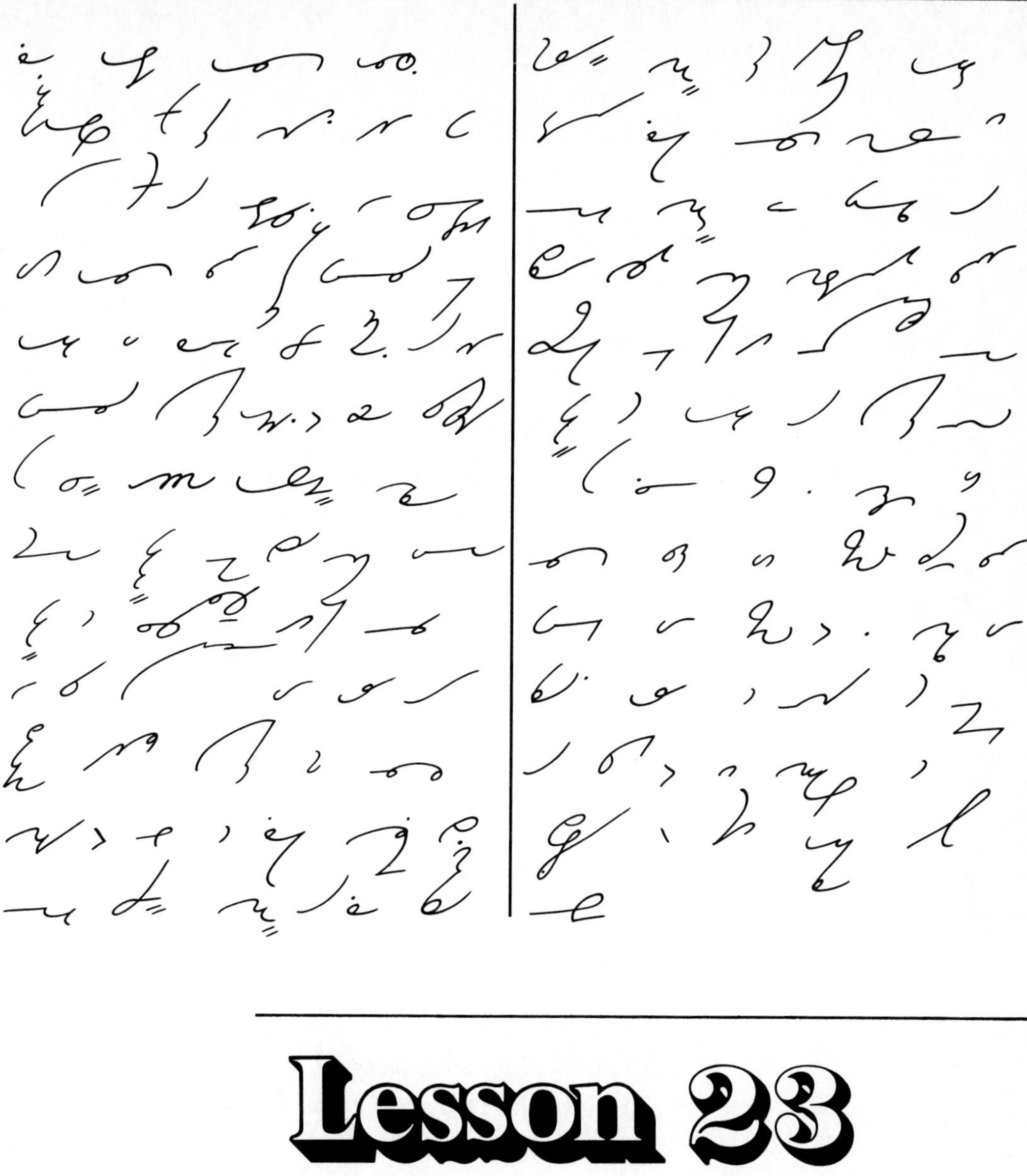

Lesson 23

BUILDING YOUR LEGAL VOCABULARY

Word Beginnings *Be-* and *bi-* are expressed by 

bestow 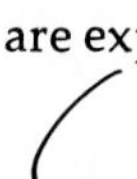 benevolences 

bilateral **bequests**

bequeath **behalf**

Word Study

adjudicated Determined judicially.

indemnification The condition of securing against loss, hurt, or damage.

instrument Any legal document.

verified Confirmed by oath.

BUILDING YOUR LEGAL TRANSCRIPTION SKILL

Transcription Aid

Capitalization: Solid Capitals

☐ Type the opening word or phrase in solid capitals in the following instances:

1. In the testimonium clause, in which the parties to a legal instrument declare their signatures are attached in testimony of the preceding parts.

   IN WITNESS WHEREOF or IN TESTIMONY WHEREOF

2. In stipulations, which list points of agreement between opposing counsel in a pending action.

   IT IS HEREBY STIPULATED AND AGREED

3. In the prayer, which constitutes the last paragraph of a document in which the counsel requests action by the court.

   WHEREFORE, this Petitioner prays . . .

   WHEREFORE, this Defendant demands judgment.

4. In a demand for bill of particulars and in notices of opposing counsel.

   SIR: (or SIRS:) PLEASE TAKE NOTICE

(Continued in Lesson 24.)

Latin and French Words and Phrases

et al. *(et al′)* And others.

in pari delicto *(in pa′rē de lik′tō)* Equally at fault.

ipso facto *(ip'so fak'tō)* By the act or fact itself.

BUILDING YOUR LEGAL DICTATION PROFICIENCY

Preview

accountability	deposition
ad damnum	predicated
circularize	modifications
covenant	verdict
discharge	without prejudice

Reading and Writing Practice

53. ANN M. LARSON, LARSON, LORD & VOORHEES, 1838 STATE STREET, BOSTON, MA 02100

54. ANN M. LARSON, LARSON, LORD & VOORHEES, 1838 STATE STREET, BOSTON, MA 02100

5

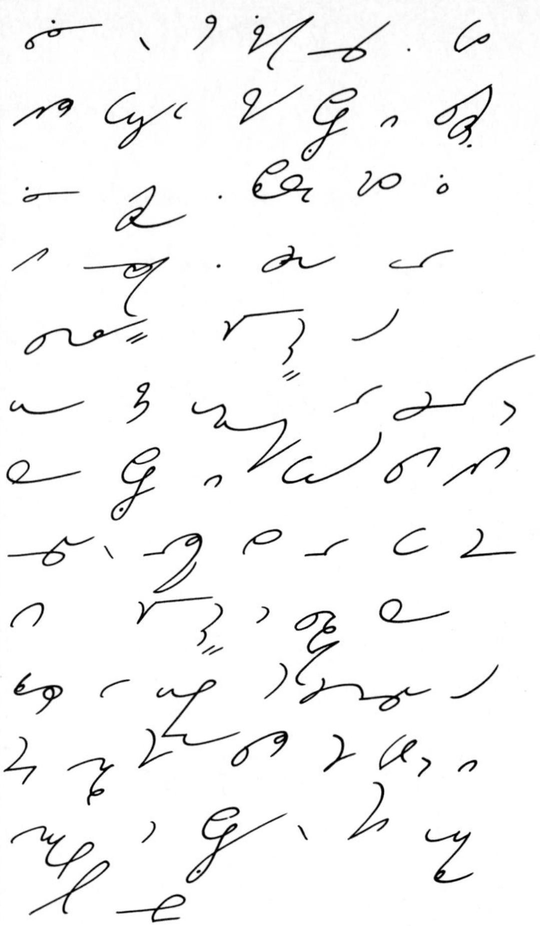

55. ANN M. LARSON, LARSON, LORD & VOORHEES, 1838 STATE STREET, BOSTON, MA 02100

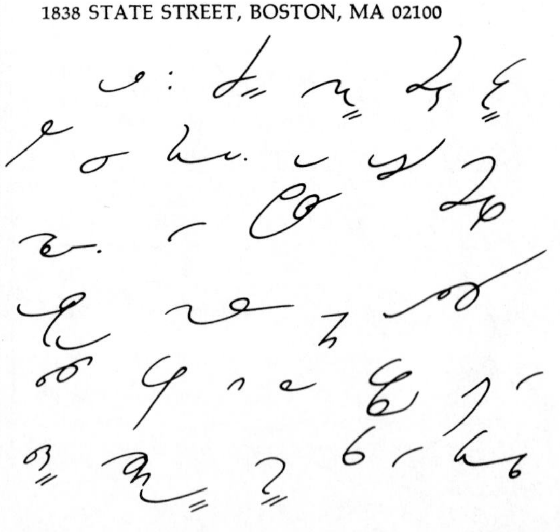

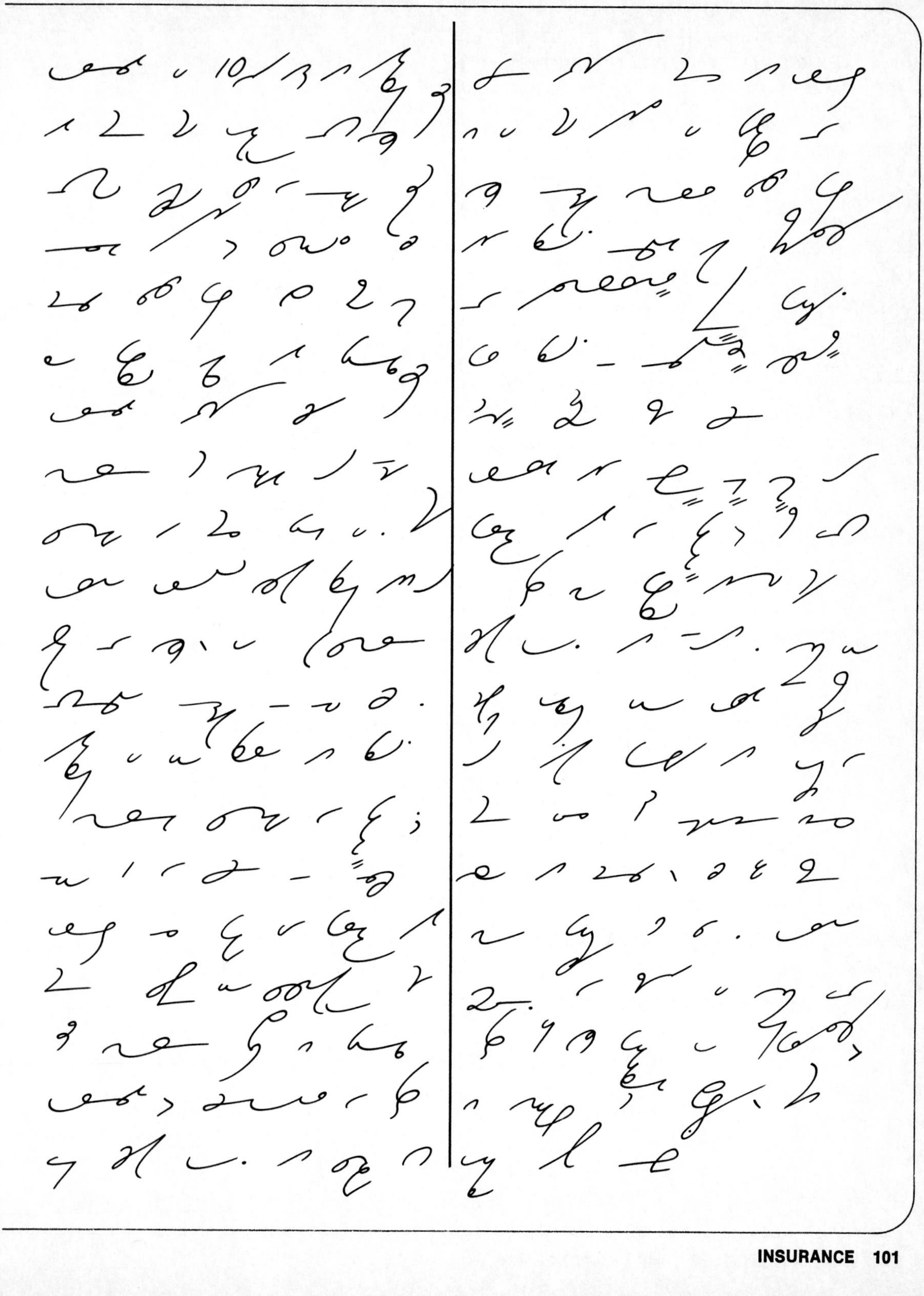

56. MR. H. I. SLATER, ESQ., NELSON, MARLEY, CORDEN & SLATER, 9 CAPITAL STREET, BOSTON, MA 02100

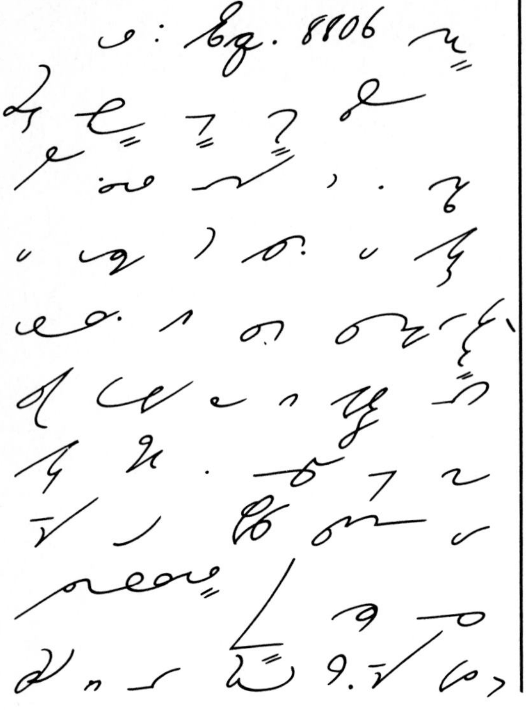

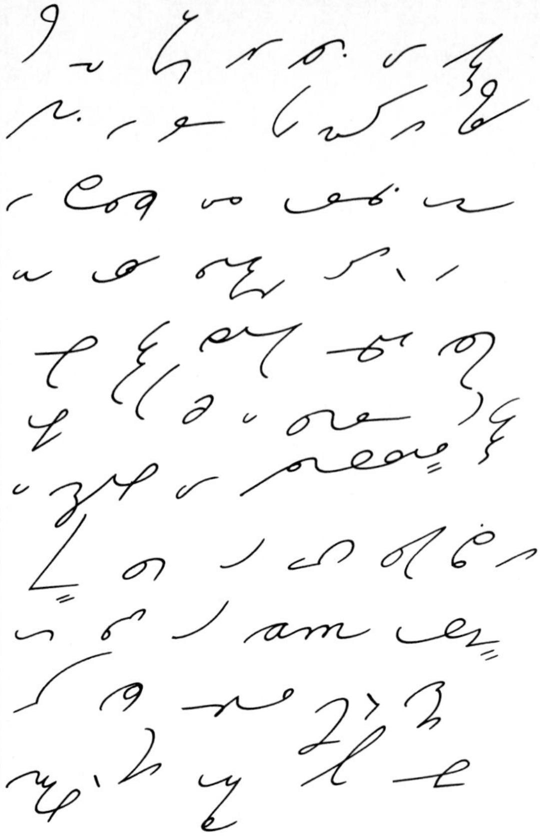

Lesson 24

BUILDING YOUR LEGAL VOCABULARY

Word Family *Pre-* is expressed by .

preexamination 

predeceased 

preliminary 

predetermined 

premeditated 

predicated 

Word Study

 **abrasions** Scrapes; injuries in which the skin is broken.

 **contusions** Bumps; bruises; injuries in which the skin is not broken.

 **fractures** Breaks; ruptures.

 **lacerations** Cuts in the skin or flesh.

BUILDING YOUR LEGAL TRANSCRIPTION SKILL

Transcription Aid

Capitalization: Solid Capitals *(Continued from Lesson 23.)*

☐ In legal papers, type in solid capitals the statement of venue, which gives the name of the state and county in which the instrument is executed or in which the trial takes place.

STATE OF TENNESSEE)
                    : ss.
COUNTY OF BEDFORD)

☐ In such instruments as wills, affidavits, certificates of acknowledgment, and verifications, type the name of the individual making the statement in solid capitals.

I, MARY POLK, of the Town of New London, County of Merrimack, State of New Hampshire. . . .

KEVIN O'BRIEN, being duly sworn, deposes and says: . . . .

Legal Collocations

 **in escrow** A situation wherein an instrument or a fund is delivered to a third person to be held until some event or until the performance of some act under the terms of a specific agreement.

 **liquidated damages** Damages of which the amount has been determined or fixed; also, damages paid off.

 **plaintiff's declaration** The plaintiff's first pleading in an action at law.

 **proximate cause** The cause nearest or most immediately connected.

 **vis-à-vis** Face to face; also, in comparison with, in relation to, or over against.

Preview

declaratory 

documents 

expedite 

excised 

photocopy 

proposed 

redrafted 

Supreme Court 

testimony 

ultimate 

Reading and Writing Practice

57. ANN M. LARSON, LARSON, LORD & VOORHEES, 1838 STATE STREET, BOSTON, MA 02100

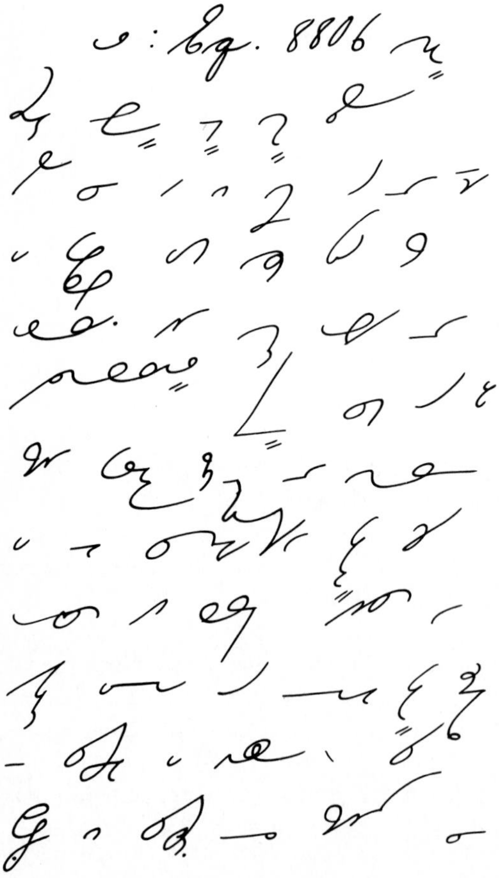

58. ANN M. LARSON, LARSON, LORD & VOORHEES, 1838 STATE STREET, BOSTON, MA 02100

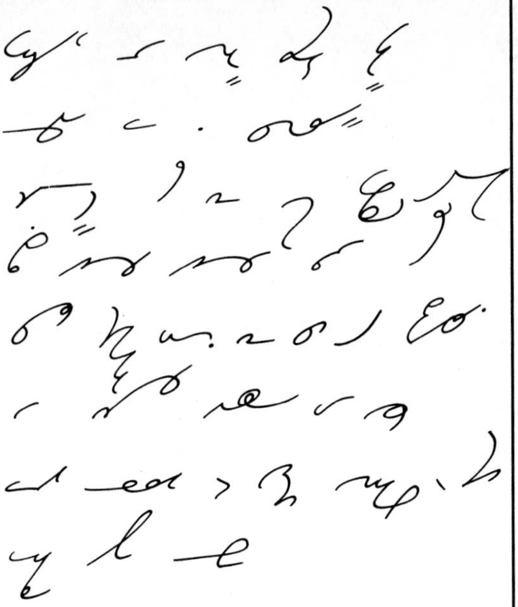

59. ANN M. LARSON, LARSON, LORD & VOORHEES,
1838 STATE STREET, BOSTON, MA 02100

5

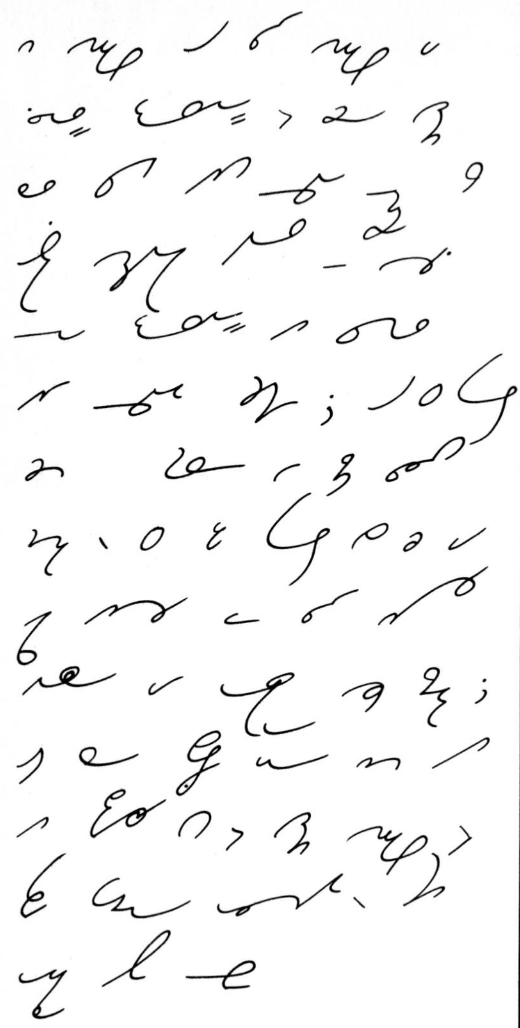

60. ANN M. LARSON, LARSON, LORD & VOORHEES,
1838 STATE STREET, BOSTON, MA 02100

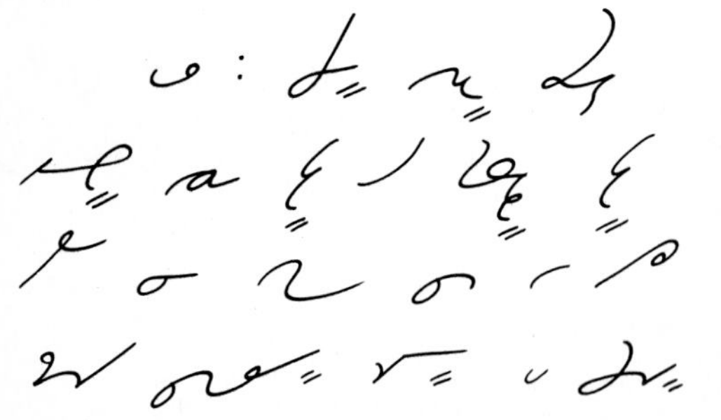

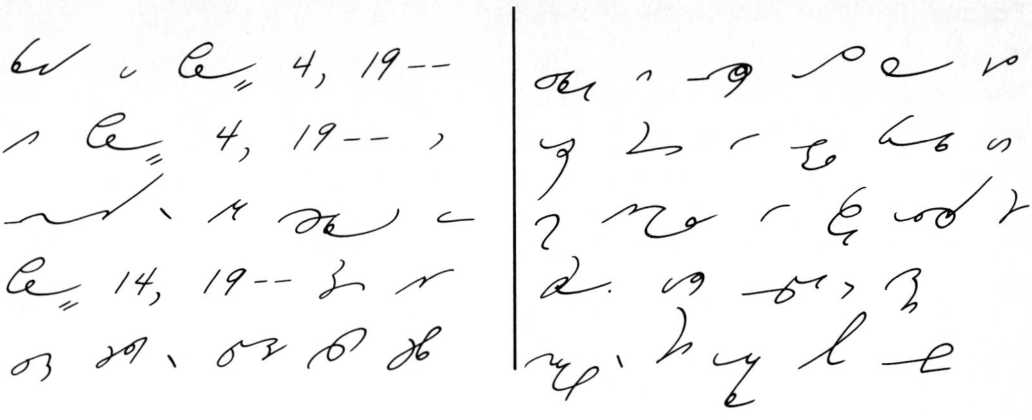

Lesson 25

BUILDING YOUR LEGAL VOCABULARY

Word Family *Pro-* is expressed by .

probationary

propounded

prorated

proviso

proxy

prohibit

Word Study

carelessness Lack of normal care to avoid harming others.

collision The act of coming together or bumping into.

disability Lack of power, strength, or capacity.

memorandum of law A supporting document for a motion.

BUILDING YOUR LEGAL TRANSCRIPTION SKILL

Transcription Aid

Capitalization in Court Papers

☐ In referring to a specific case, use initial capitals in the names of court papers such as Petition for Declaratory Judgment, Answer, Motion for Continuance; but in preparing the paper itself, the title appears in the caption or as a heading and is typed in solid capitals.

Capitalization Following "Whereas"

☐ In resolutions, contracts, agreements, and the like, the first word following *Whereas* is not capitalized; but the first word following a resolving or enacting clause is capitalized.

Whereas the Constitution provides . . .

Resolved That . . .

Be it enacted, That . . .

Latin and French Words and Phrases

 **res ipsa loquitur** *(rās ēp′sa lō′kwi tur)* The thing speaks for itself. A rebuttal presumption that the defendant was negligent.

 **sine die** *(sēn′ā dē′ā)* Without setting a day.

 **sui generis** *(sōō′ ī jen′e ris)* The only one of its own kind.

BUILDING YOUR LEGAL DICTATION PROFICIENCY

Preview

above-entitled 

aforesaid 

assignment 

automobile 

ignition 

necessitate 

petroleum 

waive 

Reading and Writing Practice

61. COMMONWEALTH OF MASSACHUSETTS MIDDLESEX, SS. SUPERIOR COURT
EQUITY NO. 8806 JANE COX V. NATIONAL INSURANCE CO., U.S. CASUALTY CO.,

THOMAS A. POPE AND FRANCES POPE, D.B.A. POPE'S GARAGE AGREED STATEMENT OF FACTS

NOW COME the parties to the above-entitled action and agree for the purposes of said action to the following[1] facts:

1. On December 20, 19—, the Plaintiff was the registered owner of a[2] 19— Ford sedan.

2. Said automobile was insured under Policy 96-38652[3] of the Defendant, The National Insurance Company, a copy of which policy is attached[4] hereto.

3. Insofar as to this material case, the pertinent provisions of said policy are:[5]

"Part I—Liability

"Persons Insured

The following are insured under Part I:

a. with respect[6] to the owned automobile,

(1) the named insured and any resident of the same household.

(2) any other person[7] using such automobile, provided the actual use thereof is with the permission of the named insured";[8]

"Definitions

"Under Part I

"....

" 'automobile business' means[9] the business or occupation of selling, repairing, servicing, storing, or parking automobiles";[10]

"Exclusions

"This policy does not apply under Part I

"....

"To an owned automobile[11] while used in the automobile business, but this exclusion does not apply to the named insured, a resident[12] of the same household as the named insured, a partnership in which the named insured or such resident is a[13] partner, or any partner, agent, or employee of the named insured, such resident or partnership";

4. Said[14] policy also provides medical payments coverage pursuant to which the Defendant The National[15] Insurance Company has paid the Plaintiff Five Hundred Dollars ($500), the limit provided for in said policy. By[16] accepting such payment the Plaintiff did not waive any of her rights under the liability provisions of[17] said policy.

5. The Defendants, Thomas A. Pope and Frances Pope, own and operate a garage in Weston,[18] Massachusetts, where they sell petroleum products and automobile accessories and also service and[19] repair automobiles.

6. On December 20, 19—, the Plaintiff called upon the[20] Defendant Thomas A. Pope to make repairs on said automobile, specifically to charge the battery and[21] repair the starter. For these purposes, the automobile was taken to said Defendant's service station. While[22] in the course of

said repair work, inside the service station, and with the permission of the Plaintiff, the said Defendant[23] turned on the ignition, whereupon the automobile lurched forward and struck the Plaintiff, resulting in bodily[24] injury to her.

7. The Plaintiff has brought suit against the Defendants Thomas A. Pope and Frances Pope,[25] for the injuries received by her and has requested the Defendant The National Insurance Company[26] to defend said suit.

8. The Defendant The National Insurance Company denies that the aforesaid[27] accident is covered under the Plaintiff's policy and has refused to defend the action against the Defendants[28] Thomas A. Pope and Frances Pope.

9. At the time of the accident, the Defendants Thomas A. Pope and Frances[29] Pope were insured by a policy issued by the U.S. Casualty Company, a copy of which is[30] attached hereto.

Jane Cox, By her attorneys, Greenberg, O'Brien, Mason & McCann, By

____

Roger L. Mason

The[31] National Insurance Company, By its attorneys, Nelson, Marley, Corden & Slater, By______________________________[32]
Henry I. Slater

The U.S. Casualty Company and Thomas A. Pope and Frances Pope, d.b.a. Pope's Garage, By their[33] attorneys, Larson, Lord & Voorhees, By

____

(670)

62. MRS. FRED J. COX, MAPLE LANE, WESTON, MA 02193

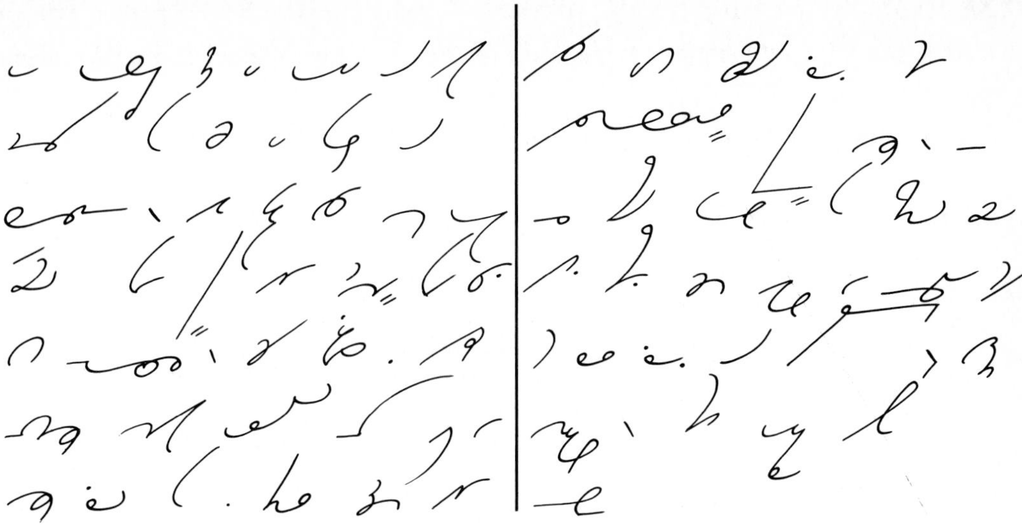

Lesson 26

BUILDING YOUR LEGAL VOCABULARY

Disjoined Word Beginnings

Ante- and *anti-* are expressed by  .

antedate 

antecedent 

antenatal 

antitrust 

antisocial 

antidote 

Word Study

 **judgment** The decision of the judge after hearing evidence or reviewing the verdict of the jury.

 **lawsuit** A dispute taken to court for settlement.

 **pertinent** Relevant; applicable.

satisfaction Giving to a person that which was granted by the judgment.

BUILDING YOUR LEGAL TRANSCRIPTION SKILL

Transcription Aid

Capitalization of Nouns With Numbers or Letters

☐ Capitalize the noun preceding a serial number or a letter indicating sequence.

Executive Order 1242   U.S. Patent No. 2,654,845   Room 112
Flight 135   Appendix B   Policy 44015

Capitalization of Trademarks, Brand Names, and Market Grades

☐ A trademark is legally reserved to the exclusive use of the owner according to statutory provisions and must be capitalized. Also capitalize other proprietary names, brand names, and market grades.

Xerox   Grade A   Choice lamb (market grade)   Steri-Pad

Legal Collocations

at issue The status of a case when pleadings in an action affirm on the one side and deny on the other.

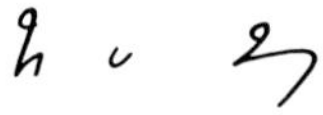
issue of execution A form issued by the clerk of the court to an officer of the law empowering him to levy against the property of the judgment debtor to satisfy judgment.

judgment creditor The party who is successful in obtaining a judgment against another.

judgment debtor The party against whom the judgment is rendered and who must pay the amount of the judgment.

supplementary proceeding A legal procedure after judgment has been entered but not satisfied by which the debtor is required to submit to examination to discover any assets that may be applied to payment of the debt.

BUILDING YOUR LEGAL DICTATION PROFICIENCY

Preview adjudicated    alleged 

battery charger	insurers
docket	obligations
exclusion	reserved
incorporating	respective
injured	thereon
instituted	transmitted

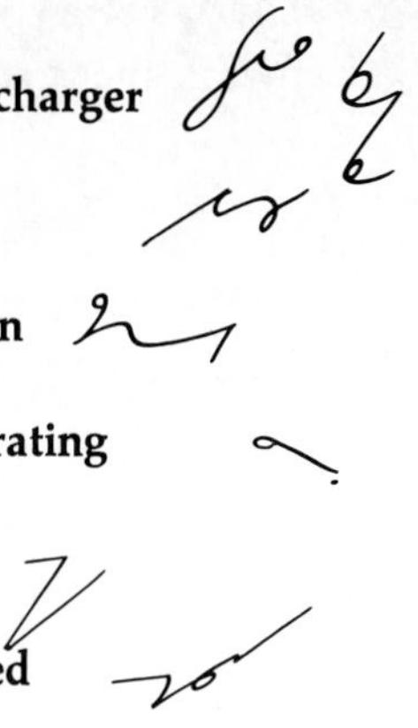

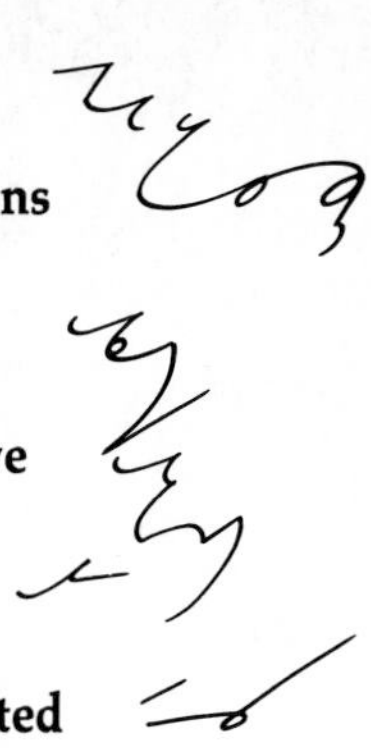

Reading and Writing Practice

63. MIDDLESEX COUNTY SUPERIOR COURT JANE COX V. NATIONAL INSURANCE CO. ET AL. NO. 6287 OPINION OF THE COURT

Petition for Declaratory Judgment by Jane Cox, Plaintiff in a pending law action against Thomas A. Pope[1] and Frances Pope, d.b.a. as Pope's Garage. She was injured December 20, 19—, when[2] struck by her own automobile in this service station as a result of the alleged negligence of Thomas Pope.[3]

Plaintiff's car was insured by the National Insurance Company under a "Family Automobile[4] Policy." Thomas A. Pope, d.b.a. Pope's Garage, was insured by U.S. Casualty Co. under[5] an "Automobile Garage Liability Policy."

Plaintiff instituted this petition to[6] have adjudicated the rights and obligations of the parties as a result of this accident. There was an[7] Agreed Statement of Facts incorporating a statement by Thomas Pope setting out the pertinent details of the[8] incident.

The Court (Miller J.) reserved and transferred without ruling the obligations of the respective[9] insurers to defend the law action and to satisfy any judgment within the limits of their[10] policy and to pay interest and costs thereon.

Greenberg, O'Brien, Mason & McCann (Mr. Roger[11] L. Mason, orally) for the Plaintiff.

Nelson, Marley, Corden & Slater and Charles F. Johnson, Jr.[12] (Mr. Slater, orally) for the National Insurance Company.

Larson, Lord & Voorhees for the[13] Casualty Co. furnished no brief.

On December 20, 19—, a very cold morning,[14] Jane Cox's automobile was towed from her home to the station, where it was determined that the starter was[15] frozen and the battery very low. When informed of the condition of the battery, she asked Pope to charge it[16] to ensure the start of her car when she left work that evening. She then drove out her car, which had been backed into the[17] south bay of the station, and headed it into the same stall to within three or four feet of the wall so that the[18] battery charger cables could reach the battery in her car.

After the charger had been connected to the[19] battery for about 20 minutes, the Plaintiff, who had been sitting in the office, came into the service part[20] of the garage and asked Pope how the battery was progressing. He advised her that she should take the car to the[21] garage where she had recently purchased it for an adjustment, as the battery could not be charged. (438)

(Continued in Lesson 27.)

64. P. H. KING, ESQ., CLERK OF SUPERIOR COURT, COURT HOUSE, BOSTON, MA 02100

65. MORSE, ALLEN, AND CURTIS, 46 HAMILTON STREET, PATERSON, NJ 07500

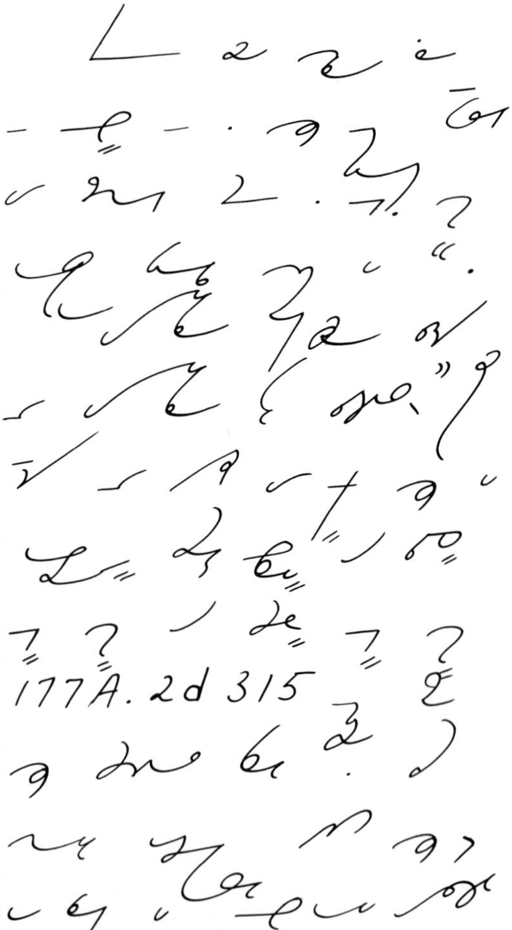

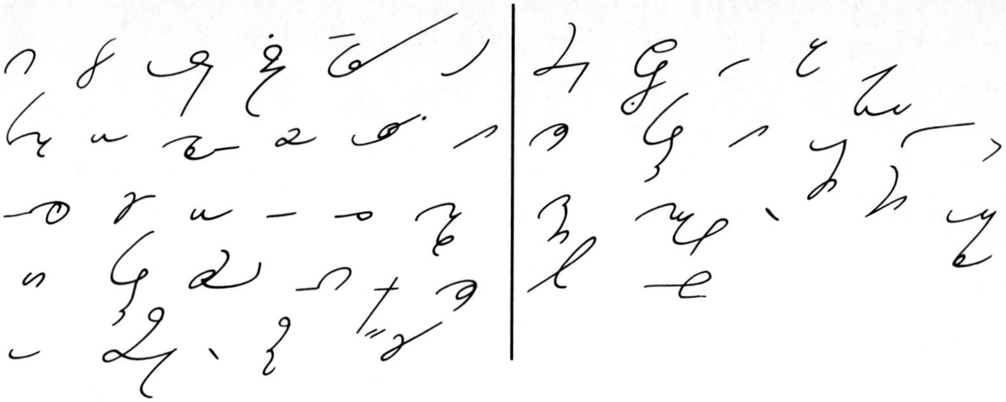

Lesson 27

BUILDING YOUR LEGAL VOCABULARY

Disjoined Word Beginnings

Inter-, *intr-*, *enter-*, and *entr-* are expressed by — .

interrogated

interplead

intervener

enterprise

intruder

interstate

Word Study

bodily injury Any physical injury.

construed Understood to be.

negligence Failure to exercise a reasonable amount of care.

vehicular Pertaining to vehicles.

BUILDING YOUR LEGAL TRANSCRIPTION SKILL

Transcription Aid

Capitalization With Points of the Compass

☐ Do not capitalize words indicating points of the compass (except in typing real property descriptions) or direction, but do capitalize definite sections of the country.

northeast southwesterly west northerly

BUT

the Middle West the East Coast the South's heritage

North forty-one (41) degrees, sixteen (16) minutes West, ten (10) feet

Capitalization to Maintain Documentary Accuracy

☐ When historic or documentary accuracy is essential, follow the style and capitalization of the original document.

Latin and French Words and Phrases

fieri facias (fi.fa.) *(fī'e rē fā'shē es)* A writ authorizing the sheriff to obtain satisfaction of a judgment from the goods and property of the defendant.

prima facie *(prī'ma fā' sē)* At first sight; on the face of it.

res gestae *(rās jes'tē)* Things done; essential circumstances surrounding the issue contested at law and that are admissible as evidence.

BUILDING YOUR LEGAL DICTATION PROFICIENCY

Preview

affirmative
applicability
comprehensive
damages
hoist
ignition
incidental

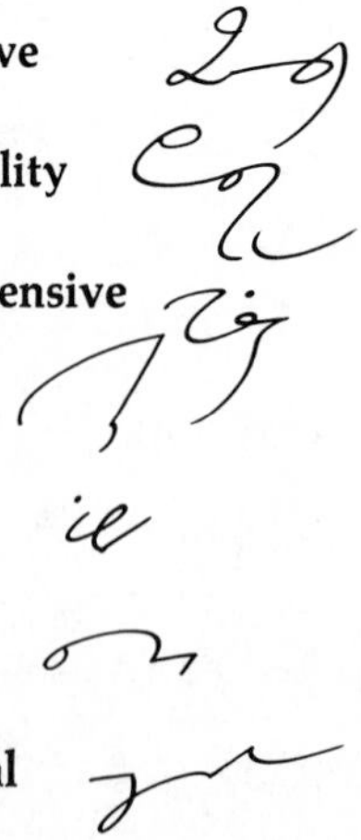

lurched
obligated
omnibus
policyholder
provision
subordinate
utilization

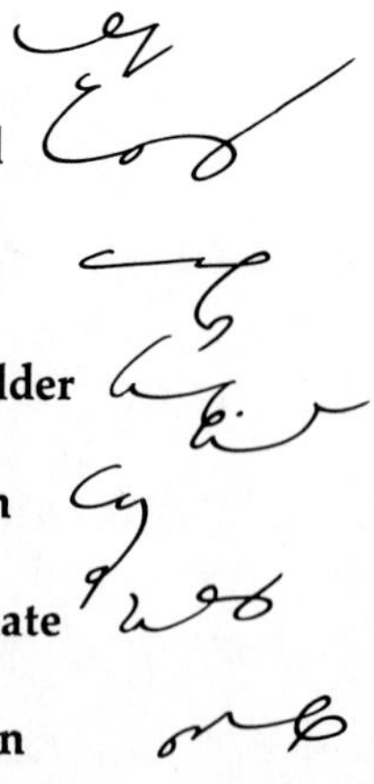

Reading and Writing Practice

66. OPINION OF THE COURT *(Continued from Lesson 26.)*

The Defendant's explanation of the accident is as follows:

"I disconnected the battery charger[1] cables from the battery. I then told Mrs. Cox to wait a minute, that I better check to see if the[2] car would start before I put the charger away. At this time, Mrs. Cox was standing on the north side of her car in[3] what I call the alley between two cars in the garage. There was room to walk between the front of the Cox car and[4] the frame lift (a hoist which was between the front of her car and the wall), so I walked around to the left front[5] door of the car. I got about three-fourths of the way into the car and turned the ignition key and . . . the[6] engine started and the car lurched forward. I don't believe I had closed the hood and think it was still up. I turned the[7] key off immediately, then started the car and backed off about three or four feet. I found Mrs. Cox had gone around[8] the front of the car, and when the car lurched forward the car had pinned her left leg against the frame lift or hoist."

The U.S.[9] Casualty Company policy agreed to pay, on behalf of Pope, damages for bodily injury[10] arising out of the "ownership, maintenance or use of the premises for the purpose of . . .[11] (a) repair shop, service station . . . and all operations necessary or incidental thereto."[12] We have been informed that this insurer has conceded, rightly in our opinion, the fact of coverage[13] and applicability of its policy to this incident. It maintains, however, that its policy[14] is subordinate to coverage by the National Insurance Company and constitutes only excess[15] protection.

The National Insurance Company, by its policy issued to Jane Cox covering the[16] automobile involved, agreed "to pay on behalf of the insured all sums which the insured shall become legally[17] obligated to pay as damages because of bodily injury . . . sustained by any[18] person . . . arising out of the ownership, maintenance or uses of the owned automobile." With[19] respect to the owned automobile, "insureds" include "(1) the named insured and any resident of the[20] same household, (2) any other person using such automobile, provided the actual use thereof is with[21] the permission of the named insured."

While conceding that Pope was acting with permission of the named insured,[22] Jane Cox, National Insurance Company takes the position that its policy affords protection to Pope[23] as an insured under the omnibus clause only if he is "using such automobile." It argues[24] that a reasonable man in the position of the insured would understand those words to mean the affirmative[25] employment of a vehicle for its vehicular qualities and maintains that Pope's acts at the time of the[26] accident did not constitute such a use.

This Court did hold in *Peerless Insurance v. Gould,* 103 N.H.[27] 134, as pointed out by National Insurance Company, that a reasonable man in the position[28] of the policyholder would not understand a provision granting coverage for the occasional[29] use for business purposes of an automobile owned by the insured to mean that it covered the use of the[30] vehicle as an article of merchandise on display in the lot of a sales agency for used cars. Rather,[31] the insured would take the language to relate to the utilization of the automobile in the ordinary[32] manner, that is, its use as a vehicle.

However, we held in *Carter v. Bergeron,* 102[33] N.H. 464, 470, that "the words 'arising out of . . . use' are very broad, general,[34] and comprehensive terms." In *Eastern Transp. Co. v. Liberty Mut. Cas.*[35] *Co.,* 101 N.H. 407, we decided that injuries sustained in a collision[36] with a tractor-trailer stopped in the highway caused by its defective lighting equipment and other negligence[37] could be found to have been caused by accident arising out of the use of the insured truck that had towed it into[38] the highway. (762)

(Continued in Lesson 28.)

Lesson 28

BUILDING YOUR LEGAL VOCABULARY

Disjoined Word Beginnings

Intra- is expressed by  .

intrastate 

intramuscular 

intracity 

intramural 

intravenous 

intracutaneous 

Word Study

indemnity Money paid to compensate for loss or injury.

irreparable So great that the loss or injury cannot be properly compensated for or made right.

liability Legal responsibility; a debt or obligation.

touchstone Standard; criterion for determining the quality or genuineness of something.

BUILDING YOUR LEGAL TRANSCRIPTION SKILL

Transcription Aid

In this and in the next ten lessons, rules for correctly transcribing numbers are presented to reinforce your knowledge of the generally accepted usage and of points that are uniquely legal in style.

Number Usage: General Rule for Numbers

☐ Spell out exact numbers under eleven with the exception of specific instances presented in this and in subsequent lessons.

This man was arrested eight months prior to his arraignment.

Number Usage: Standard Units of Measure

☐ Use figures to express numbers that precede standard units of measure such as pounds, feet, degrees, and the like.

The search produced 15 ounces, more or less, of marijuana.

Number Usage: Decimals

☐ Use figures to express decimals. A zero at the end of a decimal indicates the number of decimal places the computation has carried to, as 1.310. Use a zero preceding the decimal point to emphasize that the number is less than 1, as 0.415.

Legal Collocations

compensatory damages Damages that make equivalent return for loss or harm resulting from injury to person, property, or reputation.

due care Proper or sufficient care.

negligent operation Operation without due care.

notary public A commissioned officer of the state who may attest to or certify documents to make them authentic, such as acknowledgments, affidavits, and depositions.

personal injuries Injuries to the body of an individual.

BUILDING YOUR LEGAL DICTATION PROFICIENCY

Preview

contractor 
independent 
interpreted 
language 
mindful 
reasonably 
vehicle 
sustained 

Reading and Writing Practice

67. OPINION OF THE COURT *(Continued from Lesson 27.)*

In the Carter case, we held that if the insured vehicle was being used by an employer to regulate[1] or pace the speed of a truck following it driven by an employee, it could be found that the accident in[2] which the truck was involved arose out of the use of the vehicle driven by the employer, although it was not[3] itself physically involved in the accident. *Carter v. Bergeron,* 102 N.H. 462,[4] 471.

It seems to us that when in this case the plaintiff was injured by direct contact with the automobile,[5] which resulted from its having "lurched forward" when its engine was started by turning on the ignition[6] key by Pope, this accident all the more certainly arose out of the use of the automobile within[7] the terms of the National Insurance Company policy.

National Insurance Company argues next[8] that if Pope was using the Cox automobile with permission in making repairs, he was necessarily[9] using it in the automobile business and is excluded from coverage by the terms of its policy.[10] By its definition, " 'automobile business' means the business or occupation of selling,[11] repairing, servicing, storing, or parking automobiles." The policy provides that coverage for[12] liability does not apply, "(g) to an owned automobile while used in the automobile business,[13] but this exclusion does not apply to the named insured, a resident of the same household as the named insured,[14] a partnership in which the named insured or such resident is a partner, agent, or employee of the named insured,[15] such resident or partnership." This presents the issue of whether Pope as an independent contractor[16] was using the plaintiff's car in the automobile business at the time of this accident.

Here again we test[17] the language of the policy by the touchstone of what a reasonable person in the position of the insured[18] would have understood this exclusion to mean. *Lalos v. Tickler* 103 N.H. 292, 295.[19] We are aware of the opinion that this language is not intended to exclude coverage because the automobile[20] happens to be in the possession or under the control of a person whose business is automobiles.[21] Nor can it reasonably be interpreted to deny coverage by the mere fact that a repairperson[22] is using a customer's car in the process of servicing it. On the contrary, a reasonable person[23] in the position of the insured would understand it to mean that coverage would be excluded when the[24] automobile was employed by some purpose in connection with the automobile business. Plaintiff's car was at[25] this service station to be repaired, not to be "used in the automobile business." *McCree v. Jennings,*[26] 55 Wash. 2d 725, 727; *Chavers v. St. Paul Fire and Mar. Ins.*[27] *Co.,* 188 F.Supp. 39, aff'd 295 F.2d 812; *Le Felt v.*[28] *Nasarow,* 71 N.J.Super.Ct. 538, 549, 555, aff'd[29] 76 N.J.Super.Ct. 576; *Challis v. Commercial Standard Ins. Co.,*[30] 177 Ind. App. 180; 7 Appleman, *Insurance Law and Practice,* sec. 4372[31] (supp).

We are mindful, as pointed out by the National Insurance Company, that the facts in the above cases[32] differ in certain respects from those in this case and that some jurisdictions apply a rule of construction[33] which differs from ours. However, we are of the opinion that the exclusion of "use in the automobile[34] business" relied on by National Insurance Company does not bar coverage under our rule of[35] interpretation and on the facts of this case and we so hold.

Both U.S. Casualty Insurance Company[36] and the National Insurance Company policies afford coverage for this accident. The National[37] policy by its terms provides coverage for bodily injury "sustained by any person," which includes[38] the Plaintiff in this case. *Howe v. Howe,* 87 N.H. 338, 341; *Farm Bureau & Ins.*[39] *Co. v. Garland,* 100 N.H. 351, 352. (794)
(Continued in Lesson 29.)

Lesson 29

BUILDING YOUR LEGAL VOCABULARY

Disjoined Word Beginnings

Electr- and *electric* are expressed by 

electrocute  **electricity** 

electrocution

electric chair

electronic

electrical

Word Study

aggregate The whole or combined sum or amount.

pro rata Proportionately.

remanded Sent back for further action.

statutory Created or existing by virtue of an act of legislature.

BUILDING YOUR LEGAL TRANSCRIPTION SKILL

Transcription Aid

Number Usage: Dates

☐ Use figures to express dates unless the day of the month is mentioned without the name of the month.

On March 7, 19—, I became counsel to Jane Cox.

Number Usage: Money

☐ Use figures to express amounts of money except as noted in Lesson 38.

His bail was reduced to the sum of $5,000.

The toll charge for your telephone call is 75 cents plus tax.

Latin and French Words and Phrases

ad litem *(ad lī′tem)* During a particular litigation proceeding; while the action is pending.

ante litem *(an′tē lī′tem)* Before suit or action.

corpus delicti *(kor′pus de lik′tī)* The body of basic facts necessary to prove the commission of a crime; the damaged property; the body of the victim.

BUILDING YOUR LEGAL DICTATION PROFICIENCY

Preview

affirmation 

applicable 

collectibility 

collectible 

concurrent 

guaranteed 

homestead 

negotiations 

sheriff 

verdict 

Reading and Writing Practice

68. OPINION OF THE COURT *(Continued from Lesson 28.)*

There remains the determination of the respective obligations of the insurers. Each policy contains[1] the provision that if the insured has other insurance against a loss covered by the policy, the company[2] shall not be liable for a greater proportion of such loss than the applicable limit of liability[3] stated in the declaration bears to the total applicable limit of liability of[4] all valid and collectible insurance against such loss. Neither policy provides that in a case like the present[5] it will afford excess insurance only or have no liability if there is other valid and[6] collectible insurance. We therefore hold that since both policies have a pro rata clause and the same limit of[7] liability, each insurer is liable for its proportionate amount of any judgment recovered for this[8] accident. *Kenner* v. *Century Indemnity Co.,* 320 Mass. 6; 7 Am.Jur.2d.[9] *Automobile Insurance,* sec. 200, p. 542.

National Insurance Company and U.S.[10] Casualty policies consequently provide concurrent coverage within the limits of their policies.[11] Each is obligated to defend and pay half of the cost of the defense. 7A Appleman, Insurance[12] Law and Practice, sec. 4691, p. 511. Each company is also obligated within[13] its limit of liability to pay one-half of any judgment recovered with interest and costs.

Remanded.[14]

All concurred. (283)

69. MR. AND MRS. FRED J. COX, MAPLE LANE, WESTON, MA 02193

6

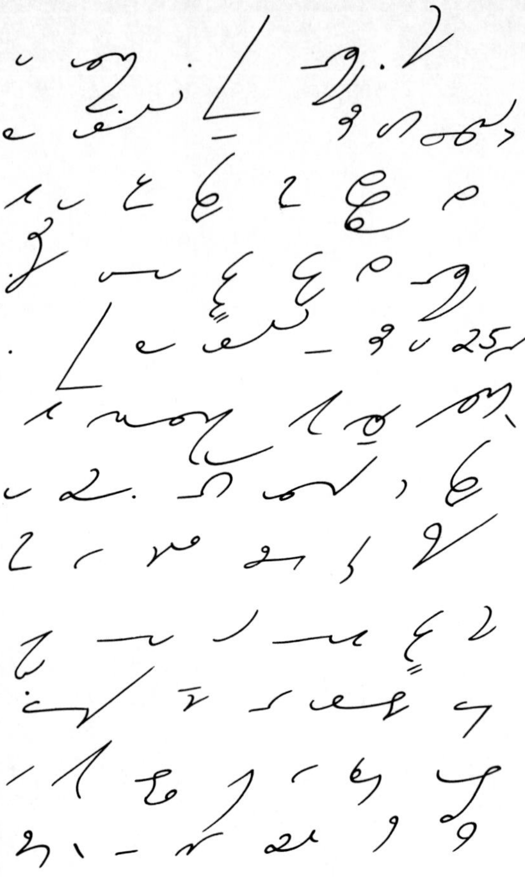

Lesson 30

BUILDING YOUR LEGAL VOCABULARY

Disjoined Word Beginnings *Par-* and *para-* are expressed by  .

paramount		**paradox**	
paramour		**paralyzed**	
parallel		**parity**	

Word Study

 **escrow** A deed, bond, money, or piece of property delivered to a third person to be held until some condition is met.

 **hand and seal** Signature and identifying mark.

 **Reporters** Books that summarize decisions of cases heard in all types of courts.

 **testimonium clause** The last clause in a legal document making reference to the signing of that document.

BUILDING YOUR LEGAL TRANSCRIPTION SKILL

Transcription Aid **Number Usage: Items Numbered Serially**

☐ Use figures to express items numbered serially. Omit the comma in typing large serial numbers except in patents.

Serial No. 4513098 Title 21, United States Code, Section 176a

Policy 445-P-9621 U.S. Patent No. 2,779,837

Number Usage: Ordinal Numbers

☐ Numbers indicating the place occupied by any item in an ordered sequence, such as first, second, and the like, should be spelled out under the following conditions:

1. Ordinal numbers that can be expressed in one or two words:

first offense   the thirty-fifth time

☐ If, however, ordinals appear in a series in which one must be expressed in figures, use figures for each member of the series:

the 2d, 6th, and 15th exhibits

2. Numbers connected with subjects to be dignified:

Eighty-first Congress   the Eighteenth Amendment   the Tenth Anniversary

Typing Citations

Reports and Reporters

Reports or Reporters are publications that list opinions of cases. Such publications include Supreme Court Reporter, Federal Reporter, Federal Supplement, state reports, and the National Reporter System (federal and state opinions published by West Publishing Co.).

In citing state reports, list state, court, and date. It is assumed that the highest court is meant when no court is indicated. Give docket number and exact date when citing unpublished decisions.

McCrees v. Jennings, 55 Wash.2d 725, 727   (state)

Chavers v. St. Paul Fire & Mar. Ins. Co., 188 F.Supp. 39 (1960)   (Federal Reporter)

Marchetti v. United States, 36 U.S.L.W. 4143 (January 29, 1968)   (unpublished ed.)

Lefelt v. Nasarow, 71 N.J.Super.Ct. 538   (listing of court)

Aetna Ins. Co. v. Peerless Ins. Co., N.J. 177 A.2d 315   (National Reporter)

BUILDING YOUR LEGAL DICTATION PROFICIENCY

Preview

accordance    expedite 

allocation    incorporate 

certificate    instruct 

empower    rendering 

respective	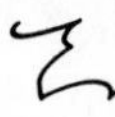	transmitted	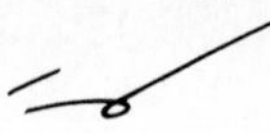
taxation		undersigned	

Reading and Writing Practice

70. ASSIGNMENT

KNOW ALL MEN BY THESE PRESENTS that for good and valuable consideration the undersigned, Fred J. Cox and Jane[1] Cox of Weston, County of Middlesex and Commonwealth of Massachusetts, do hereby assign from the net proceeds[2] that may be received by them or either of them from a particular lawsuit presently pending between[3] Jane Cox and Thomas A. Pope and Frances Pope and direct that to the extent of the unpaid balance due Dole's TV-Radio[4] & Appliances, Inc. of Weston, Massachusetts, in the amount of $266[5] at the time the proceeds of said case be received that the same be applied and paid over to[6] and for the purposes of complete and full satisfaction of any unpaid balance on said account.

And we do[7] hereby further instruct, authorize, and empower Attorney Roger L. Mason to so use and apply the[8] foregoing proceeds.

IN WITNESS WHEREOF we have hereunto set our respective hands this 26th

day of June,[9] 19__. (Witness __________) (Jane Cox __________)

(Witness __________) (Fred J. Cox __________)[10] (203)

71. OLIVER G. VANE, ESQ., CLERK OF SUPREME COURT, 20 PARK STREET, BOSTON, MA 02100

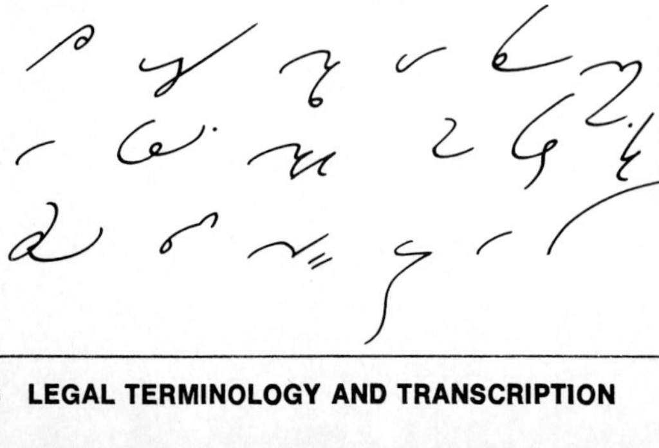

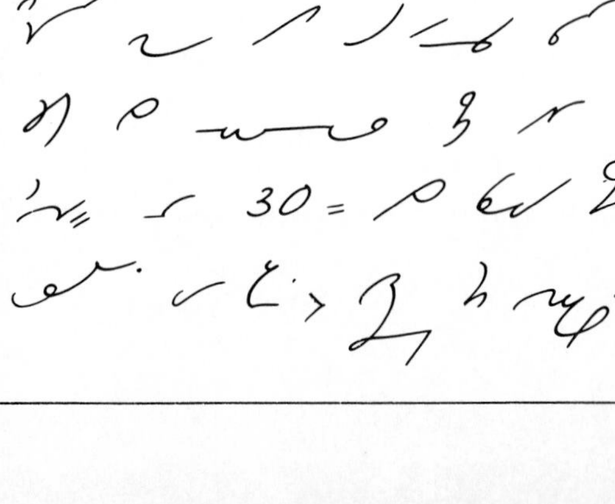

72. ROGER L. MASON, ESQ., GREENBERG, O'BRIEN, MASON & McCANN, 74 STATE STREET, BOSTON, MA 02100

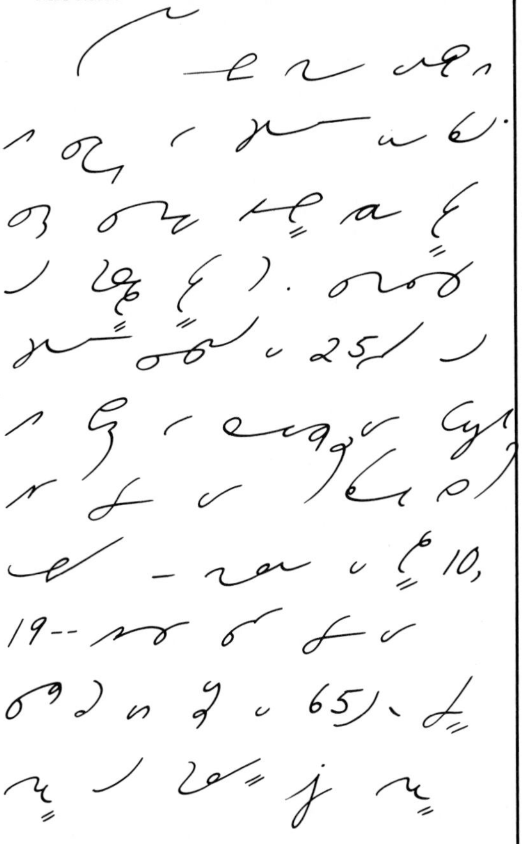

73. HENRY I. SLATER, ESQ., NELSON, MORLEY, CORDEN & SLATER, 9 CAPITAL STREET, BOSTON, MA 02100
ANN M. LARSON, LARSON, LORD & VOORHEES, 1838 STATE STREET, BOSTON, MA 02100
JAMES GAVIN, ESQ., GAVIN AND ALLEN, P. O. BOX 255, WESTON, MA 02193

74. HENRY I. SLATER, ESQ., NELSON, MORLEY, CORDEN & SLATER, 9 CAPITAL STREET, BOSTON, MA 02100

UNIT

4 Drug Smuggling

United States of America
vs.*
Robert B. Voss

This is a case concerning the criminal indictment of Robert B. Voss, charged with smuggling marijuana into the United States in violation of Title 21, United States Code, Section 176a. The case was tried in a United States District Court.

The lawyer for Mr. Voss is David E. Mason, Esq. The defense maintained that in attempting to comply with Section 176a a person would forfeit the protection against self-incrimination provided by the Fifth Amendment.

*Mr. Mason prefers the use of *vs.*

Lesson 31

BUILDING YOUR LEGAL VOCABULARY

Disjoined Word Beginnings *Post-* is expressed by . It is advisable to place the symbol on the line of writing to distinguish it from *para.*

postmarital  **postdate** 

postmortem  **postnatal** 

postponement  **post-obit** 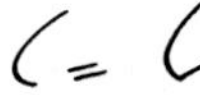

Word Study

 **affidavit** A written statement made under oath.

 **apprehended** Seized, arrested, captured.

 **arraigned** Called before a court to answer an indictment.

 **bail** Security given for the temporary release of a person under arrest.

 **customs** The duties or tariff upon merchandise exported or imported.

 **defraud** To cheat; to deprive of something by deception.

 **deponent** One who gives evidence; a witness who testifies at a deposition.

 **deposes** Testifies under oath.

 **marijuana** The dried flower clusters and leaves of the hemp plant sometimes smoked in cigarettes for their intoxicating effect.

 **warrant** A writ authorizing an arrest, search, or seizure.

BUILDING YOUR LEGAL TRANSCRIPTION SKILL

Transcription Aid

Number Usage: Numbered Paragraphs

☐ Use either arabic or roman numerals when numbering paragraphs in such papers as interrogatories, leases, motions, stipulations, and the like.

Number Usage: Roman Numerals

☐ Use roman numerals to refer to volumes and to major divisions of a publication unless they become too difficult to consult rapidly. Use arabic numerals to refer to pages, illustrations, tables, and other minor divisions. See the dictionary for the correct means of forming roman numerals.

Volume IV   Chapter II   Part III, Paragraph V (When a document is so numbered)

page 10, Table 4   Illustration 25

Typing Citations

The history of a case is indicated by the following words: "affirmed," "reversed," "affirmed or reversed on other grounds," "*certiorari*," or "rehearing denied or granted," and so on. Such words are italicized or underscored in law reviews (journals published by law schools).

Chavers v. St. Paul Fire and Mar. Ins. Co., 188 F.Supp. 39, (1960) *aff'd* 295 F.2d 812

BUILDING YOUR LEGAL DICTATION PROFICIENCY

Preview

above-mentioned    duly 

above-named    grand jury 

adjourned    identity 

aforementioned    indictment 

arrested    substituted 

commissioner    sworn 

concealment    treasury 

defraud 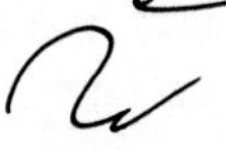   violation 

district    waived 

Reading and Writing Practice

75. UNITED STATES DISTRICT COURT DISTRICT OF MASSACHUSETTS UNITED STATES OF AMERICA VS. ROBERT B. VOSS CRIMINAL NO. 76-84-W INDICTMENT

The grand jury charges:

COUNT I

On or about January 23, 19—, at Boston in[1] the District of Massachusetts,

ROBERT B. VOSS

of New York, New York, knowingly and with intent to defraud the[2] United States, did import and bring into the United States and did facilitate the transportation and[3] concealment of 15.76 ounces, more or less, of marijuana contrary to law, in violation[4] of Title 21, United States Code, Section 176a.

COUNT II

On or about[5] January 27, 19—, at Boston in the District of Massachusetts,

ROBERT B.[6] VOSS

of New York, New York, knowingly and with intent to defraud the United States, did import and bring into[7] the United States and did facilitate the transportation and concealment of 16.64[8] ounces, more or less, of marijuana contrary to law, in violation of Title 21, United States Code, Section 176a.

COUNT III

On or about February 1, 19—, at[9] Boston in the District of Massachusetts,

ROBERT B. VOSS

of New York, New York, knowingly and with intent to[10] defraud the United States, did import and bring into the United States and did facilitate the[11] transportation and concealment of 16.26 ounces, more or less, of marijuana contrary to law,[12] in violation of Title 21, United States Code, Section 176a.

76. UNITED STATES DISTRICT COURT SOUTHERN DISTRICT OF NEW YORK UNITED STATES OF AMERICA VS. ROBERT B. VOSS, DEFENDANT. STATE OF NEW YORK COUNTY OF NEW YORK SOUTHERN DISTRICT OF NEW YORK SS. AFFIDAVIT.

GEORGE BROWN, being[13] duly sworn, deposes and says that he is an Agent of the Bureau of Customs, Department of the Treasury,[14] and further says:

On the 20th day of February, 19—, at Boston, Massachusetts,[15] in the District of Massachusetts, a Federal Grand Jury returned Indictment 76-84-W[16] against the above-named Defendant, charging violations of Title 21, United States Code,[17] Section 176a; a warrant is to be issued on this indictment today.

He believes that the[18] defendant ROBERT B. VOSS, who was apprehended in the Southern District of New York, is the same ROBERT B.[19] VOSS named in the above-mentioned indictment.

The bases for deponent's knowledge are, in part, as follows:

Communications[20] from the Boston, Massachusetts, office of the Bureau of Customs, enclosing a copy of the aforementioned[21] indictment, a copy of which is attached hereto, communications from the United States Attorney's Office[22] of the District of Massachusetts, and oral statements by the above-named Defendant, made after warning as[23] to his constitutional rights, that he is the same ROBERT B. VOSS named in the above-mentioned indictment.

STATE OF[24] NEW YORK)
) ss.
COUNTY OF NEW YORK)

JANE S. HOFFMAN, being duly sworn, deposes and says:

I am an[25] attorney duly admitted to practice law in the State of New York.

On March 7, 19—, I[26] became counsel to ROBERT VOSS who, I was informed, had been arrested on February 28,[27] 19—, in New York City by Customs Agent George Brown on a warrant issued in conection with the[28] presently pending indictment. Mr. Voss had been arraigned on March 1, 19—, in the United[29] States District Court for the Southern District of New York, at which time bail was set in the sum of $10,000[30] and the matter adjourned. At that time he was represented by Samuel J. Smith and Max H. Williams of[31] 4276 Fifth Avenue, New York, New York. On March 21, 19—, I appeared with Mr.[32] Voss in the United States District Court for the Southern District of New York before Commissioner Warren in[33] Room 615; I was formally substituted as counsel; Mr. Voss waived the issue of identity;[34] and his bail was reduced to the sum of $5,000.

Neither Mr. Voss nor I received any[35] communication from Boston until a Notice of Date for Arraignment, dated October 19,[36] 19—, was received a day or so later by Mr. Voss setting down the case for arraignment at Boston[37] on Monday, October 30, 19—.

Mr. Voss will be represented in Boston by[38] David E. Mason, of the firm of Greenberg, O'Brien, Mason & McCann. (774)

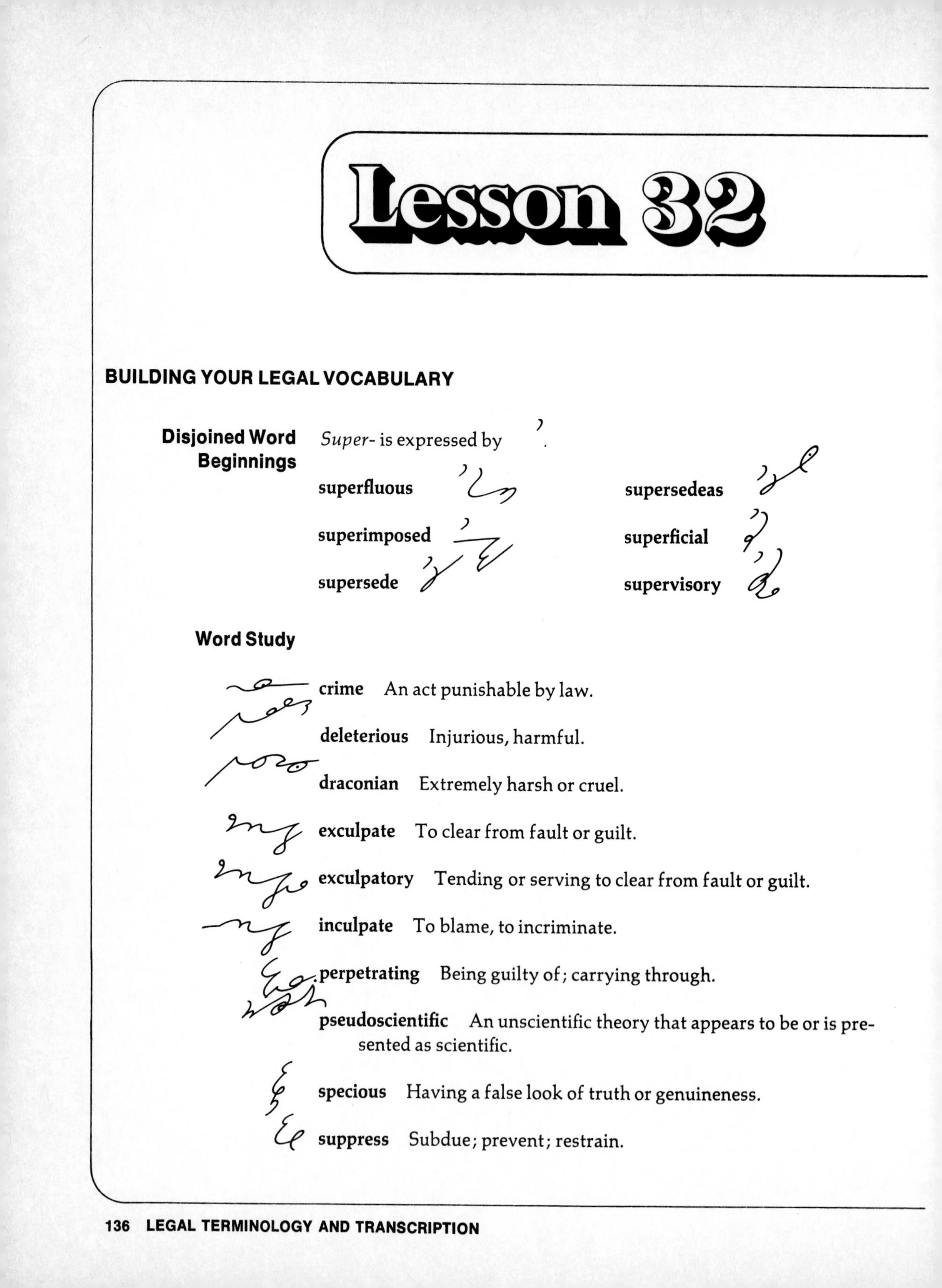

Lesson 32

BUILDING YOUR LEGAL VOCABULARY

Disjoined Word Beginnings

Super- is expressed by .

superfluous	**supersedeas**
superimposed	**superficial**
supersede	**supervisory**

Word Study

crime An act punishable by law.

deleterious Injurious, harmful.

draconian Extremely harsh or cruel.

exculpate To clear from fault or guilt.

exculpatory Tending or serving to clear from fault or guilt.

inculpate To blame, to incriminate.

perpetrating Being guilty of; carrying through.

pseudoscientific An unscientific theory that appears to be or is presented as scientific.

specious Having a false look of truth or genuineness.

suppress Subdue; prevent; restrain.

BUILDING YOUR LEGAL TRANSCRIPTION SKILL

Transcription Aid

Number Usage: Approximate Round Numbers

- ☐ Spell out approximate round numbers with the following exceptions: when used with standard units of measure, when used for emphasis, and when used to designate specific limits above 10.

  more than eleven heirs   about 6 feet tall   over 25 witnesses

  a 1- to 20-page brief

Number Usage: Clock Time

- ☐ Use figures with *a.m.* and *p.m.* when expressing time; spell out the hour when followed by *o'clock*.

  Accordingly, the motion is set for reargument on Monday, April 1, at 10 a.m.

  At ten o'clock this morning there will be a meeting in my office.

Legal Collocations

 **burden of proof** The duty of establishing facts that are in dispute in a case.

 **cause of action** Facts justifying litigation.

 **conclusion of fact** An inference drawn from the subordinate or evidentiary facts.

 **days of grace** Days allowed after the time originally limited for some act has elapsed.

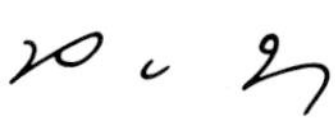 **stay of execution** A court order that delays the carrying out of a sentence.

BUILDING YOUR LEGAL DICTATION PROFICIENCY

Preview

annexed    evidence 

camel    honorable 

contraband    illegal 

documents    importation 

labeling 

marijuana 

packaging 

procedure 

pursuant 

saddles 

seizure 

substance 

tangible 

unlawfully 

Reading and Writing Practice

7

77. UNITED STATES DISTRICT COURT DISTRICT OF MASSACHUSETTS UNITED STATES OF AMERICA VS. ROBERT B. VOSS CRIMINAL NO. 76-84-W DEFENDANT'S MOTION TO SUPPRESS EVIDENCE

Defendant hereby moves this Honorable Court to direct that certain property, a schedule of which is annexed[1] hereto (which schedule Defendant believes but does not know to a certainty to be a complete schedule[2] of all such items), which property on a date or dates unknown to Defendant on a premises unknown to[3] Defendant was unlawfully seized and taken from the mails or from another location by agents of the[4] United States, be suppressed as evidence against him in any criminal proceeding.

Defendant further states that the[5] property was seized, to his knowledge and belief, without a search warrant and without probable cause for believing[6] that a crime had been committed and that the property was contraband, the search and seizure thus being in[7] violation of the Fourth Amendment to the United States Constitution.

Robert B. Voss
By his attorneys,[8]
GREENBERG, O'BRIEN, MASON & MCCANN
by:______________________
David E. Mason

78. UNITED STATES DISTRICT COURT DISTRICT OF MASSACHUSETTS UNITED STATES OF AMERICA VS. ROBERT B. VOSS CRIMINAL NO. 76-84-W SCHEDULE OF SEIZED PROPERTY

Three (3) camel saddles or similar[9] items.
Approximately 48.66 ounces of marijuana.
Packaging and labeling[10] materials, packages, and labels used for mailing parcels.

79. UNITED STATES DISTRICT COURT DISTRICT OF MASSACHUSETTS UNITED STATES OF AMERICA VS. ROBERT B. VOSS CRIMINAL NO. 76-84-W DEFENDANT'S MOTION TO INSPECT

Defendant moves this Honorable Court, pursuant[11] to Rule 16 of the Federal Rules of Criminal Procedure, to order the attorney for the Government[12] to permit the defendant to inspect and copy or photograph papers, documents, and tangible objects[13] obtained from or belonging to the Defendant or obtained from others by seizure or by process, including[14] the following items and the reasons for their materiality to the preparation of the defense:

Any[15] and all letters written by the Defendant to any persons, including his aunt, one Mrs. Wallace Monroe, which[16] letters in any way refer to the items seized and the contents thereof or any other acts of the Defendant, and[17] including any references to camel saddles, which saddles, Defendant believes, contained the marijuana[18] of which he is charged with the illegal importation.

Any and all packages, package wrappers, mailing labels,[19] camel saddles, marijuana, and any other items or parts thereof which the Government alleges or suspects[20] were used by the Defendant, or any other party, in perpetrating an illegal act.

Any other such[21] documents or items that will tend to inculpate or to exculpate the Defendant from the crime alleged in the[22] indictment.

Any and all scientific or other tests conducted by the Government, including tests of the[23] substance alleged to be marijuana.

Robert B. Voss
By his attorneys,
GREENBERG, O'BRIEN, MASON & MCCANN[24]

by:______________________________
David E. Mason

80. UNITED STATES DISTRICT COURT DISTRICT OF MASSACHUSETTS UNITED STATES OF AMERICA VS. ROBERT B. VOSS CRIMINAL NO. 76-84-W DEFENDANT'S MOTION TO DISMISS

Defendant hereby moves this Honorable Court, pursuant to Rule 48(b),[25] Federal Rules of Criminal Procedure, to dismiss the above-entitled proceeding, and Defendant assigns as[26] his reasons the following:

1. The Government unreasonably delayed prosecution of the Defendant, allowing[27] more than eight (8) months to elapse from the date of indictment and arrest to the date of[28] arraignment and eventual trial, which delay was without good and sound cause, results in oppression of the Defendant,[29] results in prejudice to the Defendant in violation of Rule 48(b) of the Federal[30] Rules of Criminal Procedure and the Fifth Amendment to the United States Constitution, in that:

a. it allows[31] the Government in effect to select those witnesses who will and those who will not appear on behalf of[32] the Defendant, and

b. it deprives the Defendant of vital exculpatory testimony and evidence[33] being introduced on his behalf, as is set forth in the attached affidavits.

2. The statute under[34] which Defendant is charged, namely Title 21, United States Code, Section 176a, is invalid[35] and unconstitutional because:

a. the statute, as it applied to cannabis (commonly[36] called marihuana or marijuana), is arbitrary and irrational and hence is in violation[37] of the due process of law guarantee of the Fifth Amendment to the United States Constitution, in that[38] the substance cannabis has not been demonstrated to be deleterious, the statute was passed pursuant[39] to specious and untrue pseudoscientific allegations, and because of enforcement of the statute,[40] liberty tends to be sacrificed for the supposedly greater advantage of health, safety, and morals; and

b.[41] the statute, as it applies to cannabis, would subject the Defendant to cruel, unusual, excessive, indeed[42] draconian penalties in violation of the Eighth Amendment to the United States Constitution.[43]

Robert B. Voss
By his attorneys,
GREENBERG, O'BRIEN, MASON & MCCANN
by:______________________________
David E. Mason (878)

Lesson 33

BUILDING YOUR LEGAL VOCABULARY

Disjoined Word Beginnings

Circum- is expressed by .

circumvent 

circumspect 

circumstantial 

circumduction 

circumscribed 

circumvention 

Word Study

arraignment In criminal practice, the process of calling of an accused by name, reading the indictment, and receiving his plea.

conviction The act of finding or proving a person guilty.

narcotics Drugs such as opium.

prosecute To follow up; to proceed against a person criminally.

BUILDING YOUR LEGAL TRANSCRIPTION SKILL

Transcription Aid

Number Usage: Numbers in Compound Adjectives

☐ When a compound adjective is formed from a number and a standard unit of measure, use figures to express the amount.

4-gram sample 15-minute interval ½-inch scar
90-degree angle

Number Usage: Numbers Preceding Compound Adjectives

☐ Spell out numbers of less than 100 preceding a compound modifier that contains a figure as its first unit.

twenty 3-ounce containers BUT 125 three-ounce containers

Latin and French Words and Phrases

in personam *(in per sō'nam)* Against for with reference to the person.

in rem *(in rem')* In or against a thing; not against the person.

inter alia *(in'ter ā'lē a)* Among other things.

BUILDING YOUR LEGAL DICTATION PROFICIENCY

Preview

arrested
assignment
client
contention
curtailed
denial
dismiss
exculpatory

Federal Bureau of Investigation | pursuance
forewent | pursued
indispensable | subsequent
justice | substantiate
potentially | suppress
prejudiced | testified

Reading and Writing Practice

81. UNITED STATES DISTRICT COURT DISTRICT OF MASSACHUSETTS UNITED STATES OF AMERICA VS. ROBERT B. VOSS CRIMINAL NO. 76-84-W DEFENDANT'S MOTION FOR CONTINUANCE

Defendant moves this Honorable Court to grant a continuance of the above-entitled proceeding until mid-[1] or late January, 19—, and defendant gives as his reason for this motion the fact that[2] a vital witness is absent from the jurisdiction and will be so absent until after the first of January,[3] 19—.

Defendant further states that he is unable to proceed with his defense in[4] the absence of said witness and his potentially exculpatory testimony.

By his attorneys,

GREENBERG,[5] O'BRIEN, MASON & MCCANN

By:______________________________

David E. Mason

(111)

82. JANE S. HOFFMAN, ESQ., 721 EAST 40 STREET, NEW YORK, NY 10000

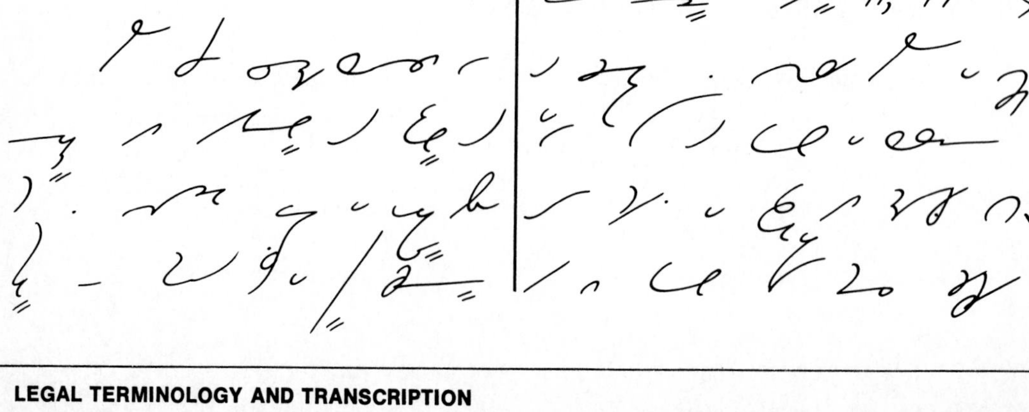

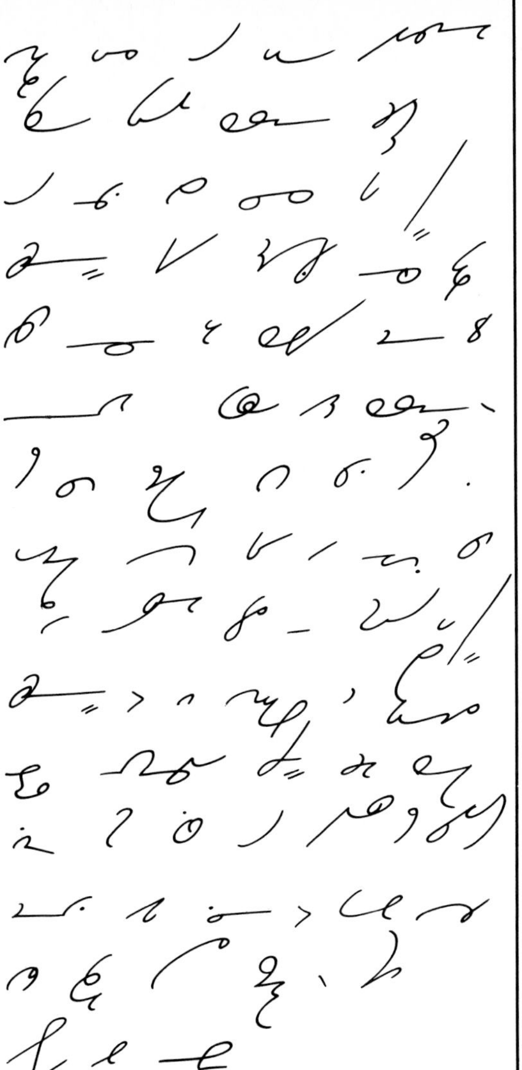

83. ALBERT F. COMPTON, ESQ., ASSISTANT UNITED STATES ATTORNEY, POST OFFICE AND COURTHOUSE BUILDING, POST OFFICE SQUARE, BOSTON, MA 02100

7

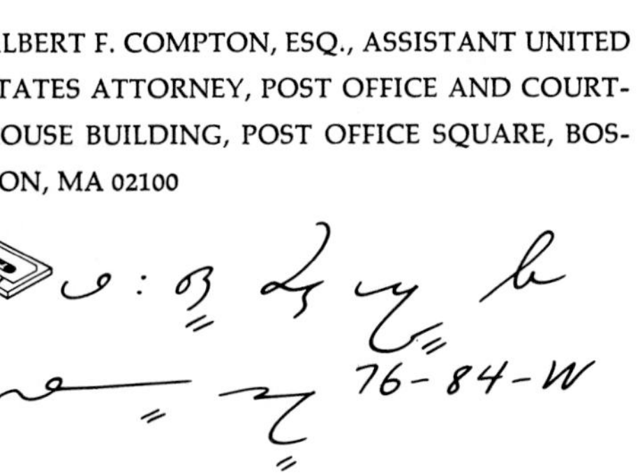

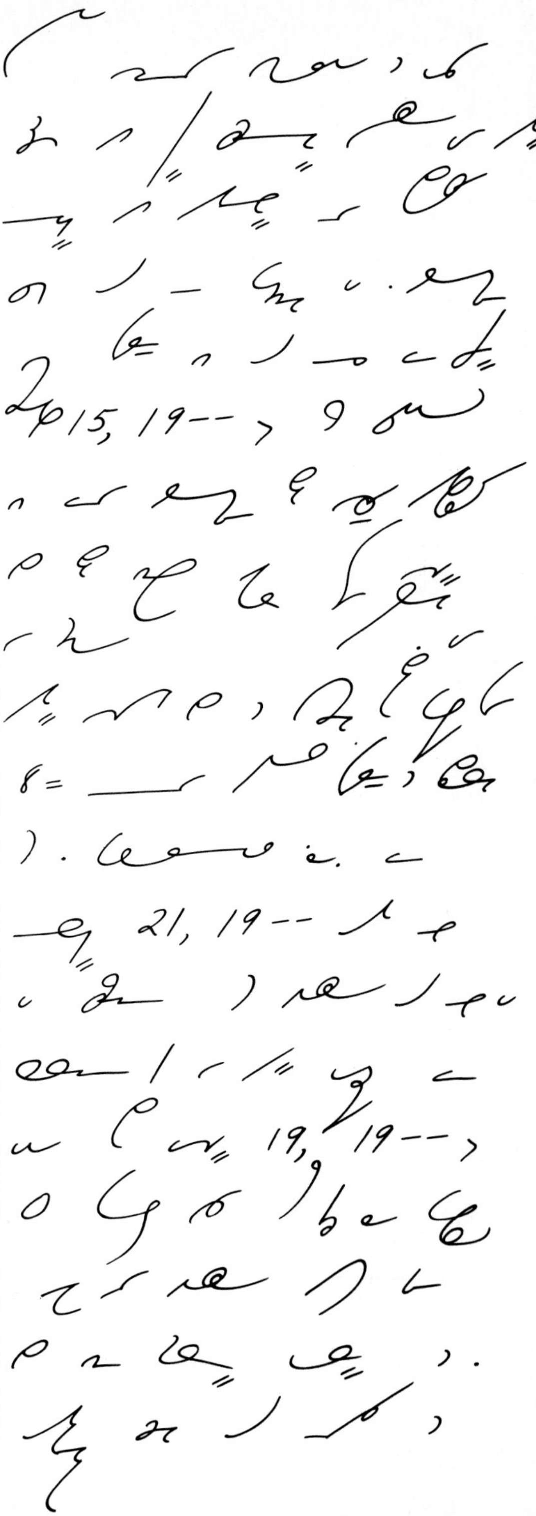

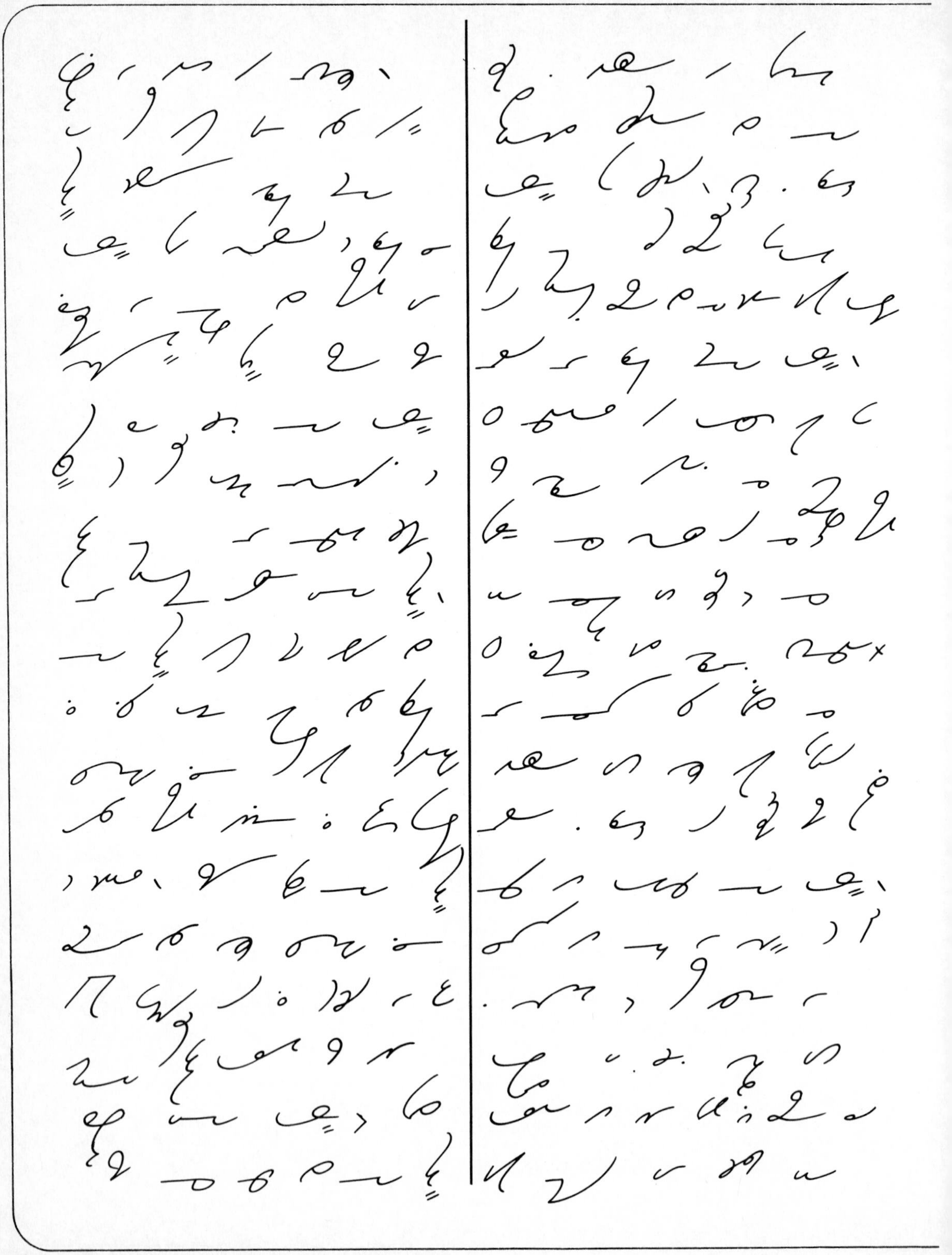

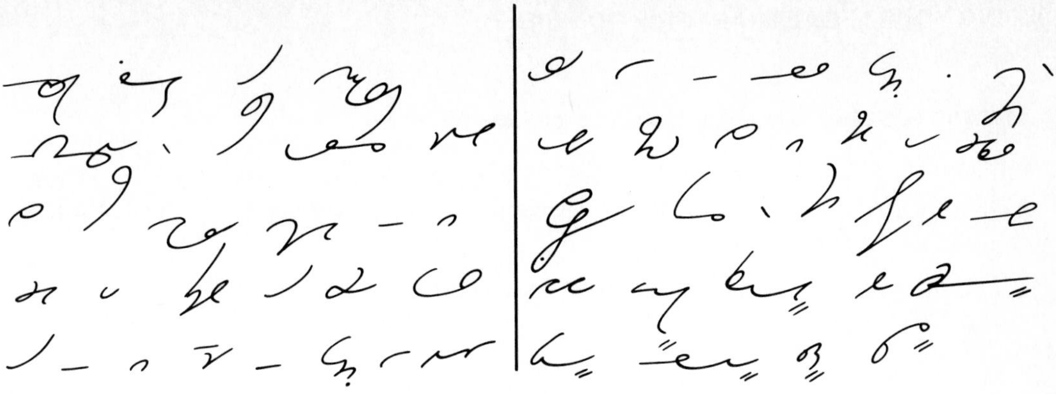

Lesson 34

BUILDING YOUR LEGAL VOCABULARY

Disjoined Word Beginnings *Self-* is expressed by .

self-defense  **self-discipline** 

self-support  **self-sufficient** 

self-preservation  **self-destruction** 

Word Study

 **customhouse** A building where customs and duties are paid or collected.

 **issuance** The act of putting out or giving out.

 **meet and just** Legally justified and fair.

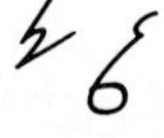 **subpoena** A writ or order commanding a person to attend court.

BUILDING YOUR LEGAL TRANSCRIPTION SKILL

Transcription Aid **Number Usage: Large Even Numbers**

☐ To avoid the use of many ciphers and to improve clarity in very large even numbers, the words *million* and *billion* may be spelled out.

The substance covered by his patent will withstand pressures of about 1 million pounds per square inch and temperatures above 3,000° F.

Number Usage: Fractions

☐ Spell out fractions that stand alone, and use a hyphen between the numerator and the denominator unless a hyphen appears in either or both.

two-thirds twenty-three thirtieths one eighty-fifth

Legal Collocations

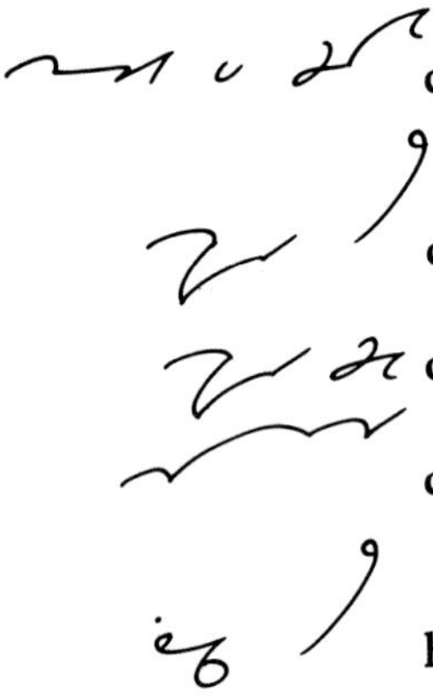

commutation of sentence The substitution of a lesser for a greater punishment by authority of law.

competent evidence Evidence that is legally admissible.

competent witness One who is legally qualified to testify in a case.

contempt of court Disobedience to the rules or orders of a court, or a disturbance of its proceedings.

hearsay evidence Evidence not proceeding from the personal knowledge of the witness.

BUILDING YOUR LEGAL DICTATION PROFICIENCY

Preview

documentary 

Grosso 

honor 

Marchetti 

prosecution 

validity 

84. UNITED STATES DISTRICT COURT DISTRICT OF MASSACHUSETTS UNITED STATES OF AMERICA VS. ROBERT B. VOSS CRIMINAL NO. 76-84-W DEFENDANT'S MOTION FOR CONTINUANCE

Defendant hereby moves this Honorable Court to continue the trial of the above-captioned case from February 6,[1] 19—, to a date approximately one month thereafter, or to whatever date which to[2] this Court appears just in the circumstances.

Defendant assigns the following reasons for his Motion:

Pursuant[3] to a conference in open court on January 31, 19—, Albert F. Compton,[4] Esq., Assistant United States Attorney, agreed to furnish Defendant with information concerning[5] efforts made and investigations conducted by federal authorities in order to locate one Frank[6] Lane, who Defendant has informed the Court appears to be a vital witness for the defense. Defendant received[7] on February 2, 19—, a Memorandum containing said information; and Defendant[8] has begun to search for said Mr. Lane on the basis of information supplied by the Memorandum[9] as well as other information. Having recently received the Memorandum, Defendant needs more time[10] to pursue his investigation.

As a further reason, Defendant says that he intends to file with this[11] Honorable Court no later than February 6, 19—, an Amended Motion to Dismiss and[12] a Memorandum of Law, in the light of the decisions of the Supreme Court of the United States in[13] *Marchetti vs. United States*, 36 U.S.L.W. 4143 (January 29,[14] 1968), *Grosso vs. United States*, 36 U.S.L.W. 4150[15] (January 29, 1968), and *Hayes vs. United States*, 36 U.S.L.W.[16] (January 29, 1968), which decisions bear on the validity[17] of this prosecution. In view of the fact that the aforesaid opinions were found and said opinions[18] did not reach Defendant's attorney in their complete text until February 2, 19—, Defendant[19] needs additional time to argue his Amended Motion to Dismiss before this Honorable Court.

By his[20] attorneys,

GREENBERG, O'BRIEN, MASON & MCCANN

by:____________________________

David E. Mason

CERTIFICATE OF SERVICE

SUFFOLK,[21] ss.

Boston, Massachusetts
February 3, 19—

I, DAVID E. MASON, attorney[22] for Robert B. Voss, do hereby certify that I have this date mailed a copy of the foregoing Motion for[23] Continuance to Albert F. Compton, Assistant United States Attorney, Post Office and Courthouse Building, Post[24] Office Square, Boston, MA 02100, Attorney for the United States.

____

David E. Mason[25]

85. UNITED STATES DISTRICT COURT DISTRICT OF MASSACHUSETTS UNITED STATES OF AMERICA VS. ROBERT B. VOSS CRIMINAL NO. 76-84-W DEFENDANT'S MOTION FOR ISSUANCE OF SUBPOENA

Defendant hereby moves this Honorable Court to issue, in accordance with Rule 17, Federal Rules of[26] Criminal Procedure, a subpoena commanding the attendance of one Frank Lane as a witness for the defense[27] in the above-entitled case; or, in the alternative, that this Honorable Court issue an order for the[28] arrest of said Mr. Lane as a material witness in the above-entitled case.

By his attorneys,

GREENBERG,[29] O'BRIEN, MASON & MCCANN

by:______________________________

David E. Mason

CERTIFICATE OF SERVICE

SUFFOLK, ss. Boston,[30] Massachusetts
February 3, 19__

I, DAVID E. MASON, attorney for Robert B.[31] Voss, do hereby certify that I have this date mailed a copy of the foregoing Motion for Issuance of[32] Subpoena to Albert F. Compton, Assistant United States Attorney, Post Office and Courthouse Building, Post Office[33] Square, Boston, MA 02100, Attorney for the United States.

____

David E. Mason (679)

86. MR. ROBERT VOSS, C/O MRS. JANE MORGAN, 685 EAST 28 STREET, APT. 905, NEW YORK, NY 10024

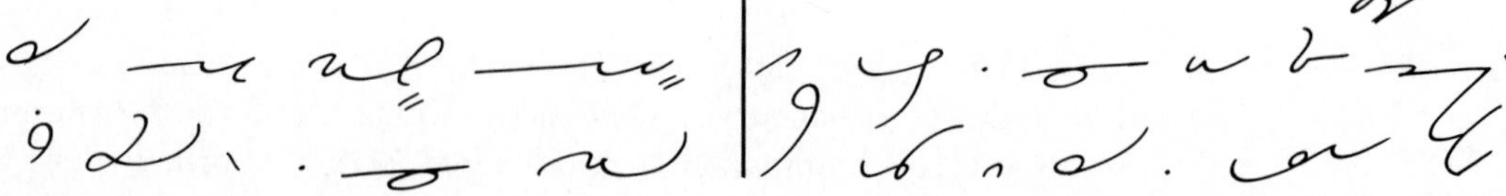

88. MR. RUSSELL H. PEEK, CLERK, UNITED STATES DISTRICT COURT, POST OFFICE AND COURTHOUSE BUILDING, POST OFFICE SQUARE, BOSTON, MA 02100

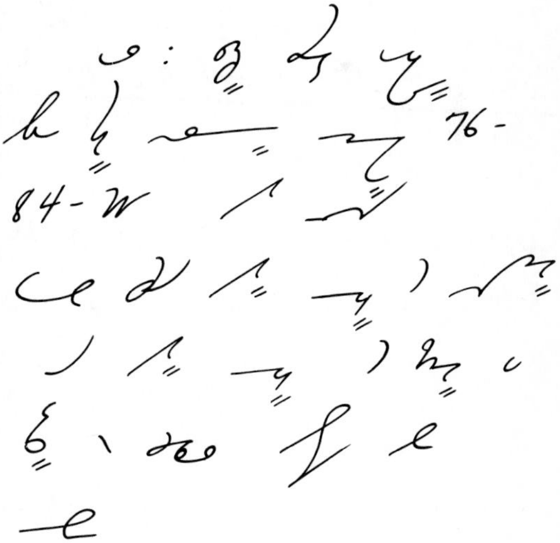

87. MISS FRANCES R. FRANKLIN, CLERK TO THE HONORABLE CHARLES E. WYMAN, UNITED STATES DISTRICT COURT, POST OFFICE AND COURTHOUSE BUILDING, POST OFFICE SQUARE, BOSTON, MA 02100

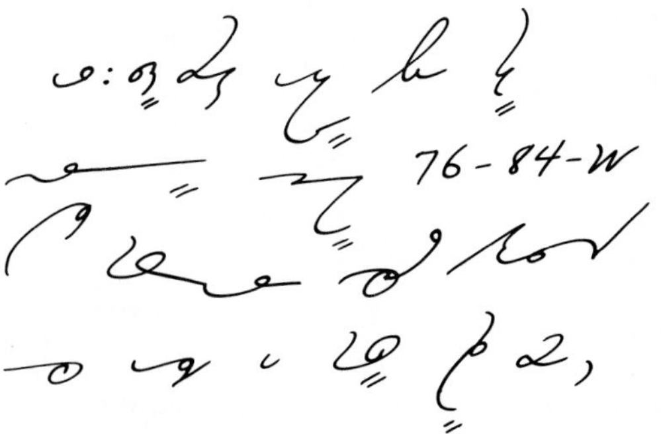

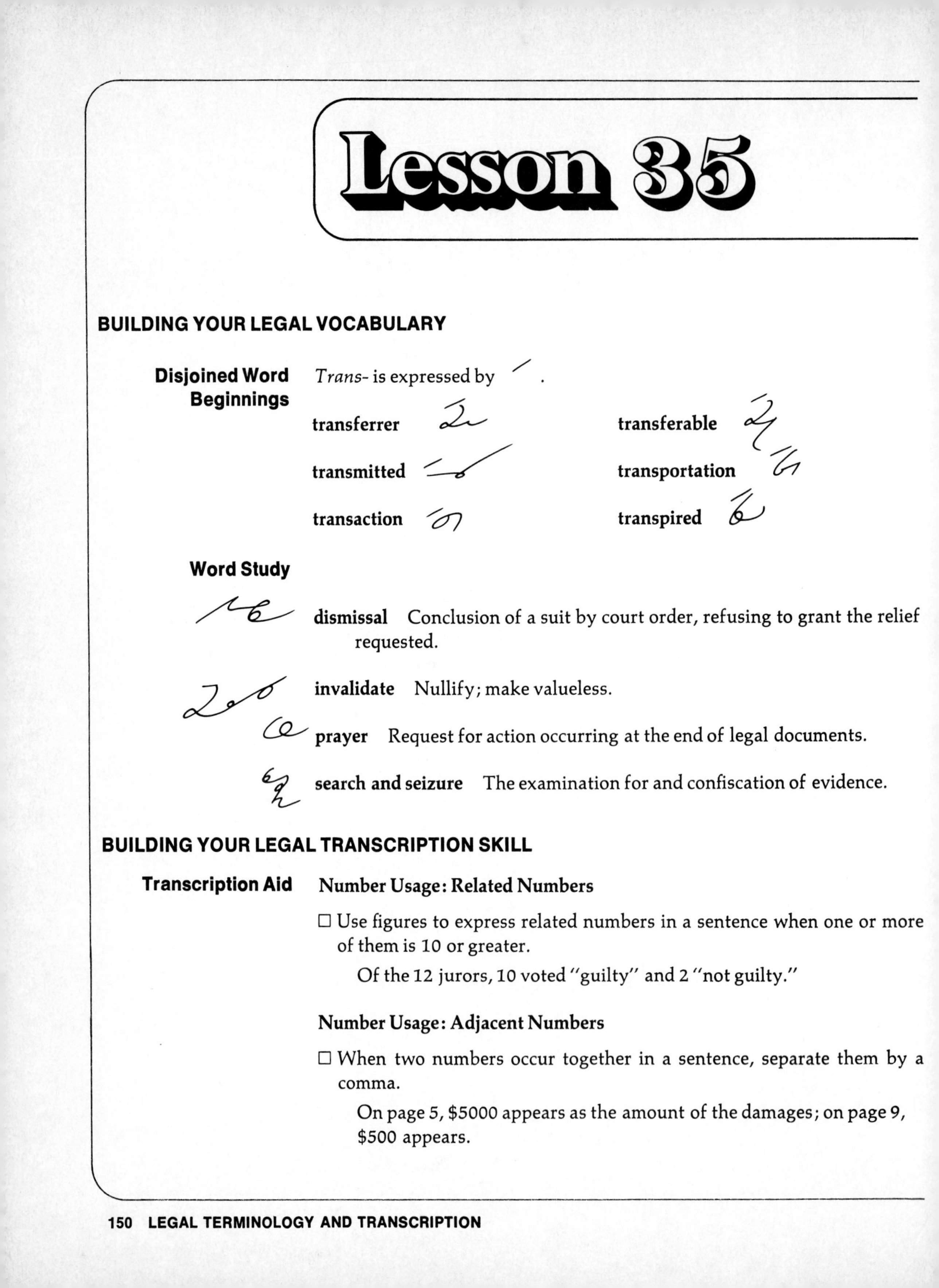

Lesson 35

BUILDING YOUR LEGAL VOCABULARY

Disjoined Word Beginnings *Trans-* is expressed by .

transferrer **transferable**

transmitted **transportation**

transaction **transpired**

Word Study

dismissal Conclusion of a suit by court order, refusing to grant the relief requested.

invalidate Nullify; make valueless.

prayer Request for action occurring at the end of legal documents.

search and seizure The examination for and confiscation of evidence.

BUILDING YOUR LEGAL TRANSCRIPTION SKILL

Transcription Aid **Number Usage: Related Numbers**

☐ Use figures to express related numbers in a sentence when one or more of them is 10 or greater.

Of the 12 jurors, 10 voted "guilty" and 2 "not guilty."

Number Usage: Adjacent Numbers

☐ When two numbers occur together in a sentence, separate them by a comma.

On page 5, \$5000 appears as the amount of the damages; on page 9, \$500 appears.

Latin and French Words and Phrases

per se *(per sā')* By himself, herself, or itself; in itself; taken alone.

subpoena ad testificandum *(su pē'na ad tes ti fi kan'dum)* A writ or order commanding a person to appear to testify.

subpoena duces tecum *(su pē'na dōō'kas tā'kum)* A writ commanding a witness to appear and bring certain papers, books, articles, or other evidence.

BUILDING YOUR LEGAL DICTATION PROFICIENCY

Preview

amend 

argument 

certify 

comprehensive 

constitution 

conviction 

inasmuch 

self-incrimination 

unconstitutional 

violation 

Reading and Writing Practice

89. UNITED STATES DISTRICT COURT DISTRICT OF MASSACHUSETTS UNITED STATES OF AMERICA VS. ROBERT B. VOSS CRIMINAL NO. 76-84-W DEFENDANT'S MOTION FOR ORAL ARGUMENT

Defendant hereby moves this Honorable Court for an order that oral arguments be heard on Defendant's Motion[1] for Leave to Amend Defendant's Motion to Dismiss the Indictment.

By his attorneys,

GREENBERG, O'BRIEN, MASON[2] & MCCANN

by:______________________________

David E. Mason

CERTIFICATE OF SERVICE

SUFFOLK, ss. Boston, Massachusetts[3]

February 5, 19__

I, DAVID E. MASON, attorney for Robert B. Voss, do hereby[4] certify that I have this date mailed a copy of the foregoing Motion for Oral Argument to Albert F.[5] Compton, Esq., Assistant United States Attorney, Post Office and Courthouse Building, Post Office Square, Boston,[6] MA 02100, Attorney for the United States.

____

David E. Mason

90. UNITED STATES DISTRICT COURT DISTRICT OF MASSACHUSETTS UNITED STATES OF AMERICA VS. ROBERT B. VOSS CRIMINAL NO. 76-84-W DEFENDANT'S MOTION FOR LEAVE TO FILE SUBSTITUTE MOTION FOR LEAVE TO AMEND DEFENDANT'S MOTION TO DISMISS INDICTMENT

Defendant[7] hereby moves this Honorable Court for leave to file a Substitute Motion for Leave to Amend Defendant's Motion[8] to Dismiss the Indictment in the above-entitled proceedings, by adding as a ground for the dismissal[9] of the indictment the following:

"Any conviction of the Defendant under 21 U.S.C.[10] 176a would be unconstitutional because to require Defendant to comply with any part[11] of said statute would deprive Defendant of his privilege against self-incrimination, in violation[12] of Defendant's rights under the Fifth Amendment of the United States Constitution."

By his attorneys,

GREENBERG,[13] O'BRIEN, MASON & MCCANN

by: __________________________

David E. Mason

CERTIFICATE OF SERVICE

SUFFOLK, ss. Boston,[14] Massachusetts

February 12, 19__

I, DAVID E. MASON, attorney for Robert B. Voss, do[15] hereby certify that I have this date delivered a copy of the foregoing Motion in hand to Albert[16] F. Compton, Esq., Assistant United States Attorney, Post Office and Courthouse Building, Post Office Square,[17] Boston, MA 02100, Attorney for the United States of America.

____

David E.[18] Mason (361)

91. MR. ROBERT B. VOSS, C/O HOLDEN, 865 ATLANTIC AVENUE, BROOKLYN HEIGHTS, BROOKLYN, NY 11200

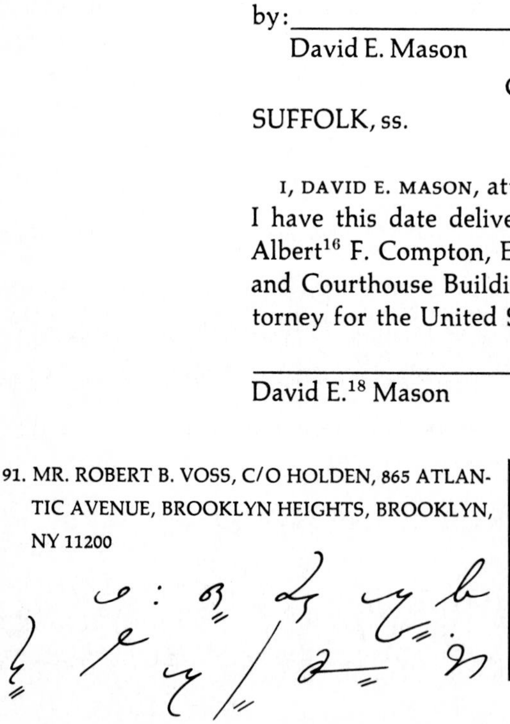

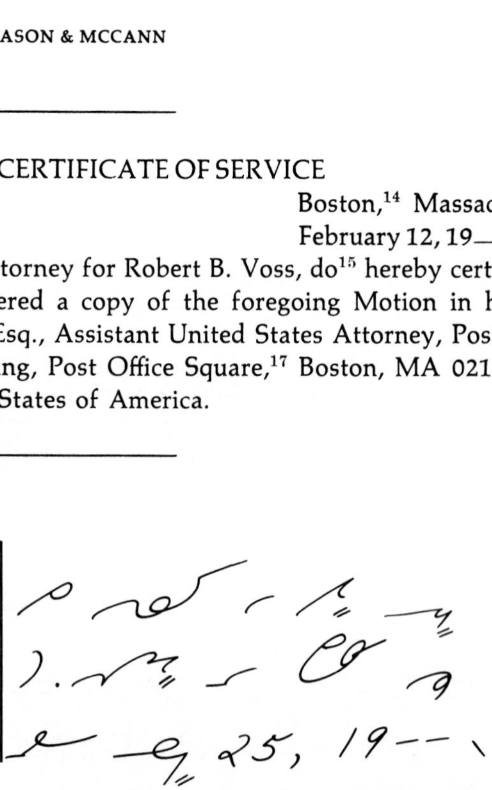

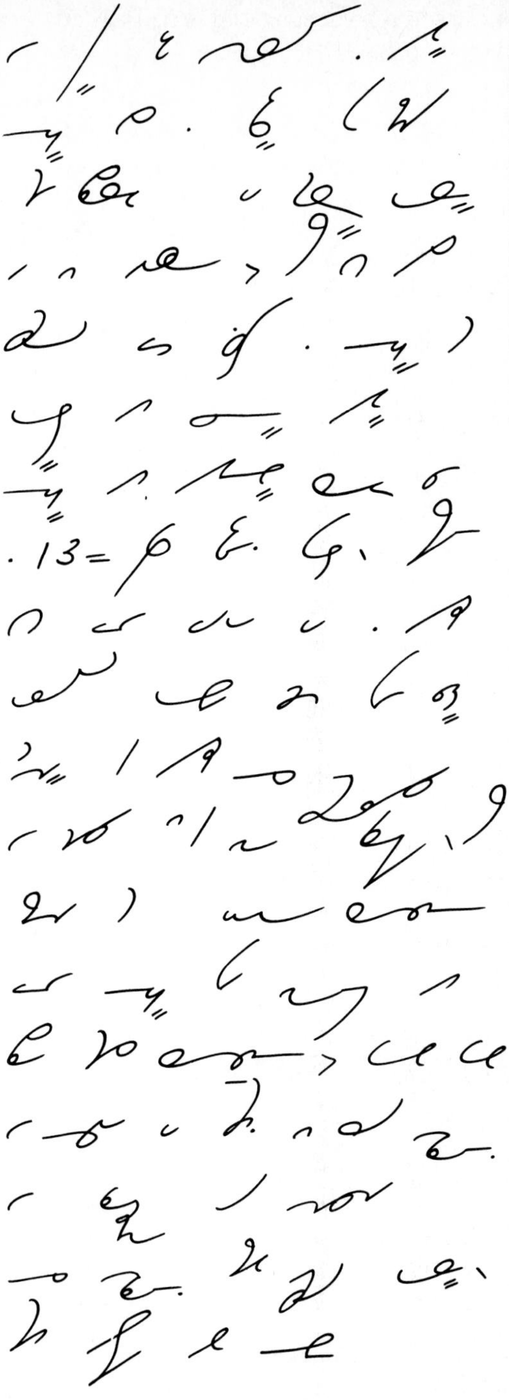

92. MR. ROBERT B. VOSS, C/O HOLDEN, 865 ATLANTIC AVENUE, BROOKLYN, NY 11200

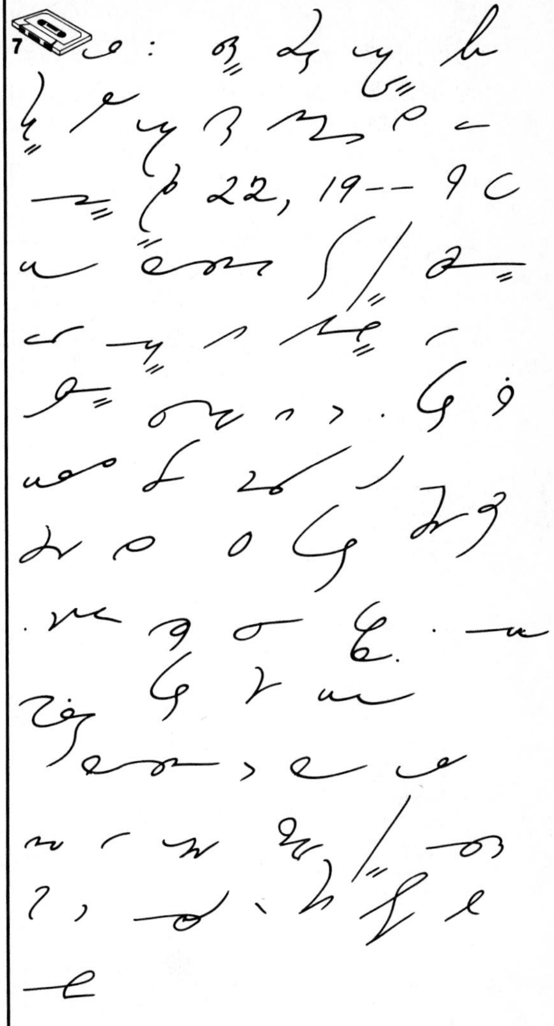

93. MR. RUSSELL H. PEEK, CLERK, UNITED STATES DISTRICT COURT, POST OFFICE AND COURTHOUSE BUILDING, POST OFFICE SQUARE, BOSTON, MA 02100

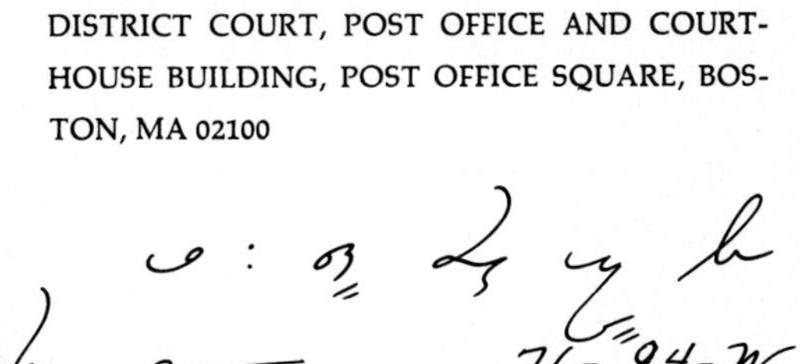

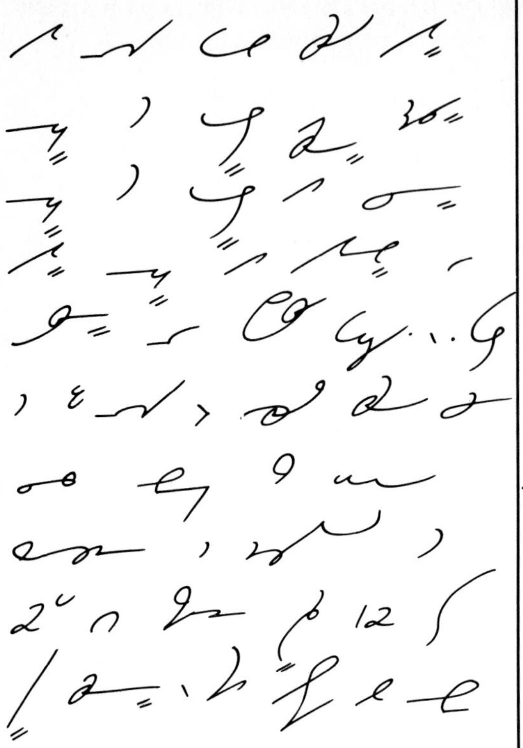

94. ALBERT F. COMPTON, ESQ., ASSISTANT UNITED STATES ATTORNEY, POST OFFICE AND COURTHOUSE BUILDING, POST OFFICE SQUARE, BOSTON, MA 02100

Lesson 36

BUILDING YOUR LEGAL VOCABULARY

Disjoined Word Beginnings

Over- is expressed by .

overassessment 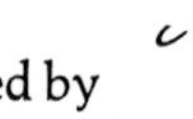

overissue

overrule 

overpriced 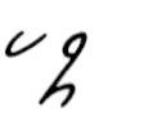

overdrawn **override**

Word Study

attorney general The chief law officer of a state or nation.

hearing A presentation of evidence before a judge for his or her approval or disapproval of a request.

order A document signed by the judge ordering an action or the stoppage of an action.

solicitor The chief law officer of a municipality, county, or government department.

BUILDING YOUR LEGAL TRANSCRIPTION SKILL

Transcription Aid

Number Usage: Percents

☐ Use figures to express percent.

The company issued bonds bearing 5 percent interest.

Number Usage: Mixed Numbers

☐ Use figures to express mixed numbers.

The defendant is alleged to have smuggled 15½ ounces of marijuana.

Legal Collocations

documentary evidence Evidence supplied by writings and documents.

expert witness One whom the law recognizes as highly trained or skilled in a particular field, having greater knowledge than an untrained person.

extraneous evidence Evidence not furnished by a document itself but derived from outside sources.

false imprisonment Imprisonment of a person without legal authority.

grand jury A body of citizens called upon to determine whether evidence warrants charging a person with a criminal offense and bringing that person before the court.

BUILDING YOUR LEGAL DICTATION PROFICIENCY

Preview

analysis 

analytical 

gambling 

incrimination 

hashish 

Justice Department 

loopholes 

perusal 

plausibility 

predicated 

reargument 

rehearing 

Reading and Writing Practice

95. UNITED STATES DISTRICT COURT DISTRICT OF MASSACHUSETTS UNITED STATES OF AMERICA VS. ROBERT B. VOSS CRIMINAL NO. 76-84-W ORDER FEBRUARY 12, 19— WYMAN, CHIEF JUDGE

Being mindful both of the plausibility of Defendant's Motion to Dismiss the Indictment and of the[1] drastic consequences which would follow if Defendant's position should be sustained, this Court defers action upon[2] the motion until the Attorney General of the United States, the Solicitor General, and any[3] other appropriate national representative of the Department of Justice have adequate opportunity[4] to brief and present arguments against the motion. Accordingly, the motion is set for reargument[5] on Monday, April 1, 19—, at 10 a.m. The Court urges that insofar as possible[6] the parties stipulate in advance of the hearing such facts as could readily be proved with respect to[7] the relation, if any, between the information secured under the federal law and its availability[8] to state officials.

Charles E. Wyman, Chief Judge (170)

96. JANE S. HOFFMAN, ESQ., 721 EAST 40 STREET, NEW YORK, NY 10000

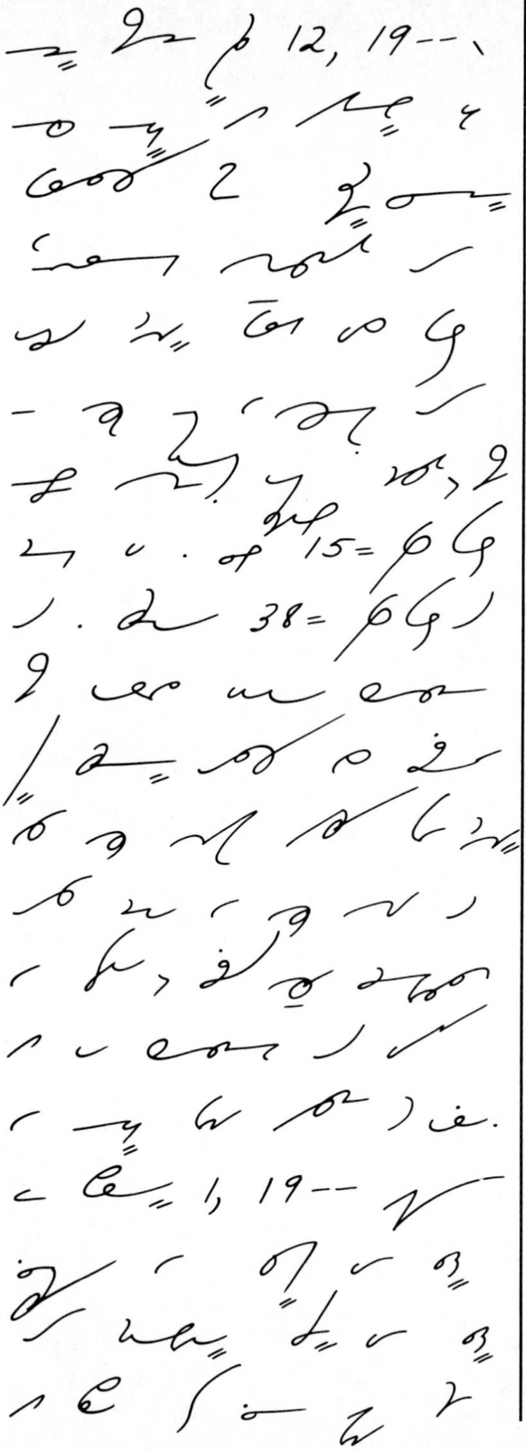

97. ALBERT F. COMPTON, ESQ., ASSISTANT UNITED STATES ATTORNEY, POST OFFICE AND COURTHOUSE BUILDING, POST OFFICE SQUARE, BOSTON, MA 02100

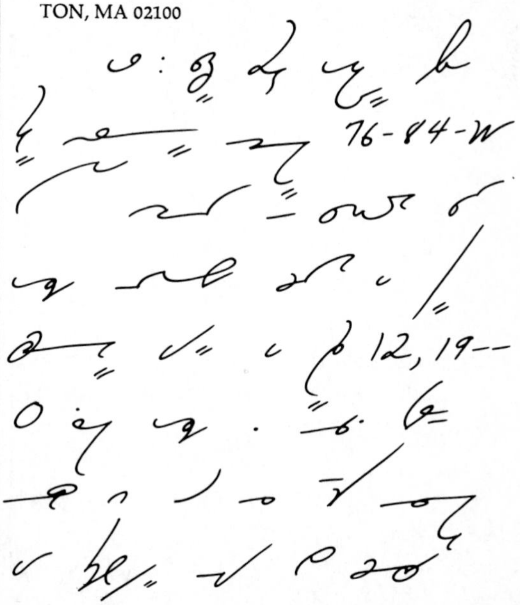

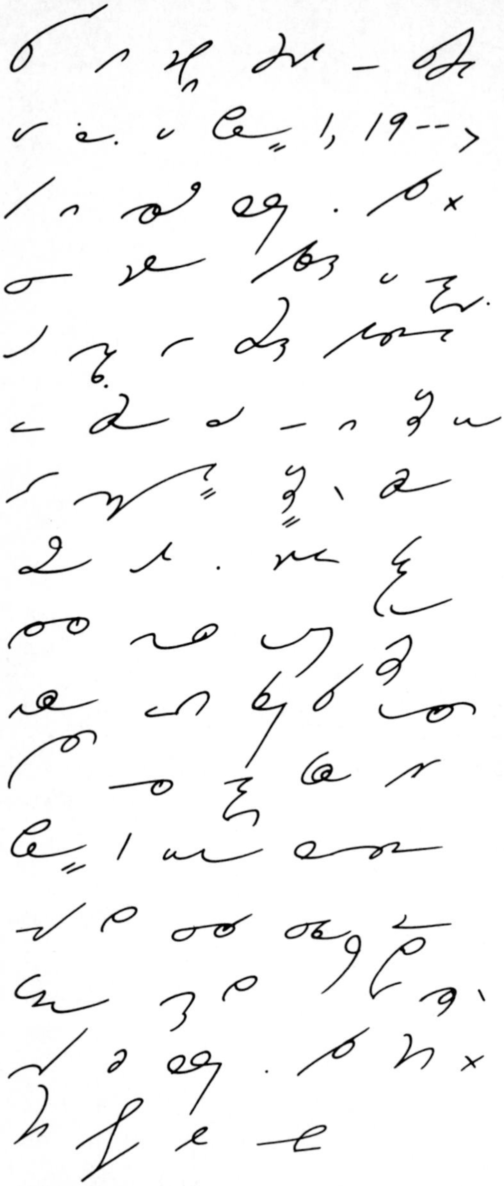

98. LEON THOMPSON, ESQ., PEARSON & THOMPSON, SUITE 204, TUCSON TITLE BUILDING, 45 WEST PENNINGTON STREET, TUCSON, AZ 85701

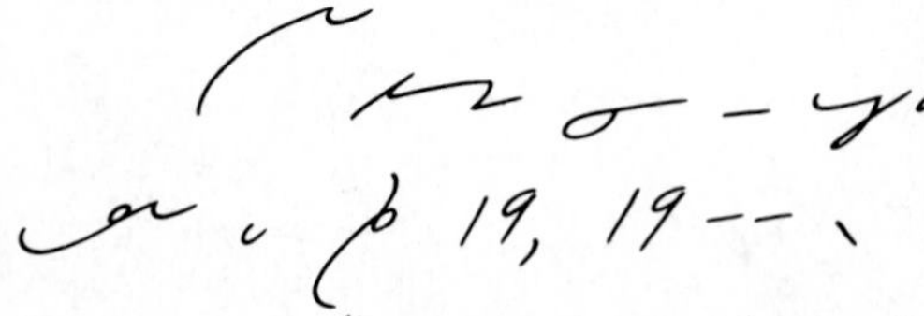

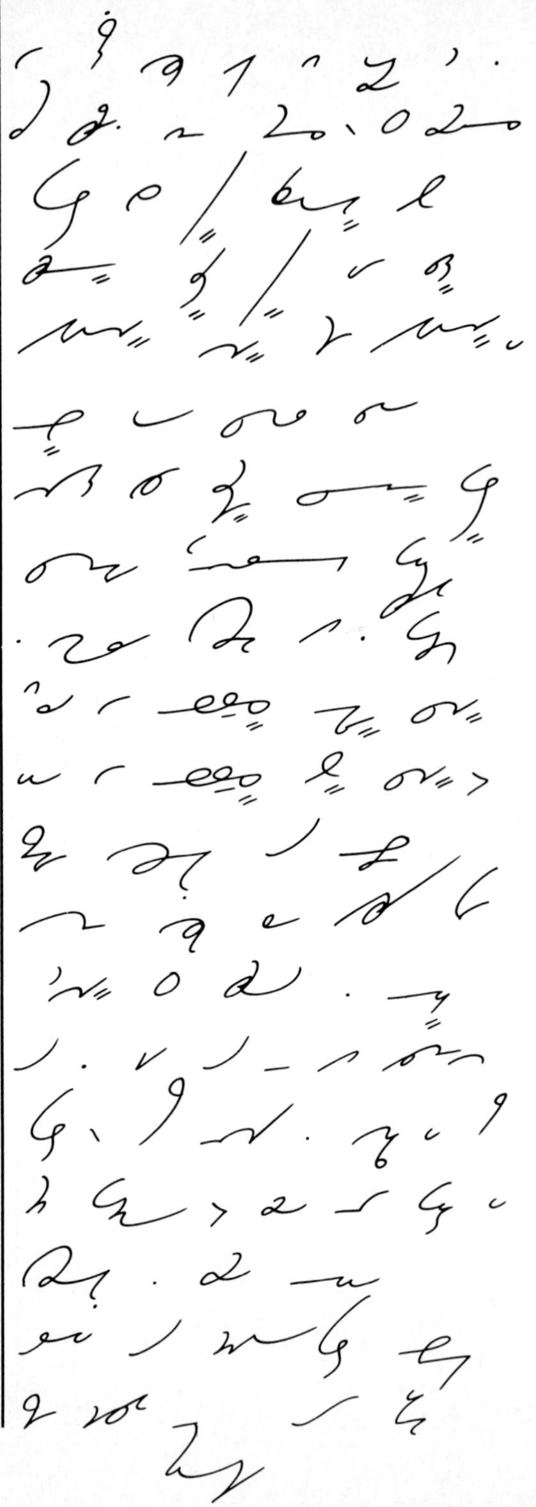

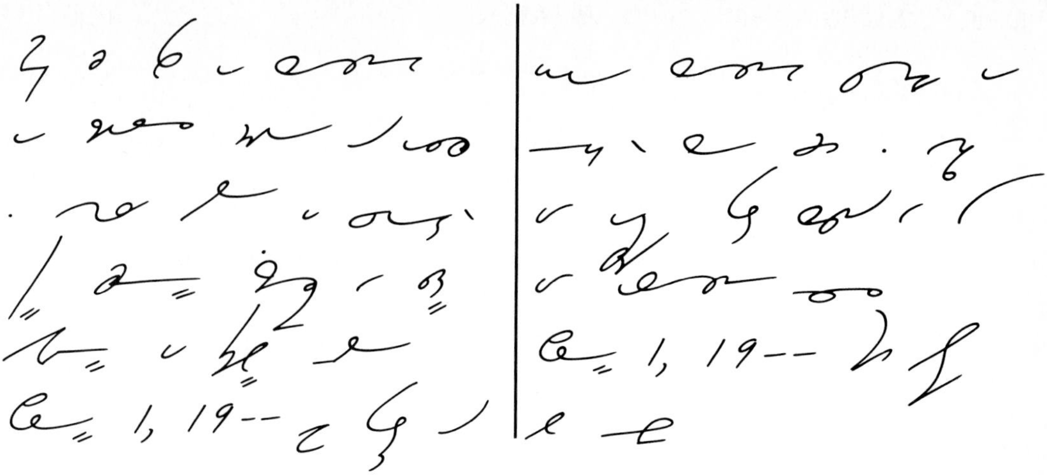

Lesson 37

BUILDING YOUR LEGAL VOCABULARY

Disjoined Word Beginnings *Under-* is expressed by  .

undercharge 

underestimate 

undersigned 

underhanded 

underwriter 

underprivileged 

Word Study

 **the accused** The person who is supposed to have violated the law and committed a crime.

 **comply** To complete, perform, or obey.

 **interrogatories** Formal questions or inquiries, usually written.

 **promulgated** Made known by open declaration; declared, proclaimed.

BUILDING YOUR LEGAL TRANSCRIPTION SKILL

Transcription Aid

Number Usage: Provisions in Wills

☐ One of the following forms of numbering provisions may be used:

1. Articles or items may be centered as titles: ARTICLE I, ARTICLE II, etc.
2. Articles or items may be introduced by the words FIRST, SECOND, etc. used as side headings.

☐ Subparagraphs may also be numbered as (1), (2), or (a), (b), etc.

Number Usage: Indexing Briefs

☐ Make an index for briefs that consist of more than 12 pages, and use lower case roman numerals for numbering index pages. Use arabic numerals for numbering the pages of the brief itself.

Latin and French Words and Phrases

pro forma *(prō for'ma)* As a matter of form; tentatively.

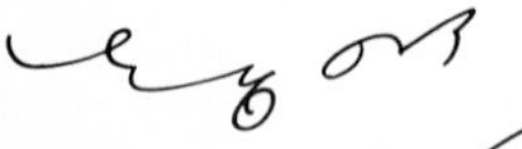
lex loci actus *(lex lō'sī ak'tus)* Law of the place of the act.

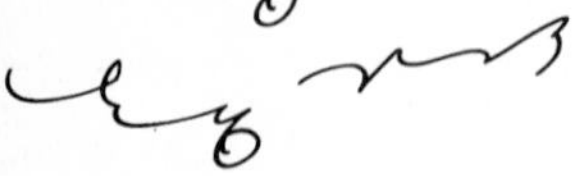
lex loci contractus *(lex lō'sī con trak'tus)* Law of the place where the contract is made.

BUILDING YOUR LEGAL DICTATION PROFICIENCY

Preview

alluded 

compliance 

conceivably 

delegate 

governmental 

propounds 

regulations 

statutory 

thereunder 

treasury 

Reading and Writing Practice

99. UNITED STATES DISTRICT COURT DISTRICT OF MASSACHUSETTS UNITED STATES OF AMERICA, PLAINTIFF, V. ROBERT B. VOSS, DEFENDANT. CRIMINAL NO. 76-84-W INTERROGATORIES

In accordance with the last sentence of the Order by Wyman, Chief Judge, dated February 12, 19—,[1] urging the parties in this proceeding to stipulate in advance of hearing such facts as could[2] readily be proved with respect to the relation, if any, between the information secured under the[3] federal law and its availability to state officials, the Defendant hereby propounds to the Plaintiff written[4] interrogatories covering those areas upon which Defendant presently intends to rely[5] in his argument:

1. What form or forms must be completed and submitted to federal authorities in[6] order for a person to import or bring marijuana into the United States in compliance with the[7] invoicing requirements associated with 21 U.S.C. 176a? Please attach to[8] your answer any such form or forms.

2. What information, other than that required on the above-referenced forms, is[9] customarily required by Bureau of Customs officials of any person attempting to comply with the above-referenced[10] invoicing requirements?

3. What is the policy of the Secretary of the Treasury or[11] his delegate as to the matter of what information might conceivably be required of a person[12] attempting to comply with the above-referenced invoicing requirements?

4. Upon the initiative of Federal[13] Customs or other authorities, what information obtained as a result of compliance with the[14] informational requirements described in the answers to Interrogatories numbered one (1)[15] through three (3) above is communicated to any other individaul or governmental[16] agency, state or federal? In answering this Interrogatory, please specify which information is[17] communicated to each individual or agency involved.

5. Upon the initiative of individuals,[18] or state or federal governmental agencies, what information is customarily released by[19] customs officials?

6. With respect to the practices alluded to in Interrogatories numbered four[20] (4) and five (5), what information might conceivably be released to individuals or state[21] or federal agencies, according to the policy or understanding of the Secretary of the[22] Treasury or his delegate?

7. What forms are required to be filled out in order for a person to comply with[23] the special registration and tax provisions of 26 U.S.C. 4742, 4751-4754?[24] Please attach to your answer any such form or forms.

8. What information, other than[25] that required on the forms referred to in Interrogatory numbered seven (7) above, is[26] customarily required by officials of the Department of the Treasury of any person attempting to comply[27] with the above-referenced statutory sections or the regulations promulgated thereunder?

9. What[28] is the policy of the Secretary of the Treasury or his dele-

gate as to the matter of what[29] information might conceivably be required of a person attempting to comply with the above-referenced 26[30] U.S.C. 4754?

10. Pursuant to 26 U.S.C. 4773, upon[31] the initiative of federal authorities, what information obtained as a result of compliance[32] with the informational, registration, or tax requirements described in the answers to Interrogatories[33] numbered seven (7) through nine (9) above is communicated to any other[34] individual or governmental agency, state or federal? In answering this Interrogatory,[35] please specify which information is communicated to each individual or agency involved.

11.[36] Pursuant to 26 U.S.C. 4773, 4775, upon the[37] initiative of individuals, or state or federal governmental agencies, what information is[38] customarily released to said individuals or agencies by Treasury officials or their delegates?[39]

12. With respect to the practices alluded to in Interrogatories numbered ten (10)[40] and eleven (11), what information might conceivably be released to individuals or[41] state or federal agencies, according to the policy or understanding of the Secretary of the[42] Treasury or his delegate?

13. Please list any other information required of any person seeking to[43] comply with any part of 21 U.S.C. 176a or any statute or regulation[44] incorporated by reference therein, or seeking to comply with any part of the Marijuana Tax Act,[45] 26 U.S.C. 4741-4775, or any regulations promulgated thereunder.[46]

14. With reference to any information referred to in Interrogatory numbered thirteen[47] (13) above, or any information dealt with in your answer to any other Interrogatory herein,[48] list and describe any practice of disclosing or communicating any such information, which practice you[49] have not yet listed or described in your answers to any of the Interrogatories above.

Robert B. Voss
By[50] his attorneys,
GREENBERG, O'BRIEN, MASON & MCCANN

by: ______________________________
David E. Mason

CERTIFICATE OF SERVICE

I[51] hereby certify that I served a copy of the within Interrogatories to the Plaintiff by mailing a[52] copy of same to the Assistant United States Attorney, Albert F. Compton, Esq., Post Office and Courthouse[53] Building, Post Office Square, Boston, MA 02100, postage prepaid on this day. dated: February[54] 27, 19__.

____
David E. Mason (1093)

Lesson 38

BUILDING YOUR LEGAL VOCABULARY

Word Endings *-ment* is expressed by ___ .

documents  **assessment** 

settlement  **bailment** 

ascertainment  **easements** 

Word Study

 **immaterial** Logically related to the matter in question, but not affecting the outcome.

 **irrelevant** Not logically related to the matter in question.

 **preponderance of evidence** The evidence having the most validity or carrying the greater weight.

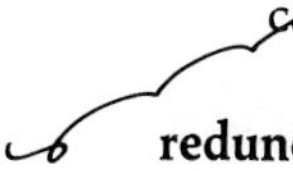 **redundant** Unnecessary; repetitious.

 **relevant** Logically related to the matter in question.

 **testify** To give information under oath regarding the knowledge one has of a case.

BUILDING YOUR LEGAL TRANSCRIPTION SKILL

Transcription Aid **Number Usage: Real Property Descriptions**

☐ In some legal papers, lawyers may require numbers to be expressed in both words and figures for verification. A typical example is the course or direction of the boundary line and the distance in real property descriptions.

The line ran south forty-five (45) degrees for one hundred twenty-five and eighty-five one-hundredths (125.85) feet.

Number Usage: Sums of Money Verified

□ Amounts of money in such legal papers as contracts, deeds, mortgages, stipulations, and so on, may be expressed in both words and figures for verification.

The libelee is ordered to pay her Seventy-five Dollars and Fifty Cents ($75.50) per week for support of the minor children.

Legal Collocations

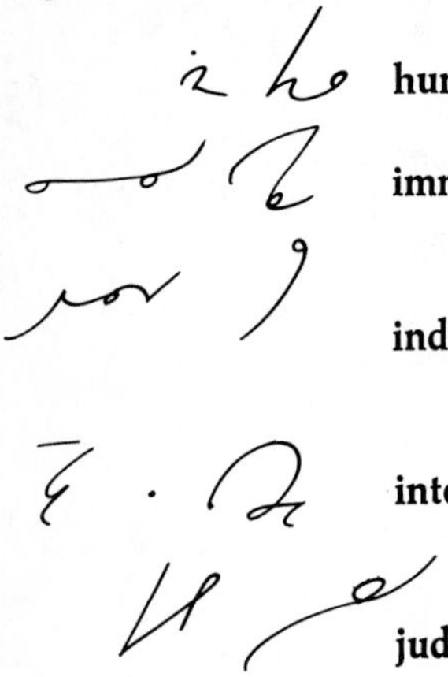

hung jury A trial jury whose members cannot reach a verdict.

imminent danger That danger which forces one into self-defense where there is no immediate assistance available.

indirect evidence Proof of facts from which inference may be drawn; circumstantial evidence.

interpose a defense To answer; to set up the defense in any manner at any stage of the action.

judicial demand The date suit is filed in a court of competent jurisdiction.

BUILDING YOUR LEGAL DICTATION PROFICIENCY

Preview

bureaus 

candor 

conformity 

customhouse 

expediting 

memorandum 

narcotics 

parties 

Reading and Writing Practice

100. ALBERT F. COMPTON, ESQ., ASSISTANT UNITED STATES ATTORNEY, POST OFFICE AND COURTHOUSE BUILDING, POST OFFICE SQUARE, BOSTON, MA 02100

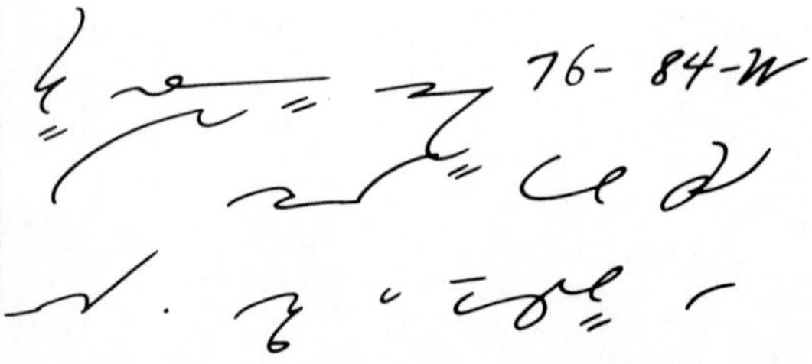

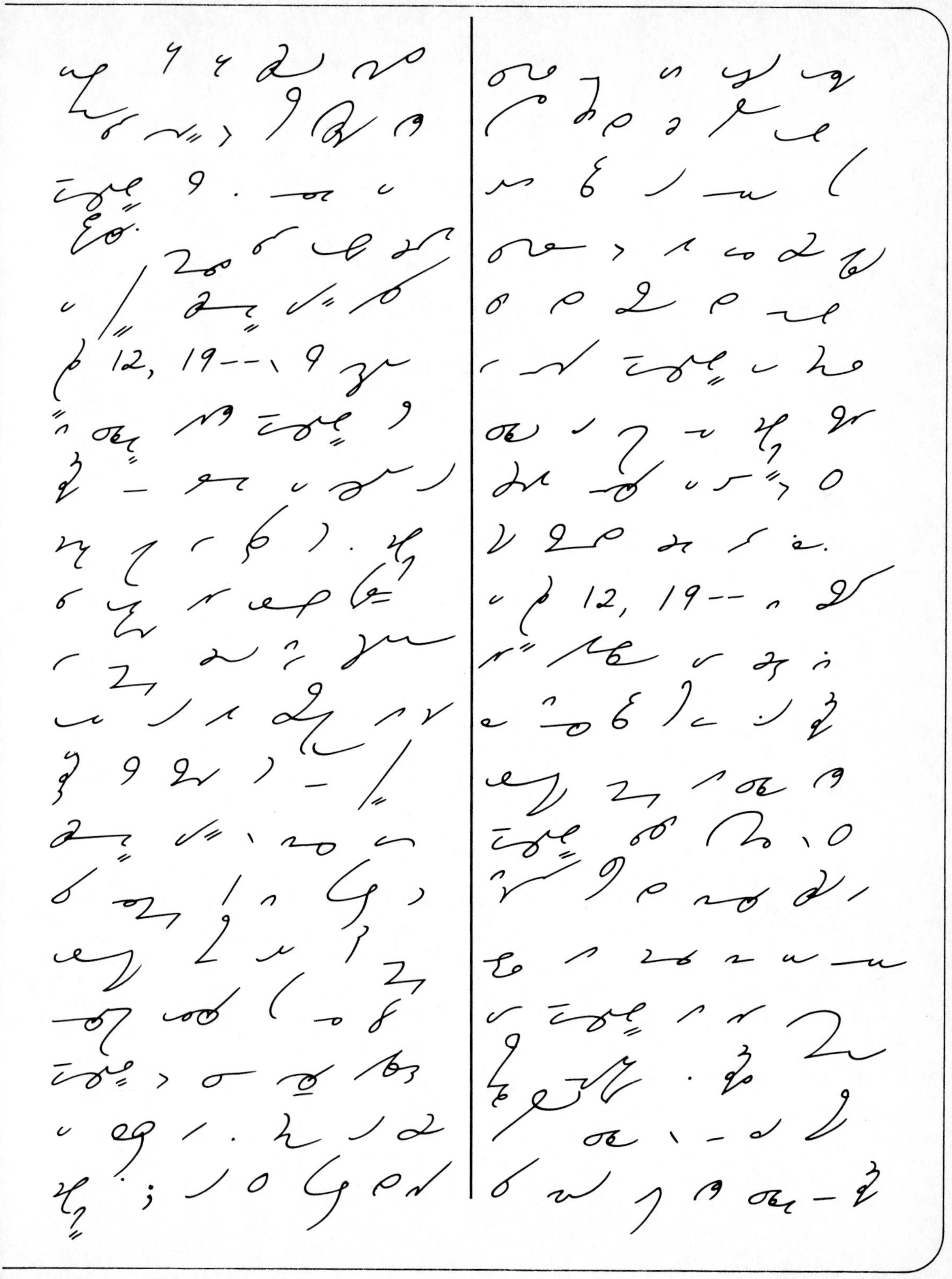
12, 19--
12, 19--

101. ALBERT F. COMPTON, ESQ., ASSISTANT UNITED STATES ATTORNEY, POST OFFICE AND COURTHOUSE BUILDING, POST OFFICE SQUARE, BOSTON, MA 02100

102. ALBERT F. COMPTON, ESQ., ASSISTANT UNITED STATES ATTORNEY, POST OFFICE AND COURTHOUSE BUILDING, POST OFFICE SQUARE, BOSTON, MA 02100

103. MR. RUSSELL H. PEEK, CLERK, UNITED STATES DISTRICT COURT, POST OFFICE AND COURT-HOUSE BUILDING, POST OFFICE SQUARE, BOSTON, MA 02100

Lesson 39

BUILDING YOUR LEGAL VOCABULARY

Word Endings -*tion*, -*sion*, -*cion*, and -*cian* are expressed by / .

apportion  **remuneration** 

reconciliation  **injunctions** 

rescission  **deposition** 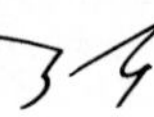

Word Study

 **declaration** Announcement; the first pleading in a common law action.

 **precedent** *(adj.)* Earlier in time. *(n.)* Something that happened previously that affects a decision on a similar current matter.

 **smuggling** Importing or exporting goods secretly without paying the duties imposed by law.

 **trafficker** One involved in commerce or trade such as the import-export business.

BUILDING YOUR LEGAL TRANSCRIPTION SKILL

Transcription Aid

In this and the next eight lessons correct usage of the hyphen is covered.

Hyphenation: Compound Adjectives

☐ Use the hyphen to join two or more words in a compound modifier when they precede a noun and convey only one idea about it. However, a two-word proper name used as an adjective is not hyphenated, nor is a modifier that contains an adverb ending in *ly*.

well-known lawyer New York office privately owned corporation
above-captioned case Supreme Court decision

Hyphenation: Prefixes

Most prefixes are joined without hyphenation directly to a word to modify its meaning. The exceptions are illustrated in this and the following two lessons.

☐ Use a hyphen following the prefix if its addition to a word results in confusion with another word as to meaning or pronunciation. Be sure to consult the dictionary when in doubt. Compare the following: pre-judicial, prejudicial re-form, reform re-sorting, resorting multi-ply, multiply.

Latin and French Words and Phrases

raison d'être *(rä'zōn det'[re])* Reason or justification for existence.

nolo contendere *(nō'lō con ten'de rā)* "I will not contest it"; without admitting guilt, this plea by the defendant subjects the person to a judgment of conviction.

viva voce *(vi'va vō'sē)* By the living voice; witness personally present and testifying.

BUILDING YOUR LEGAL DICTATION PROFICIENCY

Preview

disqualification  interchanges 

drugs  jurisdictional 

illegal  occupational 

Reading and Writing Practice

8

104. UNITED STATES DISTRICT COURT DISTRICT OF MASSACHUSETTS UNITED STATES OF AMERICA V. ROBERT B. VOSS CRIMINAL NO. 76-84-W STIPULATION

In accordance with the Order issued by this Honorable Court on February 12, 19—,[1] with respect to the Defendant's Motion to Dismiss the Indictment in the above-captioned case, the attorneys[2] for both parties have set forth and agreed to the following stipulated facts, which shall be admitted and agreed to[3] by both parties for the purpose of argument on said Motion to Dismiss and for no other purpose. The facts[4] set forth herein shall be in addition to any other facts demanded or produced up to the time of oral[5] argument on said Motion.

1. While there is cooperation and exchange of information between the Bureau[6] of Customs and the Bureau of Narcotics concerning enforcement of federal narcotics and marijuana[7] laws, there are no written rules, regulations, or memoranda setting forth the methods and procedures[8] by which such cooperation is to be effected.

2. Certain jurisdictional guidelines exist between[9] the Bureau of Customs and Bureau of Narcotics, such that if an agent of either Bureau comes in contact with[10] a violation of law which is within the jurisdiction of the other Bureau, said agent would contact that[11] other Bureau to

handle the violation. Thus, if an official of the Post Office Department finds[12] marijuana being shipped in the mails from a foreign country into the United States, and if that official[13] reports same to the Bureau of Narcotics, the Bureau of Narcotics would report the matter to the Bureau[14] of Customs for further investigation.

3. There is little past history by which to judge what procedures[15] would be used to foster cooperation between the Bureau of Customs and the Bureau of Narcotics with[16] respect to specific interchanges and exchanges of information secured, respectively, under the[17] Marijuana Import and Export Act and the Marijuana Tax Act, because as a practical matter no[18] person smuggling marijuana across the border has ever declared or invoiced such marijuana; and thus there[19] has been no information obtained under 21 U.S.C. 176a for the Bureau of[20] Customs to turn over to the Bureau of Narcotics or state agencies.

4. The United States Attorney's Office[21] believes at this time that no person who has not had some legitimate purpose for having marijuana[22] has applied for a Marijuana Occupational Tax Stamp or a transfer certificate as required by[23] the Marijuana Tax Act. No person whatsoever has invoiced marijuana in accordance with the[24] provisions of the Marijuana Import and Export Act. No person, except for lawful dealers in marijuana,[25] has ever applied for an importer's occupational tax stamp in accordance with the provisions of[26] the Marijuana Tax Act.

5. The following procedures are followed in order for an applicant to[27] comply with the provisions of the Marijuana Tax Act:

a. Applicant goes to Office of District Director[28] of Internal Revenue, fills out a form, and thus applies for a Marijuana Occupational Tax Stamp.[29]

b. The application, when completed, is sent to the Federal Bureau of Narcotics to see if applicant[30] is legally entitled to deal in marijuana.

c. Federal Bureau of Narcotics checks with state officials;[31] namely, the Massachusetts Food and Drug Division.

d. If applicant is not legally entitled,[32] the application is sent back to the District Director of Internal Revenue with a notation[33] of disapproval.

e. The disapproved application is returned to applicant.

If the applicant is an[34] ordinary person who merely does not qualify as a person entitled to deal with marijuana,[35] and if such disqualification is merely for technical reasons, nothing more is done with respect to such[36] persons as far as the Federal Government is concerned. If the applicant is a known or suspected illegal[37] trafficker in drugs, the federal official, upon receipt of the application, would usually[38] contact state police officials.

6. There are no written rules, regulations, or procedures outlining what would[39] be done with information secured by customs officials as

a result of marijuana invoicing disclosures[40] made by an importer at the border. There are no precedent situations of this type known to the[41] United States Attorney's Office. Ordinarily, records of ordinary customs declarations at a border are[42] kept on file by the Bureau of Customs and are available for inspection by other federal and state agencies.[43]

____
Attorney for the United States

____
Attorney for the Defendant

Dated:________________________
Boston, Massachusetts (878)

Lesson 40

BUILDING YOUR LEGAL VOCABULARY

Word Endings *-tial* and *-cial* are expressed by /

judicial 

nonjudicial 

circumstantial 

officials 

impartial 

marshal, martial 

Word Study

 **colloquies** Conferences; conversations.

 **impunity** Free from punishment, harm, or loss.

 **incriminate** To charge with, or to involve oneself or another person in an accusation of a crime.

 **sophistical** Plausible but false.

BUILDING YOUR LEGAL TRANSCRIPTION SKILL

Transcription Aid

Hyphenation: Prefixes With Capitalized Words

☐ Use a hyphen when the prefix is attached to a word used as a proper noun or proper adjective.

pro-British un-American non-Communist mid-December

BUT undemocratic

Hyphenation: Duplicated Prefixes

☐ Use a hyphen to join duplicated prefixes.

re-redirect examination sub-subcommittee bi-bivalent

Typing Citations

Books

The citation of books should include volume, author, title, page or section, edition (if more than one), and date.

7 Appleman, Insurance Law and Practice, 511, 1938-1942

BUILDING YOUR LEGAL DICTATION PROFICIENCY

Preview

constitutionality 

legislative 

export 

plausability 

farsighted 

retrospective 

import 

territorial 

Reading and Writing Practice

105. UNITED STATES DISTRICT COURT, DISTRICT OF MASSACHUSETTS UNITED STATES OF AMERICA, PLAINTIFF, V. ROBERT B. VOSS, DEFENDANT. CRIMINAL NO. 76-84-W DEFENDANT'S REPLY BRIEF

It cannot seriously be contended that the legislative hearing referred to in pages[1] 24-27 of Defendant's Amended Memorandum of Law do not refer to Section 176a[2] of the Marijuana Import and Export Act. In fact, those hearings, and the colloquies between Senator[3] Paul Donne, Chairman of the Subcommittee on Improvement in the Federal Criminal Code of the Senate[4] Committee on the Judiciary, and Messrs. Evers and

Kent of the Bureau of Customs, were discussing[5] Section 1404 of S. 3760 (84th Congress, 2d sess.), which was enacted[6] and codified as 21 U.S.C. 176a. A copy of these hearings is appended[7] hereto.

It should be noted in passing that it is clear from the context of the hearings that the words *addicts* was[8] used loosely to refer not only to narcotics addicts, but more often to traffickers, dealers, and users[9] of marijuana.

It is clear from the hearings that there is cooperation between state and federal officials[10] with regard to controlling marijuana traffic and that information obtained as a result of[11] border declarations or even border observations are turned over to state and federal police to[12] aid in the prosecution of marijuana trafficking offenses. See especially pages 22-26[13] of the hearings appended hereto.

In contending the contrary, the Government seems to[14] imply that individuals who are proceeding with due haste to the customs checkpoint may smoke marijuana with[15] impunity so long as the marijuana is totally consumed before reaching the checkpoint. There is certainly[16] no authority supporting such a preemption of a state's jurisdiction over its territorial waters,[17] docks, or airports.

If indeed the state does have criminal jurisdiction over its airports, territorial[18] waters, and docks, then customs declaration of marijuana would be an admission of having possessed[19] marijuana within a state's jurisdiction immediately prior to that declaration, which possession is[20] a criminal offense in every state in the Union.

The Supreme Court's farsighted holding in *Marchetti* that swept away[21] the sophistical distinction between retrospective and prospective self-incrimination renders any[22] question of concurrent jurisdiction in airports or seaports unnecessary. All that is required to meet[23] the *Marchetti* test of self-incrimination is that forced compliance with a federal statute increase the[24] likelihood of prosecution for either past or *future* violations. *Marchetti vs. United States,*[25] 36 U.S.L.W. 4143. See Defendant's Amended Memorandum of Law, pp. 4-5.[26]

On page 3 of the Government's brief, the Government contends that "by complying fully with the requirements[27] of the statute which he is now accused of having violated, the defendant would have insulated himself[28] entirely from both federal and state sanctions and would have subjected himself to no possible danger[29] of self-incrimination." This cannot be asserted except on the most sophistical level. It is[30] true that pursuant to procedures of the customs regulations—which have absolutely no statutory[31] authority to support them—an individual is not *allowed* to comply with the federal[32] statutes until he is cleared as a legal possessor under state laws.

It should first be noted that there is no[33] federal statutory authority for refusing application for the federal tax stamp on the[34] basis of state law. It would indeed be strange if 176a or the Marijuana Tax Act could be[35] saved because, through unauthorized administrative practice which might be changed at any time, no one was allowed to[36] comply with them.

Second, it shows less than good faith to argue that the federal practice of "checking" with[37] the state authorities with respect to an individual *attempting* to comply with the federal statutes,[38] amounts to less of a real hazard of self-incrimination than would result if compliance through registration[39] itself were allowed.

106. UNITED STATES DISTRICT COURT, DISTRICT OF MASSACHUSETTS UNITED STATES OF AMERICA V. ROBERT B. VOSS CRIMINAL NO. 76-84-W OPINION APRIL 2, 19___ WYMAN, CHIEF JUDGE

The indictment charges Voss as a principal with having imported into the United[40] States marijuana in violation of 21 U.S.C. 176a. Government[41] counsel specified orally that the Government's proof would show that the marijuana was produced abroad and was[42] transported into the United States unlawfully by Voss as principal.

Defendant has moved to dismiss[43] the indictment on the ground that in order to have complied with the requirements of 176a, he[44] would have been forced to incriminate himself, contrary to the Fifth Amendment to the United States Constitution.[45]

Indubitably, 21 U.S.C. 176a does not have on its face any requirement[46] of self-incrimination. Read literally, therefore, the statute does not conflict with the United States Constitution.[47]

However, it is asserted that at least the implications of *Marchetti vs. United*[48] *States* and *Haynes vs. United States* and *Grosso vs. United States,* three decisions rendered by the Supreme[49] Court of the United States, suggest that 21 U.S.C. 176a as here sought to be applied[50] would violate the Fifth Amendment. The argument has a certain plausibility, particularly because[51] of the construction placed upon the majority opinions in the three cases cited by Chief Justice[52] Warren dissenting from the judgments in those cases.

However, it behooves a United States District Judge to[53] remember that he is only one man and that there is a strong presumption of constitutionality of[54] acts of Congress which, after all, have always commanded a majority in each House of Congress and frequently,[55] as here, the approval of the President of the United States. Of course, a United States District Judge,[56] like every other public officer, has taken an oath to support the Constitution of the United States.[57] But that oath may reasonably be interpreted as including a modest awareness of one's own limited[58] competence.

Motion to dismiss the indictment denied.

Charles E. Wyman, Chief Judge (1177)

UNIT

5 Probate

Estate of John W. Dunn

This unit concerns the settlement of the estate of John W. Dunn. Lester L. Greenberg, Esq., serves as Executor. In this capacity he appointed the National Bank of Boston as his agent to perform certain financial duties in connection with the settlement of the estate according to the directions of the Executor.

Lesson 41

BUILDING YOUR LEGAL VOCABULARY

Word Endings *-ly* is expressed by ; *-ily* is expressed by .

allegedly

falsely

uneasily

illegally

equitably

unsteadily

Word Study

dividend A share of profits given to shareholders.

estate All possessions, including property and debts, left by a person at death.

executor A person designated in a will to administer an estate.

executrix Feminine form of executor.

inheritance That which is acquired from an ancestor or another person by legal succession or will.

inter vivos Between living persons.

probate Relating to proof, such as official proof of a will.

remaindermen Ones who are entitled to an estate after possession is surrendered by another.

securities Stock certificates, bonds, and so on.

BUILDING YOUR LEGAL TRANSCRIPTION SKILL

Transcription Aid

Hyphenation: Prefixes Ending in a Vowel

☐ Use a hyphen to prevent mispronunciation and to increase ease of reading when a prefix ending in *a* or *i* is joined to a word beginning with the same vowel; usually omit the hyphen when the prefix ends with *e* or *o*.

semi-invalid anti-inflation ultra-atomic naso-orbital
preempt reelect coordinate co-owner

Hyphenation: Prefixes "Quasi-" and "Self-"

☐ Use a hyphen with the prefixes *quasi-* and *self-*, except in the words *selfish, selfsame, selfhood,* and *selfless.*

quasi-argument quasi-corporation self-incrimination

Typing Citations

The series number must be included in a citation of a series that has more than one. Abbreviations of the series number are preferred.

Consolidated Elec. Corp. v. Panhandle Ed. Co. 189 F.2d 777

BUILDING YOUR LEGAL DICTATION PROFICIENCY

Preview

administration
appraisers
coexecutor
concurrently
coordinate
distributees
facilitate
joint
petition
procedural
recall
tenancy
therewith
ultimate

Reading and Writing Practice

107. MR. JOHN R. TAYLOR, NATIONAL BANK, 40 WATER STREET, BOSTON, MA 02100

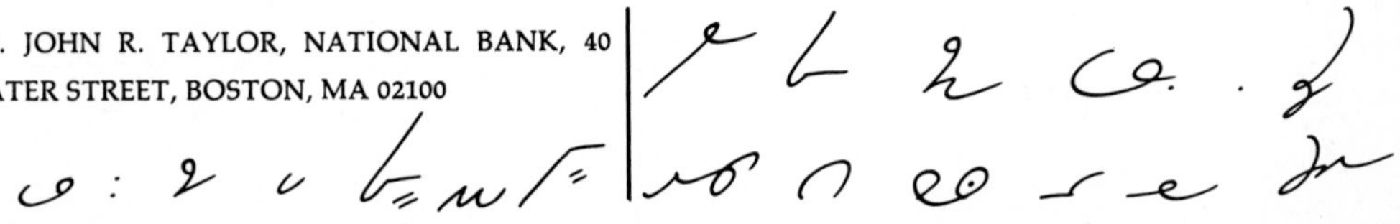

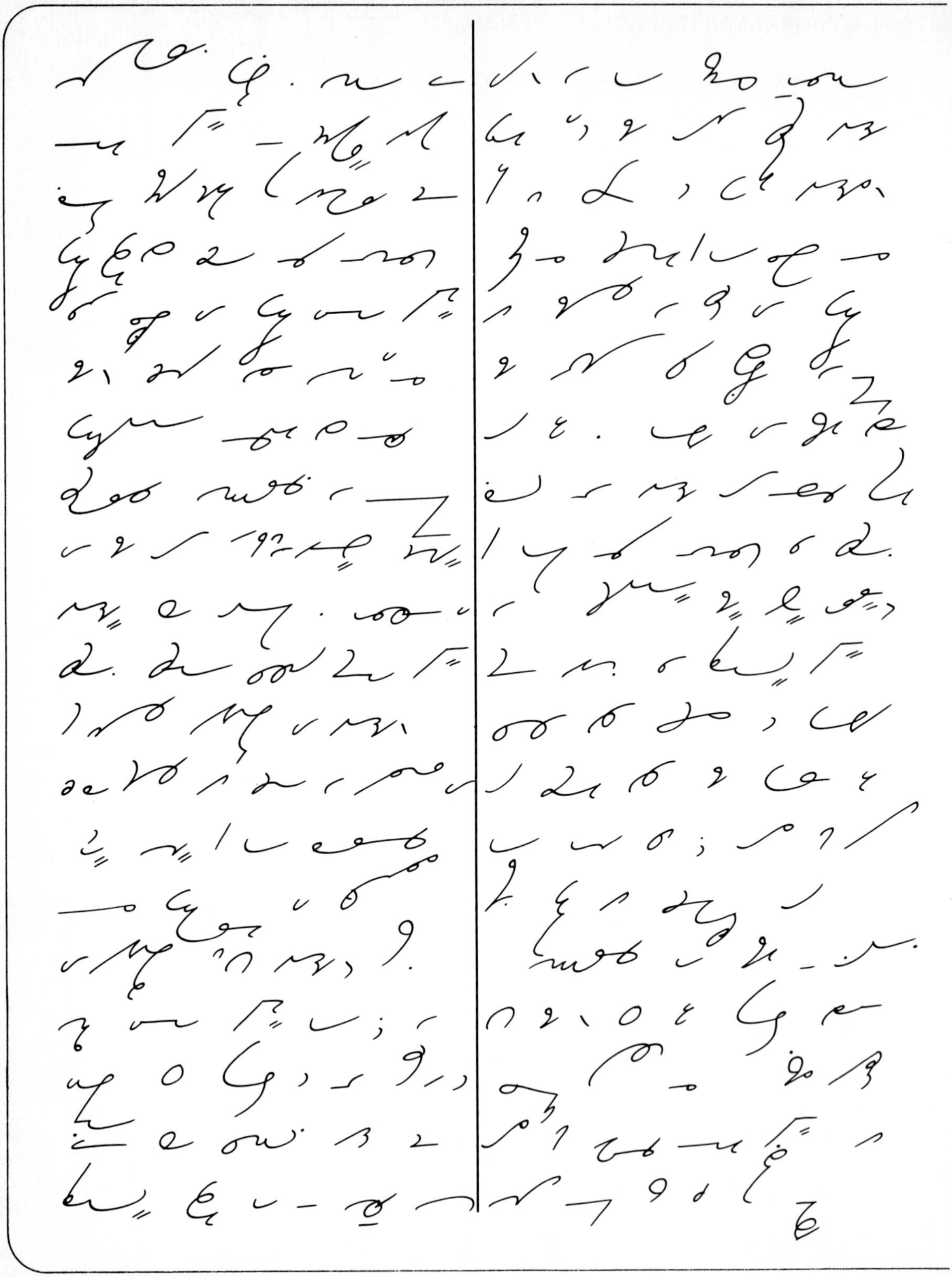

108. MR. JOHN R. TAYLOR, NATIONAL BANK, 40 WATER STREET, BOSTON, MA 02100

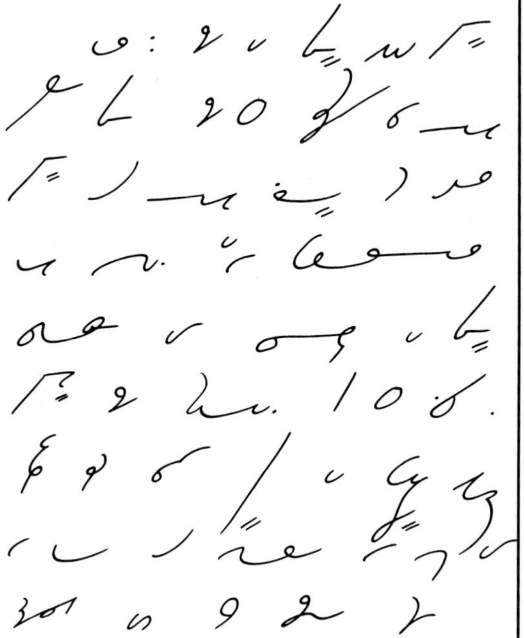

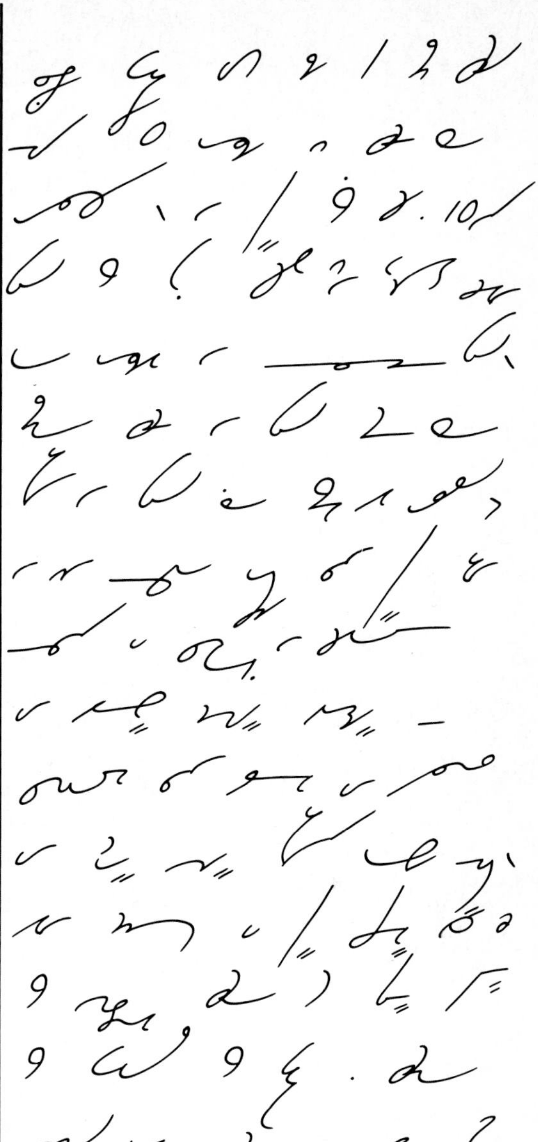

109. MR. JOHN R. TAYLOR, NATIONAL BANK, 40 WATER STREET, BOSTON, MA 02100

9

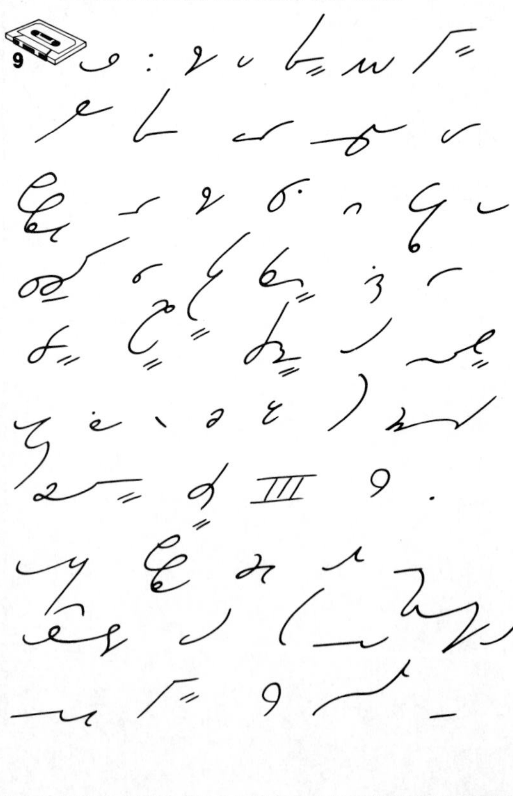

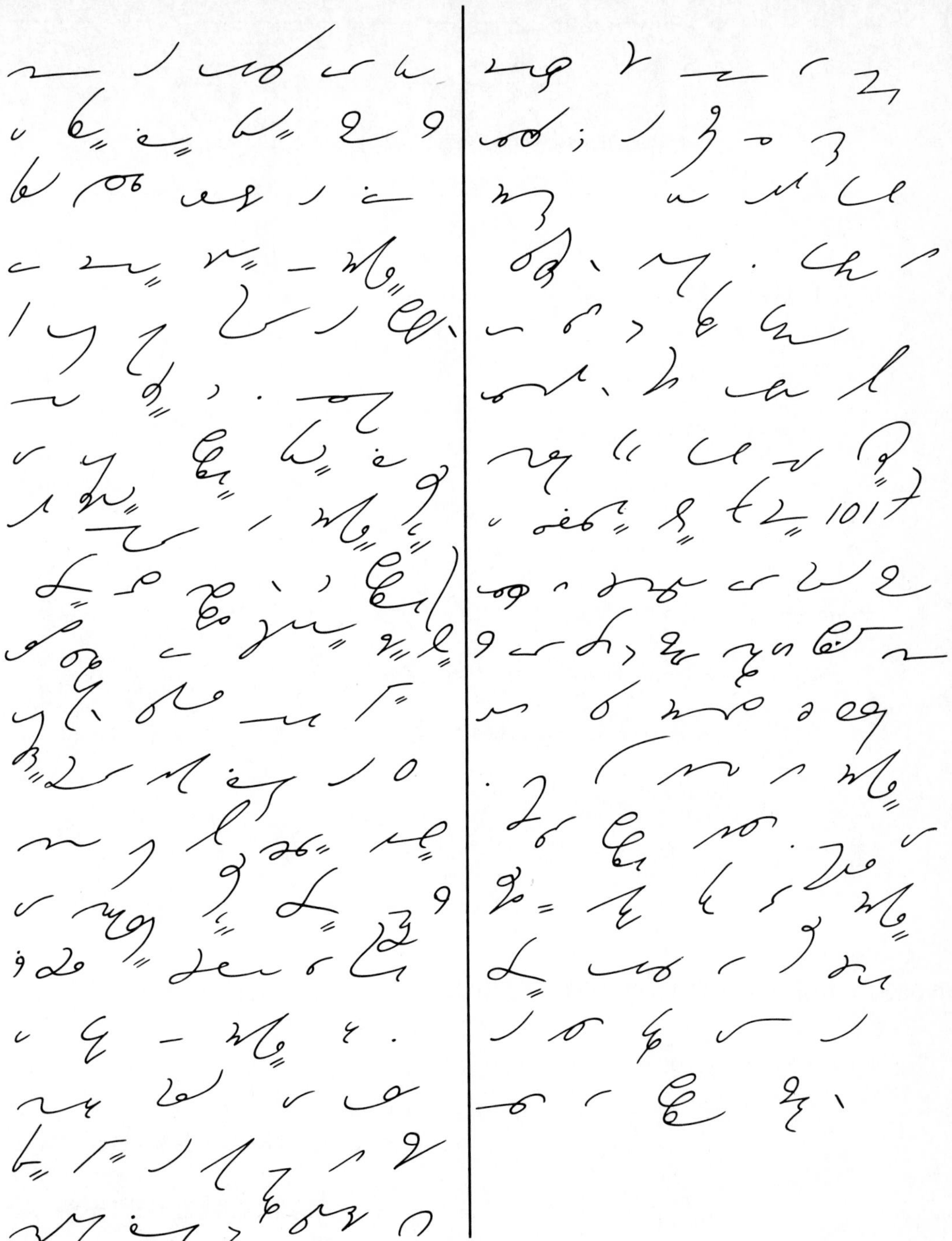

Lesson 42

BUILDING YOUR LEGAL VOCABULARY

Word Endings *-ful* is expressed by  .

lawful 

unlawfully 

forceful 

willfully 

mindful 

powerful 

Word Study

 **affixed** Fastened, attached.

 **decedent** One who has died.

 **declination** A formal refusal.

 **legacies** Gifts by will; bequests.

 **oath** A solemn attestation of the truth of one's words.

BUILDING YOUR LEGAL TRANSCRIPTION SKILL

Transcription Aid **Hyphenation: Compound Words**

☐ Use the hyphen to make a compound word when:

1. Building a verb: blue-pencil double-check quick-freeze cross-license
2. Building a noun containing a preposition: right-of-way patent-in-fee
3. Spelling out compound numerals below one hundred: seventy-one
4. Improvising words for specialized use: know-how know-it-all

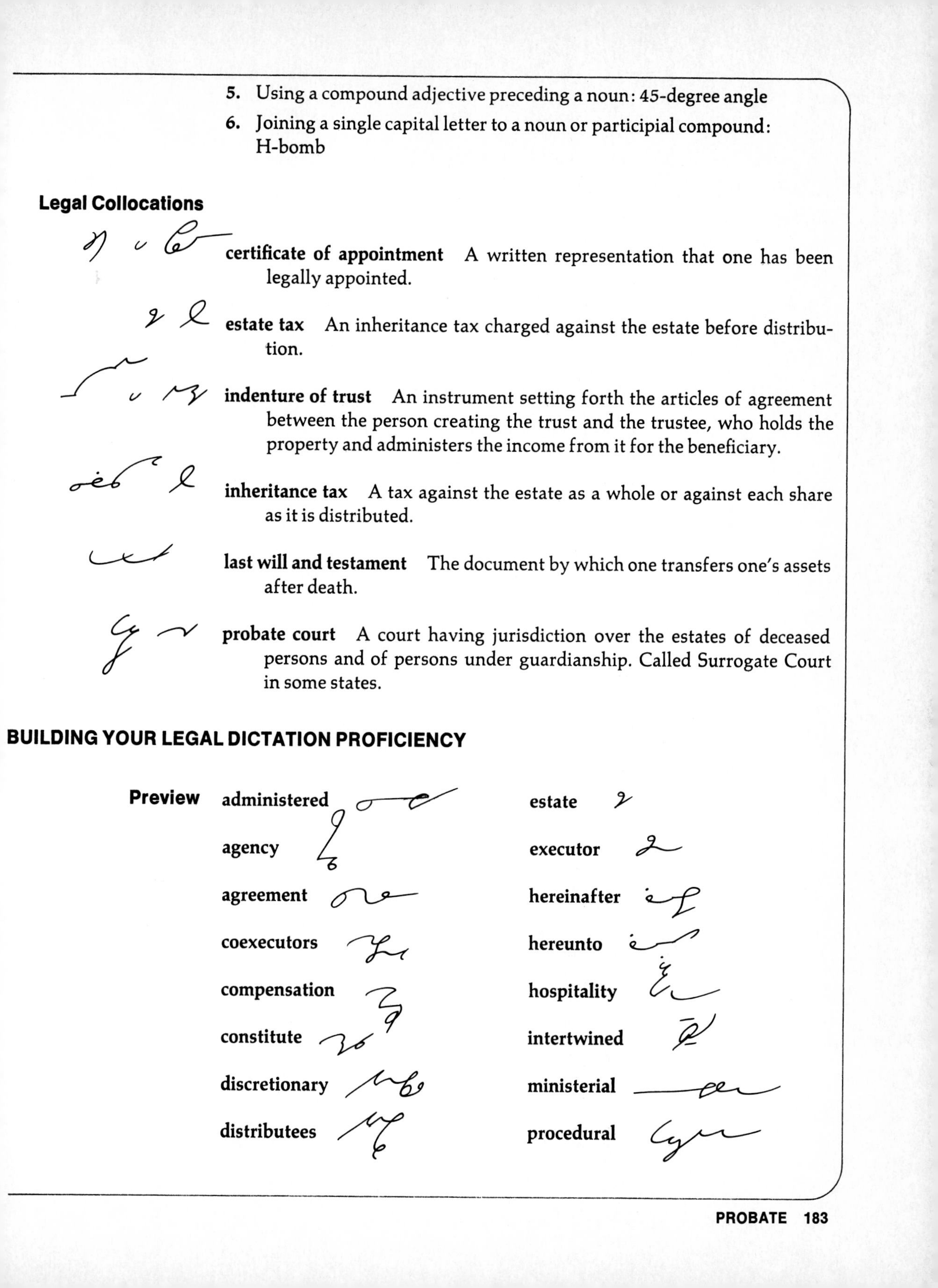

5. Using a compound adjective preceding a noun: 45-degree angle
6. Joining a single capital letter to a noun or participial compound: H-bomb

Legal Collocations

certificate of appointment A written representation that one has been legally appointed.

estate tax An inheritance tax charged against the estate before distribution.

indenture of trust An instrument setting forth the articles of agreement between the person creating the trust and the trustee, who holds the property and administers the income from it for the beneficiary.

inheritance tax A tax against the estate as a whole or against each share as it is distributed.

last will and testament The document by which one transfers one's assets after death.

probate court A court having jurisdiction over the estates of deceased persons and of persons under guardianship. Called Surrogate Court in some states.

BUILDING YOUR LEGAL DICTATION PROFICIENCY

Preview

administered
agency
agreement
coexecutors
compensation
constitute
discretionary
distributees
estate
executor
hereinafter
hereunto
hospitality
intertwined
ministerial
procedural

submission 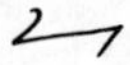 therefrom 

Superior Court  thereunder 

Reading and Writing Practice

110. AGENCY AGREEMENT

KNOW ALL MEN BY THESE PRESENTS that I, LESTER L. GREENBERG, of Boston, County of Suffolk, and Commonwealth of[1] Massachusetts, Executor of the will of John W. Dunn, late of Sudbury, Massachusetts, hereby constitute and[2] appoint National Bank of Boston, Massachusetts, as my Agent.

Said Agent agrees to perform all such duties of the[3] Executor in his name and on his behalf, as the Executor may from time to time direct, but only[4] to the extent that the law permits. No action, which is not of a ministerial nature, shall be taken[5] by the Agent without the approval of the Executor. The Executor assumes responsibility[6] for all acts of the Agent authorized hereby.

The compensation to be paid to the Agent for its performance of[7] the duties hereinafter set forth shall be one-half of the fee allowed to the Executor by the Middlesex[8] County Probate Court for the Commonwealth of Massachusetts, under whose jurisdiction this estate is[9] administered.

The duties to be performed by the Agent under this agreement include: 1. The retention of the[10] assets delivered by the Executor of the estate. 2. The physical custody and safekeeping of[11] securities. 3. Collection of income. 4. The maintenance of all necessary bookkeeping records. 5.[12] Estimating cash requirements for the purpose of payment of debts, expenses, legacies, and taxes, and the[13] advising of the Executor with regard to raising of the necessary cash therefor. 6. Payment of the[14] debts, expenses, legacies, and tax obligations of the estate or of the decedent preceding his death[15] as required by the estate. 7. Advising the Executor with regard to any other investment problems[16] that may from time to time arise. 8. Buying and selling of securities and other property. 9. The[17] distribution of the estate to the beneficiaries in accordance with the will, including the making[18] of any transfers required thereunder. 10. The submission to the Executor to prepare and file therefrom the[19] probate accounts required.

This agreement may be terminated by either party by written notice delivered[20] to the other. IN WITNESS WHEREOF, I have hereunto set my hand and seal this 28th day of February,[21] 19__.

John W. Dunn Estate
By Lester L. Greenberg

______________________ ______________________
Executor Witness

National Bank[22] of Boston, Massachusetts, agrees to act as Agent under the foregoing appointment.

Dated ______________________ [23] ______________________

Vice President (462)

111. MRS. JOHN W. DUNN, 17 SUMMER STREET, SUDBURY, MA 01776

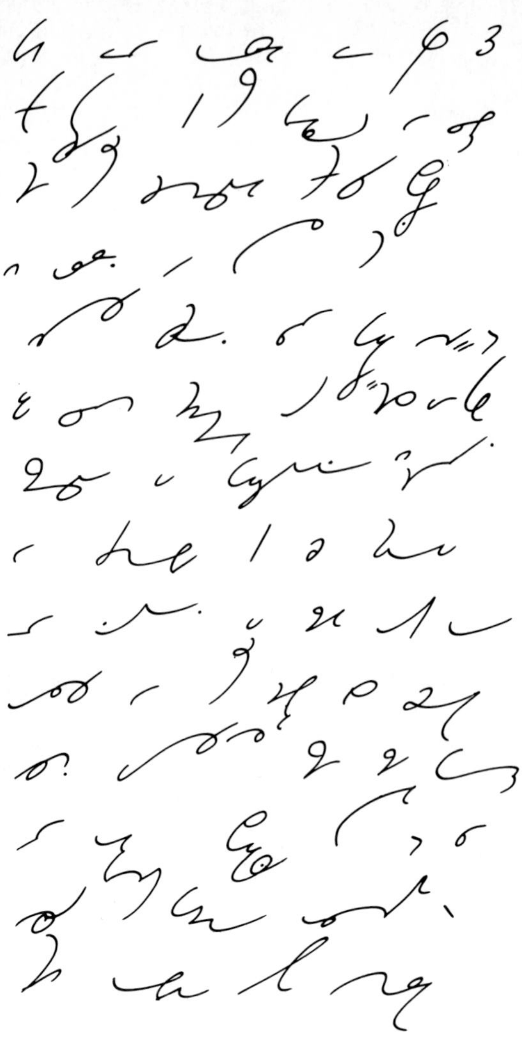

112. MR. JOHN R. TAYLOR, NATIONAL BANK, 40 WATER STREET, BOSTON, MA 02100

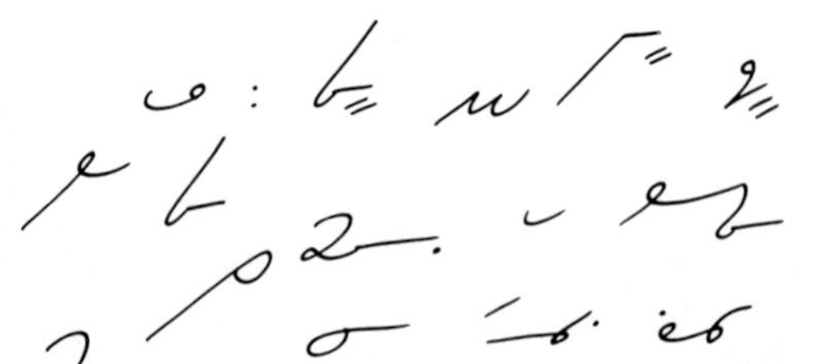

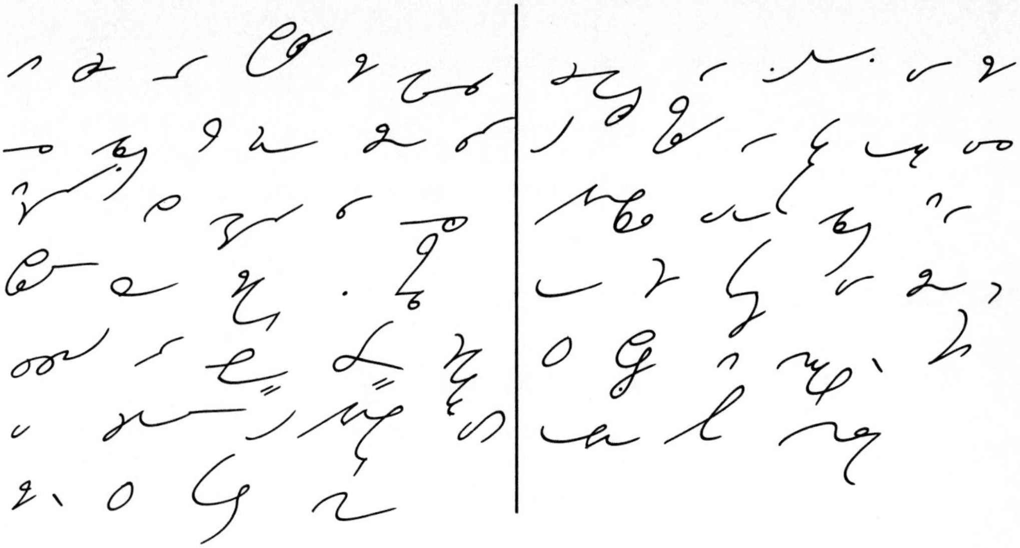

Lesson 43

BUILDING YOUR LEGAL VOCABULARY

Word Endings -*sume* is expressed by ; -*sumption* is expressed by .

resume 

assumption 

assumpsit 

consumed 

consummated 

presumptive 

Word Study

 **authorization** The act of establishing legal power.

 **inventory** A list of the property of a person or an estate.

portfolio The securities held by an investor.

resolution A decision reached by formal action.

statutes Laws enacted by a legislative branch of the government.

BUILDING YOUR LEGAL TRANSCRIPTION SKILL

Transcription Aid

Hyphenation: Combining Form "Cross"

☐ The word *cross* used as a combining form to make a compound word is usually written without a hyphen, as in *crossbreed* and *crosscurrent*. The following frequently used expressions require the hyphen:

cross-examine, -er, -ation cross-interrogate, -atory cross-check
cross-index cross-action cross-purpose cross-reference
cross-question, -ed, -ing cross-license *(v.)*

Latin and French Words and Phrases

cestui que trust *(ses'twē kē)* He who has a beneficiary interest in an estate or trust fund.

et ux. (uxor) *(et ux)* And wife.

ex post facto *(ex pōst fak'tō)* After the fact or act; subsequently.

BUILDING YOUR LEGAL DICTATION PROFICIENCY

Preview

agent	**percentage**
appraisers	**photocopy**
declination	**prudent**
dividend	**redrafted**
formula	**securities**
license	**transmittal**

Reading and Writing Practice

113. MR. JOHN R. TAYLOR, NATIONAL BANK, 40 WATER STREET, BOSTON, MA 02100

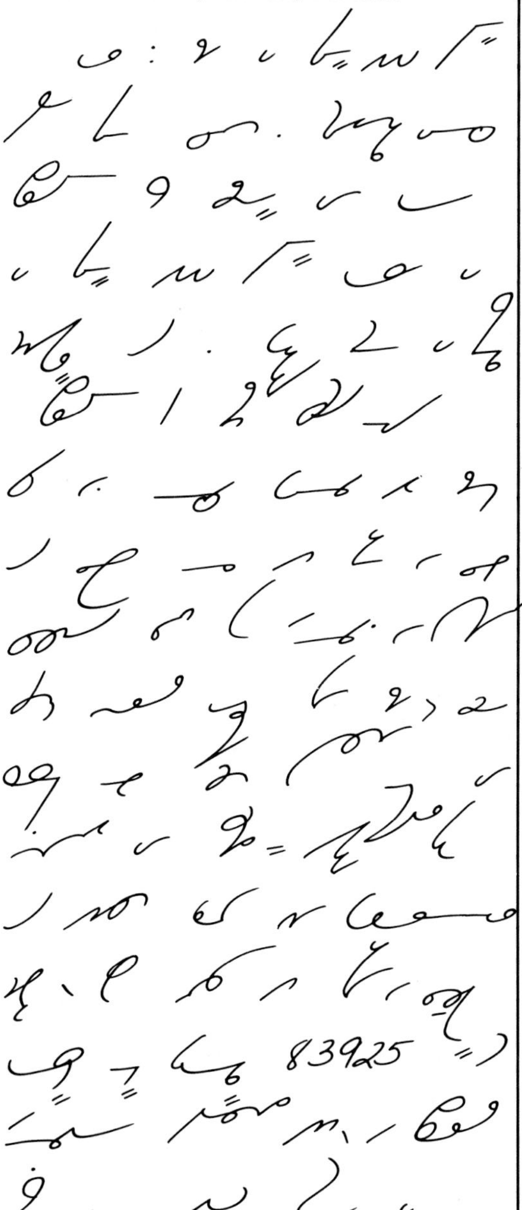

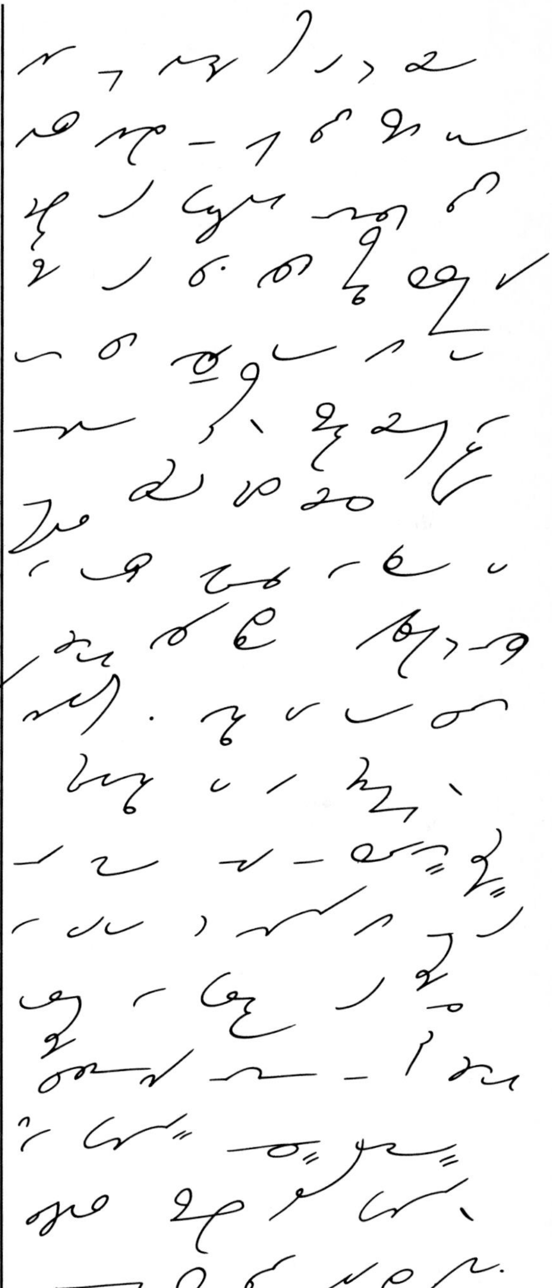

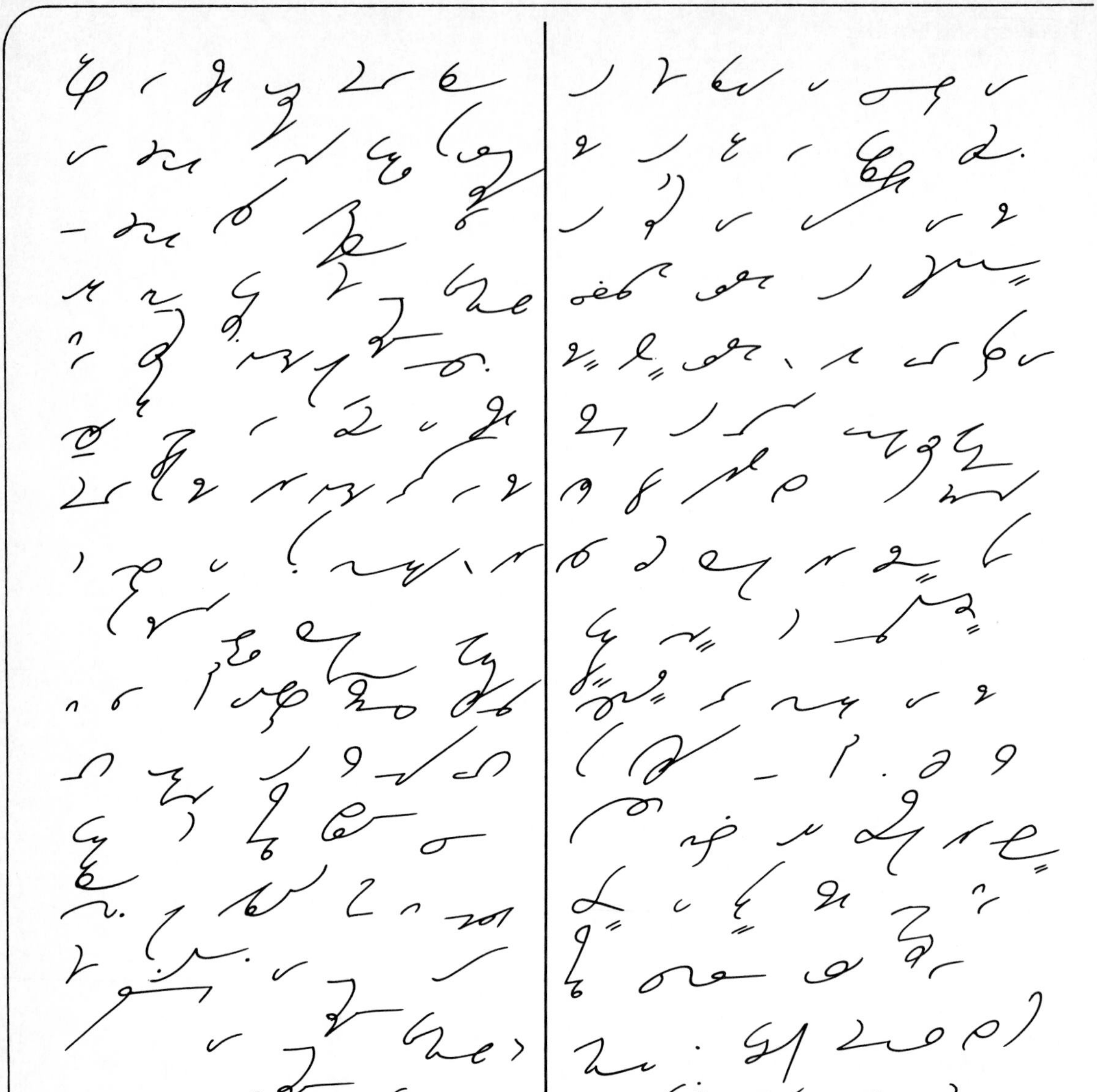

114. MRS. FRANCES D. POST, REGISTER OF PROBATE, 65 CHURCH STREET, MAYNARD, MA 01754

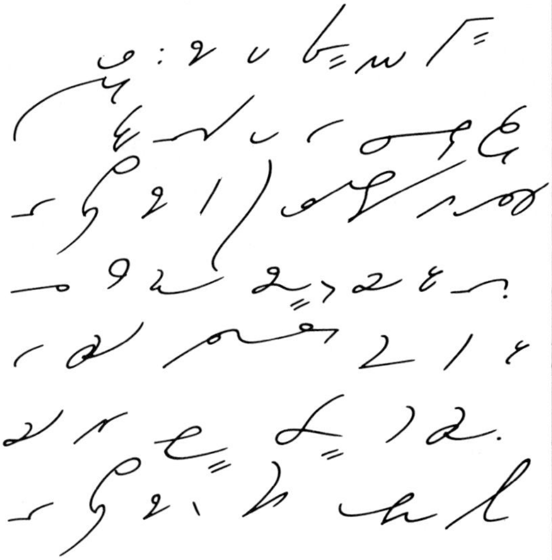

115. MRS. JOHN W. DUNN, 17 SUMMER STREET, SUDBURY, MA 01776

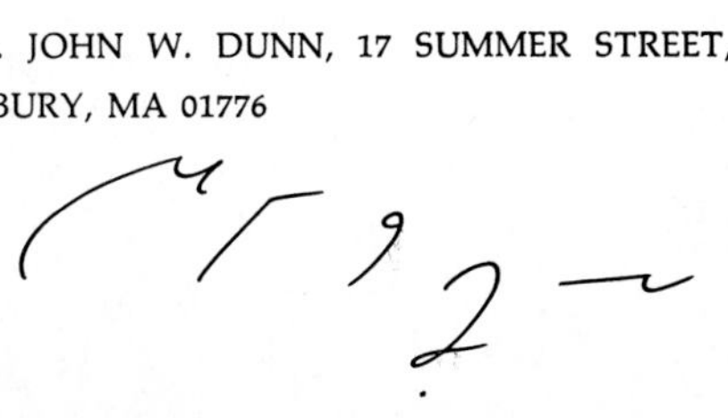

116. MR. L. KENNETH THOMAS, COOPERATIVE SAVINGS BANK, SUDBURY, MA 01776

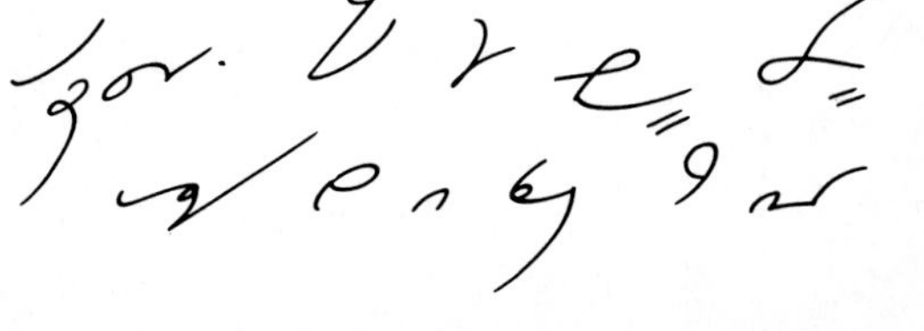

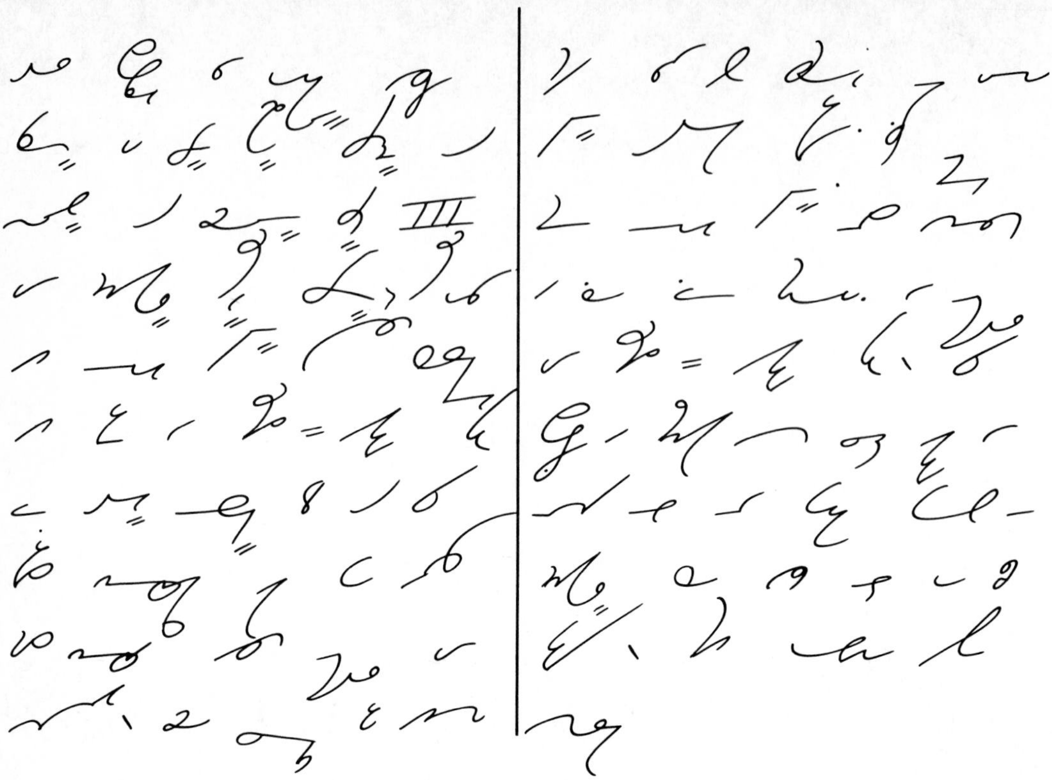

Lesson 44

BUILDING YOUR LEGAL VOCABULARY

Word Endings *-ble* is expressed by .

revokable 

untenable 

taxable 

contestable 

ascertainable 

unassailable 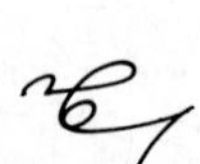

Word Study

devise To give or leave by will.

indenture A formal document executed in two or more copies; a document prepared for purposes of control.

issue Children.

last will and testament The document by which one transfers assets after one's death.

promissors Ones who make promises.

stockholders Ones who own stock; shareholders.

BUILDING YOUR LEGAL TRANSCRIPTION SKILL

Transcription Aid

Hyphenation: Foreign Phrases

☐ Do not use a hyphen in a compound adjective consisting of a foreign phrase.

prima facie evidence   *per diem* employee   bona fide transaction

Hyphenation: Two-Unit Compound Adjectives

☐ Use only one hyphen in compound adjectives composed of two-unit expressions.

post-World War II treaties   vitamin C-deficient patient

Legal Collocations

heir at law The person to whom the law would give the property of an individual who dies without a will.

heir apparent One who is sure to inherit provided the heir outlives the ancestor.

joint tenancy Holding of real estate, personal property, or money by two or more persons whereby the survivor gets the whole.

personal property Property other than real estate.

 **promissory note** A written promise to pay on demand or at a fixed future time a sum of money to the person specified.

BUILDING YOUR LEGAL DICTATION PROFICIENCY

Preview

agency		preliminary	
appraisal		situate	
certificates		statute of limitations	
collectible		subsequently	
devise		successive	
funeral		survived	
inventory		testamentary	
legacies		ultimate	
practicable		unto	

Reading and Writing Practice

117. LAST WILL AND TESTAMENT

Be it remembered that I, H. ELIZABETH DUNN, of the Town of Sudbury, County of Middlesex, and the Commonwealth[1] of Massachusetts, being of sound mind and memory, do hereby make, publish, and declare this to be my[2] last Will and Testament, hereby specifically revoking all prior Wills and testamentary instruments[3] by me made.

FIRST: I direct my Executor, hereinafter named, to pay my just debts and funeral[4] expenses as soon as practicable after my death.

SECOND: In the event at the time of my death I am survived by[5] my three sons, Gerald, Morton, and David Dunn, I give, devise, and bequeath unto each of them one-third of all of[6] my estate of whatsoever name and nature and wheresoever situate, whether real, personal, or mixed,[7] to them and their heirs forever.

THIRD: In the event that any of my sons shall have predeceased me, I then give, devise,[8] and bequeath that share of my estate to their issue by right of representation, to them and their heirs forever.[9]

FOURTH: I nominate and so far as I legally may appoint as my Executor Lester L. Greenberg, Esq.,[10] and the National Bank in Boston, Massachusetts, as coexecutors of my Will. I direct that my[11] Executors be permitted to serve with the minimum bond required by law and without sureties. In the[12] event that either is unable, unwilling, or unavailable so to serve, I direct that the other shall serve alone.

IN[13] WITNESS WHEREOF, I hereunto set my hand and seal this ____________

____________ day of March, 19__[14]

____

H. Elizabeth Dunn

Signed, sealed, published and declared by the above-named H. Elizabeth Dunn to be her last Will and Testament in the[15] presence of us, who at her request, in her presence, and in the presence of each other, hereunto

subscribe our[16] names as witnesses thereto on this ______________ day of March, 19__.

____

____

____

(340)

118. MRS. JOHN W. DUNN, 17 SUMMER STREET, SUDBURY, MA 01776

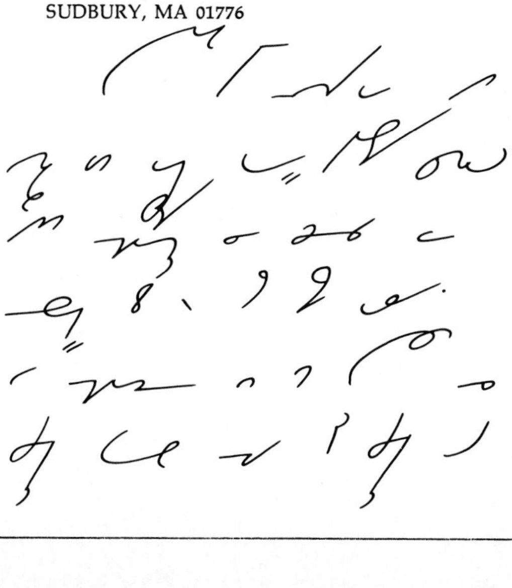

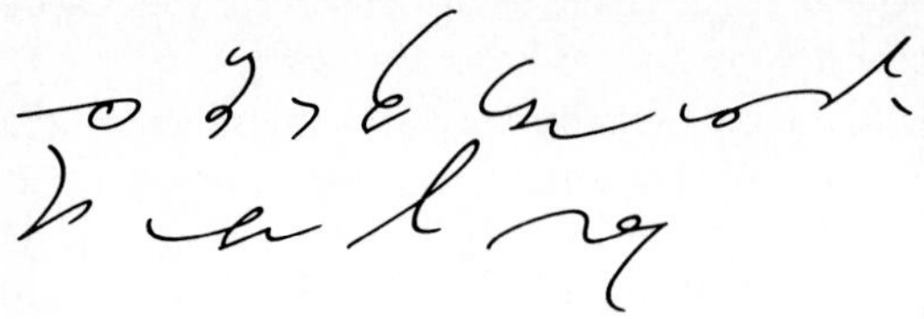

119. MR. JOHN R. TAYLOR, NATIONAL BANK, 40 WATER STREET, BOSTON, MA 02100

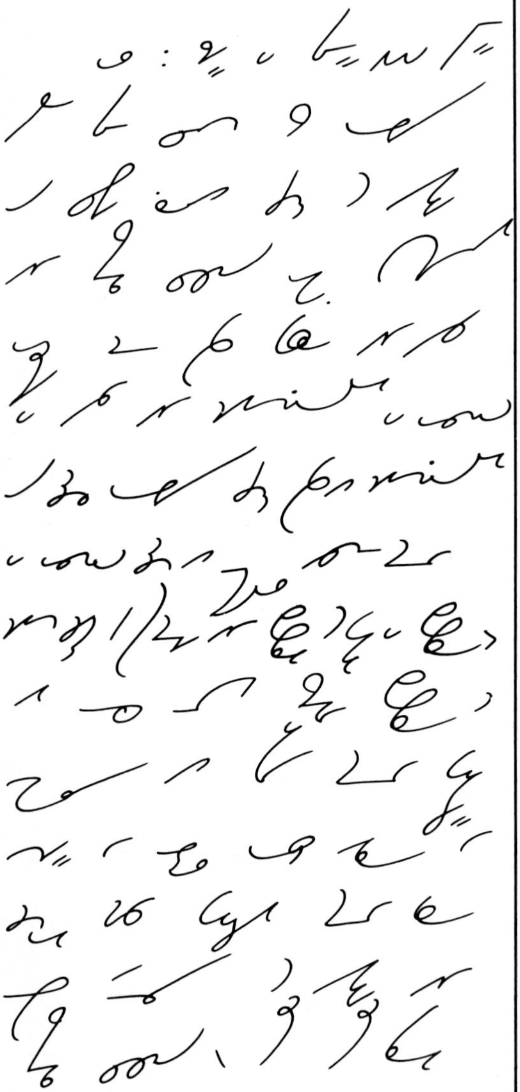

120. MRS. JOHN W. DUNN, 17 SUMMER STREET, SUDBURY, MA 01776

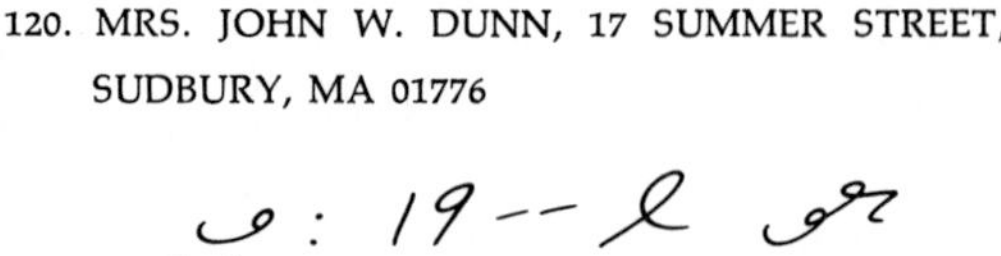

121. MRS. JOHN W. DUNN, 17 SUMMER STREET, SUDBURY, MA 01776

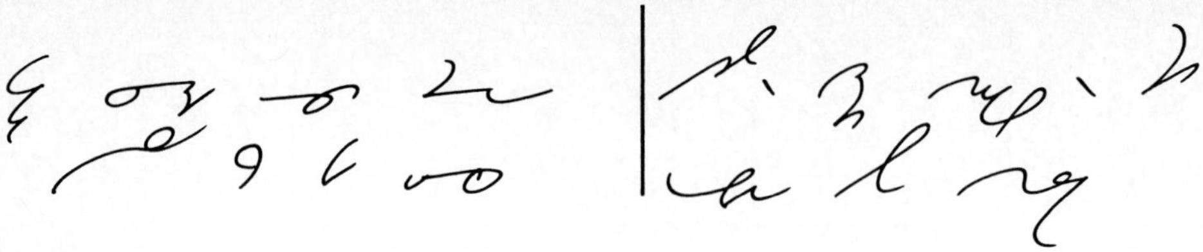

Lesson 45

BUILDING YOUR LEGAL VOCABULARY

Word Endings *-ual* and *-ule* are expressed by .

contractual  residual 

factual  conceptual 

individually  scheduled 

Word Study

 **bequeath** To give or leave by will.

 **bequest** Something given or left by a will.

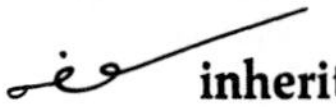 **inherited** Acquired by gift or succession.

 **residue** The remainder of the estate after other bequests are made.

BUILDING YOUR LEGAL TRANSCRIPTION SKILL

Transcription Aid Hyphenation: Letters or Figures in Compound Adjectives

☐ The compound adjective that contains a letter or a figure as its second element is not hyphenated.

Article 3 provisions Grade A meat Section 6 reference
Exhibit B evidence

- ☐ When the letter or figure is the first element of the unit modifier, use the hyphen.

  40-acre plot   L-shaped scar   A-frame house   15-story building

Latin and French Words and Phrases

a fortiori *(a for'shē o'rē)* From the strongest reason or more convincing force.

nunc pro tunc *(nunk prō tunk)* Now for then; to have effect as of the former date.

per stirpes *(per stir'pāz)* Method of dividing an estate whereby a group takes the share that their deceased ancestor would have taken.

BUILDING YOUR LEGAL DICTATION PROFICIENCY

Preview

appraisal	**notification**
authorization	**outlawed**
authorize	**policy**
cited	**protective**
clarify	**subsequent**
harmonious	**supplement**
insoluble	**tenancy**
legally	**widow**

Reading and Writing Practice

122. MRS. JOHN W. DUNN, 17 SUMMER STREET, SUDBURY, MA 01776

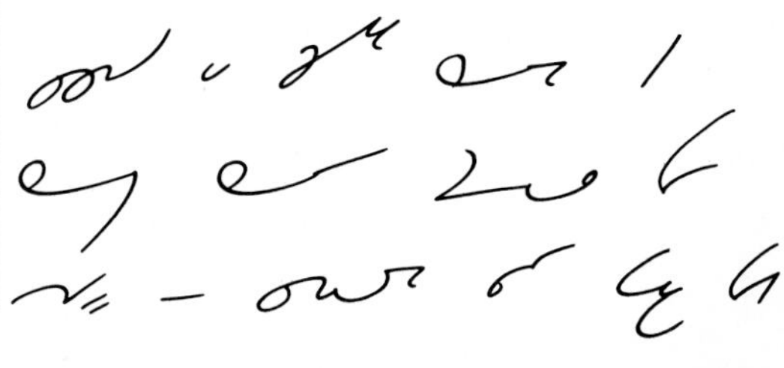

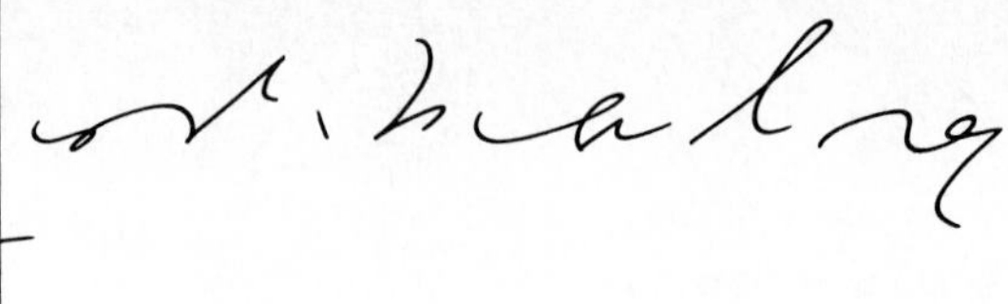

123. MR. C. PAUL DUNN, MAIN STREET, SPRINGFIELD, VT 05156, AND MR. RALPH DUNN, SPRING STREET, SPRINGFIELD, VT 05156

124. MRS. JOHN W. DUNN, 17 SUMMER STREET, SUDBURY, MA 01776

125. MR. L. KENNETH THOMAS, SUDBURY SAVINGS BANK, SUDBURY, MA 01776

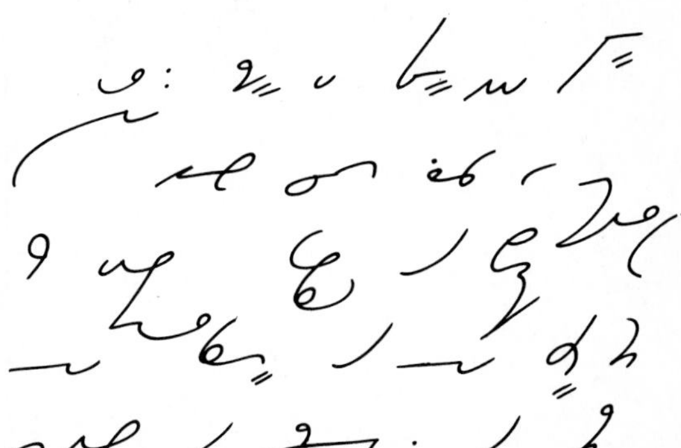

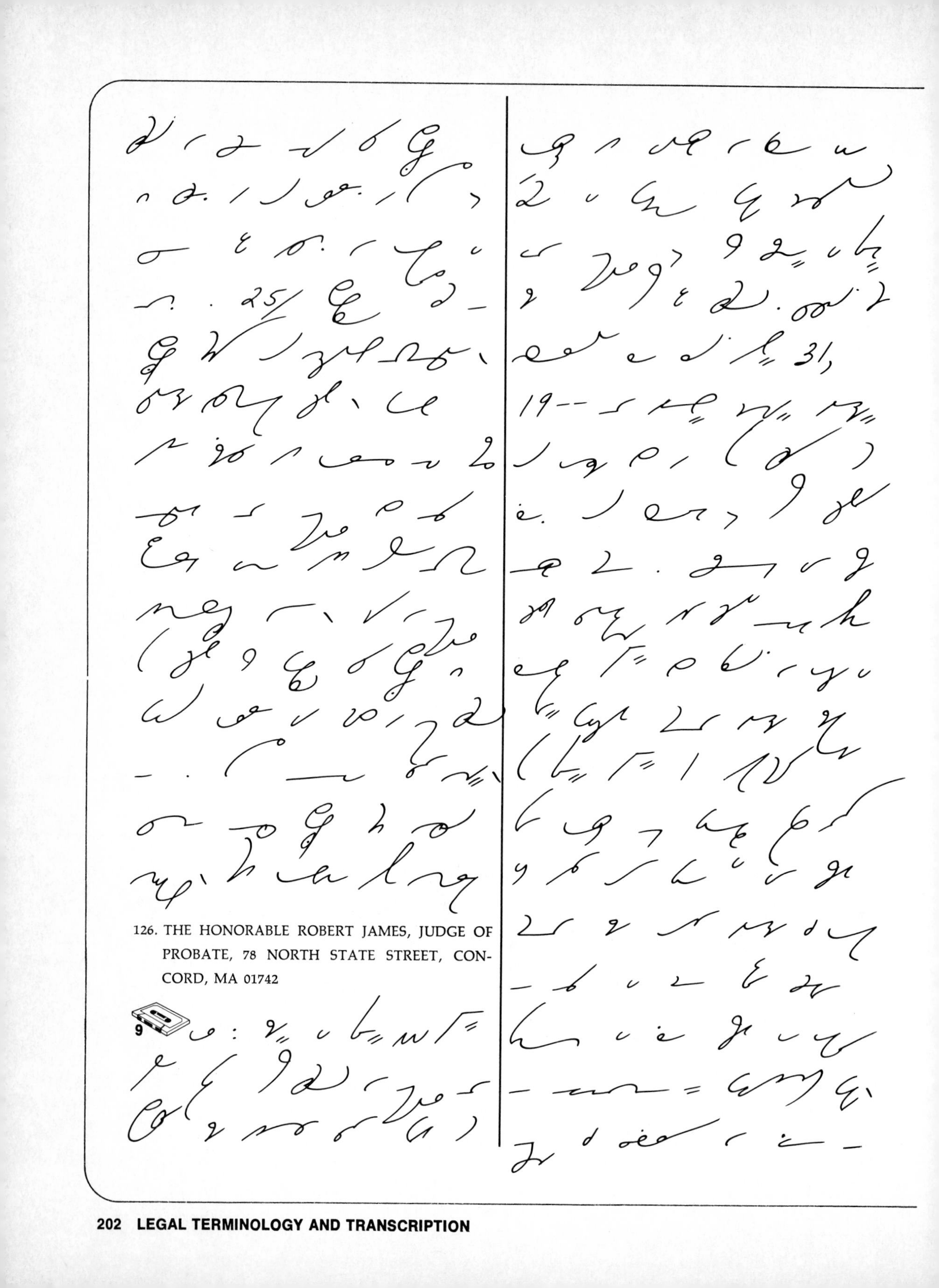

126. THE HONORABLE ROBERT JAMES, JUDGE OF PROBATE, 78 NORTH STATE STREET, CONCORD, MA 01742

9

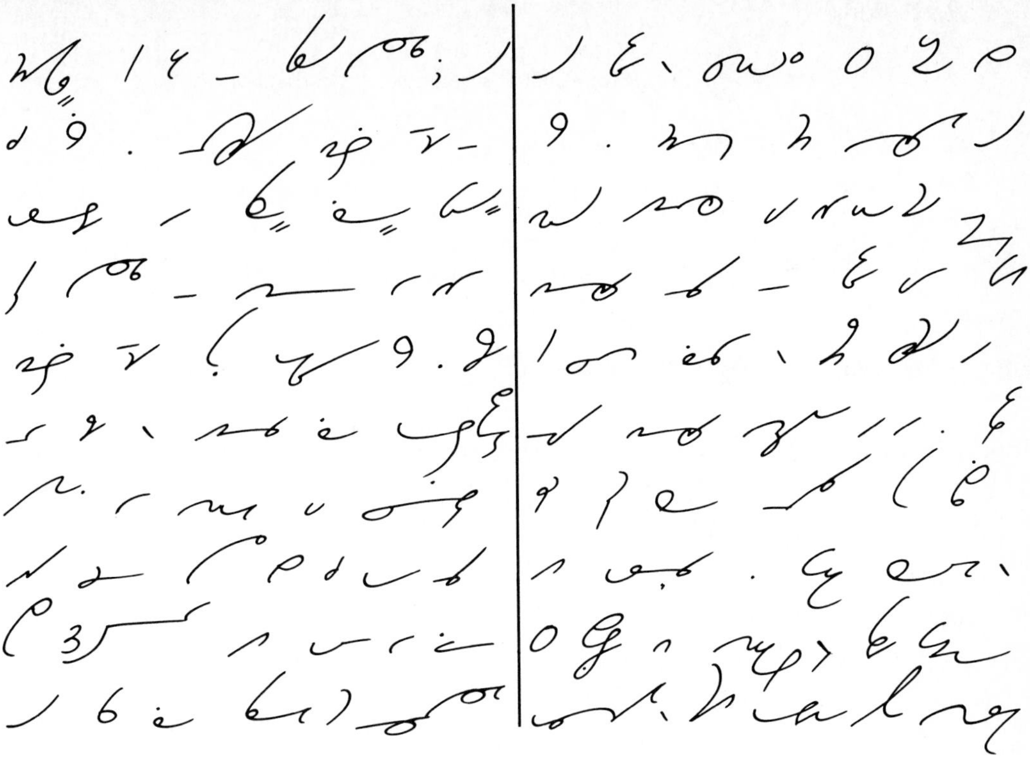

Lesson 46

BUILDING YOUR LEGAL VOCABULARY

Word Endings *-ure* is expressed by unless it follows a downstroke.

debentures	unsecured
indentures	assured
procedural	fracture

Word Study

 **concur** To act together in a common end; to agree.

 **intestate** Without a will.

 **testator** The maker of a will.

 **testatrix** Feminine form of testator.

BUILDING YOUR LEGAL TRANSCRIPTION SKILL

Transcription Aid

Hyphenation: "Suspending" or Spaced

☐ Use the hyphen followed by a space when two or more hyphenated compounds have a common basic element.

five- or six-page report   long- and short-term loans

Hyphenation: Plural of Hyphenated Compounds

☐ To make the plural of hyphenated compound words, add the plural sign to the most important element or to the last word if the elements are equal.

rights-of-way   go-betweens   courts-martial *(n.)*   mothers-in-law

Legal Collocations

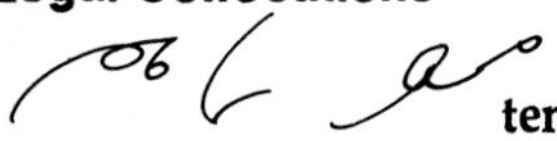 **tenancy by the entirety** Joint ownership of real property by husband and wife with survivor of the marriage to become sole owner.

 **tenancy in common** Joint ownership (not necessarily by husband and wife) in which survivor does not get the whole; deceased's interest goes to his distributees.

 **residuary clause** The clause in a will which disposes of the remainder.

 **spendthrift trust** A trust created to provide a fund for the beneficiary that is secure against reckless spending or against the beneficiary's incapacity to manage his or her affairs.

 **surrogate's office** Office of a judicial official in some states with jurisdiction over the probate of wills, the settlement of estates, and supervision of guardians.

BUILDING YOUR LEGAL DICTATION PROFICIENCY

Preview

- accelerate
- accrued
- affirmation
- associates
- canceled
- certified
- chattels
- compromise
- distributable
- distributive
- execution
- feasible
- fund
- guaranty
- herewith
- manufacturers
- refinancing
- subsequently
- technically
- transfer

Reading and Writing Practice

127. MRS. FRANCES D. POST, REGISTER OF PROBATE, 65 CHURCH STREET, MAYNARD, MA 01754

128. MR. JOHN R. TAYLOR, NATIONAL BANK, 40 WATER STREET, BOSTON, MA 02100

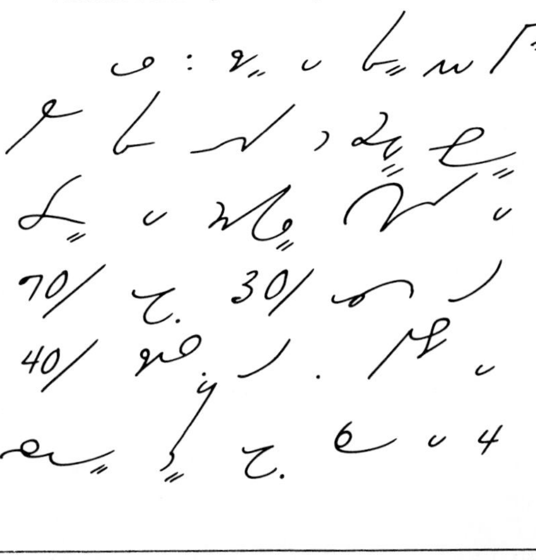

129. MR. JOHN SLOAN, JOHNSON & COMPANY, 10 POST OFFICE SQUARE, BOSTON, MA 02100

130. MR. C. PAUL DUNN, MAIN STREET, SPRINGFIELD, VT 05156

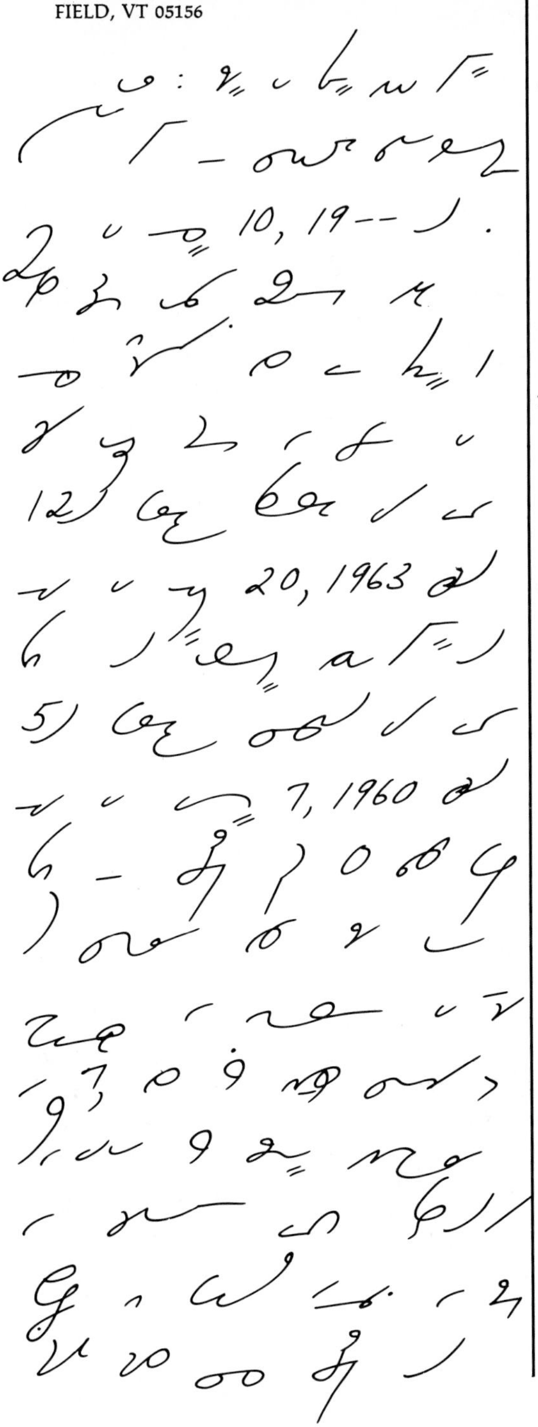

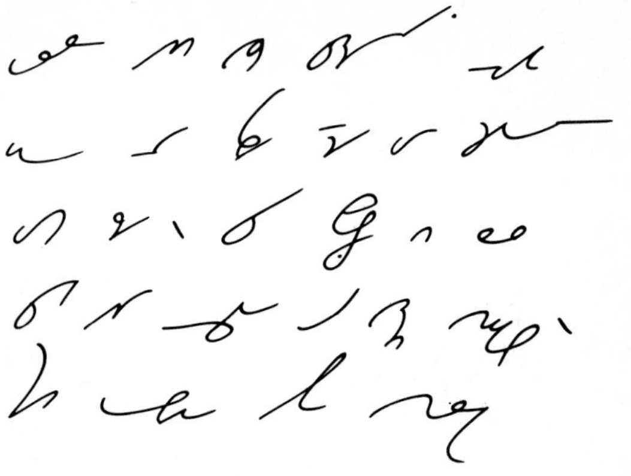

131. MR. DAVID E. DUNN, 780 ELM STREET, MAYNARD, MA 01754

Lesson 47

BUILDING YOUR LEGAL VOCABULARY

Word Endings -*tain* is expressed by  .

retainer		**unobtainable**	
sustained		**maintaining**	
detainer		**appertaining**	

Word Study

beneficiary A person benefiting under a will, trust, or agreement.

liquidity Capability of being readily converted into cash.

valuations The estimated market values of a thing.

waiver The act of intentionally giving up a known right, claim, or privilege.

waiving Giving up voluntarily; abandoning.

BUILDING YOUR LEGAL TRANSCRIPTION SKILL

Transcription Aid **Hyphenation: Word Division at the End of a Line**

☐ Consult a good reference manual to master the rules for word division at the end of a line of typing, and always consult a dictionary when in doubt. Many errors can be avoided by following the basic principles given below.

1. Divide only between syllables.

knowl-edge indict-ment fea-sance mis-de-meanor par-tial stat-utes

2. Never divide two letters from the end of a word, and avoid dividing two letters at the beginning of a word whenever possible.

3. Divide a word that is spelled with a hyphen only at the hyphen.

   anti-intellectual   self-incriminating   quasi-judicial

4. While most reference manuals state that a page should never end with a hyphenated word, in legal work the last word on a page may be divided in order to guard against the insertion of a page that might alter the intention of the person signing the document.

Latin and French Words and Phrases

in extremis *(in ex tre' mis)* In the last extremity; near death.

scilicet *(sil'e set)* Abbreviation, ss. or SS. (Latin for "to wit" or namely). The statement of the venue or place where an action is brought or an affidavit is signed.

pari passu *(pa'rē pa'soo)* Equally, without preference; at an equal rate.

BUILDING YOUR LEGAL DICTATION PROFICIENCY

Preview

applicability	funds
compromise	herewith
concur	investments
desirability	memorials
distributions	optional
federal estate tax	surrender
forthcoming	treasurer

Reading and Writing Practice

132. MR. KENNETH CASS, TAX COMMISSION, STATE HOUSE, BOSTON, MA 02100

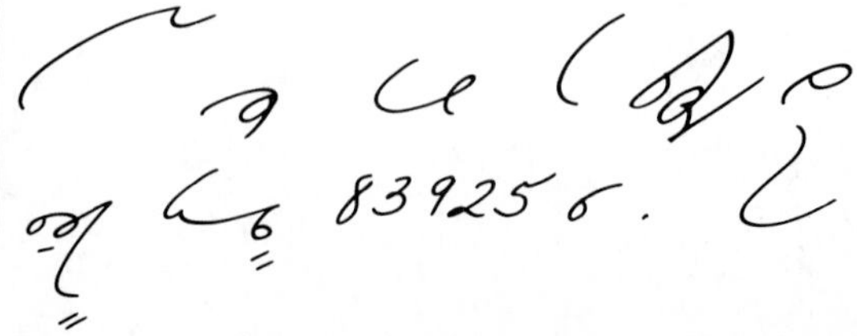

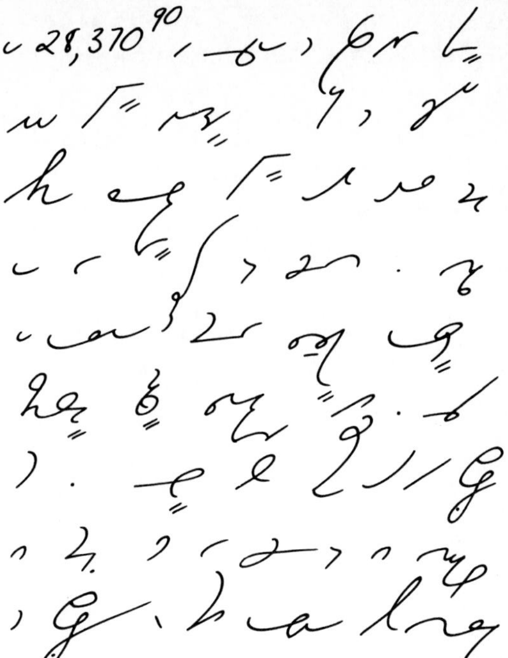

133. MRS. JOHN W. DUNN, 17 SUMMER STREET, SUDBURY, MA 01776

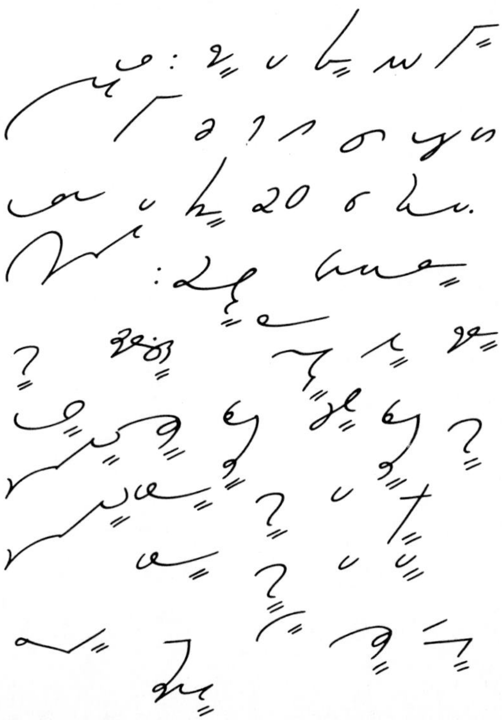

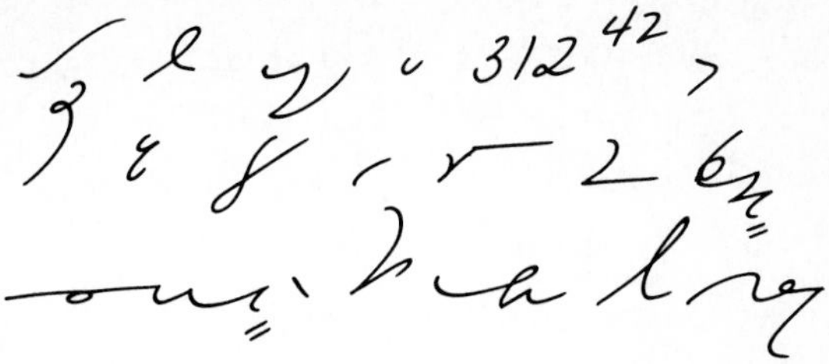

134. MR. JOHN TAYLOR, NATIONAL BANK, 40 WATER STREET, BOSTON, MA 02100

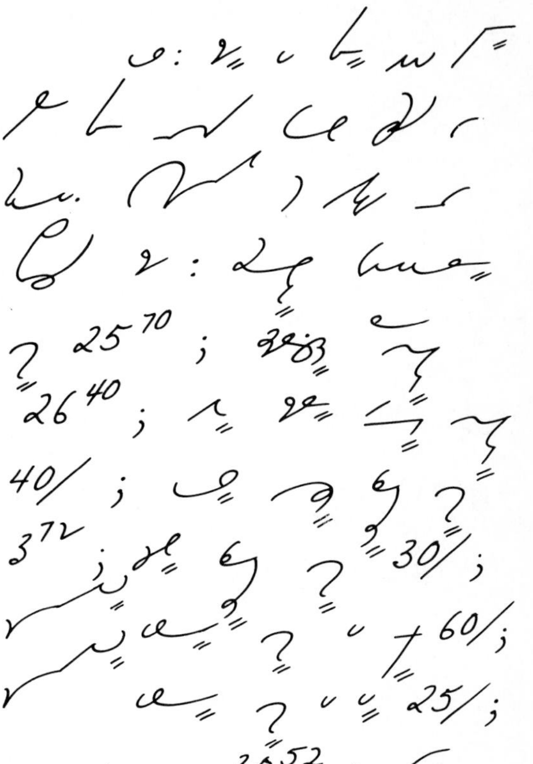

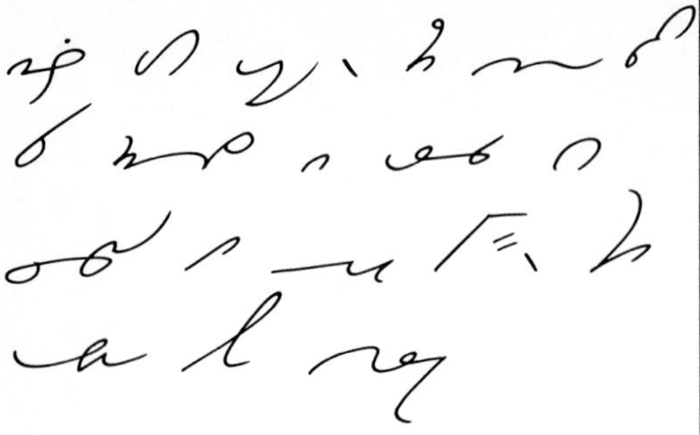

135. MR. C. PAUL DUNN, MAIN STREET, SPRINGFIELD, VT 05156

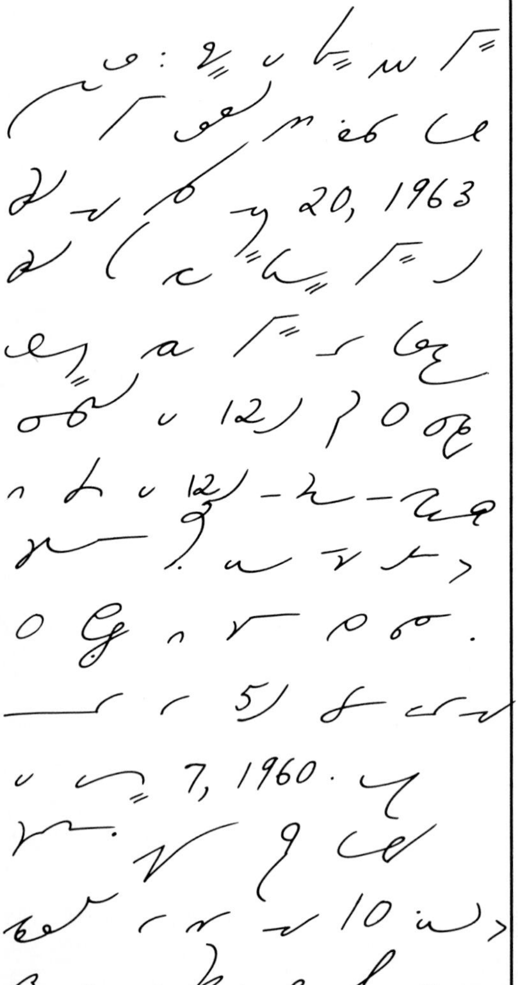

136. MR. JOHN R. TAYLOR, NATIONAL BANK, 40 WATER STREET, BOSTON, MA 02100

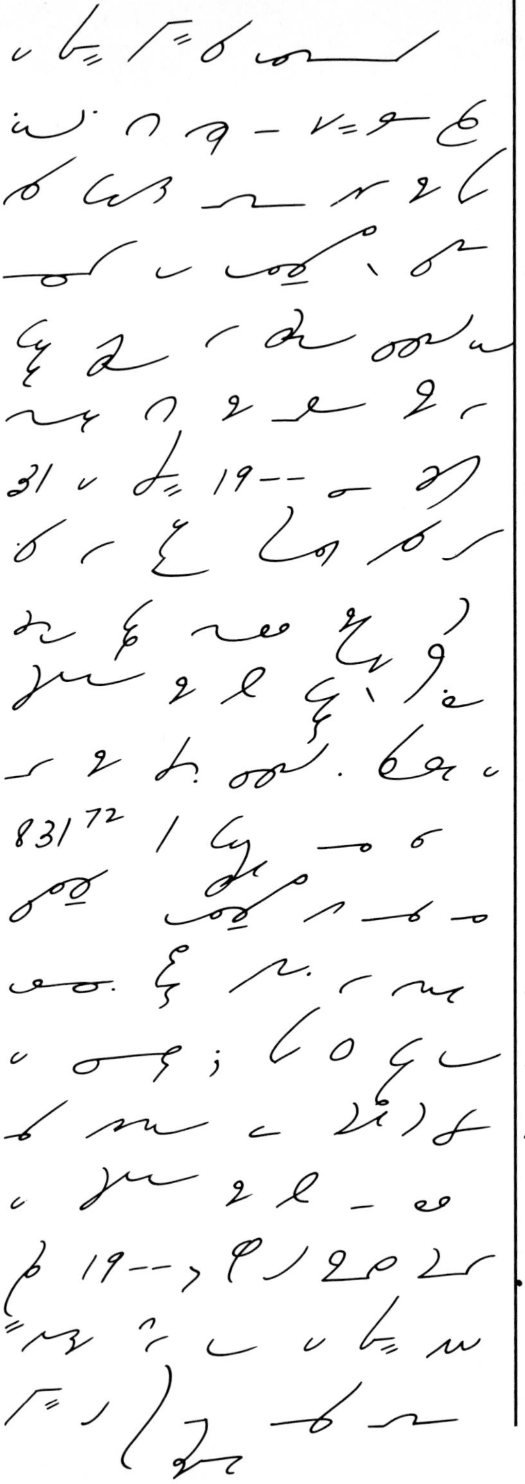

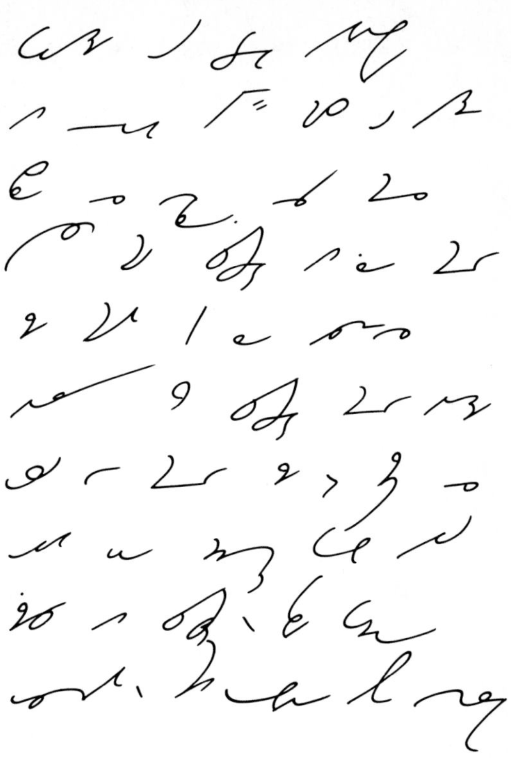

137. MR. DAVID C. DUNN, 780 ELM STREET, MAYNARD, MA 01754

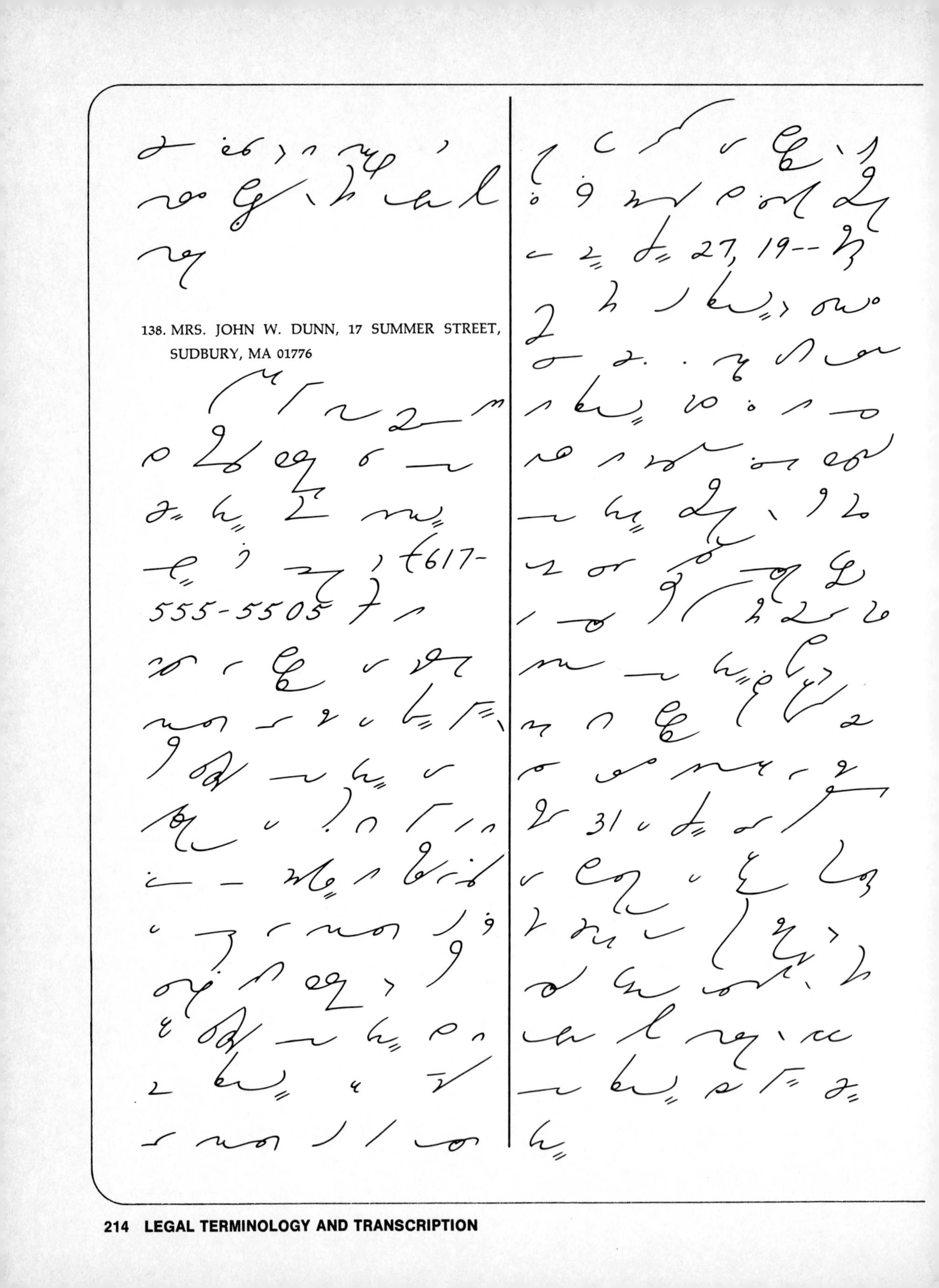

138. MRS. JOHN W. DUNN, 17 SUMMER STREET, SUDBURY, MA 01776

Lesson 48

BUILDING YOUR LEGAL VOCABULARY

Word Endings *-tient* and *-cient* are expressed by  ; *-ciency* is expressed by  .

deficient		**insufficient**	
deficiencies		**patients**	
inefficiently		**efficiency**	

Word Study

 **arrearage** That which is unpaid and overdue.

 **legatees** Ones to whom a bequest is made.

 **quitclaim deed** A deed used to release one person's title, right, or interest to another without providing a warranty of title.

 **salability** The quality or state of being able to be sold.

BUILDING YOUR LEGAL TRANSCRIPTION SKILL

Transcription Aid **Underscore and Italics**

☐ Use the underscore as a substitute for italics in typed material or to indicate to the printer what is to be italicized.

☐ Underscore capital letters when they are used to represent proper names of hypothetical parties or places.

The Buy and Sell Agreement set forth that <u>A</u> agrees to sell and <u>B</u> agrees to buy the hotel property of <u>A</u> consisting of . . . in <u>X</u> township.

☐ Underscore foreign words and phrases that have not become part of the English language.

<u>capias</u> <u>a fortiori</u> <u>nolo contendere</u>

Legal Collocations

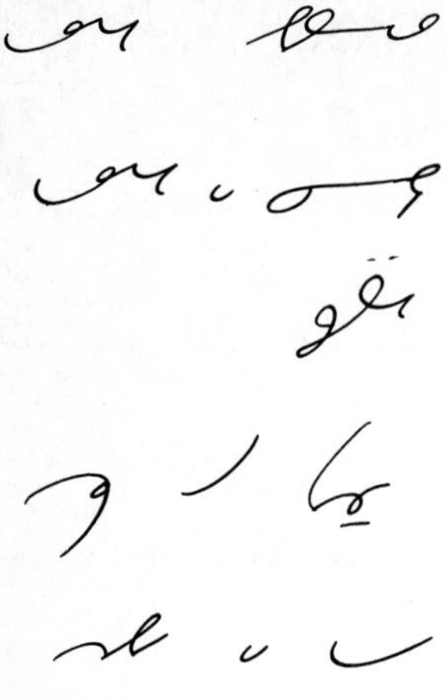

letters testamentary The instrument of authority granted by a court to an executor or executrix.

letters of administration The instrument of authority granted by a court to an administrator or administratrix.

assent of heirs An acknowledgment by the heirs of a willingness to comply with a request; consent; approval.

give and bequeath Term used in a will, leaving certain property to certain heirs.

contest of will A proceeding opposing rights to legatees in the estate of the testator.

BUILDING YOUR LEGAL DICTATION PROFICIENCY

Preview

aggregate

certified

deposit

institution

insured

inter vivos

legal

tentatively

triplicate

waiver

Reading and Writing Practice

139. MR. JOHN R. TAYLOR, NATIONAL BANK, 40 WATER STREET, BOSTON, MA 02100

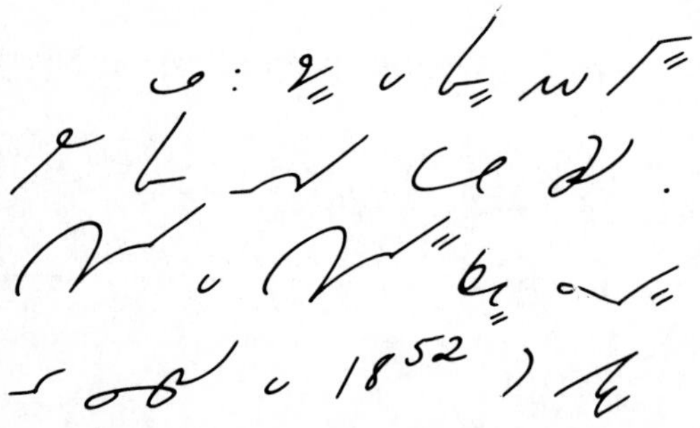

140. MR. WALLACE GREYSTONE, 78 BOSTON POST ROAD, SUDBURY, MA 01776

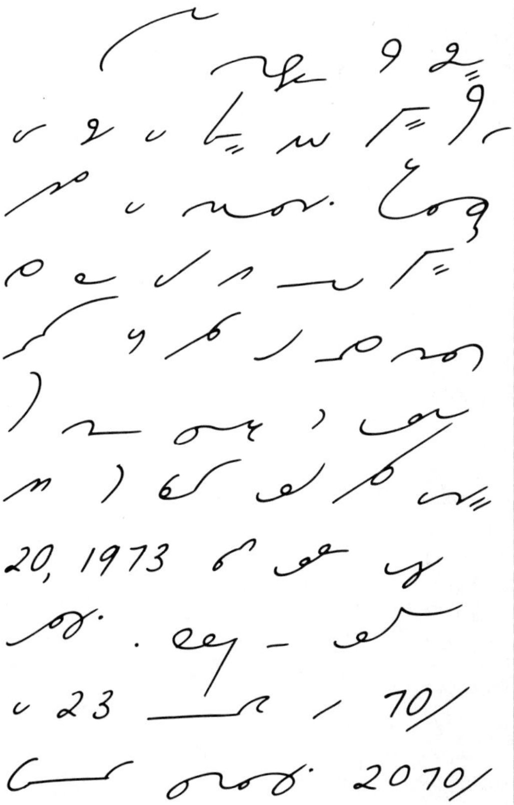

141. VETERANS ADMINISTRATION, 798 MAIN STREET, CONCORD, MA 01742

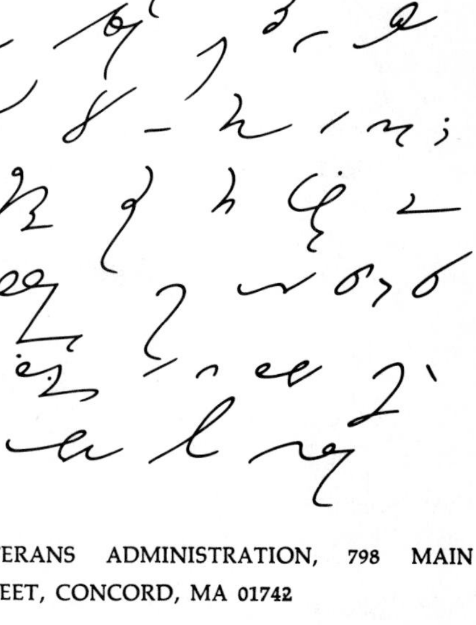

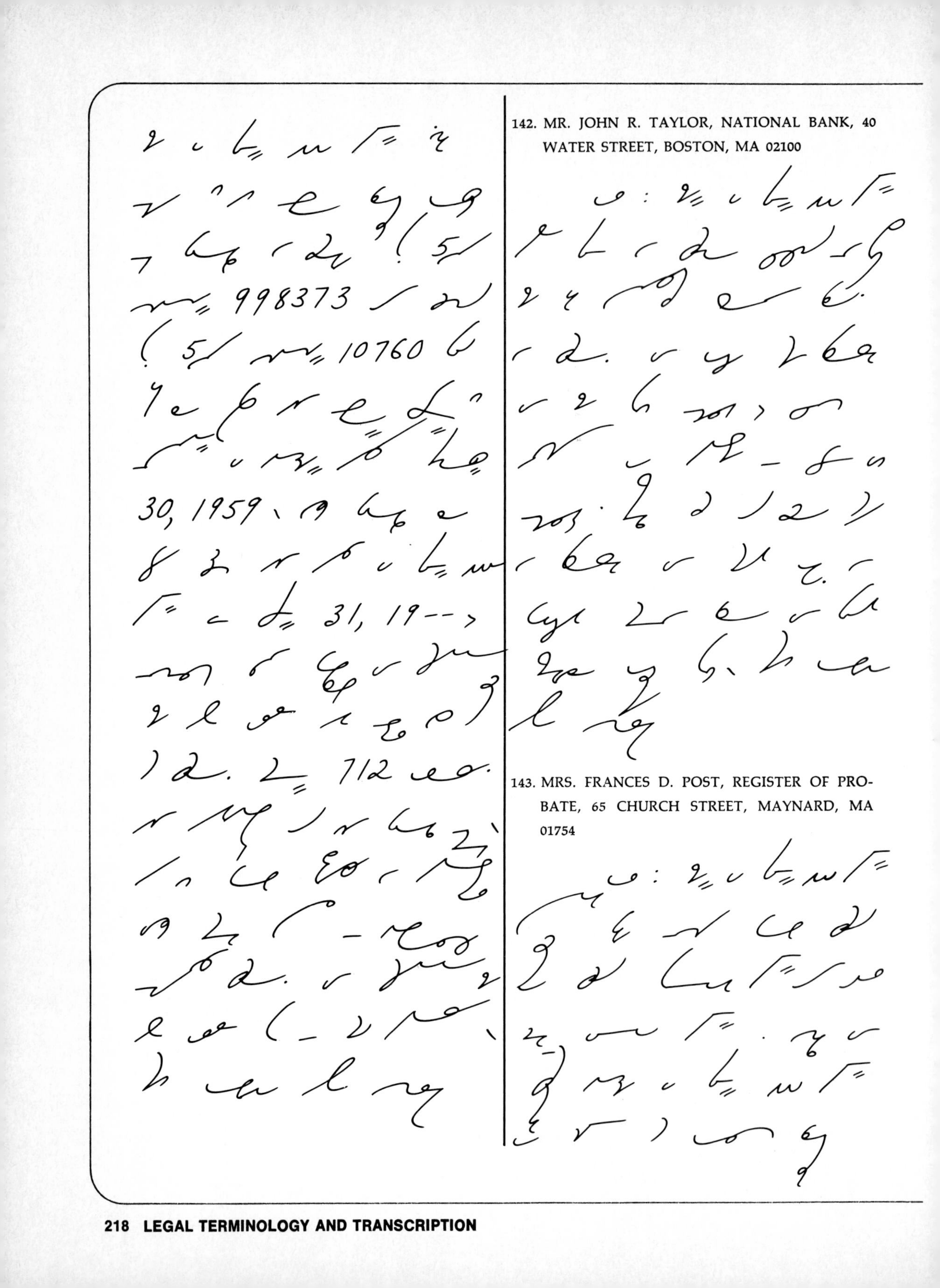

142. MRS. JOHN R. TAYLOR, NATIONAL BANK, 40 WATER STREET, BOSTON, MA 02100

143. MRS. FRANCES D. POST, REGISTER OF PROBATE, 65 CHURCH STREET, MAYNARD, MA 01754

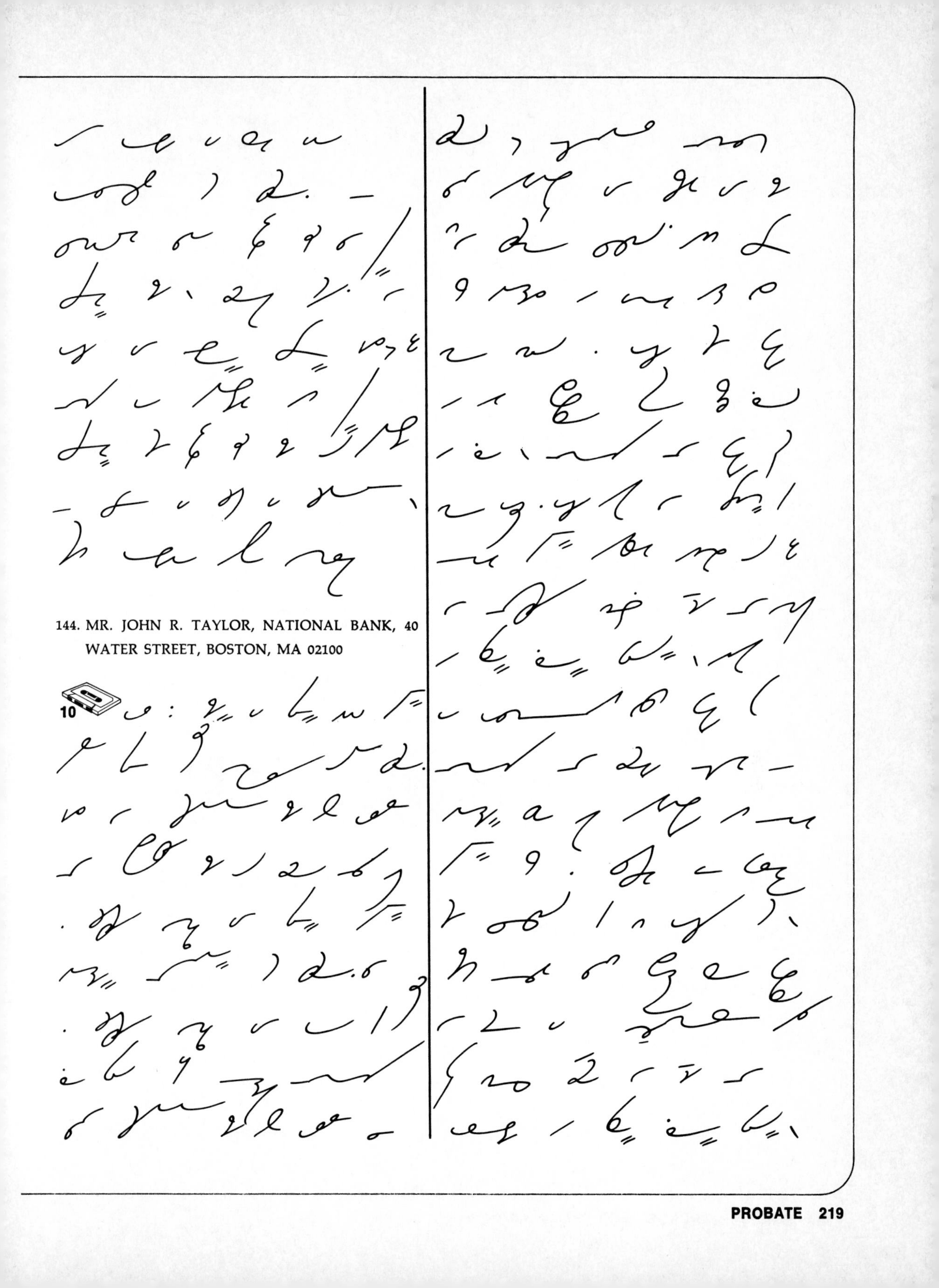

144. MR. JOHN R. TAYLOR, NATIONAL BANK, 40 WATER STREET, BOSTON, MA 02100

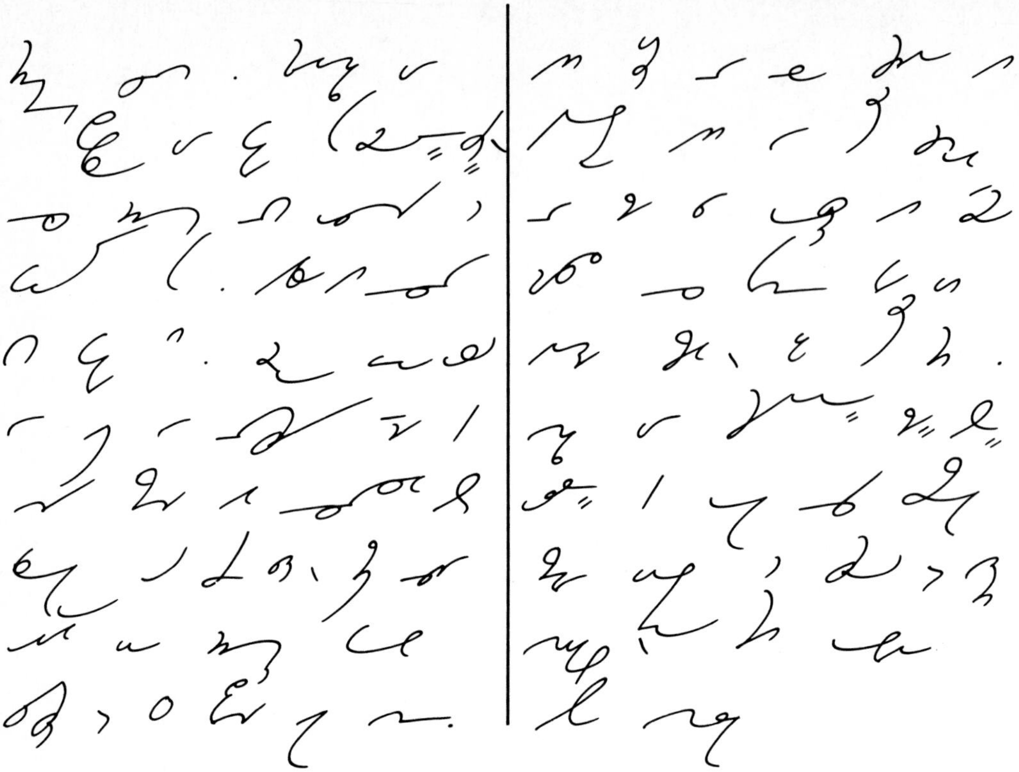

Lesson 49

BUILDING YOUR LEGAL VOCABULARY

Word Endings *-uate* is expressed by ; *-uation* is expressed by .

extenuating

extenuation

situated

actuate

insinuations

fluctuations

Word Study

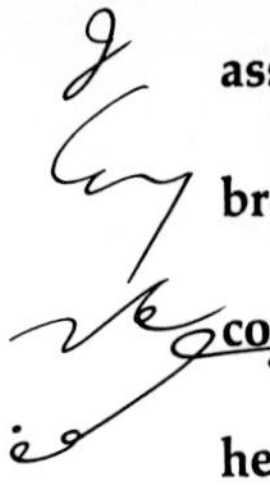

asset Anything owned.

brokerage The fee for transacting business as a broker.

codicil An addition to a will made after the will is executed.

hereditaments Property that can be inherited by another.

BUILDING YOUR LEGAL TRANSCRIPTION SKILL

Transcription Aid

Underscore With Titles of Publications

☐ Underscore the titles of books, periodicals, plays, operas, and the like. In typing citations, however, it is common practice to omit the underscore when referring to periodicals.

> The Manual for the Legal Secretarial Profession was prepared by the National Association of Legal Secretaries.

Underscore for Emphasis

☐ Underscore words, phrases, clauses, or sentences to give them greater prominence or emphasis.

> As Executor, I accept your check for $1200 in full compromise settlement, waiving all interest thereon.

Latin and French Words and Phrases

pur autre vie *(por ō'ter vē')* For or during another's lifetime.

cestui que vie *(ses'twē kē vē')* The person whose life measures the duration of the estate.

cestui *(ses'twē)* (*plu.* **cesuis**) Beneficiary.

BUILDING YOUR LEGAL DICTATION PROFICIENCY

Preview

amended 

computed 

compensate 

depose 

enrichment	official
necessitated	omissions
notification	recomputed

Reading and Writing Practice

10

145. AFFIDAVIT

NOW COMES LESTER L. GREENBERG and in support of the amended Federal Estate Tax return of the John W. Dunn[1] estate filed herewith, does hereby certify and depose as follows:

1. That with respect to assets returned in[2] Schedule B of the original Federal Estate Tax return 60 shares of Tidewater Oil Company were[3] included as an asset of the estate and have subsequently been determined to have been delivered[4] erroneously to the Executor by Johnson & Company, a brokerage company acting for the[5] National Bank of Boston, which bank was servicing an agency account for the late John W. Dunn, Trustee; said Johnson[6] & Company having failed to complete the sale of assets of the Thomas Scott Trust, of which John W. Dunn was[7] trustee during his lifetime and holding inadvertently or by error in its account under the name of[8] John W. Dunn individually 60 shares of Tidewater Oil Company, which shares were delivered on[9] August 8, 19—, to the undersigned as Executor of the estate. That said Executor[10] then and at all times up to the filing of the final account and closing said estate believed the same to[11] have been sole property of John W. Dunn.

That subsequent to the filing of the original Federal Estate[12] Tax return and final accounting in the estate, correspondence from Johnson & Company to the[13] National Bank has determined this was not a proper asset of the estate and as such the estate has been obliged[14] to return the same, for which reason it should not have been properly included in the original return. (299)

(Continued in Lesson 50.)

146. MR. M. E. DOWNS, ASSISTANT TRUST OFFICER, NATIONAL BANK, 40 WATER STREET, BOSTON, MA 02100

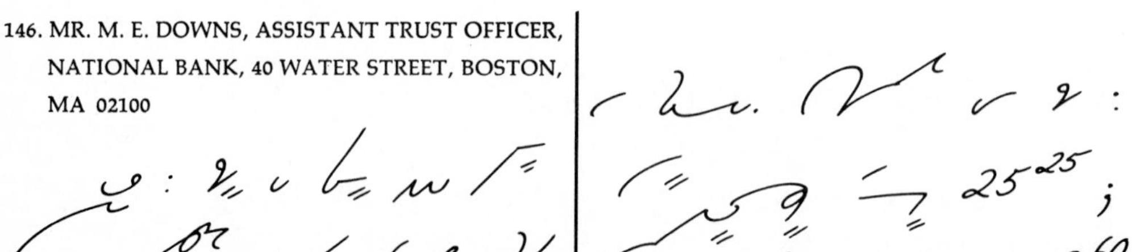

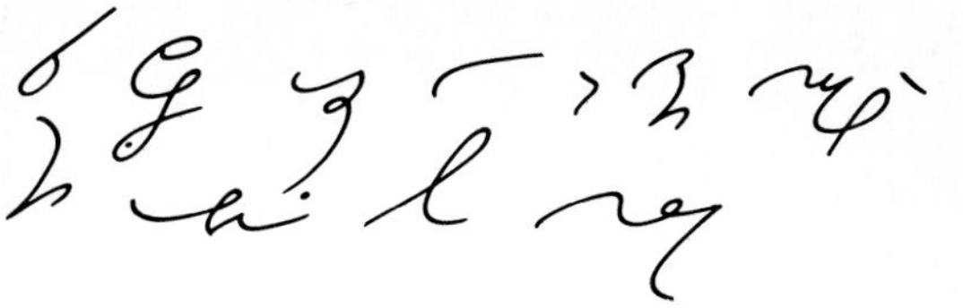

147. MR. M. E. DOWNS, ASSISTANT TRUST OFFICER, NATIONAL BANK, 40 WATER STREET, BOSTON, MA 02100

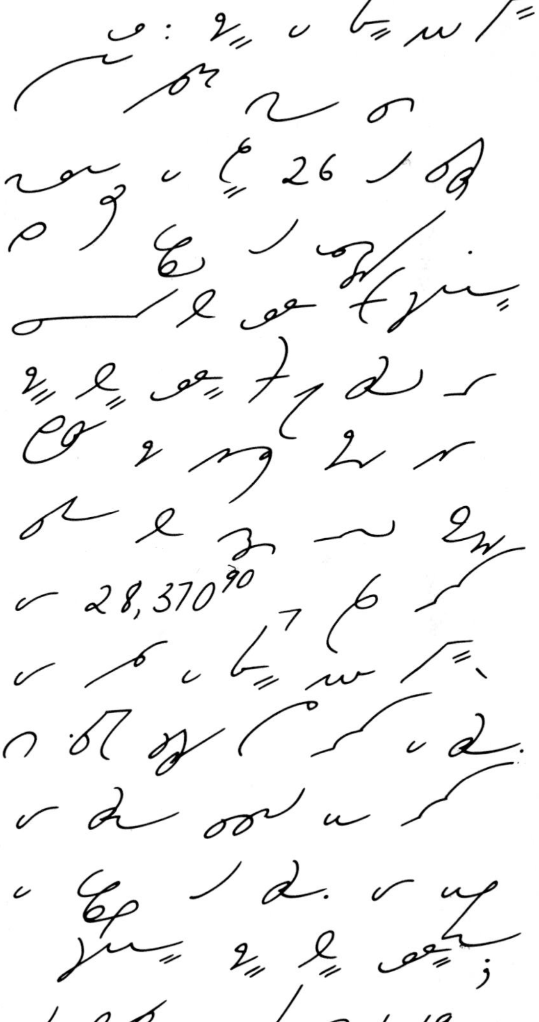

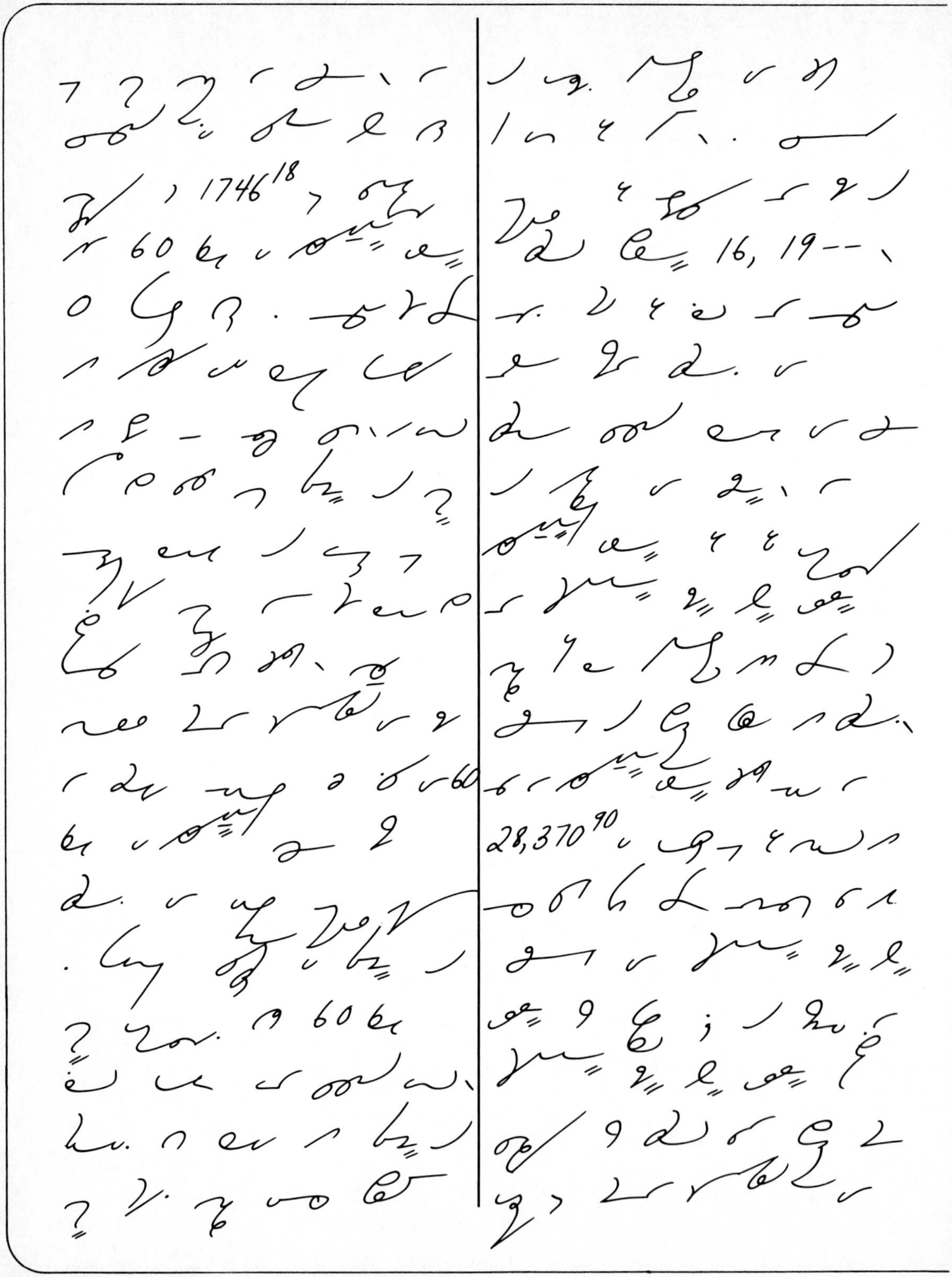

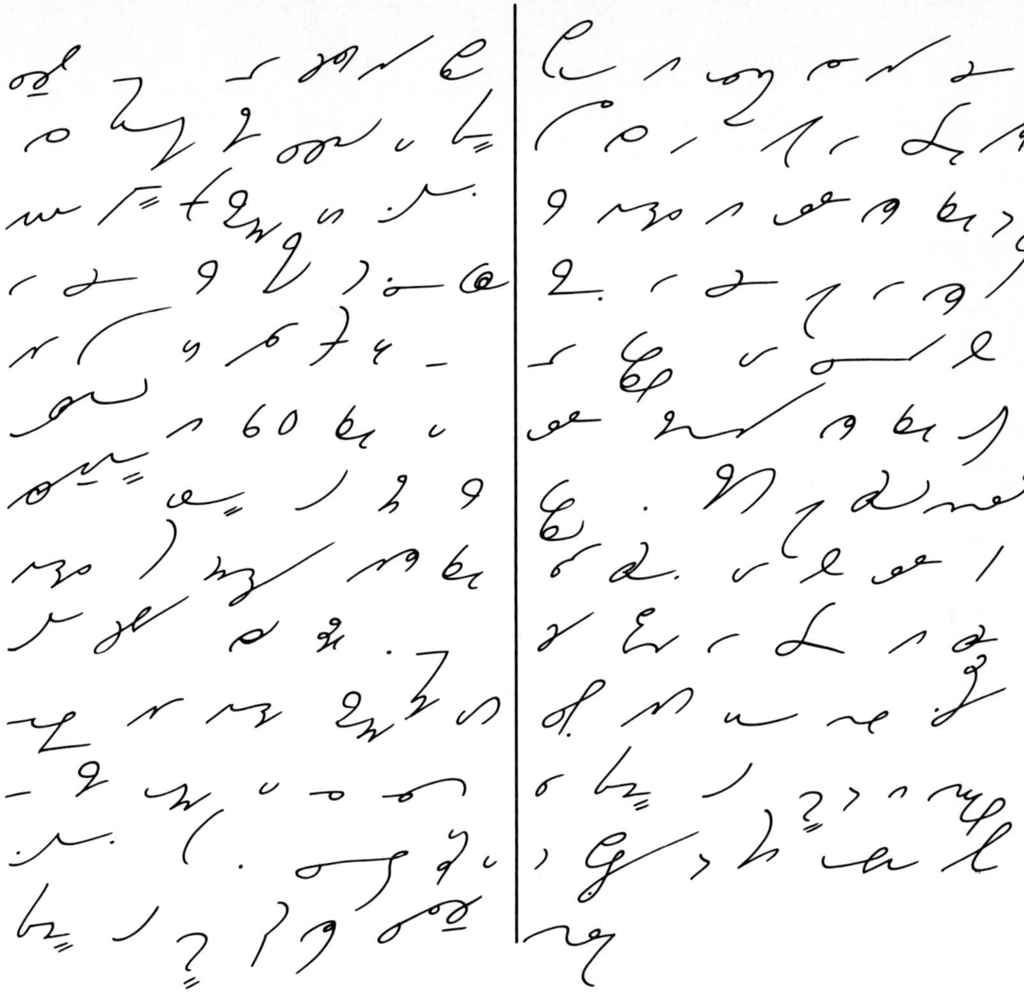

Lesson 50

BUILDING YOUR LEGAL VOCABULARY

Word Family *-age* is expressed by .

demurrage  marriage 

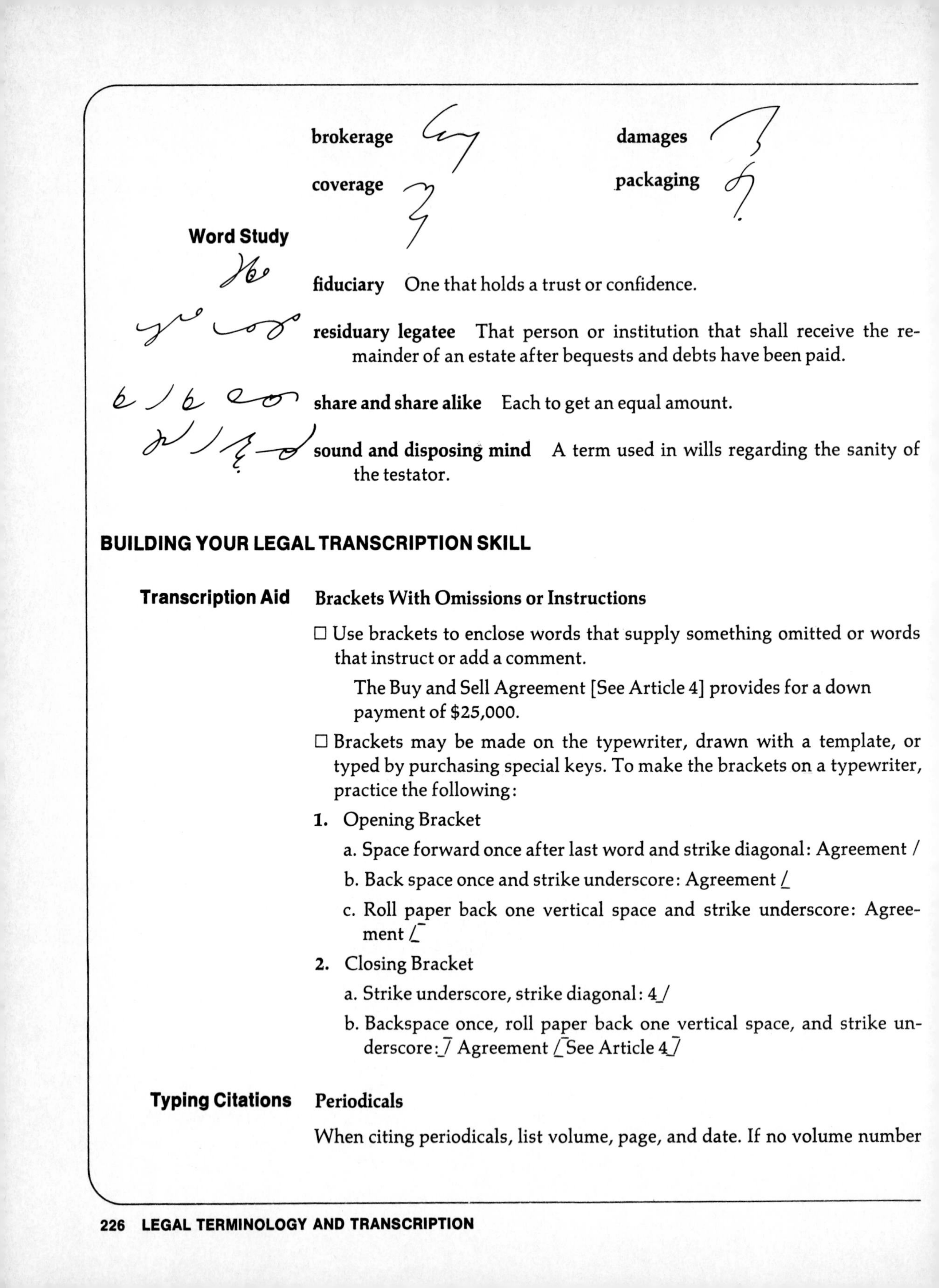

brokerage **damages**

coverage **packaging**

Word Study

fiduciary One that holds a trust or confidence.

residuary legatee That person or institution that shall receive the remainder of an estate after bequests and debts have been paid.

share and share alike Each to get an equal amount.

sound and disposing mind A term used in wills regarding the sanity of the testator.

BUILDING YOUR LEGAL TRANSCRIPTION SKILL

Transcription Aid

Brackets With Omissions or Instructions

☐ Use brackets to enclose words that supply something omitted or words that instruct or add a comment.

The Buy and Sell Agreement [See Article 4] provides for a down payment of $25,000.

☐ Brackets may be made on the typewriter, drawn with a template, or typed by purchasing special keys. To make the brackets on a typewriter, practice the following:

1. Opening Bracket

a. Space forward once after last word and strike diagonal: Agreement /

b. Back space once and strike underscore: Agreement /_

c. Roll paper back one vertical space and strike underscore: Agreement /‾

2. Closing Bracket

a. Strike underscore, strike diagonal: 4_/

b. Backspace once, roll paper back one vertical space, and strike underscore: _7 Agreement /‾See Article 4_7

Typing Citations

Periodicals

When citing periodicals, list volume, page, and date. If no volume number is given, show the date of publication. Use standard abbreviations for periodicals from reference books listed in Lesson 10.

9 J. Legal Ed. 344 (1967)

When citing articles appearing in periodicals, cite by author, title, volume, and page. Underscore the title of the article. Do not give initials of the author unless they are needed to prevent misunderstanding.

Brimmer, Drug Procedures Re-Examined, 9 J. Legal Ed. 344 (1967)

BUILDING YOUR LEGAL DICTATION PROFICIENCY

Preview

advise 

assessed 

calendar 

diligently 

intelligence 

legatee 

registered 

subscribed 

supplementary 

waived 

Reading and Writing Practice

10

148. AFFIDAVIT *(Continued from Lesson 49)*

2. That under Schedule D of the Federal Estate Tax return as originally filed, were included all[1] insurance policies known to the Executor as having been originally affixed to an *inter vivos*[2] trust indenture dated July 30, 19—, into which the assets of the estate[3] of John W. Dunn were poured in connection with his will dated July 30, 19—, that at[4] the outset of administration the Executor wrote to the National Bank, Trustee, requesting the necessary[5] Forms 712 from the several insurance companies relating to all insurance to[6] be scheduled and included in the Federal Estate Tax return; that the Forms 712 were checked against the[7] original trust and appeared to be complete; and the Executor diligently filed the same together with[8] all then furnished supporting documents, said Bank having obtained and furnished the same during the months of March and[9] April of 19— and May of 19—.

Subsequent to the filing of[10] the Federal Estate Tax return and the closing of the estate, the Executor was advised of the existence[11] of a further Equitable Life Insurance Contract 4689, which had been delivered by John W.[12] Dunn to the Trustee without knowledge of the Executor during his lifetime and subsequent to the execution[13] of the original trust. Proceeds of this policy should have been included as a proper asset under[14] Schedule D, and the Executor accordingly wrote to the company for the necessary Form[15] 712 and attached hereto amended Schedule D in accord therewith.

The foregoing changes relate to the[16] only matters known to the Executor not originally included in the filing of the original tax[17] return and payment of the tax required, and the Executor in filing the amended tax return including[18] the foregoing assets and adjustments does pay herewith the sum of $1,742.68[19] representing the difference in tax from that originally computed and filed and[20] accepted earlier by Internal Revenue Service. Since the foregoing has turned up through accident,[21] mistake, and misfortune and out of circumstances over which the Executor had no control, he respectfully[22] requests that the interest and penalties thereon be waived.

COMMONWEALTH OF MASSACHUSETTS

Subscribed and sworn to,[23] before me, this 12th day of December, 19—.

____

Notary Public

My commission expires[24] February 15, 19—. (489)

149. MR. M. E. DOWNS, ASSISTANT TRUST OFFICER, NATIONAL BANK, 40 WATER STREET, BOSTON, MA 02100

150. MR. M. E. DOWNS, ASSISTANT TRUST OFFICER, NATIONAL BANK, 40 WATER STREET, BOSTON, MA 02100

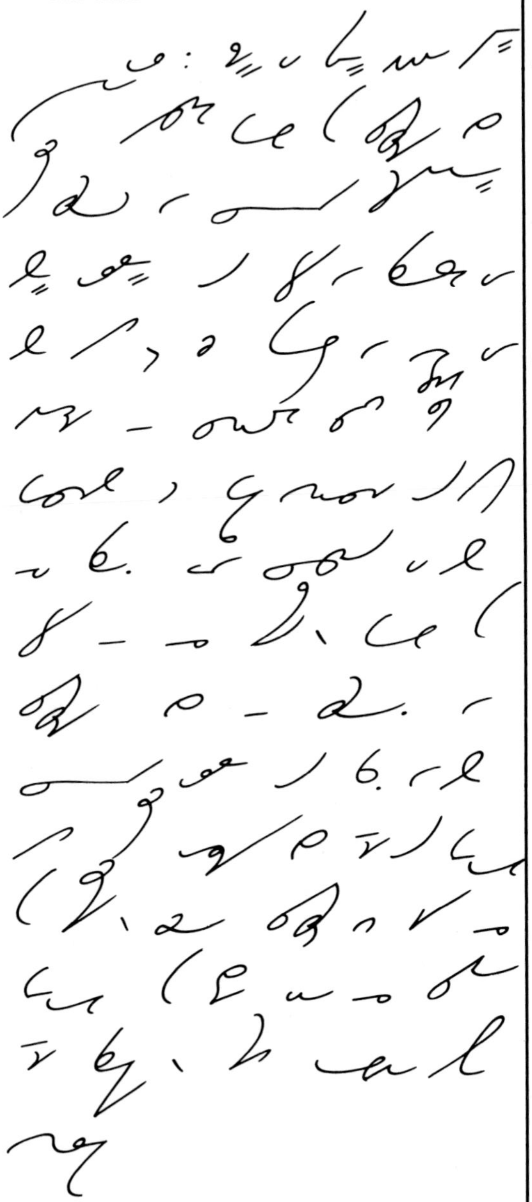

151. MR. M. E. DOWNS, ASSISTANT TRUST OFFICER, NATIONAL BANK, 40 WATER STREET, BOSTON, MA 02100

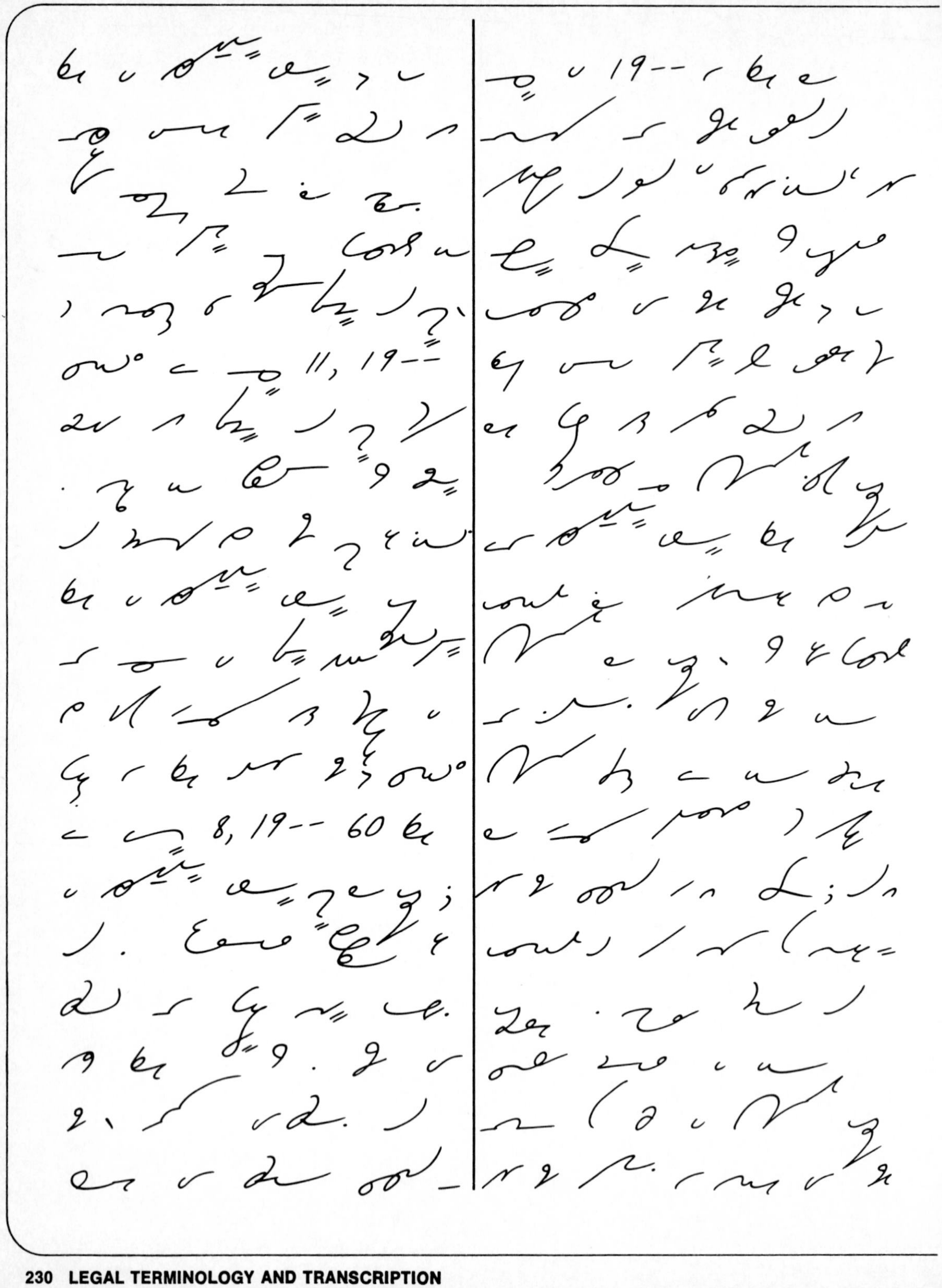

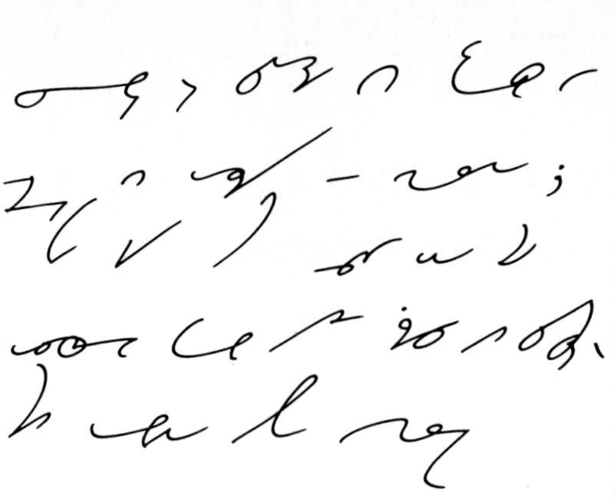

152. MR. JOHN R. TAYLOR, NATIONAL BANK, 40 WATER STREET, BOSTON, MA 02100

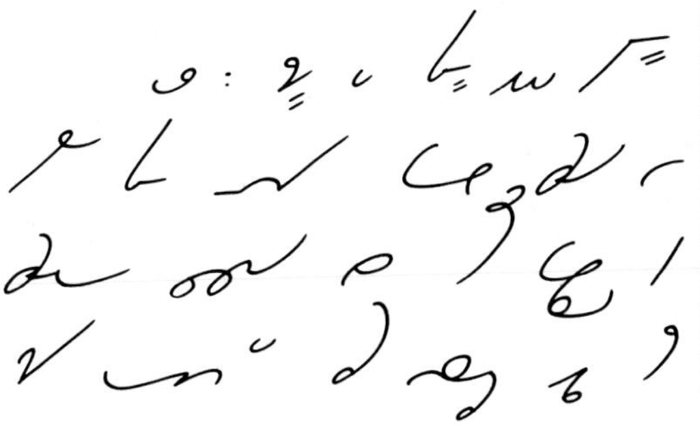

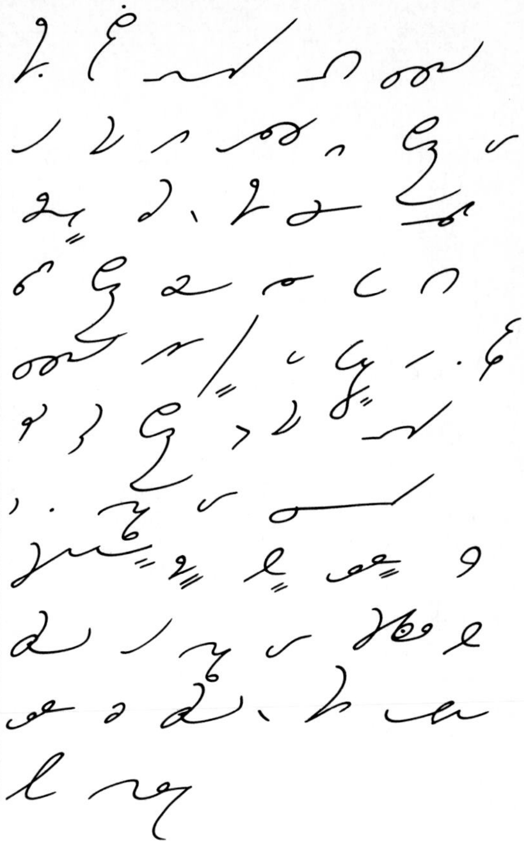

UNIT

6 Corporations

Hunter's, Inc.

The memoranda, correspondence, and legal papers in this unit concern the formation, operation, and dissolution of a small corporation, Hunter's, Inc. The assets of the corporation consist of a resort hotel with a golf course and ski tow facilities and of farm property to be developed into building lots.

Roger L. Mason, Esq., is the attorney and clerk for the corporation.

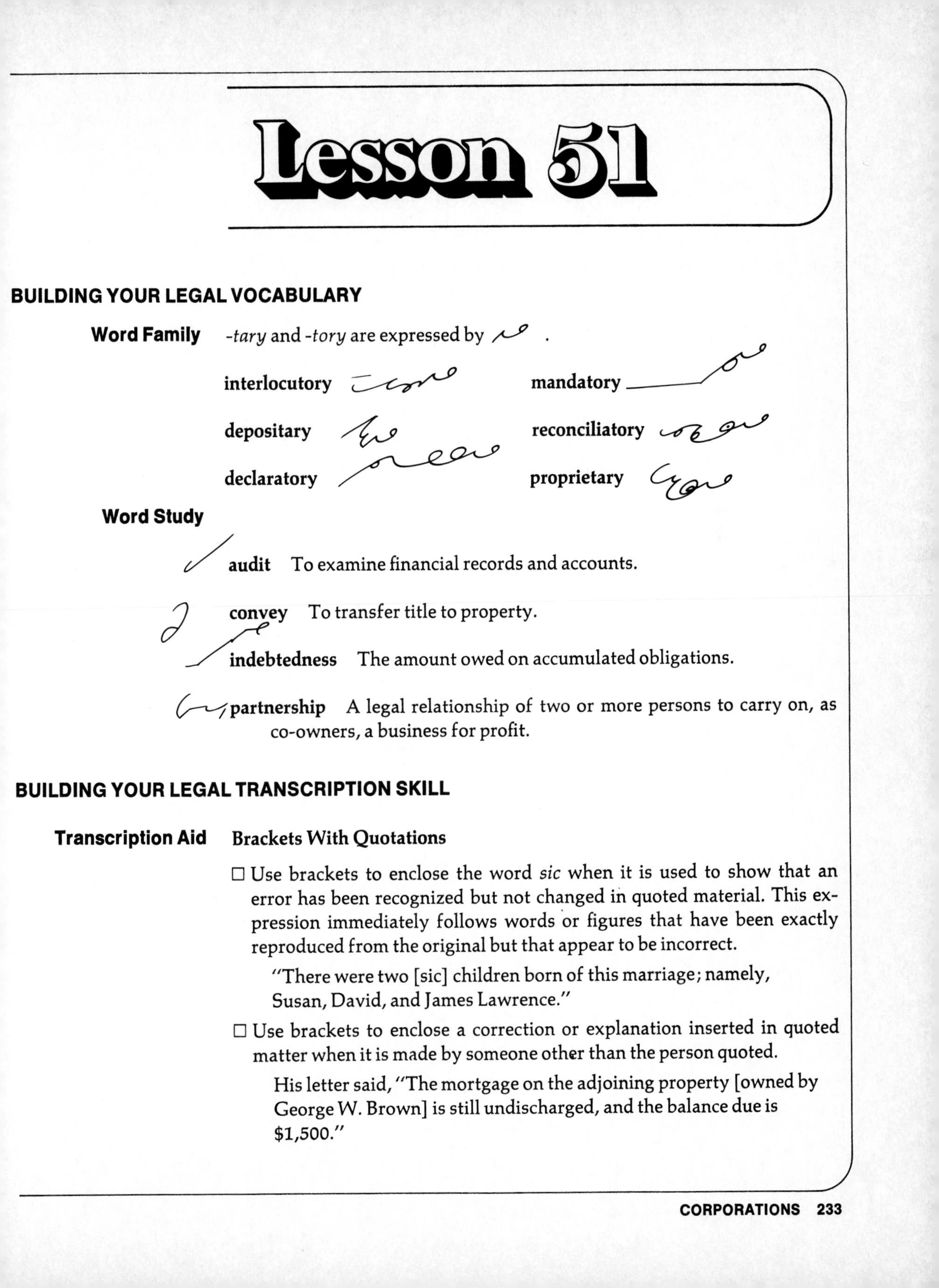

Lesson 51

BUILDING YOUR LEGAL VOCABULARY

Word Family -*tary* and -*tory* are expressed by .

interlocutory

mandatory

depositary

reconciliatory

declaratory

proprietary

Word Study

audit To examine financial records and accounts.

convey To transfer title to property.

indebtedness The amount owed on accumulated obligations.

partnership A legal relationship of two or more persons to carry on, as co-owners, a business for profit.

BUILDING YOUR LEGAL TRANSCRIPTION SKILL

Transcription Aid **Brackets With Quotations**

☐ Use brackets to enclose the word *sic* when it is used to show that an error has been recognized but not changed in quoted material. This expression immediately follows words or figures that have been exactly reproduced from the original but that appear to be incorrect.

> "There were two [sic] children born of this marriage; namely, Susan, David, and James Lawrence."

☐ Use brackets to enclose a correction or explanation inserted in quoted matter when it is made by someone other than the person quoted.

> His letter said, "The mortgage on the adjoining property [owned by George W. Brown] is still undischarged, and the balance due is $1,500."

Typing Citations Contractions may be used instead of abbreviations in most legal work, but they are preferred in law reviews. In a contraction, an apostrophe indicates missing letters; the last letter must be the same as the one in the full word; and the contraction is not followed by a period.

Lefelt v. Nasarow 71 N.J. Super. Ct. 438, 549, 555, aff'd 76 N.J. Super Ct. 576

BUILDING YOUR LEGAL DICTATION PROFICIENCY

Preview

audited
bequeathed
cancellation
conveying
corporation
disbursements
forthwith
heretofore

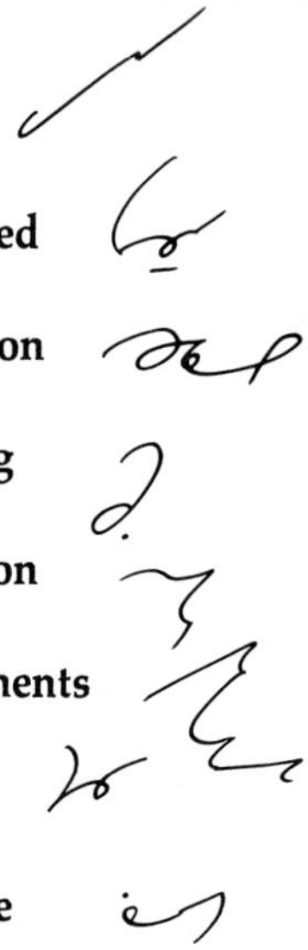

legatee
presumed
property
proprietor
refinancing
residuary
revoked
supervision

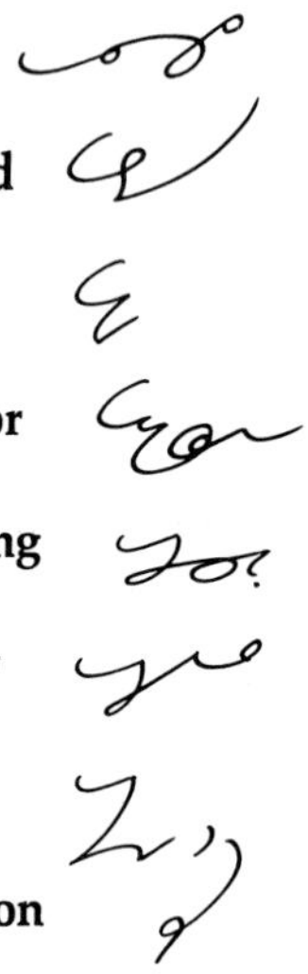

Reading and Writing Practice

153. MEMORANDUM RE: HUNTER'S

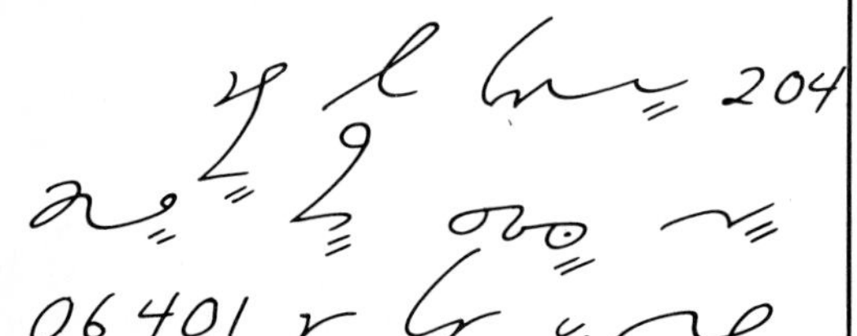

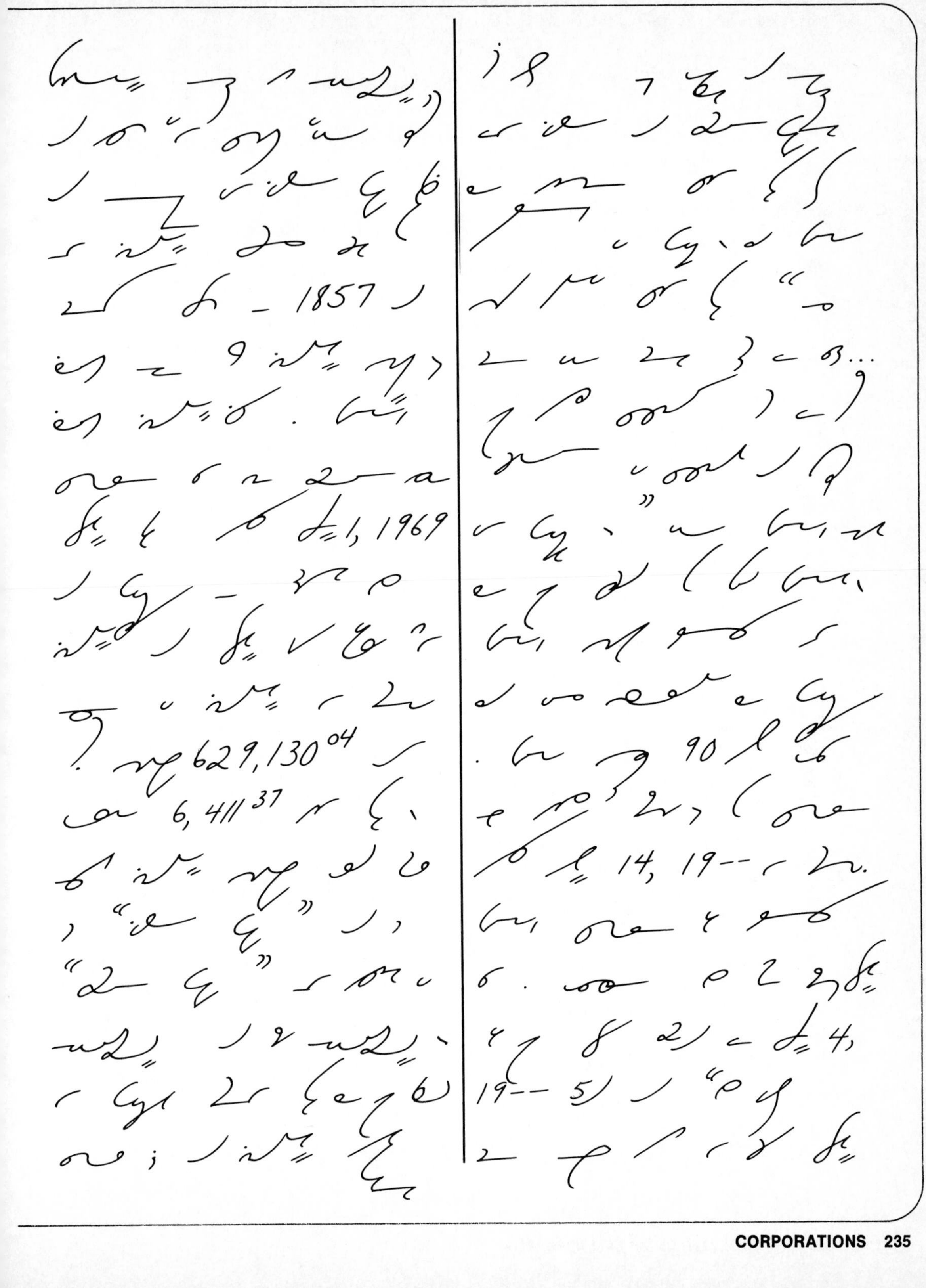

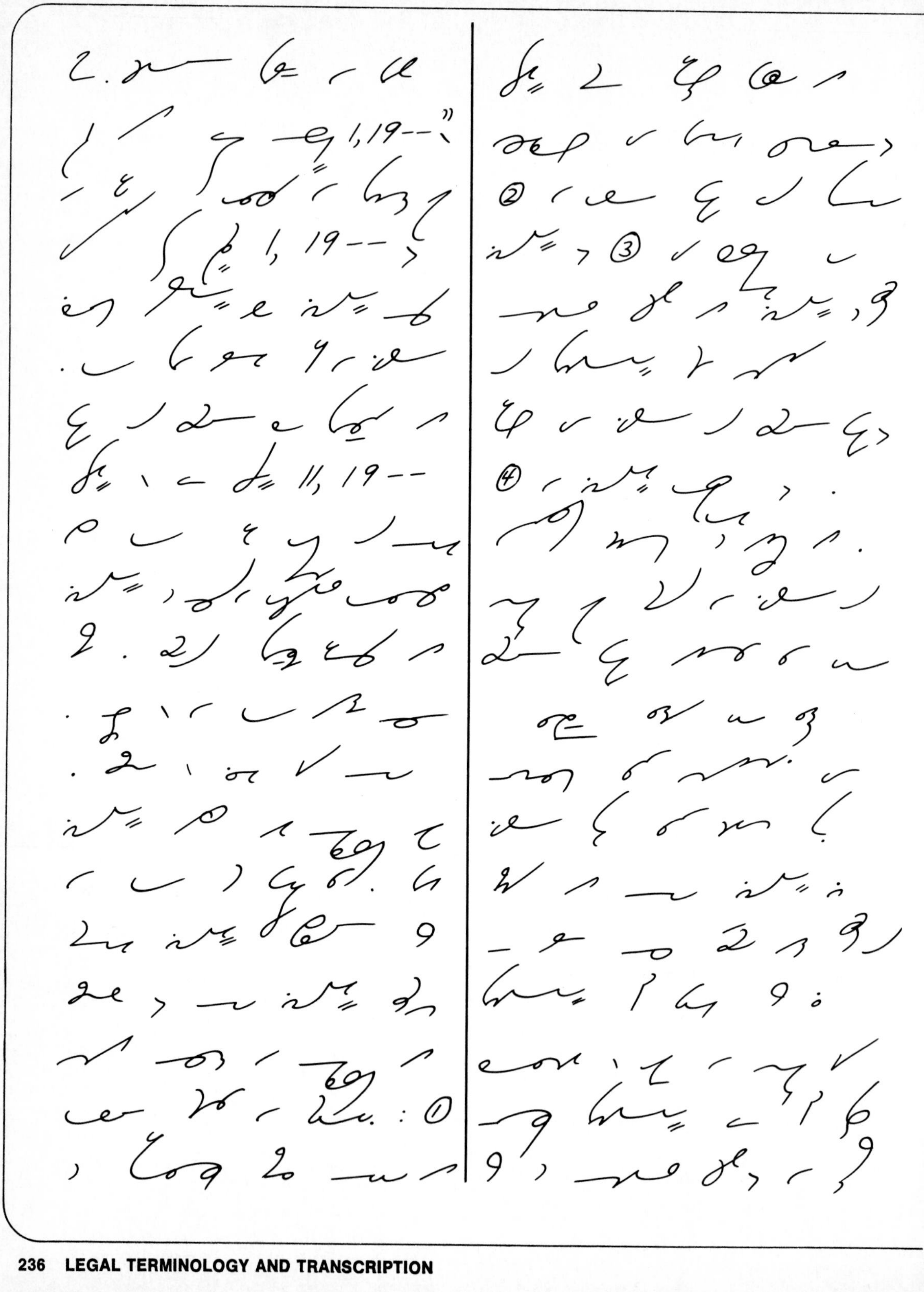

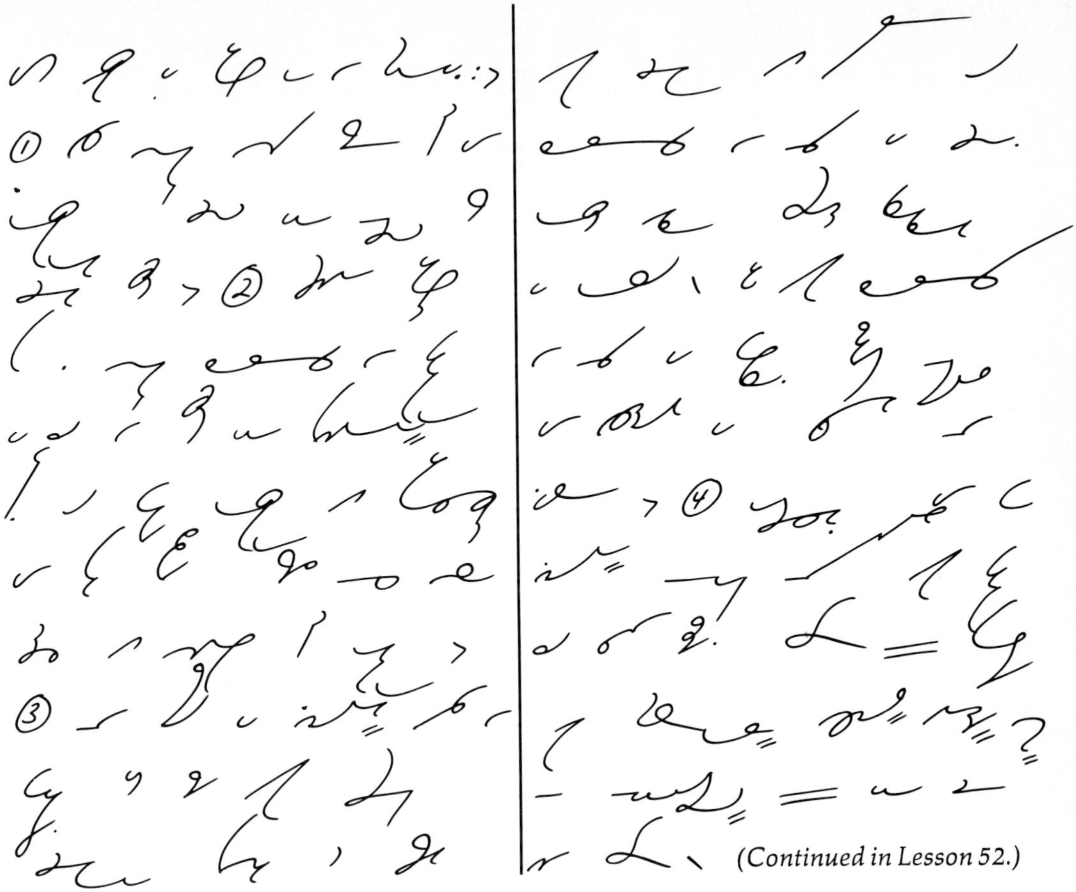

(Continued in Lesson 52.)

Lesson 52

BUILDING YOUR LEGAL VOCABULARY

Word Family *-or* is expressed by or .

lessor	contractor
assignor	minor
guarantor	survivor

Word Study

bylaws Self-enacted rules governing an organization.

conveyance An instrument used to transfer titles to property.

countersigned A signature added to attest authenticity.

debenture Bond; corporate security.

deed An instrument used in transferring title to real property.

BUILDING YOUR LEGAL TRANSCRIPTION SKILL

Transcription Aid

Correct use of the possessive case marks the careful writer. The rules for good usage of possessives are presented in this and in the next four lessons.

Possessive: Compound Nouns

☐ The possessive form of a compound noun is formed by adding the apostrophe and *s* to the last element.

The Secretary-Treasurer's report   the Notary Public's seal

Possessive: Abbreviations

☐ The possessive of an abbreviation is formed by adding the apostrophe and *s* if the abbreviation is singular but only the apostrophe if the abbreviation is plural.

W. N. Page, Jr.'s accident   CIA's representative

the M.D.s' testimony *(plu.)*

Legal Collocations

articles of incorporation The instrument constituting and organizing a private corporation under general corporation laws.

attorney in fact Person appointed to have the authority to act for another in specified matters.

board of directors The body entrusted with authority to conduct the business of a corporation.

fee simple "Estate in fee simple," an absolute title to land clear of any limitations or restrictions on right of transfer.

waiver of notice An instrument evidencing the act of voluntarily relinquishing the right to receive notice.

BUILDING YOUR LEGAL DICTATION PROFICIENCY

Preview

accounts payable 

depreciated 

acquisition 

outstanding 

assessed 

secured 

delegated 

valuation 

Reading and Writing Practice

154. MEMORANDUM *(Continued from Lesson 51.)*

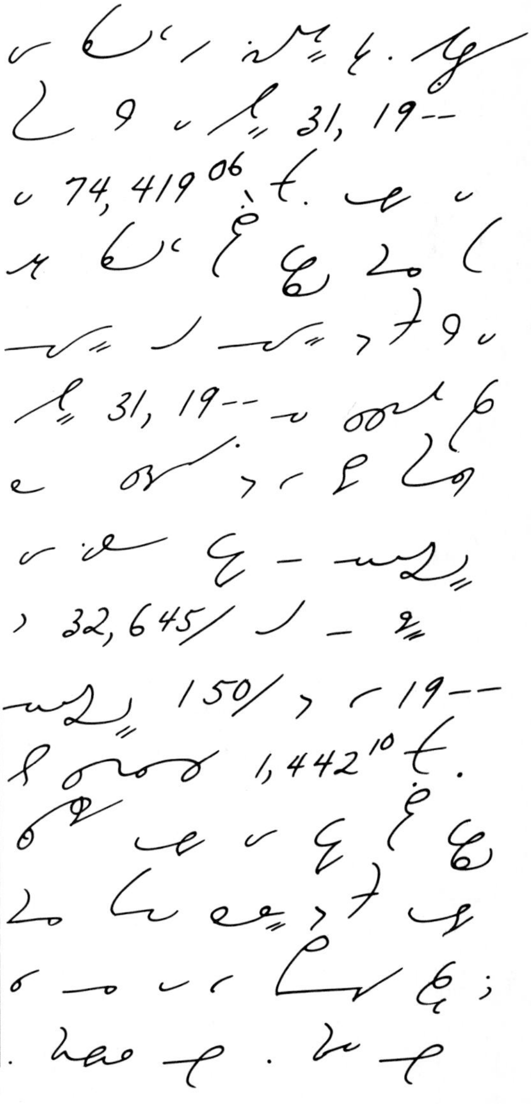

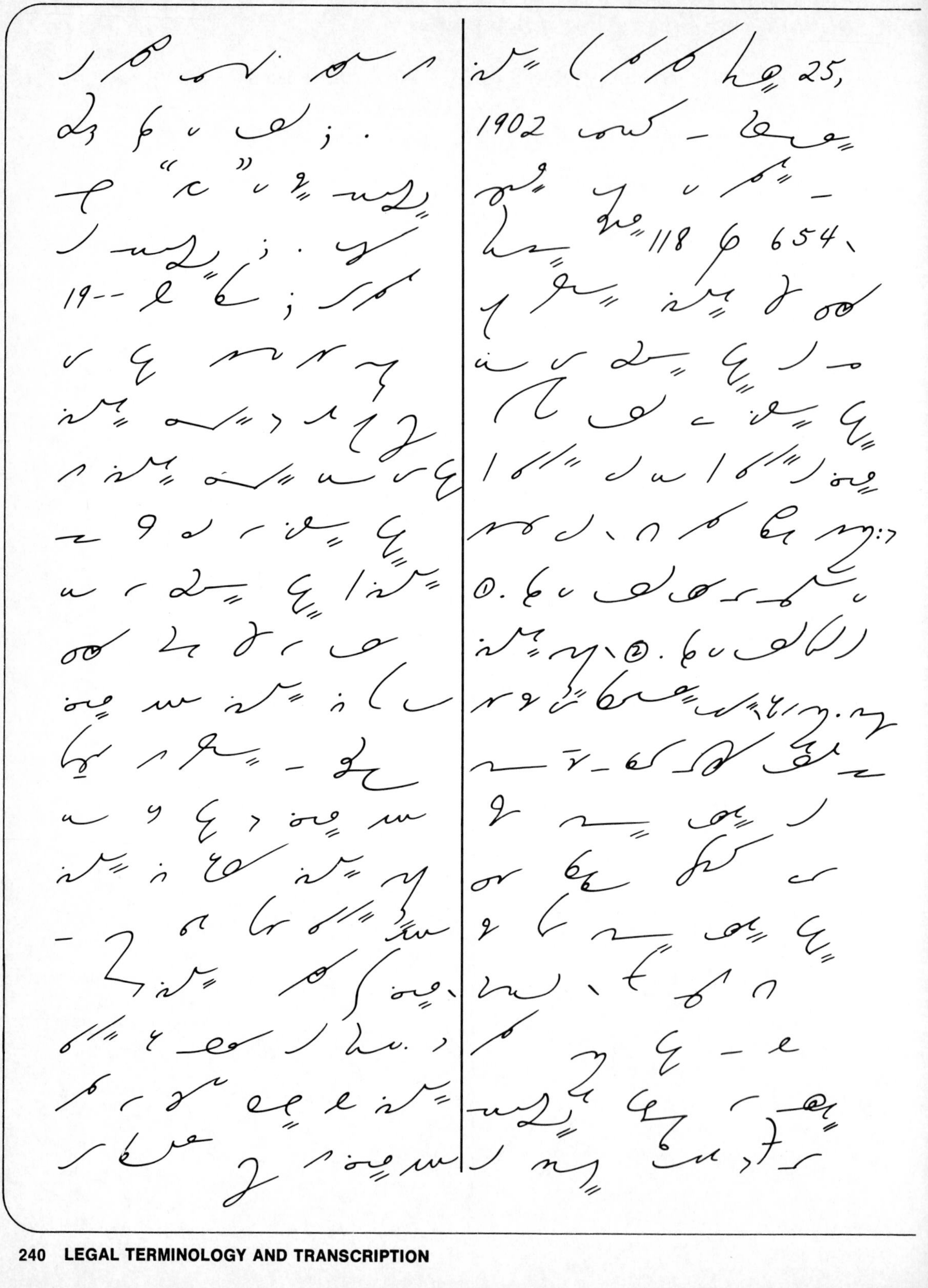

155. MR. STEVEN L. BUTLER, NORTHFIELD, MA 01360

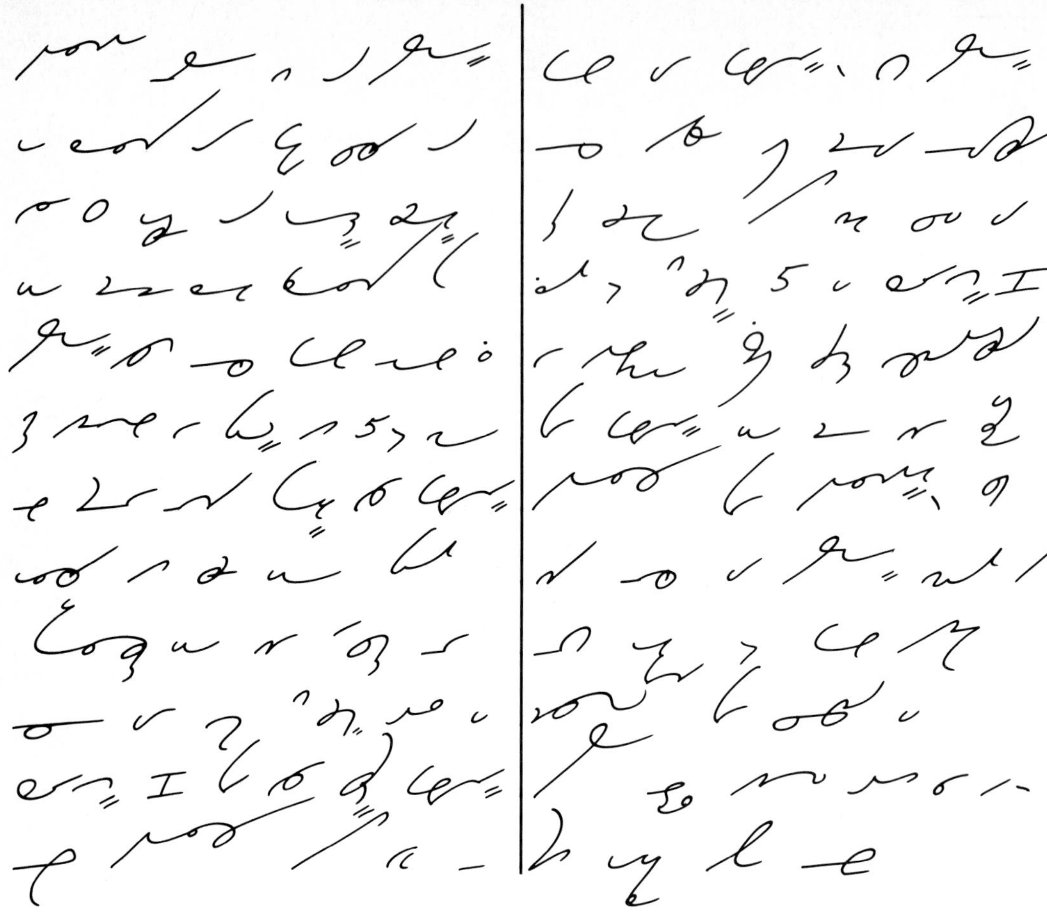

Lesson 53

BUILDING YOUR LEGAL VOCABULARY

Word Family *-ous*, *-eous*, and *-ious* are expressed by or .

erroneously 

felonious 

libelous 

slanderous 

infamously 

polygamous 

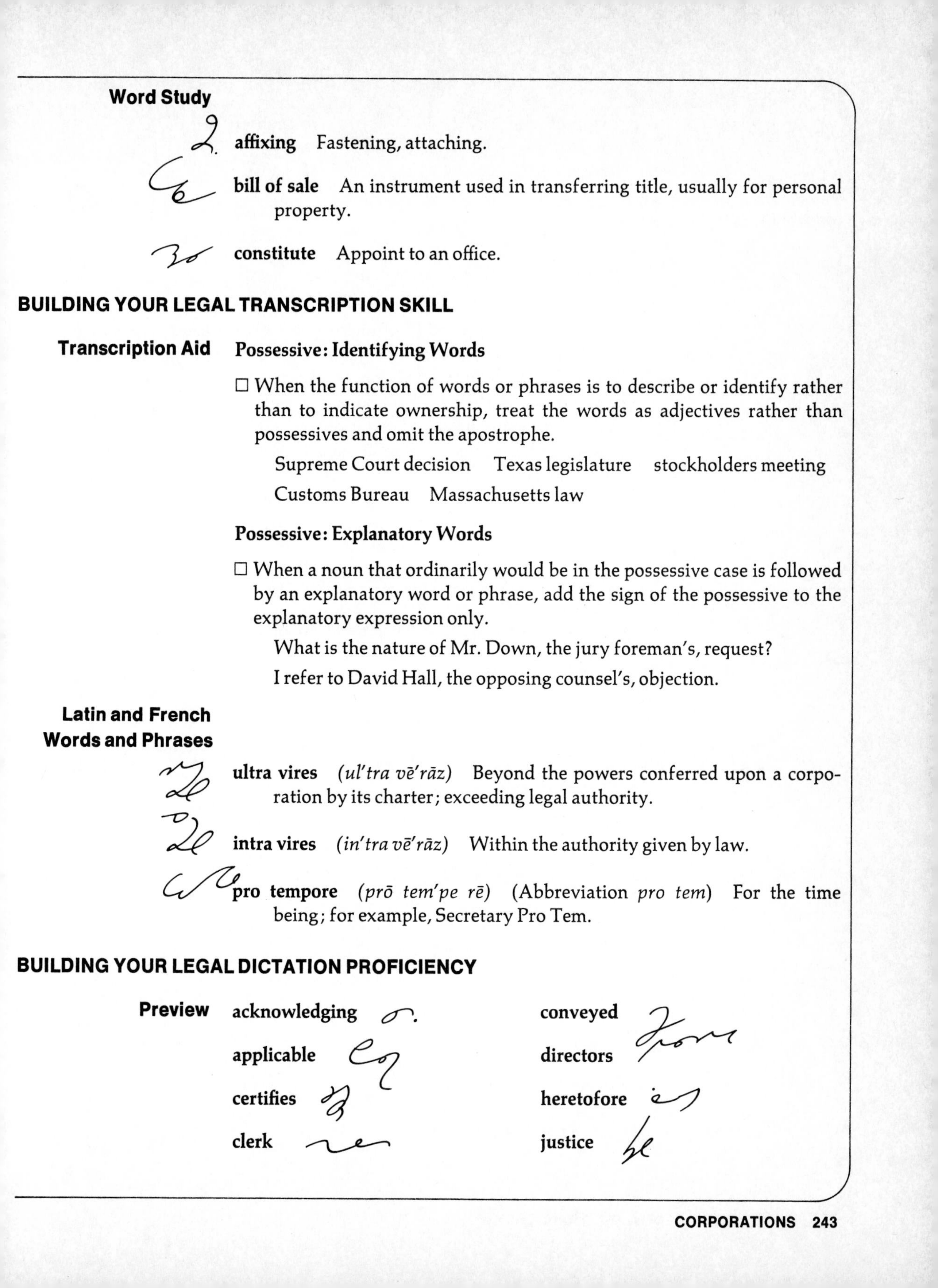

Word Study

affixing Fastening, attaching.

bill of sale An instrument used in transferring title, usually for personal property.

constitute Appoint to an office.

BUILDING YOUR LEGAL TRANSCRIPTION SKILL

Transcription Aid

Possessive: Identifying Words

☐ When the function of words or phrases is to describe or identify rather than to indicate ownership, treat the words as adjectives rather than possessives and omit the apostrophe.

Supreme Court decision   Texas legislature   stockholders meeting
Customs Bureau   Massachusetts law

Possessive: Explanatory Words

☐ When a noun that ordinarily would be in the possessive case is followed by an explanatory word or phrase, add the sign of the possessive to the explanatory expression only.

What is the nature of Mr. Down, the jury foreman's, request?

I refer to David Hall, the opposing counsel's, objection.

Latin and French Words and Phrases

ultra vires *(ul'tra vē'rāz)* Beyond the powers conferred upon a corporation by its charter; exceeding legal authority.

intra vires *(in'tra vē'rāz)* Within the authority given by law.

pro tempore *(prō tem'pe rē)* (Abbreviation *pro tem*) For the time being; for example, Secretary Pro Tem.

BUILDING YOUR LEGAL DICTATION PROFICIENCY

Preview

acknowledging
applicable
certifies
clerk
conveyed
directors
heretofore
justice

partners  **resolution** 

partnership  **secretary** 

Reading and Writing Practice

156. COMMONWEALTH OF MASSACHUSETTS FRANKLIN, SS.

The undersigned hereby certifies that the Partnership, heretofore doing business in the Town of Northfield, County[1] of Franklin, Commonwealth of Massachusetts, under the name of Hunter's, of which Partnership Daniel E. Hunter[2] and William A. Bates were partners, by agreement between said partners was dissolved, effective December 14,[3] 19—; that said Partnership has ceased to do business, and that hereby is withdrawn the name of[4] Hunter's as a trade name and consent is hereby given to the use of the name Hunter's, Inc., by[5] a corporation of which the undersigned is a sole stockholder and to which corporation there has been conveyed[6] by the undersigned the property heretofore owned by said Partnership.

____

Steven L. Butler

COMMONWEALTH[7] OF MASSACHUSETTS) SS.
FRANKLIN)

Subscribed and sworn to before me this 1st day of February 19—[8]

______________________________. (162)

157. MR. STEVEN L. BUTLER, NORTHFIELD, MA 01360

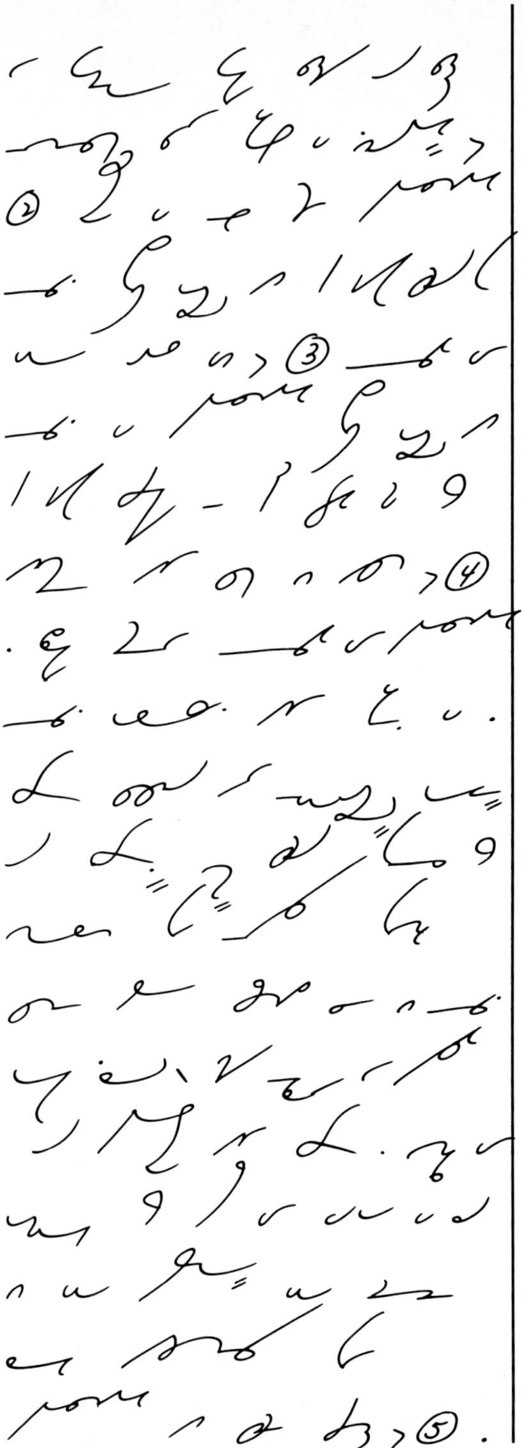

158. MR. STEVEN L. BUTLER, NORTHFIELD, MA 01360

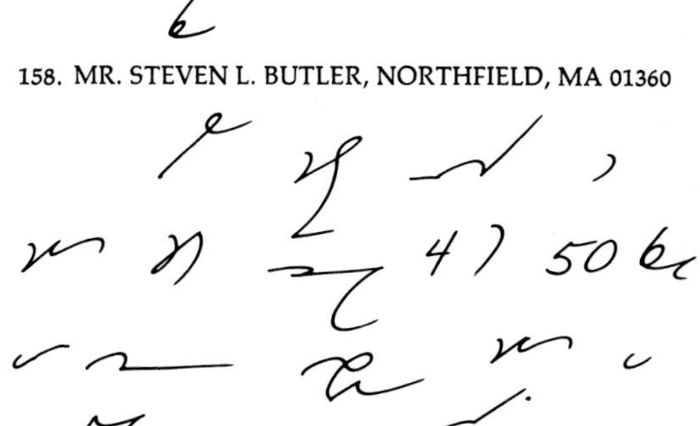

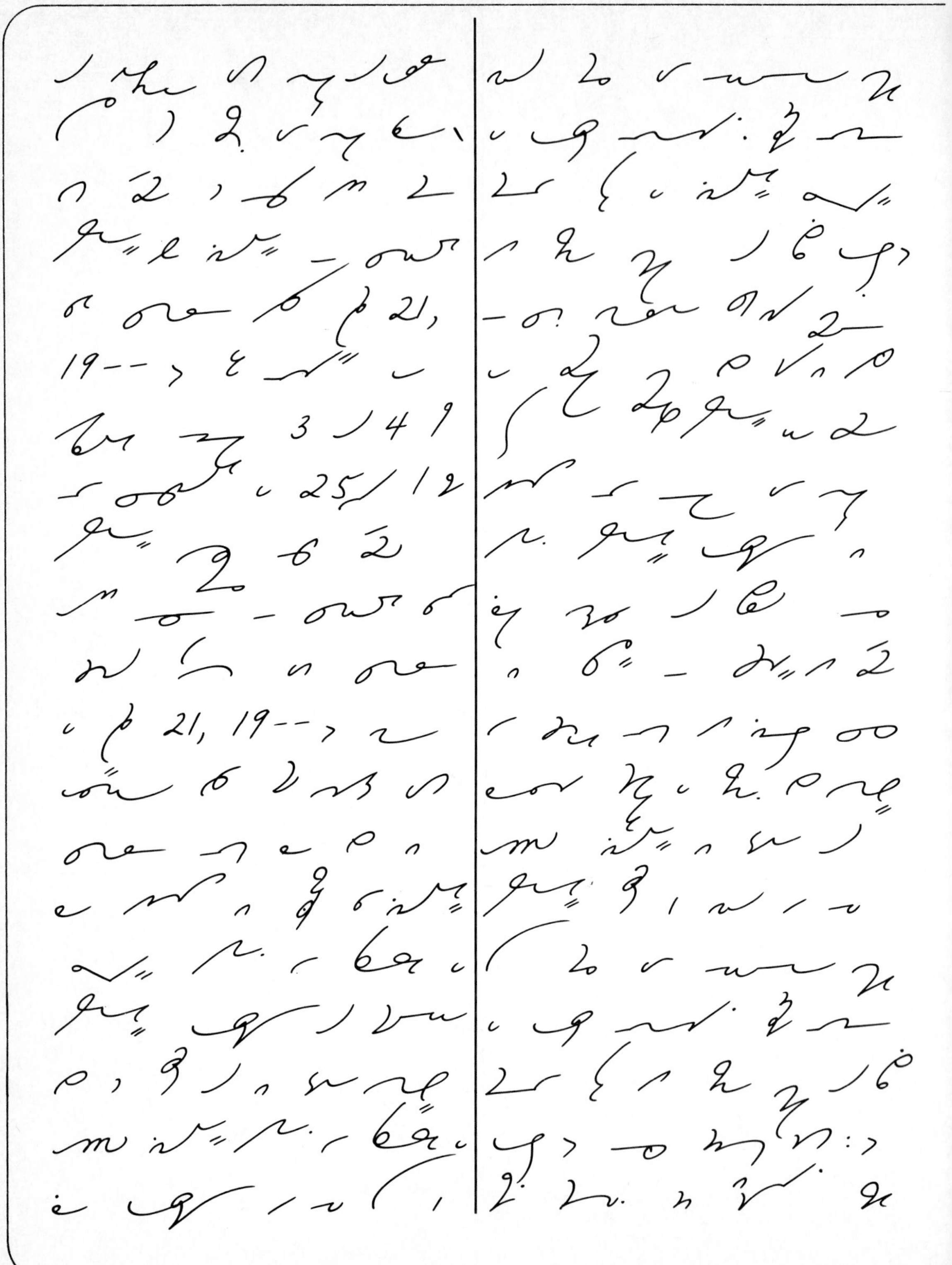

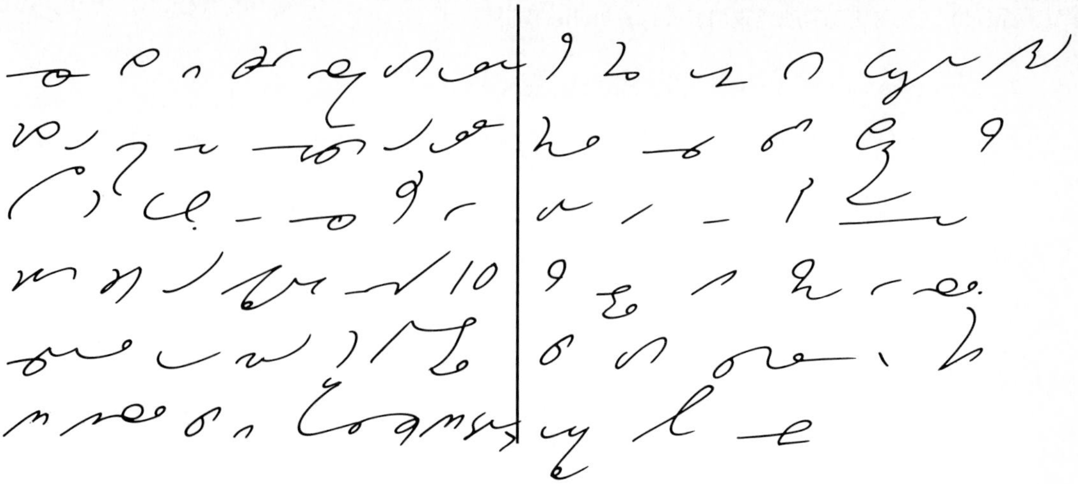

Lesson 54

BUILDING YOUR LEGAL VOCABULARY

Word Family *-ance* is expressed by [shorthand] or [shorthand].

grievances	surveillance
disallowance*	appurtenances
ordinance	maintenance

Word Study

franchise A special privilege granted to an individual or group.

lease A contract to rent property.

pro tem For the time being.

proxy Authority or power to act for another.

ratified Confirmed; sanctioned.

*Derivative of a shortcut.

BUILDING YOUR LEGAL TRANSCRIPTION SKILL

Transcription Aid

Possessive: Joint Ownership

☐ The possessive of two or more nouns representing joint ownership is formed by adding the sign of the possessive to the last noun only.

Patrol Officers Johnson and Frank's report

Barnes and Russell's inventory

Possessive: Individual or Alternative Possession

☐ The possessive of nouns representing individual or alternative possession is formed by adding the sign of the possessive to each name.

Mr. Stover's or Mr. Fox's suggestions

the president's or the treasurer's signature

Mr. Clark's and Mr. Lawson's votes

Legal Collocations

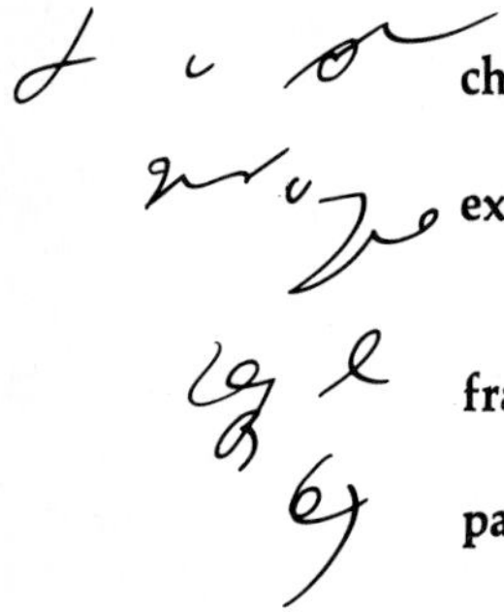

chain of title Successive conveyances of certain property.

extract of inventory A portion of a formal inventory prepared by a notary, used when the entire inventory is irrelevant to the issue.

franchise tax A tax a corporation must pay in order to carry on business.

par value Value equal to the face of a bond or a stock certificate.

BUILDING YOUR LEGAL DICTATION PROFICIENCY

Preview

acknowledgment  **tenant** 

authorizing  **treasurer** 

president  **vice president** 

Reading and Writing Practice

159. MR. STEVEN L. BUTLER, NORTHFIELD, MA 01360

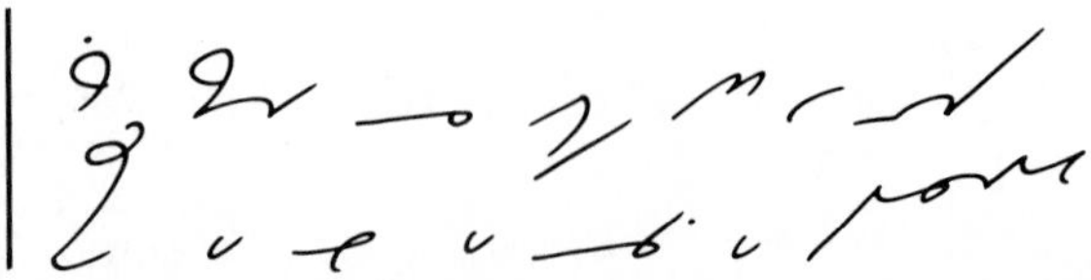

160. MR. STEVEN L. BUTLER, TREASURER, HUNTER'S, INC., NORTHFIELD, MA 01360

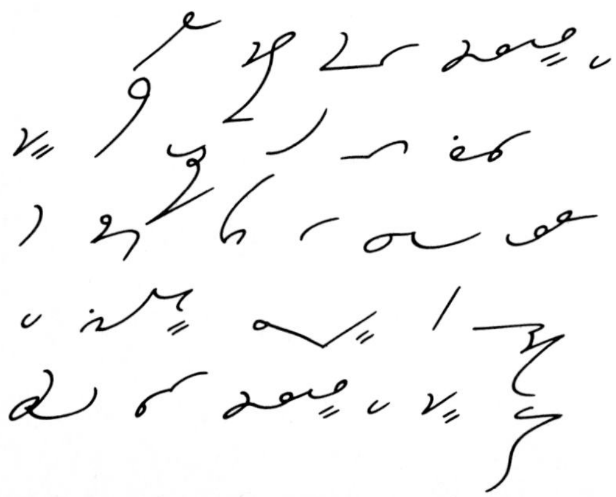

161. MR. STEVEN L. BUTLER, NORTHFIELD, MA 01360

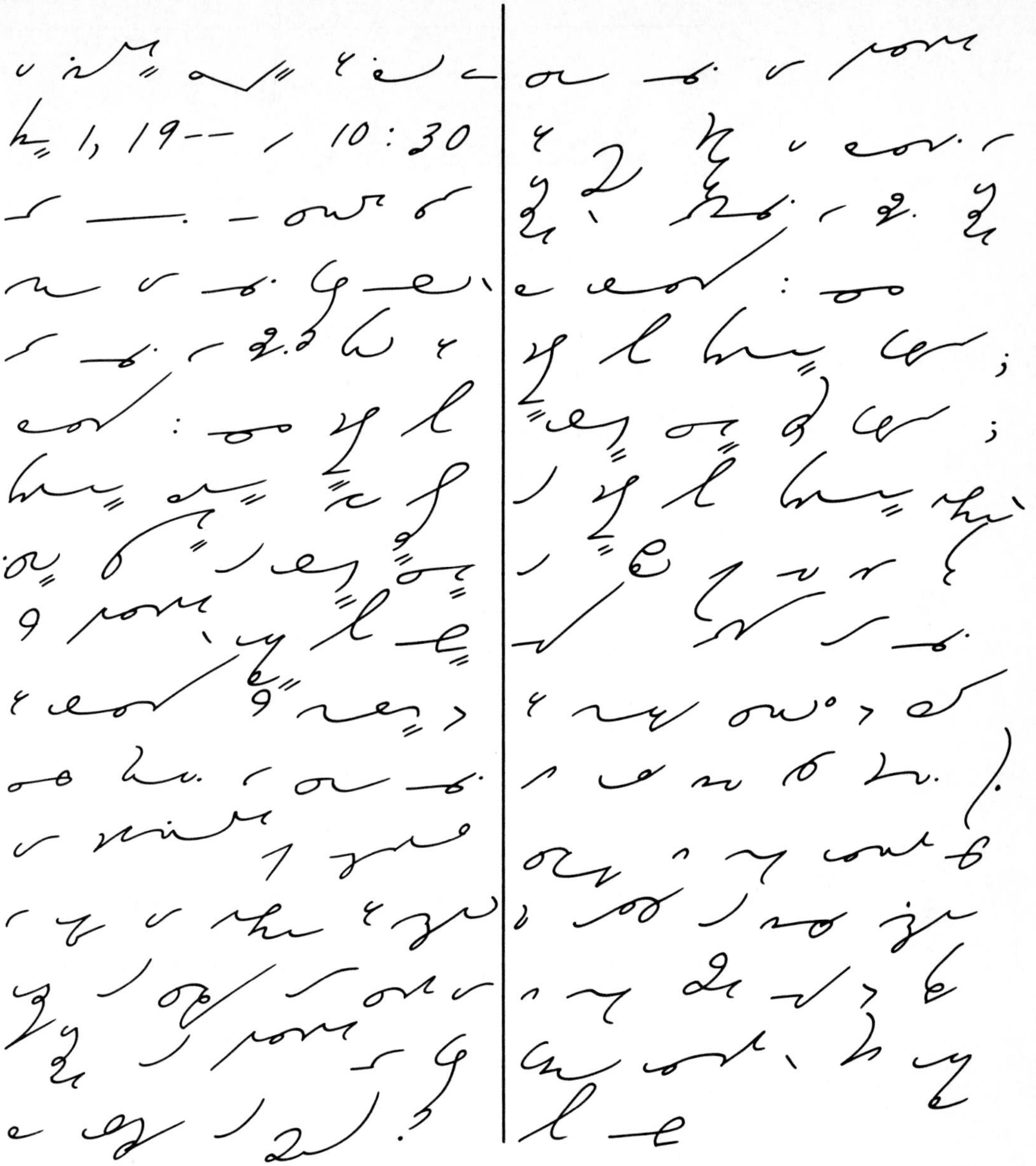

Lesson 55

BUILDING YOUR LEGAL VOCABULARY

Word Family *-ant* is expressed by  or .

appellant 

infant 

warrant 

warranty 

tenant 

immigrant 

Word Study

 **alien corporation** A corporation formed outside the United States.

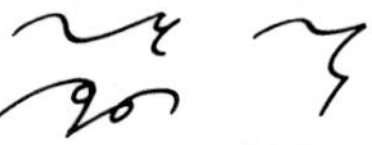 **close corporation** A corporation owned by a few people.

 **domestic corporation** A corporation formed under the laws of a state.

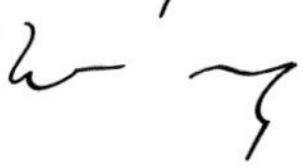 **foreign corporation** A corporation formed under the laws of another state.

BUILDING YOUR LEGAL TRANSCRIPTION SKILL

Transcription Aid Possessive With Gerunds

☐ Use the possessive case when a noun or pronoun precedes a verb form used as a noun *(gerund).*

I shall appreciate your returning the enclosed waiver of notice as soon as possible.

Dr. Brown's testifying for the defense was a surprise to the prosecution.

Possessive: Personal Pronouns

☐ Do not use the apostrophe in the possessive forms of the personal pronouns and of the pronoun *who*.

its whose ours hers his theirs yours

Latin and French Words and Phrases

ad vitam *(ad vē′tam)* For life.

circa *(ser′ka)* About, concerning, at, in, or of approximately.

ex officio *(ex′ō fish′ō)* From or by virtue of the office.

BUILDING YOUR LEGAL DICTATION PROFICIENCY

Preview

- aforementioned
- authorizing
- board of directors
- boundary
- commitment
- duly
- easterly
- execute
- frontage
- monument
- northeasterly
- northerly
- parallel
- procure
- requisite
- simultaneously
- southerly
- subdivide
- tracts
- westerly

Reading and Writing Practice

162. MR. RALPH AMES, GREENFIELD TRUST CO., GREENFIELD, MA 01301

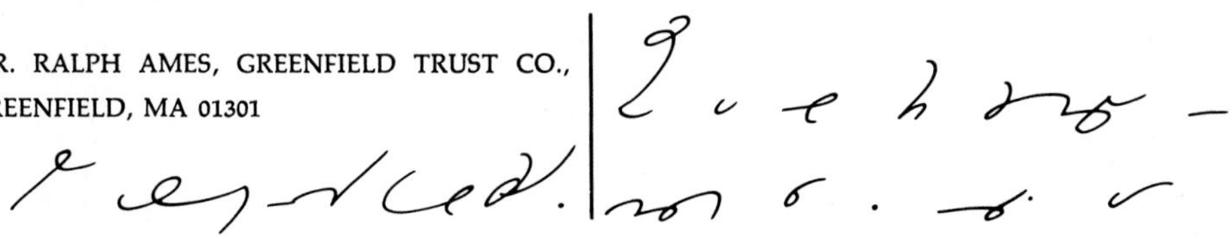

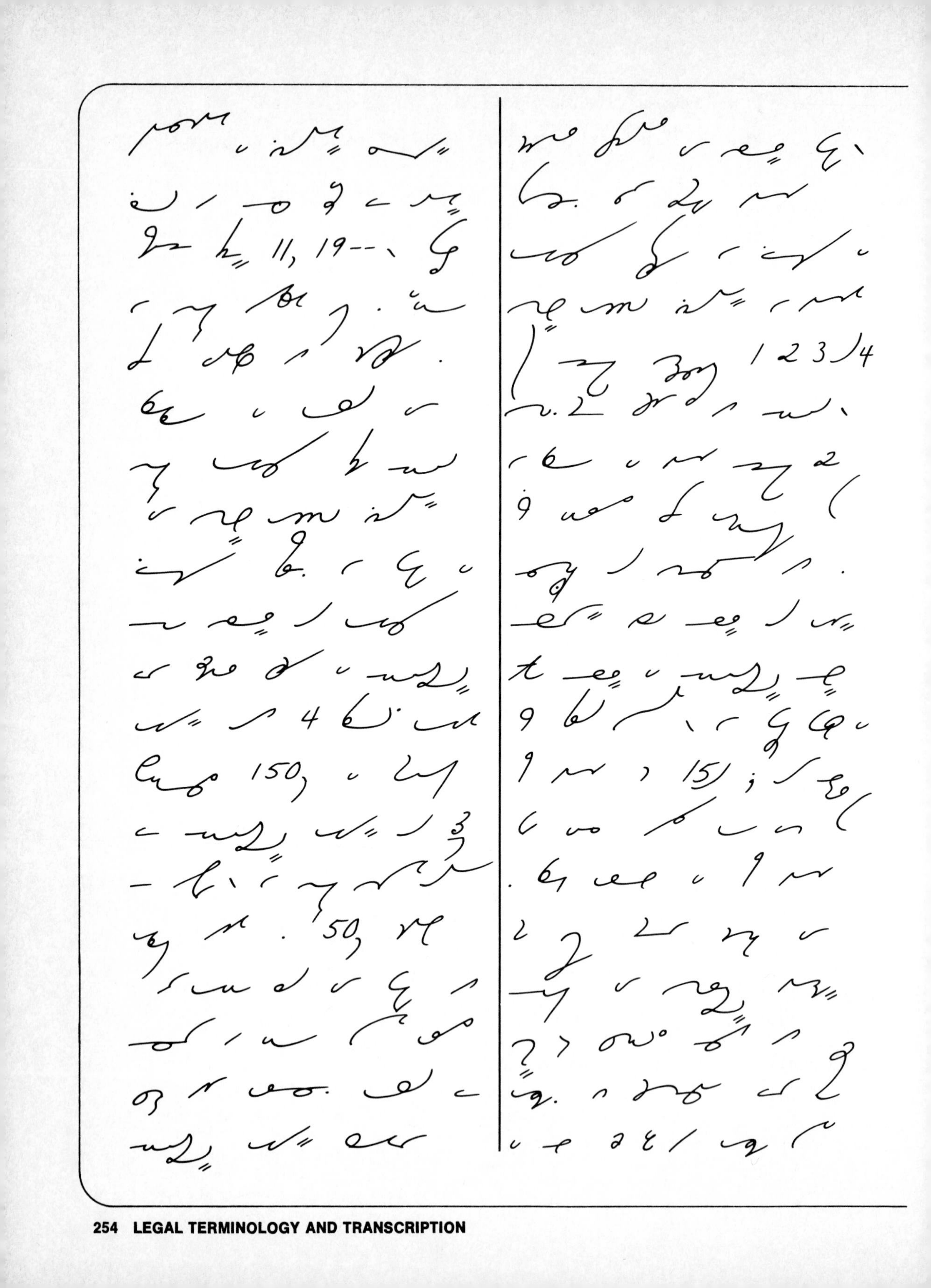

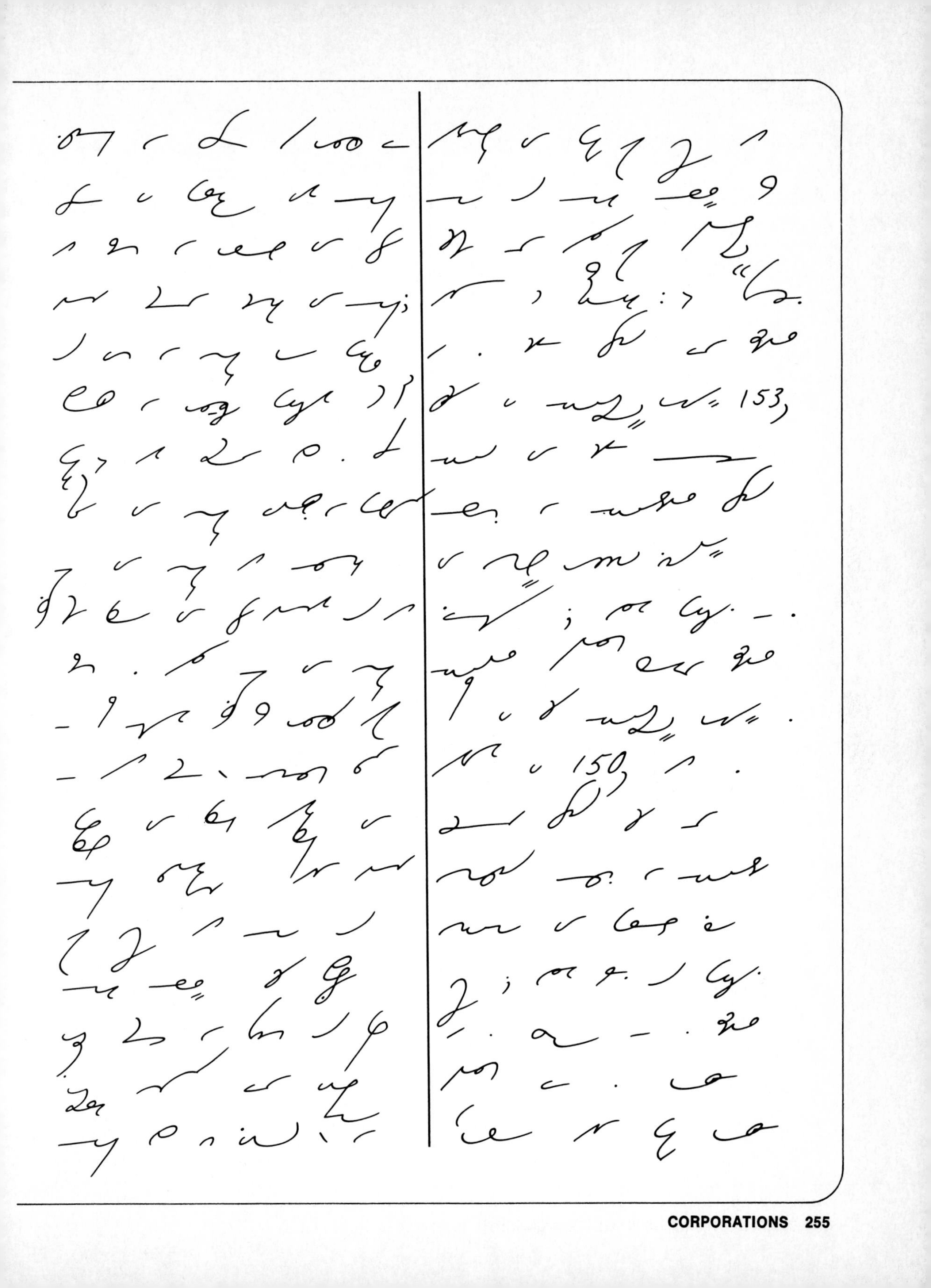

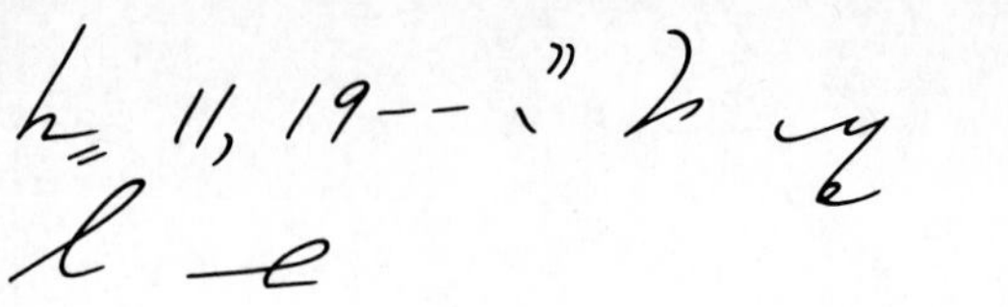

163. MR. RALPH AMES, GREENFIELD TRUST CO., GREENFIELD, MA 01301

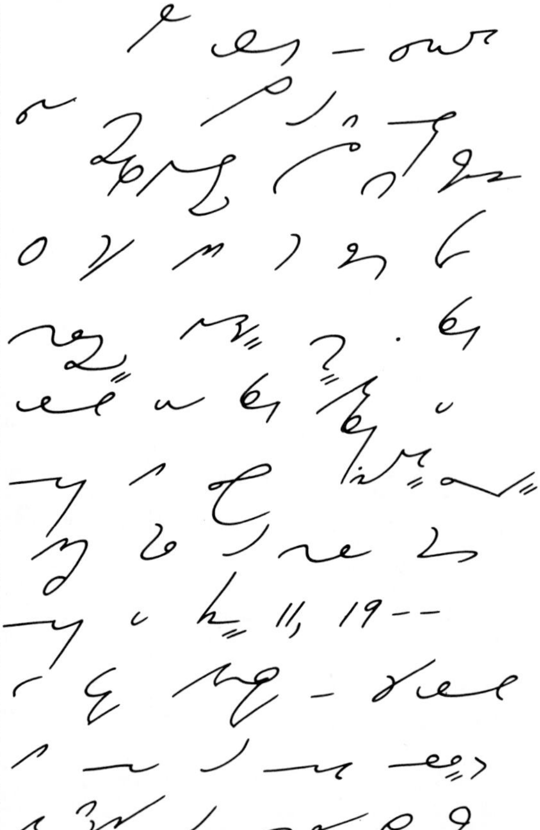

164. MR. RALPH AMES, GREENFIELD TRUST CO., GREENFIELD, MA 01301

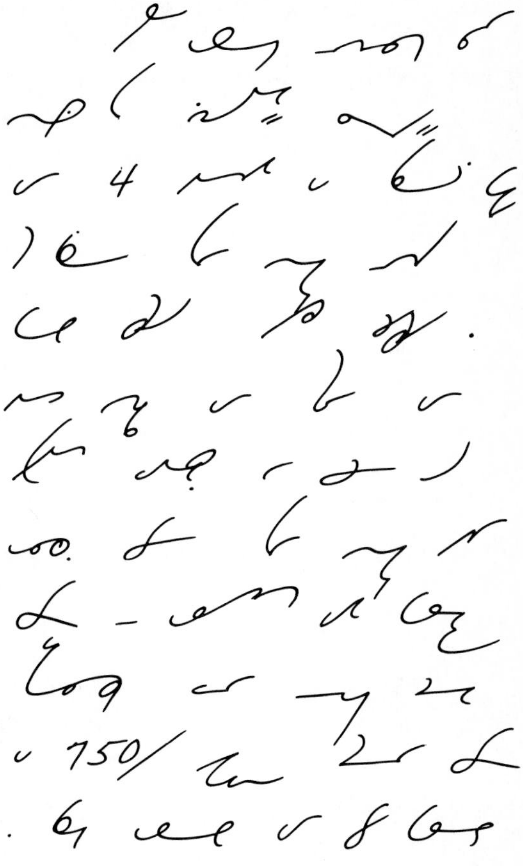

Lesson 56

BUILDING YOUR LEGAL VOCABULARY

Word Family *-tation* and *-tition* are expressed by  .

citations  **commutation** 

deportation  **limitations** 

petitioner  **premeditation** 

Word Study

 **ambiguity** Uncertainty as to meaning.

 **leasehold** Land or property held by lease.

 **mortgage** *(n.)* The document by which one pledges security for a loan.

 **recording** Copying an instrument into the public records, usually in the office of the county clerk.

BUILDING YOUR LEGAL TRANSCRIPTION SKILL

Transcription Aid **Possessive: Words Ending in "s"**

☐ According to most authorities, it is acceptable to add the apostrophe alone to form the possessive of words ending in *s* if the addition of *'s* would cause an unpleasant sound when spoken or be difficult to pronounce. When a singular noun ends in *s*, the *'s* is usually added if a new syllable is formed in the pronunciation of the possessive.

Moses' not Moses's   Larkins' not Larkins's   Alexis' not Alexis's

BUT

Jones's   Davis's   Adams's   Ross's   Harris's

☐ When the proper name is used as an adjective, no apostrophe is needed.

the Haynes ruling the Francis patents the Davis house

Possessive: Idiomatic Expressions

☐ The possessive case is frequently used in place of an objective phrase even though no ownership is involved. In such expressions the modifier indicates whether to use the singular or plural form.

four hours' overtime pay 90 days' notice a stone's throw away

a dollar's worth one day's labor three weeks' vacation

Legal Collocations

frozen assets Assets that cannot be quickly converted into cash.

corporate franchise A corporation's right to organize, exist, and act as granted by the sovereign or absolute power of the state.

sight draft A bill or draft payable on presentation.

sinking fund A sum of money set aside at fixed intervals and deposited or invested to pay off a debt.

tax certificate A certificate showing taxes have been paid for the past three years.

BUILDING YOUR LEGAL DICTATION PROFICIENCY

Preview

contemplation recorded

conveyance registry

easterly revenue

premiums simultaneously

Reading and Writing Practice

165. MR. RALPH WIGGIN, PARKWOOD DRIVE, BAY CITY, MI 48706

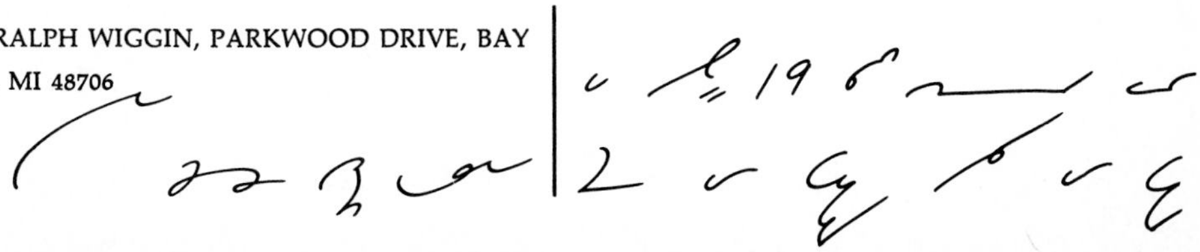

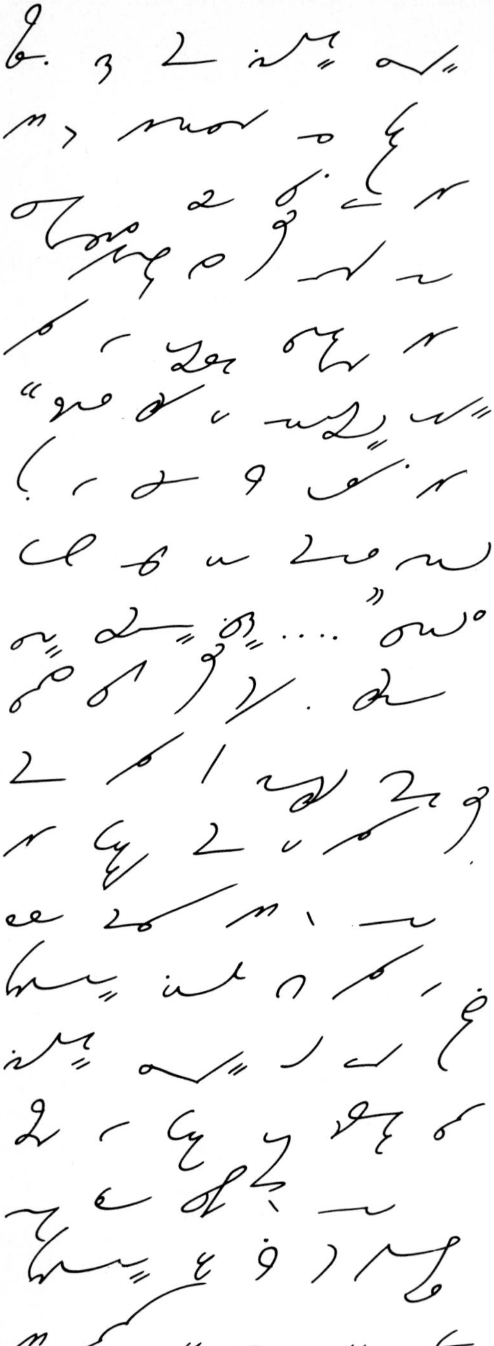

166. MR. ALFRED CAMPBELL, 136 WASHINGTON STREET, BOSTON, MA 02100

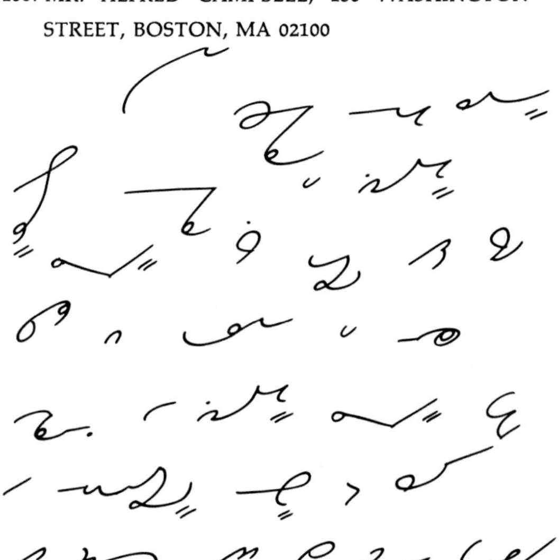

167. MRS. ETHEL DAVIS, HUNTER'S, INC., NORTHFIELD, MA 01360

11

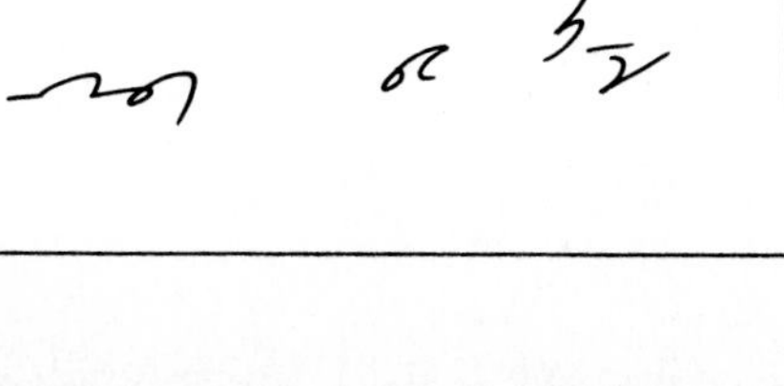

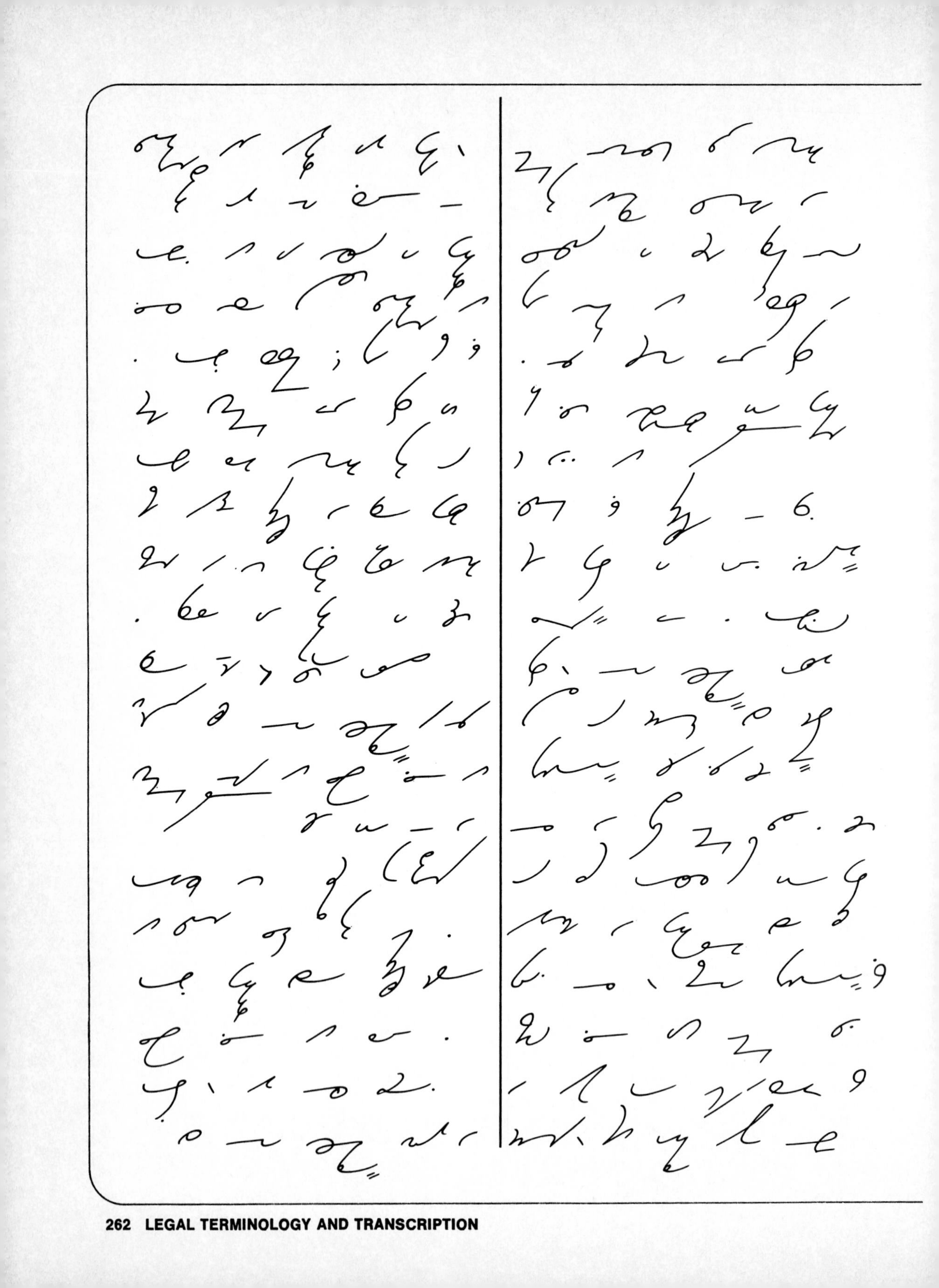

168. MRS. ETHEL DAVIS, HUNTER'S, INC., NORTHFIELD, MA 01360

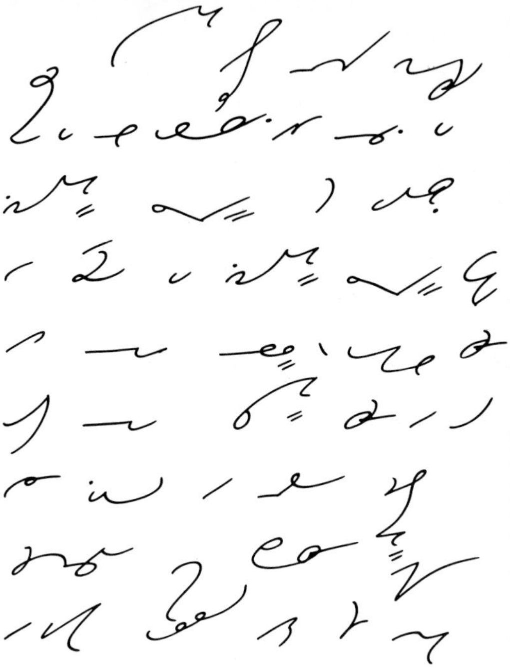

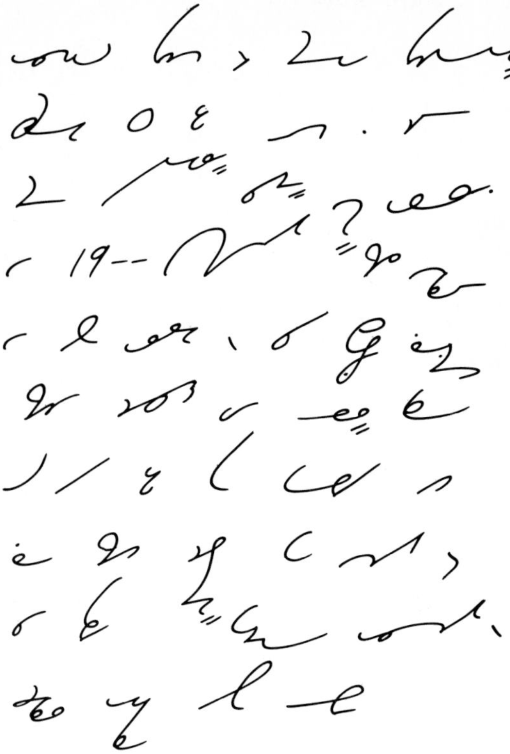

Lesson 57

BUILDING YOUR LEGAL VOCABULARY

Word Family *-dition* and *-dation* are expressed by  .

conditional 

recommendations 

reconditioned 

consolidation 

liquidation 

invalidation 

Word Study

abstract of title A condensed history of the title to land.

amortization The act or process of providing for payment of debt by creating a sinking fund or paying in installments.

lien A claim upon property, usually because money was lent and the property was pledged as security.

precinct A part of a territory with definite bounds or functions often established for administrative purposes.

prorating Distributing or assessing proportionately.

severally Pertaining separately to each party of a bond or note; several persons or things; a few.

BUILDING YOUR LEGAL TRANSCRIPTION SKILL

Transcription Aid

Indicating Omissions

☐ Omissions in quoted matter are indicated by ellipses made with periods or asterisks. Use three spaced periods to show omission of words within or at the beginning of a sentence. Use four spaced periods to show omission at the end of a sentence that would close with a period.

> The Agreement stated that either partner could draw out of the business "any sum or sums for his own use . . . to be duly accounted for on every settlement of accounts and division of the profits."

☐ Indicate the omission of one or more paragraphs by typing a line of periods five spaces apart.

☐ Some offices prefer to show the omission of paragraphs by using the asterisk. Three asterisks may be centered on a line by themselves to indicate the point of omission.

* * *

Latin and French Words and Phrases

ad hoc *(ad hok)* For this; for this purpose; particularly.

in toto *(in tō'tō)* In the whole; completely.

quid pro quo *(kwid prō kwō)* Something for something; something in return.

BUILDING YOUR LEGAL DICTATION PROFICIENCY

Preview effectuate, empowered, insofar, instruments, modernizational, president, proposed, substantial

Reading and Writing Practice

169. WAIVER OF NOTICE OF MEETING OF DIRECTORS OF HUNTER'S, INC.

We, the undersigned, being all the duly elected directors of Hunter's, Inc., hereby severally[1] waive notice of time, place, and purpose of a meeting of the directors of said corporation and consent[2] that the same be held at the office of the Clerk, 74 State Street, Boston, Massachusetts, on May 1,[3] 19—, at two o'clock in the afternoon for purpose of considering the borrowing[4] by the corporation of the sum of $5,000 with interest from Greenfield Trust Co., Greenfield,[5] Massachusetts, for purpose of starting the summer season of 19—, and for such other[6] and further business as may properly come before the meeting.

173. CERTIFIED COPY OF VOTING

I, ROGER L. MASON, Clerk of Hunter's, Inc.,[7] hereby certify that at a meeting of the directors of said corporation held on May 1,[8] 19—, the following is a true copy of their vote: "Voted that the President and/or[9] Treasurer, Steven L. Butler, be and hereby is authorized, directed, and empowered to borrow on[10] behalf of the corporation from the Greenfield Trust Co., Greenfield, Massachusetts, the sum of $5,000[11] and to execute such instruments necessary to effectuate such borrowing."

____

Roger L.[12] Mason, Clerk (243)

170. MR. STEVEN L. BUTLER, HUNTER'S, INC., NORTHFIELD, MA 01360

11

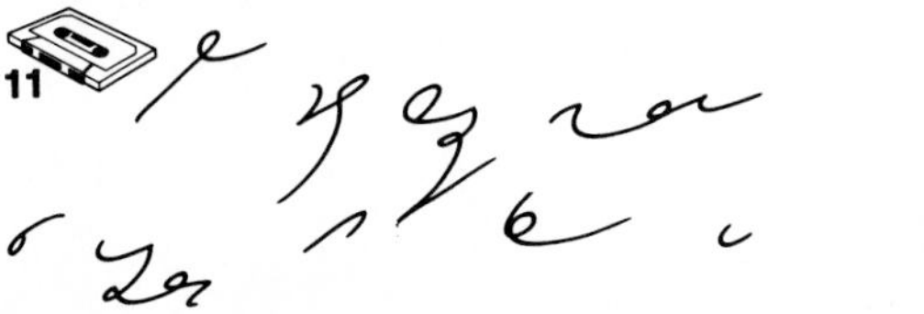

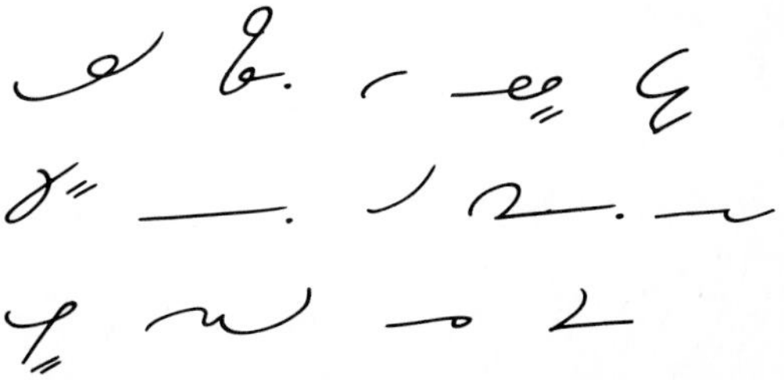

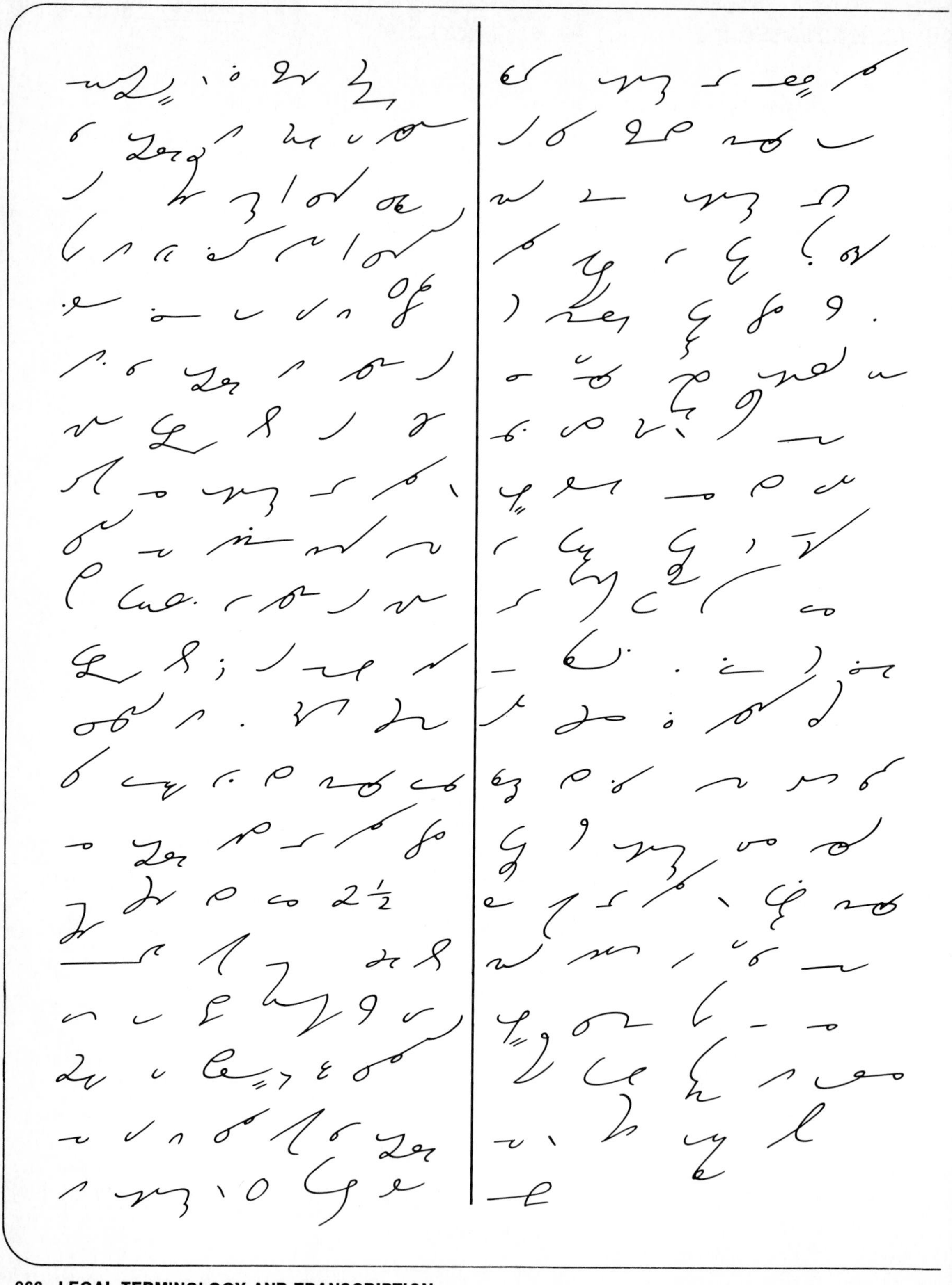

168. MRS. ETHEL DAVIS, HUNTER'S, INC., NORTHFIELD, MA 01360

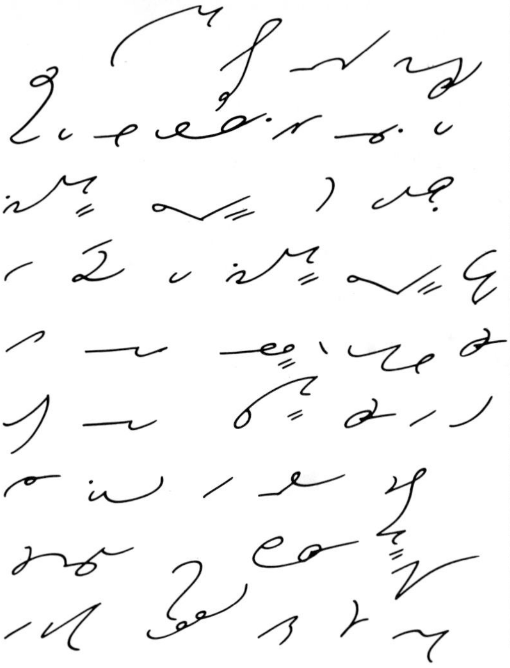

Lesson 57

BUILDING YOUR LEGAL VOCABULARY

Word Family *-dition* and *-dation* are expressed by  .

conditional 

consolidation 

recommendations 

liquidation 

reconditioned 

invalidation 

Word Study

abstract of title A condensed history of the title to land.

amortization The act or process of providing for payment of debt by creating a sinking fund or paying in installments.

lien A claim upon property, usually because money was lent and the property was pledged as security.

precinct A part of a territory with definite bounds or functions often established for administrative purposes.

prorating Distributing or assessing proportionately.

severally Pertaining separately to each party of a bond or note; several persons or things; a few.

BUILDING YOUR LEGAL TRANSCRIPTION SKILL

Transcription Aid

Indicating Omissions

☐ Omissions in quoted matter are indicated by ellipses made with periods or asterisks. Use three spaced periods to show omission of words within or at the beginning of a sentence. Use four spaced periods to show omission at the end of a sentence that would close with a period.

> The Agreement stated that either partner could draw out of the business "any sum or sums for his own use . . . to be duly accounted for on every settlement of accounts and division of the profits."

☐ Indicate the omission of one or more paragraphs by typing a line of periods five spaces apart.

☐ Some offices prefer to show the omission of paragraphs by using the asterisk. Three asterisks may be centered on a line by themselves to indicate the point of omission.

* * *

Latin and French Words and Phrases

ad hoc *(ad hok)* For this; for this purpose; particularly.

in toto *(in tō'tō)* In the whole; completely.

quid pro quo *(kwid prō kwō)* Something for something; something in return.

BUILDING YOUR LEGAL DICTATION PROFICIENCY

Preview

effectuate
empowered
insofar
instruments

modernizational
president
proposed
substantial

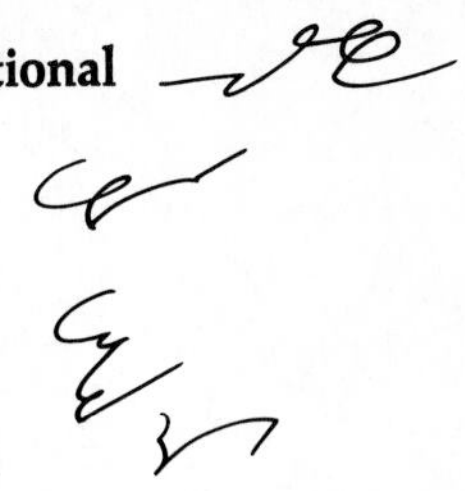

Reading and Writing Practice

169. WAIVER OF NOTICE OF MEETING OF DIRECTORS OF HUNTER'S, INC.

We, the undersigned, being all the duly elected directors of Hunter's, Inc., hereby severally[1] waive notice of time, place, and purpose of a meeting of the directors of said corporation and consent[2] that the same be held at the office of the Clerk, 74 State Street, Boston, Massachusetts, on May 1,[3] 19—, at two o'clock in the afternoon for purpose of considering the borrowing[4] by the corporation of the sum of $5,000 with interest from Greenfield Trust Co., Greenfield,[5] Massachusetts, for purpose of starting the summer season of 19—, and for such other[6] and further business as may properly come before the meeting.

173. CERTIFIED COPY OF VOTING

I, ROGER L. MASON, Clerk of Hunter's, Inc.,[7] hereby certify that at a meeting of the directors of said corporation held on May 1,[8] 19—, the following is a true copy of their vote: "Voted that the President and/or[9] Treasurer, Steven L. Butler, be and hereby is authorized, directed, and empowered to borrow on[10] behalf of the corporation from the Greenfield Trust Co., Greenfield, Massachusetts, the sum of $5,000[11] and to execute such instruments necessary to effectuate such borrowing."

Roger L.[12] Mason, Clerk (243)

170. MR. STEVEN L. BUTLER, HUNTER'S, INC., NORTHFIELD, MA 01360

11

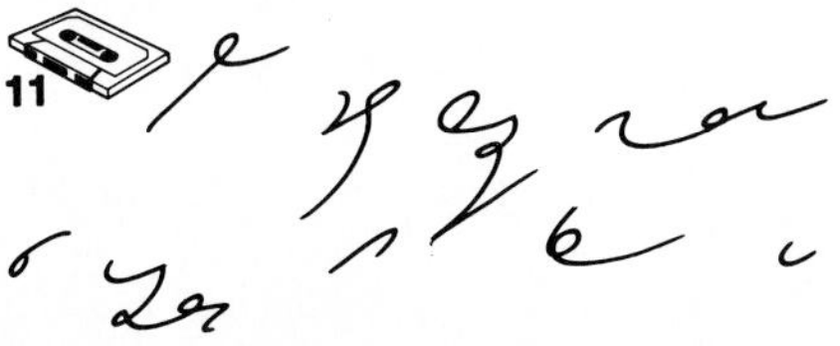

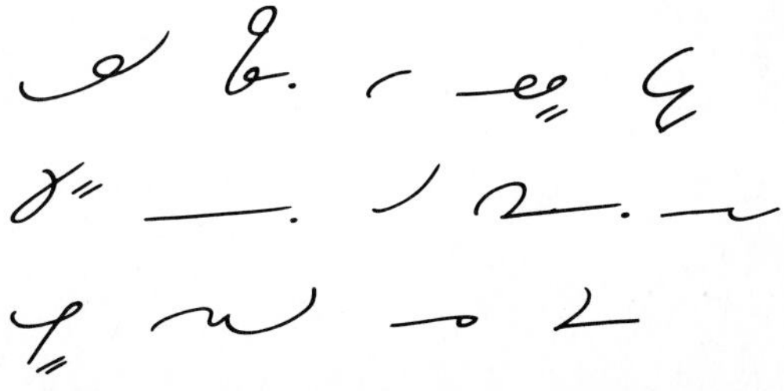

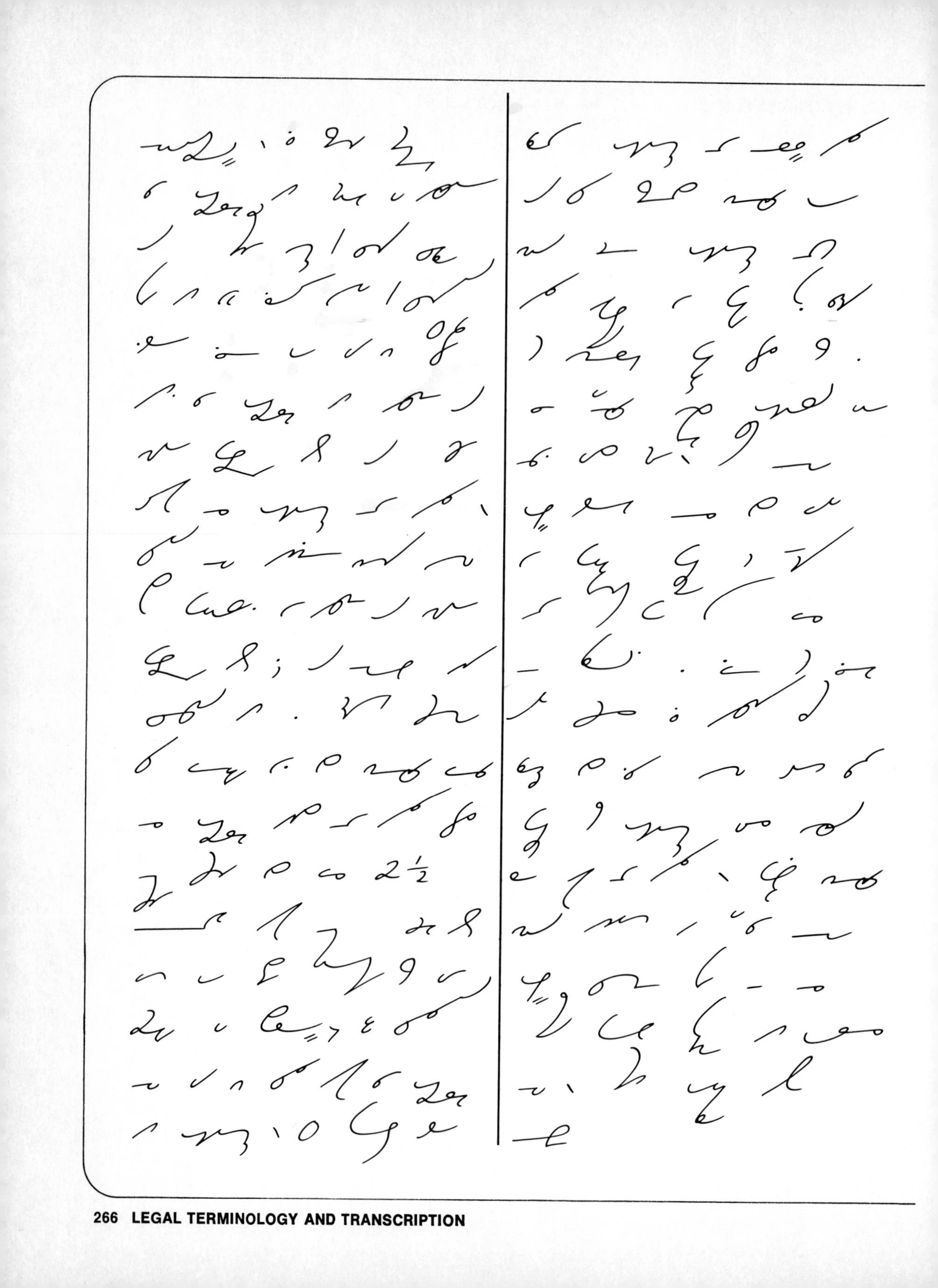

171. MR. STEVEN L. BUTLER, HUNTER'S, INC., NORTHFIELD, MA 01360

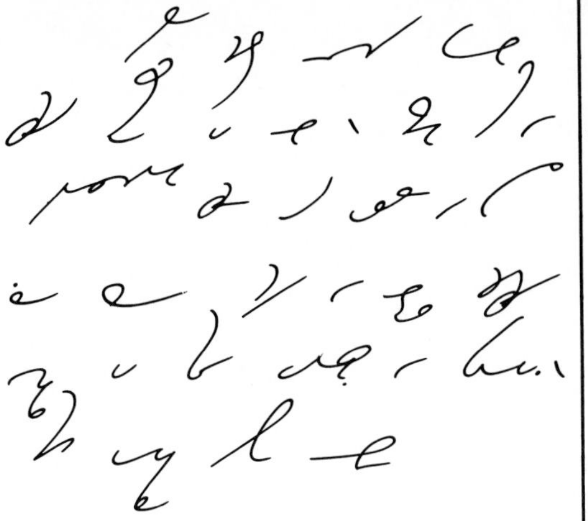

172. MR. RALPH AMES, GREENFIELD TRUST CO., GREENFIELD, MA 01301

173. MR. RALPH AMES, GREENFIELD TRUST CO., GREENFIELD, MA 01301

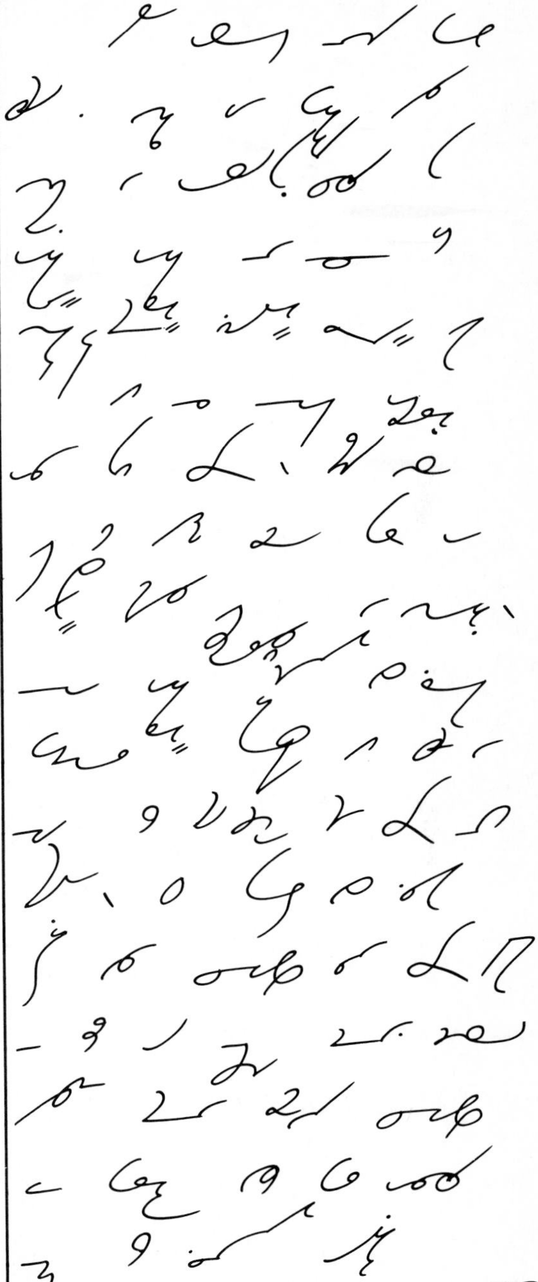

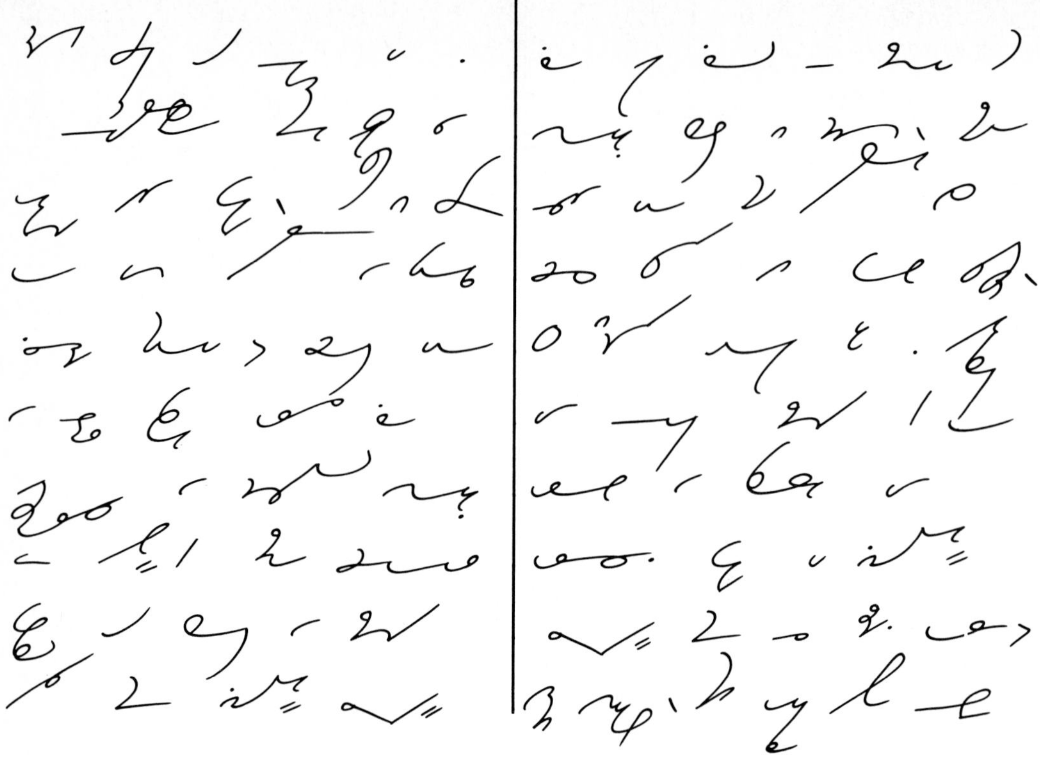

Lesson 58

BUILDING YOUR LEGAL VOCABULARY

Word Family *-mission* and *-mation* are expressed by .

summation

commissioner

reclamation

declamation

proclamation

submission

Word Study

mortgagee One who pledges security.

mortgagor One who makes a loan.

prorate To divide or assess proportionately.

tender Offer.

BUILDING YOUR LEGAL TRANSCRIPTION SKILL

Transcription Aid

The Dash: Before a List

☐ The dash may be used instead of the colon before a list or a summarizing statement, particularly when the introductory word that precedes the list is not expressed.

> There are three essential characteristics of a corporation—creation by the state, legal entity, and perpetual life.

The Dash: Before Summarizing Statement

☐ The dash is used before *all* or *these* when the word introduces a summary of a preceding list or series of ideas.

> Educational, religious, social, and charitable organizations—all may be incorporated as nonstock corporations.

Legal Collocations

acceleration clause A clause in a note or mortgage stipulating that the debt secured thereby shall become due and payable upon the breach or violation of some condition.

unearned increment Added value to property due to natural causes that bring about an increased demand for it.

unlawful detainer Possession of real property after the right to possess it has lapsed.

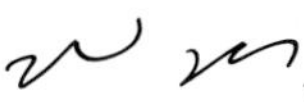
watered stock Stock issued by a corporation as fully paid up when in fact it is not.

lands, tenements, and hereditaments Inheritable lands or interest therein.

BUILDING YOUR LEGAL DICTATION PROFICIENCY

Preview

commonwealth		per annum	
default		precinct	
easterly		southerly	
enterprise		subordinate	
essence		therefrom	
herein		tract	
hereof		westerly	
hereunder		whereof	

Reading and Writing Practice

12

174. BUY AND SELL AGREEMENT

KNOW ALL MEN BY THESE PRESENTS, that Hunter's, Inc., a Massachusetts corporation with principal[1] place of business in Northfield, County of Franklin, and Commonwealth of Massachusetts, SELLER, and Robert Rogers[2] of Brookline, County of Norfolk, and Commonwealth of Massachusetts, BUYER, for and in consideration of[3] the sum of One Thousand Dollars ($1,000) this 28th day of October, 19—,[4] paid by the buyer to the seller, do hereby stipulate and agree as follows:

1. Seller agrees[5] to sell and buyer agrees to buy for the sum of Sixty-five Thousand Dollars ($65,000)[6] the hotel property of the seller consisting of the Morgan House, Main House, Annex, Ellis House, bowling[7] alleys, and two garages located on the westerly side of the road of East Northfield to Northfield together[8] with the golf course, recreation hall, and ski tow facilities located on the easterly side of said[9] highway, reserving and excluding therefrom the tract or parcel of land known as the Easterly Mountain Lot, lying[10] east of said golf course tract, as more particularly described in a deed and map on which a red line has been[11] used to encircle the aforementioned property to be sold.

2. The buyer agrees to pay the remaining of the[12] purchase price crediting the $1,000 aforesaid against the Sixty-five Thousand Dollars[13] ($65,000) stated[13] price by refinancing within 30 days the first mortgage if possible to the[14] amount of Forty Thousand Dollars ($40,000) and cash

payment to the seller of[15] Twenty-five Thousand Dollars ($25,000) including therein the aforesaid One Thousand Dollars[16] ($1,000) down payment.

3. Taxes on the property including the real property taxes,[17] water precinct charges, and any rentals received by the seller extending beyond the date of the sale shall[18] be prorated to the date of the deed but not later than December 1, 19—.

4. The[19] parties hereto do further agree, subject to the approval of the present mortgagee, Greenfield Trust Co.,[20] nevertheless that in the event the buyer is unable to locate the first mortgage financing specified in[21] paragraph 2 above within the 30-day specified time interval from the date hereof, that the seller shall[22] receive and the buyer shall pay the sum of Twenty-five Thousand Dollars ($25,000)[23] in cash, buyer shall assume without recourse the outstanding first mortgage at the said Greenfield Trust Co. and[24] tender a note and mortgage on the premises subordinate to the aforesaid first mortgage and any second mortgage[25] lien securing the Twenty-five Thousand Dollars ($25,000) cash payment above[26] recited from the buyer to the seller in the amount of Fifteen Thousand Dollars ($15,000)[27] with interest at the rate of six (6) percent per annum to be paid in full not later in[28] any event than June 1, 19—.

5. It is further understood and agreed that the aforesaid purchase[29] price shall include and the seller does hereby agree to sell all of the furnishings, fixtures, exclusive of food and[30] perishables, equipment, and the like contained on the premises of the seller generally used in connection[31] with the enterprise.

6. In the event of the performance of the terms and conditions of the aforesaid agreement strictly[32] in accordance with the terms aforesaid, time being of the essence, by the buyer, and tender and delivery[33] by the seller of a good and sufficient warranty deed to the aforesaid property subject to the within[34] recited terms and conditions hereof, the transaction shall at that time be declared final and completed. In[35] the event of default, however, on the part of the buyer in the performance of the terms and conditions herein[36] recited, the seller shall be entitled to retain the aforesaid One Thousand Dollars ($1,000)[37] as part of the liquidated damages arising out of this transaction.

7. It is understood and[38] agreed that within the date of this contract there has been subjected to a Buy and Sell Agreement a small tract or parcel[39] of land located along the Riverside crossroad in the tract of property of the seller lying on the[40] westerly side of Northfield Road so-called, said Buy and Sell Agreement running between Hunter's, Inc., and[41] one Peter J. and Ruth G. Sherman consisting of 200 feet frontage on said Riverside Road and[42] 150-foot depth to the southerly side thereof, for which the said Shermans are to pay Hunter's, Inc.,[43] the sum of Fifteen Hundred Dollars ($1,500). Payment of the Fifteen Hundred Dollars[44]

($1,500) aforesaid by the Shermans to Hunter's, Inc., shall be credited[45] against the obligation of the Sixty-five Thousand Dollars ($65,000) purchase[46] price which the buyer is obligated hereunder to the seller.

8. The seller agrees that upon performance[47] in full by the buyer of the terms and conditions of the within agreement, which in any event shall be completed[48] not later than December 1, 19__, that the buyer may use and operate under the[49] name of Hunter's, Inc., and the seller further agrees to furnish all necessary papers and[50] permissions required to permit the buyer to register the said name to him.

It is further understood and agreed[51] that upon completion of the within agreement that ten (10) percent of the purchase price will be paid[52] to James B. Sawyer, Real Estate.

IN WITNESS WHEREOF, the parties have hereunto set their hands and seals the day and[53] year first above written.

SELLER:
Hunter's, Inc.

____________________ By: ____________________
Witness President

BUYER:

____________________ ____________________
Witness[54]

(1081)

Lesson 59

BUILDING YOUR LEGAL VOCABULARY

Word Family *-nition* and *-nation* are expressed by  .

ignition 

termination 

discrimination 

determination 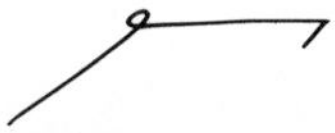

recognition 

condonation 

Word Study

 **apportion** Divide and distribute in a planned ratio.

 **empowered** Given legal authority; enabled.

 **liquidation** Settlement of the affairs of a business; sale of assets and distribution of moneys to creditors in order to terminate a business.

 **quorum** The number of people that must be present at a meeting to make decisions regarding the activities of an organization.

BUILDING YOUR LEGAL TRANSCRIPTION SKILL

Transcription Aid

The Dash: With Parenthetic Elements

☐ Dashes may replace commas used to set off a parenthetic element when more emphatic separation from the rest of the sentence is desired or when the parenthetic element itself contains commas.

I do not believe it would be wise—and I am sure you would not—to fill in the discharge on the mortgage itself until you have the money in hand.

The Dash: With Abrupt Change in Thought

☐ The dash is used to mark a sudden break or abrupt change in thought.

If the buyer defaults—which heaven forbid!—we must delay petitioning the court for dissolution.

Latin and French Words and Phrases

 **sans recours** *(sans rē cor')* Without recourse.

 **debitum fundi** *(de'bi tum fun'dī)* A lien or mortgage on land.

 **status quo** *(stā'tus kwō')* The state in which anything is; state existing.

BUILDING YOUR LEGAL DICTATION PROFICIENCY

Preview adjourn  authority 

attest  constituting 

dissolution 

pursuant 

forenoon 

surviving 

negotiate 

unanimously 

Reading and Writing Practice

175. WAIVER OF NOTICE OF MEETING OF DIRECTORS OF HUNTER'S, INC.

We, the undersigned, being all the duly elected directors of Hunter's, Inc., hereby waive notice[1] of time, place, and purpose of a meeting of the directors of said corporation and consent that the same be[2] held at the office of the Clerk, 74 State Street, Boston, Massachusetts, on August 11,[3] 19—, at ten o'clock in the forenoon for the purpose of authorizing the President in behalf[4] of the corporation to sell house lots on the real estate of the corporation on the Riverside Road[5] upon such terms and conditions and at such times as he shall deem advantageous for the corporation and to[6] negotiate satisfactory releases of mortgage with the Greenfield Trust Co. and for such other[7] and further business as may properly come before the meeting.

176. MINUTES OF SPECIAL MEETING OF DIRECTORS OF HUNTER'S, INC.

Pursuant to a waiver of notice, a meeting[8] of the directors of Hunter's, Inc., was held at the office of the Clerk, 74 State[9] Street, Boston, Massachusetts, on August 11, 19—, at ten o'clock in the forenoon.[10]

The Directors present were Steven L. Butler and Ethel Davis, constituting a quorum of the board. Howard[11] Adams was absent on account of illness.

The President, Steven L. Butler, presided.

The Clerk, Roger[12] L. Mason, kept the records of the meeting.

The President pointed out to the meeting that from time to time persons[13] desiring to purchase house lots on the Riverside Road had approached him and that it was desirable that he[14] have authority to close such transactions as quickly as possible for the benefit of the corporation.[15] After full discussion upon motion duly made and seconded, it was unanimously

Voted that the[16] President be and hereby is duly authorized to sell lots on that portion of the real estate of this corporation[17] as adjoins the highway known as the Riverside Road to such persons upon such terms and conditions and[18] for such consideration as he shall deem advantageous to the interest of the corporation and[19] to execute for and on behalf of this corporation all contracts, deeds, and other documents necessary[20] or incidental to the foregoing and to negotiate with the Greenfield Trust Co. for releases[21] of mortgage of such lots on terms which he may deem advantageous to this corporation.

There being no[22] further business to come before the meeting, it was

Voted to adjourn, a true record, attest: Clerk ______________________

I, ROGER[23] L. MASON, Clerk of Hunter's, Inc., hereby certify that the foregoing is a true copy of the[24] minutes of the meeting of directors held on August 11, 19___.

177. MINUTES OF MEETING OF STOCKHOLDERS AND DIRECTORS OF HUNTER'S, INC.

Pursuant to[25] a waiver of notice, a combined meeting of the stockholders and directors of Hunter's, Inc.,[26] was held at the office of the Clerk, 74 State Street, Boston, Massachusetts, on May 24,[27] 19___, at eleven o'clock in the forenoon.

The Directors present were: Steven L. Butler and Ethel[28] Davis, being the surviving directors and constituting a quorum, and Mr. Butler, being the[29] holder of all the presently issued and outstanding stock of the corporation was present in person.

The[30] President, Steven L. Butler, presided.

The Clerk, Roger L. Mason kept the records.

The President brought to[31] the attention the vacancy on the Board of Directors created by the sudden death of Howard Adams.[32] Following discussion, upon motion duly made and seconded, it was

Voted that Mary Butler be elected[33] Director to fill the unexpired term of Howard Adams.

The President announced that a contemplated plan[34] of liquidation had been carefully considered by the Directors and was herewith presented to the[35] Directors to provide for a winding up of the corporation's affairs, the sale of its physical assets if[36] feasible, a provision for the payment of liabilities, if any, and an ultimate distribution[37] of the remaining property to the stockholders on a pro rata basis apportioned to their existing[38] holdings. The proposed plan of liquidation was reviewed and discussed in full, and its relationship to Section[39] 337 of the Internal Revenue Code was detailed. Following discussion, upon motion duly[40] made and seconded, it was

Voted that the corporation adopt the proposed plan of liquidation under Section[41] 337 of the International Revenue Code, and that the President, by and in behalf of the[42] corporation be authorized and empowered to make, execute, and deliver all necessary instruments,[43] papers, and other documents necessary to give effect to the foregoing, together with the further[44] right, and power, by and in behalf of the corporation to sell and transfer the physical assets of the[45] corporation upon such terms and conditions as he may most advantageously obtain, and to provide[46] for the payment of all liabilities and to accomplish a distribution of the remaining assets[47] of the corporation on a pro rata basis among the present stockholders, following which a petition[48] for a decree of dissolution to the Superior Court for Franklin County accomplishing a complete[49] wind-up of the corporate affairs is authorized.

There being no further business to come before the meeting,[50] it was Voted to adjourn

A true record, attest: ______________________________, Clerk.

I, ROGER L. MASON, Clerk of Hunter's,[51] Inc., hereby certify that the foregoing is a true copy of the minutes of the meeting of[52] Stockholders and Directors held on May 24, 19—. (1054)

Lesson 60

BUILDING YOUR LEGAL VOCABULARY

Word Family *-iety* is expressed by writing through the accented *i*.

sobriety 

variety 

propriety 

society 

notoriety 

impropriety 

Word Study

 **attest** To affirm; to declare to be true.

 **ratify** To give approval to.

 **revocation** Something made void that had previously been permitted.

 **to wit** Namely; that is to say.

BUILDING YOUR LEGAL TRANSCRIPTION SKILL

Transcription Aid

Parentheses: With Interrupting Elements

☐ Parentheses may be used to set off explanatory matter, references, directions, and other interrupting elements that are independent of the main thought.

This hotel and real estate was advertised for two weeks in the Springfield (Massachusetts) *Times.*

The trademark Hush Puppies (shoes) is protected by law.

Parentheses: With Confirming Figures

☐ Use parentheses to enclose a figure inserted to confirm a number given in words if the double form is requested.

The enclosed promissory note is due in sixty (60) days.

Typing Citations

Newspapers

When citing cases that have appeared in a newspaper, cite the name of the paper, volume or date, page number, column, and court (when needed). A signed article is cited by author and title. Underscore the title of the newspaper.

Boston Globe, Jan. 17, 1968, at 12, col. 4.

BUILDING YOUR LEGAL DICTATION PROFICIENCY

Preview

adjournments
affirmative
certifying
constitutes
county

dissolving
hereby
negative
presided
undersigned

Reading and Writing Practice

178. P R O X Y HUNTER'S, INC.

KNOW ALL MEN BY THESE PRESENTS, that the undersigned, a stockholder of Hunter's, Inc., hereby constitutes[1] and appoints ______________________ ____________ and ______________________________ or both of them, the attorney and proxy of the undersigned[2] to attend and represent the undersigned at the annual meeting of the stockholders of said corporation[3] to be held at the office of the Clerk, 74 State Street, Boston, Massachusetts, on June 7,[4] 19—, at eleven o'clock in the forenoon and at all adjournments thereof, and for and on[5] behalf of the undersigned to vote according to the number of shares of stock of the said corporation which[6] the undersigned would be entitled to vote if there personally present.

Hereby ratifying and confirming[7] all that said attorneys and proxies shall do in the premises and giving unto said attorneys and proxies[8] full power of substitution and revocation.

______________________________, Stockholder

179. MINUTES OF MEETING OF STOCKHOLDERS AND DIRECTORS OF HUNTER'S, INC.

Pursuant to a foregoing[9] waiver of notice, a meeting of the stockholders and directors of Hunter's, Inc., was held[10] at the office of the Clerk, 74 State Street, Boston, Massachusetts, on June 7, 19—,[11] at eleven o'clock in the forenoon.

All the Directors were present, and the holder of all of the[12] outstanding and issued stock of the corporation was present in person.

The President, Steven L. Butler, presided.[13]

The Clerk, Roger L. Mason, kept the records.

The President brought to the attention of the meeting that[14] all the assets of the corporation had now been disposed of or transferred to the stockholder and all the[15] outstanding obligations of the corporation taken care of, and that the corporation would now be in a[16] position to petition the Court for dissolution, and accordingly, following discussion, upon motion[17] duly made and seconded, it was unanimously

Voted that whereas there are no existing liabilities[18] against the corporation Hunter's, Inc., and no assets thereof requiring distribution,[19] said assets having been fully disposed of, it is advisable that said corporation be dissolved and wound up[20] and the President and the Clerk be and they hereby are directed to petition the Superior Court for[21] Franklin County for a decree dissolving Hunter's, Inc., and ordering the cancellation of[22] its capital stock and the winding up of its affairs, and the Treasurer certifying to said Court that there[23] are no outstanding obligations of the corporation remaining.

There being no further business to come[24] before the meeting, it was

Voted to adjourn,

A true record, attest: ______________________________

Roger L. Mason, Clerk

180. THE COMMONWEALTH OF MASSACHUSETTS FRANKLIN, SS. SUPERIOR COURT PETITION FOR DISSOLUTION OF HUNTER'S, INC.

HUNTER'S, INC.,[25] a corporation duly organized under the Business Corporation Law of Massachusetts, with[26] its principal place of business in Northfield, County of Franklin and Commonwealth of Massachusetts, by its[27] President and its Clerk, respectfully represent at a meeting of the stockholders, duly called for the purpose, held[28] on June 7, 19—, in Boston, Massachusetts, fifty (50) share of stock[29] voting in the affirmative and no shares of stock voting in the negative, the holders of all of the[30] outstanding stock consisting of a single class of common capital stock entitled to vote, being then present[31] or represented in person or by proxy at said meeting, adopted a vote of which the following is a[32] true copy, to wit:

"Voted that whereas there are no existing liabilities against the corporation Hunter's,[33] Inc., and no assets thereof requiring distribution, said assets having been fully disposed[34] of, it is advisable that said corporation be dissolved and wound up and the President and the Clerk be and[35] they hereby are directed to petition the Superior Court for Franklin County for a decree dissolving[36] Hunter's, Inc., and ordering the cancellation of its capital stock and the winding up[37] of its affairs, and the Treasurer certifying to said Court that there are no outstanding obligations of[38] the corporation remaining."

WHEREFORE, your petitioner prays that an order may issue decreeing the[39] dissolution of Hunter's, Inc., the cancellation of its capital stock and the winding up[40] of its affairs, subject to such conditions and limitations as justice may require, and of such other and[41] further relief as to the Court may seem just.

HUNTER'S, INC.

by______________________________President

by[42]______________________________Clerk

COMMONWEALTH OF MASSACHUSETTS)
MIDDLESEX) ss.

Personally appeared STEVEN L.[43] BUTLER and ROGER L. MASON, who acknowledged themselves to be the President and Clerk of said corporation,[44] and that they, as such officers, being authorized so to do, executed the foregoing instrument for[45] the purpose therein contained, by signing the name of the corporation by themselves as such officers, and[46] certifying that the statements therein contained are true.

Before me,______________________________Notary Public
June 6,[47] 19—

My commission expires____________________

And I, STEVEN L. BUTLER, Treasurer of said[48] Hunter's, Inc., further certify that there are no outstanding liabilities of said corporation.[49]

____

Subscribed and sworn to, before me.

______________________________Notary Public
June 6,[50] 19—
My commission expires______________________________ (1010)

UNIT

7 Equity

Lease Violation

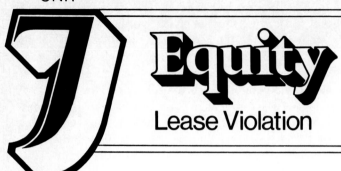

Baldwin's, Inc., Plaintiff
v.
Gardiner Shopping Center, Inc., Stetson Stores, Inc., and Lovett Shoe Co., Inc., Defendants

This case concerns a dispute involving the owner of Gardiner Shopping Center and two firms leasing space in the center.

Baldwin's, Inc., a firm selling shoes and handbags exclusively, contends that a provision in its lease is violated by permitting the Defendant Stetson Stores, Inc., to operate a department selling shoes and handbags in competition.

Counsel for Gardiner Shopping Center, Inc., is John H. Nichols, Esq.

Counsel for Stetson Stores, Inc., is Lester L. Greenberg, Esq.

Counsel for Lovett Shoe Company, Inc., is Norma H. Starr, Esq.

Counsel for Baldwin's, Inc., is G. Peter Gary, Esq.

Lesson 61

BUILDING YOUR LEGAL VOCABULARY

Word Family *-ology* is expressed by  .

criminology  pathological 

criminologist  psychologist 

psychology  toxicology 

Word Study

 **allegations** Statements of fact in a pleading.

 **concession** A voluntary grant; e.g., the leasing of a portion of premises for a particular purpose.

 **demised** Conveyed by will or lease.

 **inequitable** Unfair.

 **lessee** A tenant under lease.

 **lessor** One who grants a lease.

 **privity** Mutual or successive relationship to the same rights of property.

BUILDING YOUR LEGAL TRANSCRIPTION SKILL

Transcription Aid **Footnotes: Books**

☐ In typing a footnote that refers to a book, include the following: footnote number, author's name in normal order, the title underscored, the edition (if not the first one), the publisher, the place of publication, year of publication, and page reference.

1. William J. Casey, Lawyer's Desk Book, 4th ed., Prentice-Hall, Inc., Englewood Cliffs, NJ, 1975, p. 8.

☐ When the name of the organization responsible for publishing the book is more important than the names of the contributors or when the author is anonymous, list the organization's name instead of the author.

2. Bar Association of the City of New York, Law of Presidential Impeachment, Harper & Row Pubs., Inc., New York, 1974, p. 32.

Typing Citations Signals used in citations, such as *e.g., accord, see, cf., but see, but cf., see generally,* and *see also* indicate the purpose for which an authority is cited or the degree of support the authority gives to a proposition. Such signals are italicized in law reviews but not in other legal writing.

See, e.g., *Peerless Ins. Co. v. Gould,* 103 N.H. 134

BUILDING YOUR LEGAL DICTATION PROFICIENCY

Preview

alleged
competitive
infringement
landlord
leasehold
maxims

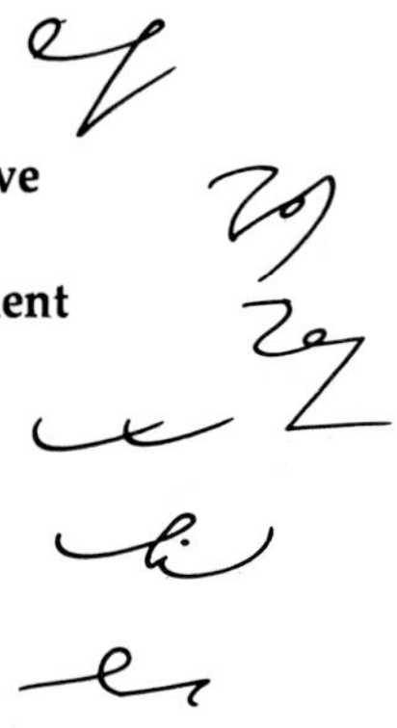

memorandum
monetary
registry of deeds
remedy
revenues
subleasing

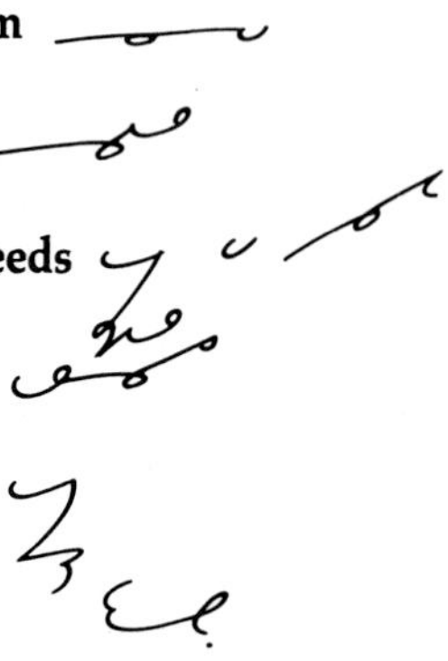

Reading and Writing Practice

181. COMMONWEALTH OF MASSACHUSETTS ESSEX, SS. SUPERIOR COURT BALDWIN'S, INC., V. GARDINER SHOPPING CENTER, INC., STETSON STORES, INC., LOVETT SHOE CO., INC., DEFENDANT. STETSON STORES, INC.'S MEMORANDUM OF LAW

Plaintiff, Baldwin's, Inc., and Defendant Stetson Stores, Inc., are each lessees under separate[1] written indentures with the Defendant Gardiner Shopping Center, Inc., lessor, common[2] to both.

Each lease has been duly recorded in the Essex County Registry of Deeds. Several other tenants,[3] including Blue & White, Inc., Brent's division of Nugents, and Bailey's Dairy Bar, are also tenants[4] under written leasehold interests from the Defendant Gardiner Shopping Center, Inc.

The[5] Plaintiff's 15-year lease was dated January 12, 19__, and recorded on August 8,[6] 19__, Essex County Registry Book 285, page 156. The Defendant Stetson[7] Stores, Inc., holds under written lease dated August 5, 19__, recorded[8] Essex County Registry of Deeds in Book 287, page 175, on October 16,[9], 19__. It provides for a term of 20 years (Article II, Section I) and contains[10] options for two successive five-year renewal terms (Lease Article III) at specified rentals.[11]

Among its more important operative terms is the phrase, "The demised premises shall be used for the conduct[12] of a department store business which business may include the sale of such items as are presently sold by tenant[13] in its stores." (Article VIII, Section I.) This business of a general department store has been[14] conducted under the firm and style of Cabot's.

While the lease contains limitations against assignment or subleasing[15] without the prior written consent of the landlord (Article XI), these terms are specifically[16] limited "not to include the granting of concessions, licenses, and the like." (Article[17] XI.)

The Plaintiff's lease included a provision contemplating its use of the leased premises[18] for a retail shoe business (Article VIII, Section I of Plaintiff's Lease). It further provided,[19] "No other store or operation whose sales shall consist principally of shoes or handbags shall be permitted[20] in the shopping center."

The Plaintiff's action therefore assumes the burden to prove that the operation of[21] Cabot's store by the Defendant Stetson Stores, Inc., constitutes the operation of a store "whose[22] sales . . . consist principally of shoes or handbags." The Plaintiff has failed to satisfy this burden[23] of proof.

While it is perfectly true that under the firm and style of Cabot's store the Defendant Stetson Stores,[24] Inc., in one of its several departments has merchandised shoes and handbags, its gross revenues[25] from such operation are considerably less than 5 percent of the total gross revenues from the operation[26] of the entire store.

Even if the Plaintiff's proof were consistent with its allegations that Stetson Stores,[27] Inc., was indeed conducting a store whose sales consist "principally of shoes or handbags," the[28] present action should be dismissed because the Plaintiff would have a clear and adequate remedy at law against the[29] Defendant Gardiner Shopping Center, Inc., for damages. Equity has no jurisdiction[30] where the plaintiff has an adequate remedy at law. *Exeter Realty Co. v. Buck*, N.H.[31] 199; *Rockwell v. Dow*, 85 N.H. 58; *Hatch v. Hillsgrove*, 83 N.H. 91. The leasehold[32] covenants between the Defendant, the landlord, and the Plaintiff tenant do not create privity between the[33] Plaintiff and other tenants and do not therefore entitle the Plaintiff to maintain this action against the Defendant[34] Stetson Stores, Inc., *Boston & M.R.R. v. Boston & L.R.R.*, 65 N.H.[35] 393. Merely because there may be several actions against several defendants does not establish that the[36] remedy at law is inadequate. *Town of Hampton v. Palmer*, 99 N.H. 143.

Interestingly,[37] it appears from the evidence that Brent's division of Nugents, also a tenant of the Defendant[38] Gardiner Shopping Center, Inc., conducts a department store type of operation quite like that[39] of Cabot's.

Similarly Brent's is conceded as having conducted, among other things, the sale of shoes and handbags[40] which the Plaintiff's president, George Martin, acknowledged damaged Baldwin's, Inc., up to an estimated[41] extent of 10 percent. No action has been brought nor complaint made to bring Brent's into these proceedings. How[42] can the Plaintiff be permitted to maintain the present action against Stetson Stores, Inc., in such complete[43] disregard of fundamental maxims of equity including that "he who seeks equity must do[44] equity"? *Fowler v. Taylor*, 97 N.H. 294. To complain and seek monetary[45] damages from Defendant Stetson Stores, Inc., for alleged competitive infringement (even[46] assuming the Plaintiff's strained construction of its lease) and yet acknowledge damage from another tenant, Brent's,[47] but refrain from seeking the same remedy from it is most inequitable. Such a proceeding suggests that although[48] the Plaintiff has been damaged by others as well, Stetson Stores, Inc., must pay the plaintiff for[49] it all and cease the sale of shoes and handbags, while Brent's as a next-door tenant to the Plaintiff goes free and continues[50] the sale of shoes and handbags. (1006)

(Continued in Lesson 62.)

Lesson 62

BUILDING YOUR LEGAL VOCABULARY

Disjoined Word Endings

-hood is expressed by  .

falsehood  **livelihood** 

childhood  neighborhood 

parenthood  manhood 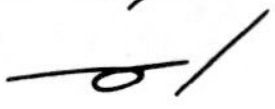

Word Study

 **fraud** Misrepresentation intended to deprive another of his or her rights.

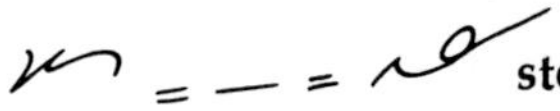 **stock-in-trade** The equipment necessary to, or used in, a trade.

 **sublease** Agreement between a tenant and a third party to rent the property described in the original lease.

BUILDING YOUR LEGAL TRANSCRIPTION SKILL

Transcription Aid

Footnotes: Periodicals

☐ In typing a footnote that refers to an article in a periodical, include the following: author's name in natural order, title of the article in quotes, title of the periodical underlined, series number (if given), volume number, issue number (if given), page numbers inclusive, and publication date.

1. William L. Hungate, "Changes in the Federal Rules of Criminal Procedure," American Bar Association Journal, Vol. 61, pages 1203-1207, October 1975.

Legal Collocations

 **express warranty** A guarantee that is established in writing, as distinguished from an implied warranty.

 **implied warranty** A guarantee presumed by the law.

 **implied agreement** An inferred understanding between parties, as distinguished from written or spoken words.

 **unilateral contract** Agreement binding only one side or party, lacking mutual obligations.

 **general release** A surrender of one's claim to the obligated party.

BUILDING YOUR LEGAL DICTATION PROFICIENCY

Preview

allegedly		merchandising	
allocated		monetary	
asserted		proposition	
complex		restraint	
conspiracy		restriction	
contradictory		retained	
departmentalized		terminable	
logically		uncontroverted	

Reading and Writing Practice

182. MEMORANDUM OF LAW *(Continued from Lesson 61.)*

Hardly less contradictory is the proposition that while the basis of the Plaintiff's complaint is that the[1] Defendant Lovett Shoe Co., Inc., has allegedly enjoyed profits from what the Plaintiff[2] claims to be operation of a store (within the Cabot's complex) whose sales consist "principally[3] of shoes or handbags" and with Lovett Shoe Co., Inc., having the same constructive knowledge[4] of the terms of the Plaintiff's lease as all other defendants, the Plaintiff seeks no monetary damages[5] from Lovett Shoe Co., Inc., but insists the Defendants,Stetson Stores, Inc., and[6] Gardiner Shopping Center, Inc., respond in monetary damage for all the Plaintiff's losses.[7] Neither fraud nor conspiracy has been either alleged or asserted, and certainly the evidence would not[8] support such a contention.

The evidence as to the operation of the Cabot's Store by Stetson Stores, Inc.,[9] and the sale of shoes and handbags at its premises is uncontroverted as to the following[10] important points:

1. All fixtures and furnishings in the area where shoes and handbags were sold were owned by Stetson[11] Stores, Inc.

2. All customers and personnel were covered by the insurance policies purchased[12] and maintained by Stetson Stores, Inc.

3. All sales to customers on credit were recorded and[13] billed by Stet-

son Stores, Inc., and all records and accounts relating to this were solely kept by this[14] Defendant.

4. Determination of credit and all risk of loss resulting from unpaid bills to credit[15] customers was solely that of Stetson Stores, Inc.

5. All advertising of shoes, handbags, and other[16] wares at Cabot's was originated and paid for by Stetson Stores, Inc.

6. Stock-in-trade and[17] other taxes on inventory including shoes and handbags were paid by Stetson Stores, Inc.

7.[18] Selection of lines of shoes to be carried was made by Stetson Stores, Inc.

8. Control over all[19] personnel in the shoe and handbag department was strictly retained by Stetson Stores, Inc. Hiring[20] or firing was the sole privilege of Stetson Stores, Inc.

9. Control of the inventory of[21] shoes was retained by Stetson Stores, Inc.

10. Arrangements for the purchase and delivery of shoes to[22] Stetson Stores, Inc., by Lovett Shoe Co., Inc., was terminable at will by[23] Stetson Stores, Inc.

11. Bookkeeping and accounts for all departments at Cabot's were kept by[24] Stetson Stores, Inc., and no different system or method was used in connection with records of[25] the shoe department from any other department.

The mere fact that the payment to Lovett Shoe Co., Inc.,[26] by Stetson Stores, Inc., for its ability to purchase shoes and provide consulting service[27] for Cabot's was guaranteed and based upon a percentage received from the actual sales of shoes in no[28] way establishes that this operation consisted of a sublease arrangement or any arrangement that[29] constituted a violation of any provision of the Plaintiff's lease with Gardiner Shopping Center, Inc.[30] No rent was paid or received; no term existed with respect to such arrangement. No writing defined[31] any relationship out of which sublease or independent operation by Lovett Shoe Co.,[32] Inc., could be construed. No retail sale of shoes has been made by Lovett Shoe Co., Inc.,[33] at Cabot's store to any member of the public at any time.

The Defendant Gardiner Shopping Center, Inc.,[34] by visiting at other stores and seeking the resultant tenancy, was fully aware of the[35] operation of the type of department store by the Defendant Stetson Stores, Inc., prior to any[36] lease with Baldwin's, Inc. Blueprints and plans calling for specific area allocated to the shoe[37] department and all places of construction were known to Gardiner Shopping Center, Inc. As lessor[38] it retained the right to examine records and accounts of the lessee (Lease Article IV, pages[39] 5 and 6). From such records the examination of "gross sales figures of Stetson Stores, Inc."[40] clearly indicated to this landlord that the store was not principally engaged in the sale of shoes[41] and handbags.

To grant the relief requested by the Plaintiff and require Stetson Stores, Inc., to refrain[42] from retail merchandising of shoes and handbags would require the Court to enlarge the scope of the Plaintiff's lease[43] and the plain meaning of its language beyond reasonable construction. It would result in an unfair restriction[44] on a phase of the Defendant Stetson Stores, Inc.'s, departmentalized operation.

The validity[45] of a restriction or an agreement depends upon the reasonableness of the restraint as applied to[46] the particular circumstances of the case. *Bancroft v. Co.*, 72 N.H. 402, 41 ALR[47] (2d) 15, 43 ALR (2d) 94. The construction which the Plaintiff[48] seeks to apply extends beyond the plain meaning of the contract of the lease. The Plaintiff insists it has an[49] exclusive right to the sale of shoes or handbags in the Gardiner Shopping Center area. Such construction is[50] forced and does not logically flow from terms that provide no other tenant will be permitted "whose sales shall[51] consist principally of shoes or handbags." By no fair import of the language of the lease can the Plaintiff[52] extend its scope to prevent the sale at Cabot's of shoes or handbags where such sale is such a small portion of the[53] department store's total gross sales. To do so would impose a restriction in restraint of trade or competition.[54] The law does not look with favor upon contracts in restraint of trade or competition. *Eastern Express Co.*[55] *v. Meserve*, 60 N.H. 198; *Dunfy v. Enwright*, 101 N.H. 195. (1118)

Lesson 63

BUILDING YOUR LEGAL VOCABULARY

Disjoined Word Endings

-ward is expressed by 

inward 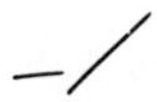

outward 

forward 

onward 

backward 

upward 

Word Study

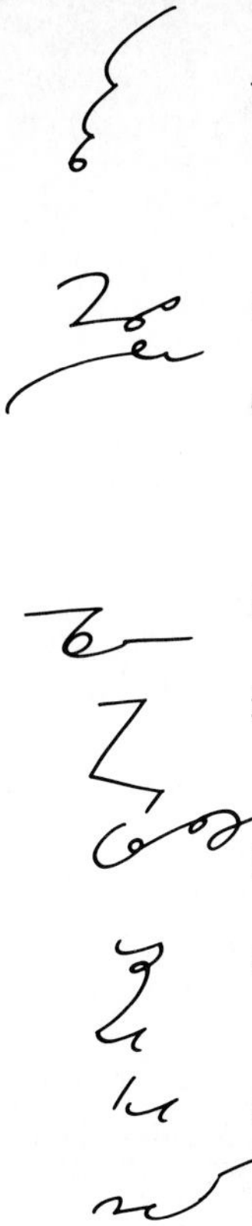

bankruptcy Legal status under which the court administers a person's assets for the benefit of his creditors, distributing the assets and thus paying off the debts.

conformity Agreement.

demurrer A pleading that assumes the truth of the allegations but holds that it is insufficient to sustain the claim or that there are other defects.

impairment Damage.

injunction A court order requiring a person to do or refrain from doing an act.

predicate To affirm, declare.

receivers Persons appointed by the court to receive and hold in trust properties in legal process.

sureties Insurers of a debt, obligation, or responsibility of another.

unwarranted Not justifiable, inexcusable.

BUILDING YOUR LEGAL TRANSCRIPTION SKILL

Transcription Aid

Footnotes: Works Previously Cited

☐ In typing a footnote that refers to a work already cited, select the appropriate one from the following expressions:

1. For reference to the same page of a source just cited, use the expression *Ibid.*
2. For the same source as the footnote *immediately preceding* but on a different page, use *Ibid.*, followed by the page number.
3. For the same source as a work previously cited when other footnotes intervene, use the author's surname followed by *op. cit.* and the page number:

   Landon, op. cit., pp. 100-110.

Latin and French Words and Phrases

allonge *(a lōnj′)* A piece of paper attached to a bill of exchange or a promissory note on which to add endorsements when there is insufficient space on the instrument itself.

infra *(in fra′)* Below, under; appearing later.

res judicata *(rās ju di ca′ta)* A thing judicially acted on or decided.

BUILDING YOUR LEGAL DICTATION PROFICIENCY

Preview

amended 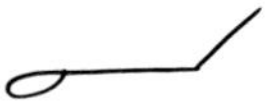

commodities 

conformity 

demised 

denies 

indemnify 

landlord 

licensing 

merchandising 

paragraphs 

responsive 

thereto 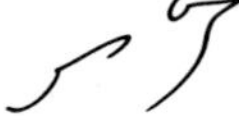

Reading and Writing Practice

13

183. COMMONWEALTH OF MASSACHUSETTS ESSEX, SS. SUPERIOR COURT EQUITY NO. 16,205 BALDWIN'S, INC., V. GARDINER SHOPPING CENTER, INC., STETSON STORES, INC., LOVETT SHOE COMPANY, INC. ANSWER OF DEFENDANT, STETSON STORES, INC.

Without waiving demurrer, motion to dismiss, and the reservation of rights herewith filed to plead and further[1] answer, now comes Stetson Stores, Inc., a Massachusetts corporation, and in response to the Petition[2] filed by Baldwin's, Inc., a Massachusetts corporation with principal place of business[3] in Peabody, states that with respect to the allegations contained in paragraphs 1 through 8 the Defendant is[4] without adequate information or belief on which to predicate responsive pleadings and accordingly[5] neither admits nor denies the same but puts the Plaintiff on its proof with respect thereto.

Stetson Stores, Inc.,[6] under its lease and under the firm and style of

Cabot's conducts the business of a department store on[7] the demised premises which include the sale of such items as are presently sold by Stetson Stores, Inc.,[8] in its other stores, all in conformity with the provisions of Article VII of its lease with Gardiner[9] Shopping Center, Inc., but denies that this constitutes an operation whose sales consist[10] principally of shoes or handbags.

The allegations of paragraphs 10 through 14 are denied.

And further[11] answering, the defendant Stetson Stores, Inc., states that shoes or handbags do not constitute the[12] principal sales but only a small portion of the total retail sales of the commodities marketed under[13] the firm and style of Cabot's by said Stetson Stores, Inc., all in conformity with and in accordance[14] with the rights reserved to it under indenture of lease dated August 23, 19—,[15] by and between Gardiner Shopping Center, Inc., and said Stetson Stores, Inc.; and[16] that

The said Stetson Stores, Inc., has at no time since the date of said lease altered, amended, or varied[17] the method of merchandising shoes or handbags which has been the retail selling under an oral licensing[18] arrangement with the Defendant, Lovett Shoe Company, Inc., whose shoe products have been marketed,[19] at the Cabot's store in the Gardiner Shopping Center by Stetson Stores, Inc.; and

That the said Stetson[20] Stores, Inc., on or about April 4, 19—, filed a petition in the[21] United States District Court for the District of Massachusetts under Chapter XI of the Bankruptcy Act[22] for an arrangement, which plan was confirmed on or about September 27, 19—, since[23] which time the operation of its business, including that subject to the lease with Gardiner Shopping Center,[24] Inc., is under the direct supervision of the Receivers appointed by said Bankruptcy[25] Court who are thereby necessary parties to any action or proceeding involving the rights of parties governed[26] by leases affecting the method or area of retail merchandising.

WHEREFORE, the Defendant Stetson Stores,[27] Inc., prays that this proceeding be dismissed, that it be awarded just and suitable counsel fees, that no[28] restraining order or injunction be issued or decreed without a hearing and an adequate bond with[29] independent sureties to indemnity the defendant from all loss, costs, and damages that would result therefrom,[30] including without limiting the generality thereof the loss of customers, accounts, business volume,[31] good will, and the unwarranted impairment of existing business relationship, and

For such other and further[32] relief as may be just.

Stetson Stores, Inc. By its attorneys By:____________________

Lester L. Greenberg

July[33] 7, 19—

I hereby certify that a copy of the foregoing has this day been forwarded[34] to Maine, Carlson, Galey, Gene & Bonn, Esquires, counsel for the Plaintiff, and Willis, Norris, Sutherland, Nichols[35] & Polk, counsel for Gardiner Shopping Center, Inc.

Lester L. Greenberg (717)

184. FREDERICK G. FRANKLIN, ESQ., HARRIS AND DONAVON, 160 STATE STREET, BOSTON, MA 02109

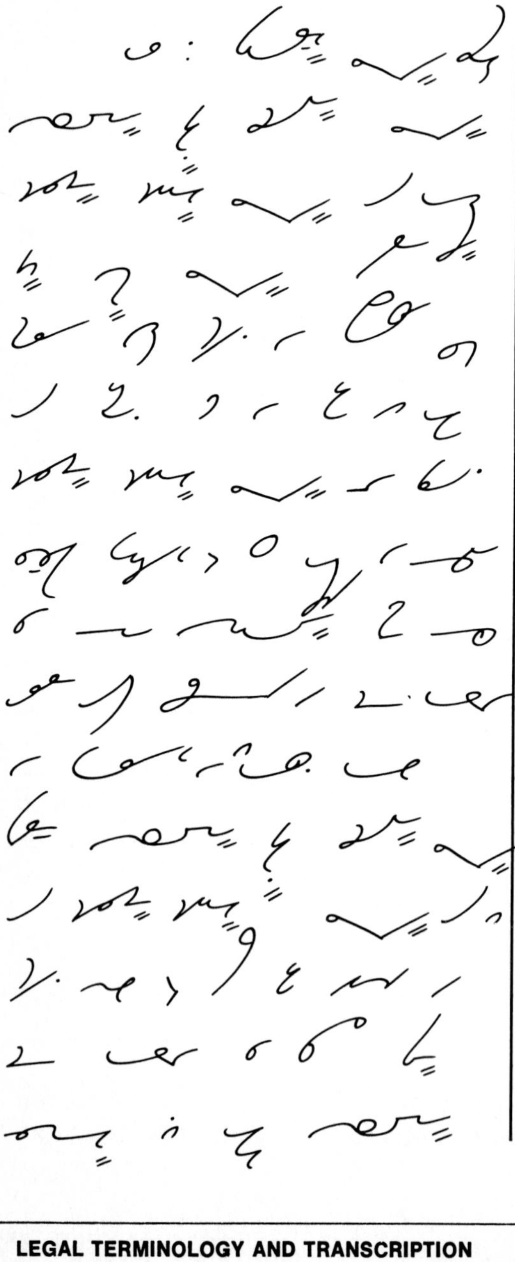

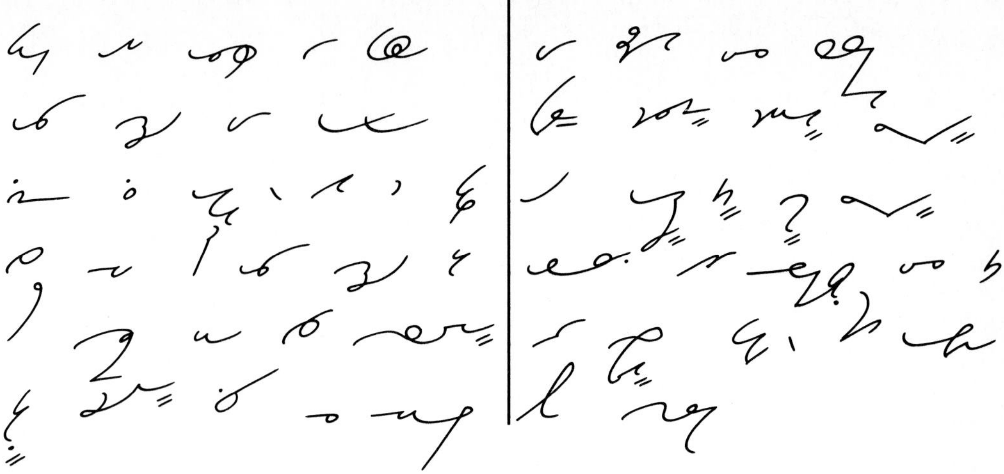

Lesson 64

BUILDING YOUR LEGAL VOCABULARY

Disjoined Word Endings

-ship is expressed by / .

receivership	**censorship**
guardianship	**suretyship**
citizenship	**township**

Word Study

estop To stop; prevent.

induce To influence; persuade.

insolvency State of being unable to pay one's debts.

 **restraining order** A court order stating that a person or group cease an activity, usually for a specified time.

BUILDING YOUR LEGAL TRANSCRIPTION SKILL

Legal Collocations

 **escalator clause** A clause in leases or contracts providing for increase or reduction of rents or salaries under certain conditions.

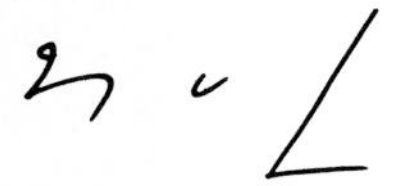 **execution of judgment** Enforcement of an order, decree, or judgment granted by a court of law.

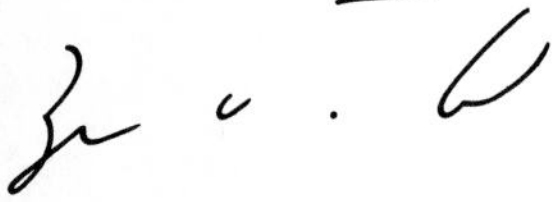 **forfeiture of a bond** Loss of bond (money or property) through failure of the bonded person to appear in court or to perform the act for which he or she was bonded.

 **involuntary bankruptcy** Legal proceedings filed by creditors without the consent of the debtor.

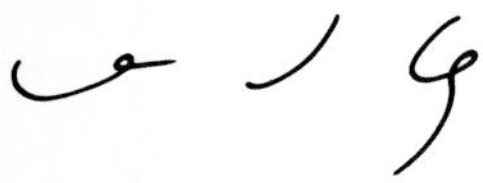 **lien and privilege** The right of a creditor to proceed against the property of a debtor.

BUILDING YOUR LEGAL DICTATION PROFICIENCY

Preview

align 
bankruptcy 
concession 
defenses 
detrimental 
forewarned 
injunction 
interpreted 

modifications 
mountainous 
parenthetically 
precedent 
receivers 
responsive 
substantial 
terminate 

Reading and Writing Practice

185. FREDERICK G. FRANKLIN, ESQ., HARRIS AND DONAVON, 160 STATE STREET, BOSTON, MA 02109

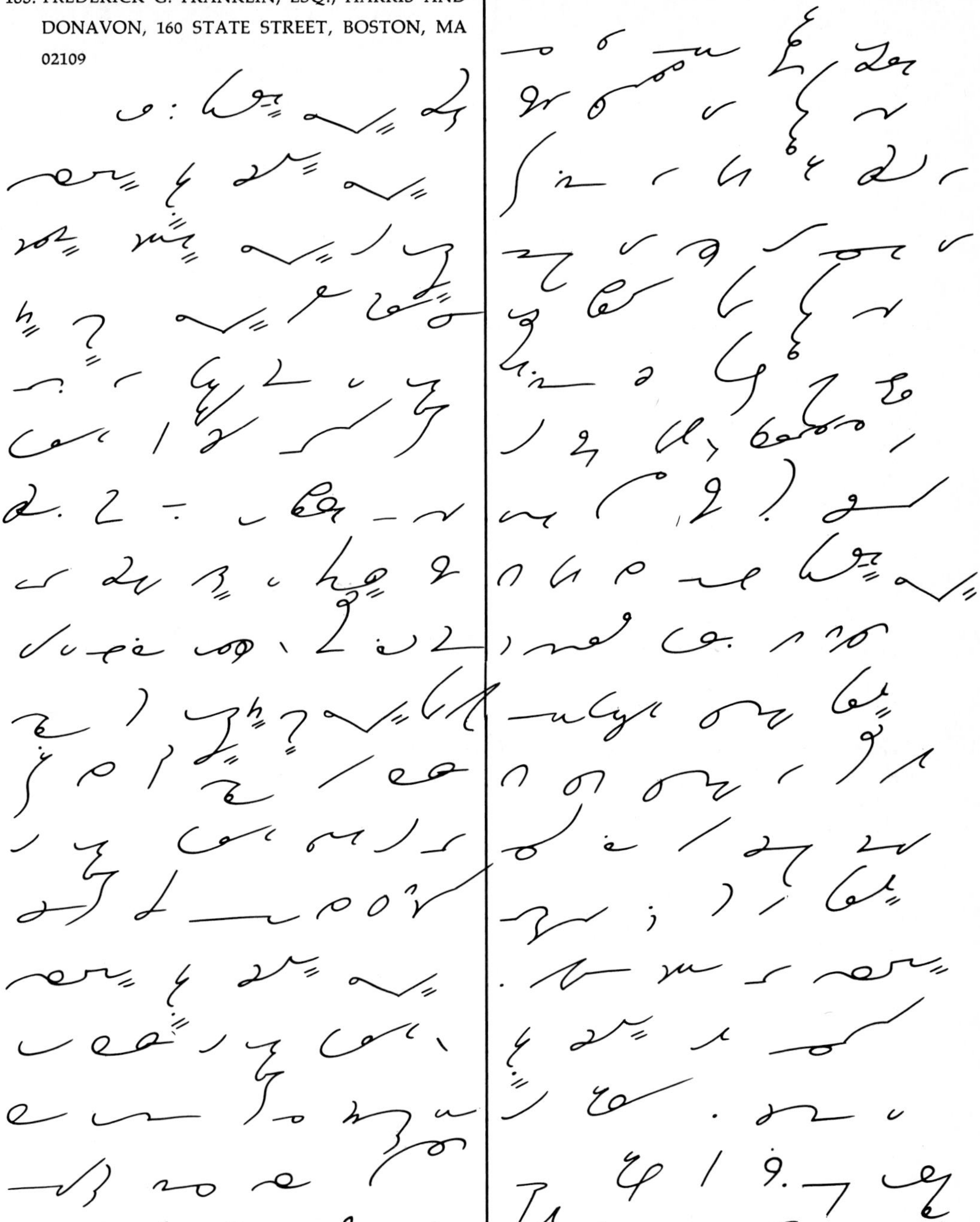

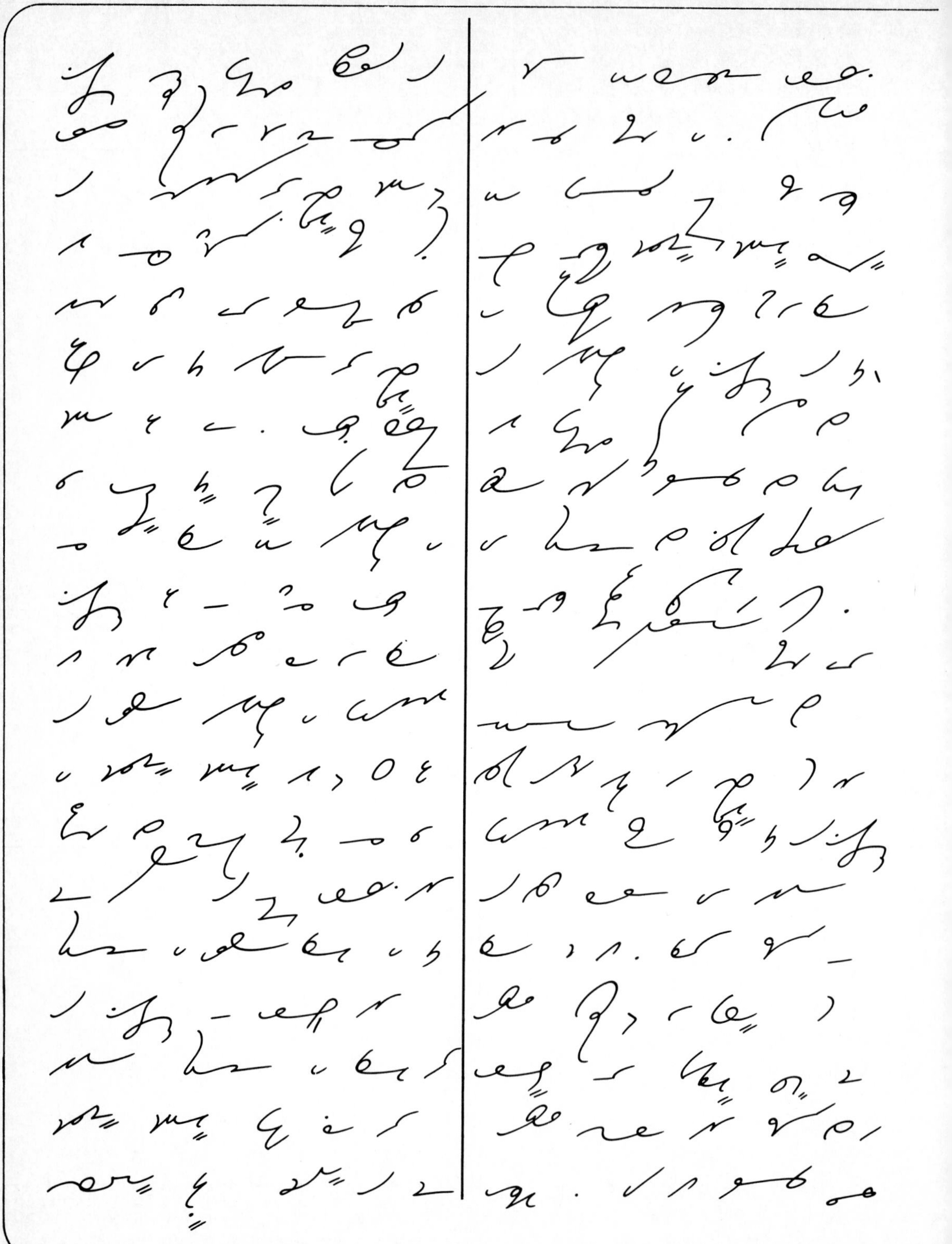

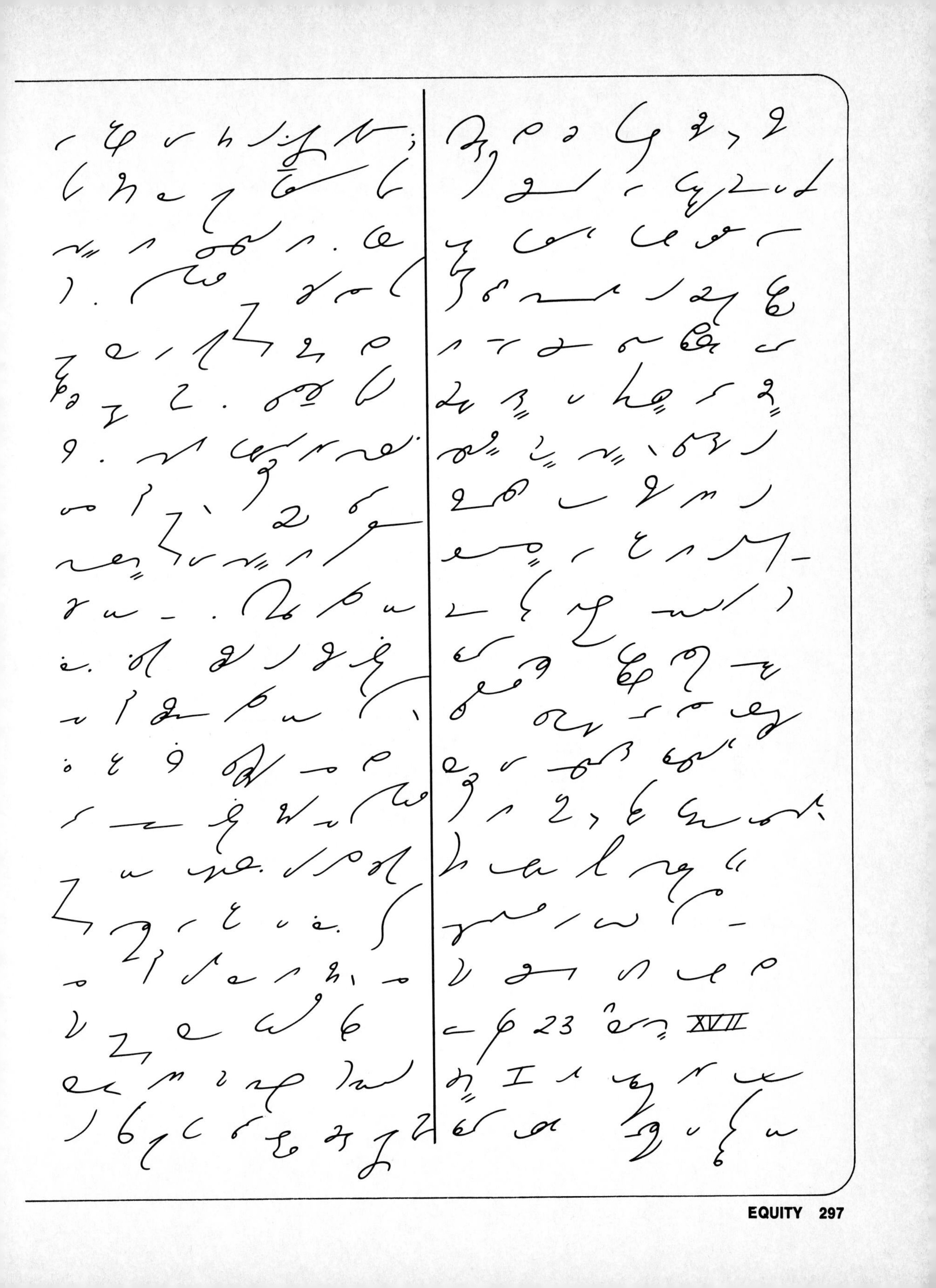

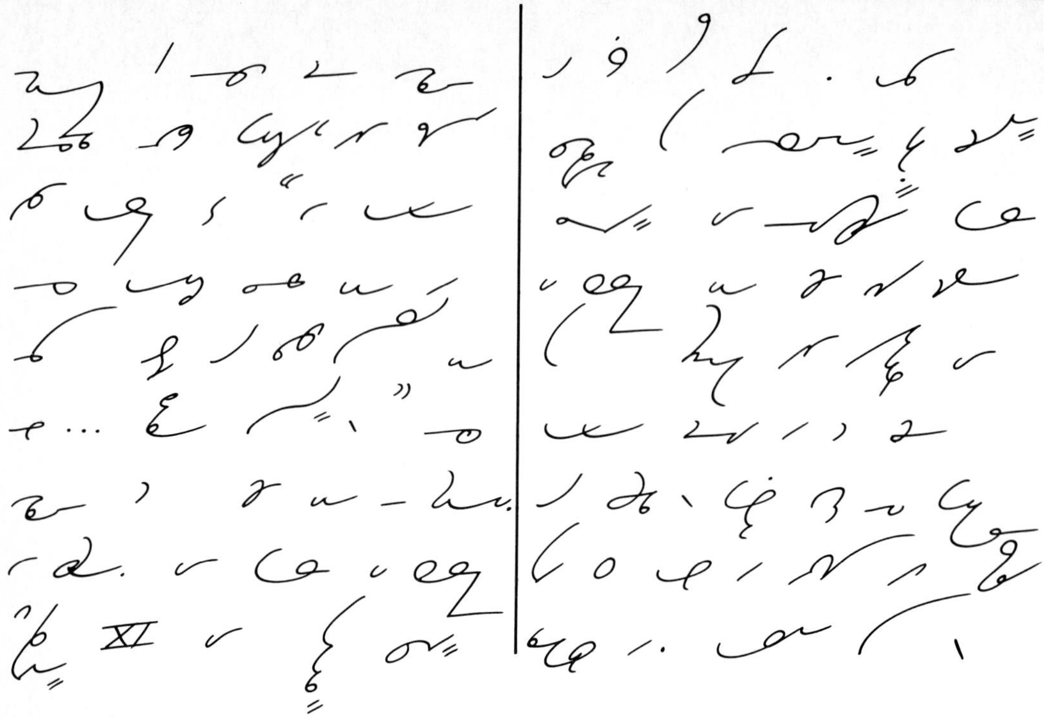

Lesson 65

BUILDING YOUR LEGAL VOCABULARY

Disjoined Word Endings

-cal and *-cle* are expressed by ⌒ .

empirical	critically
medical	identical
articles	emphatically

Word Study

litigation A contest in law.

replication A plaintiff's reply to a defendant's answer.

revested Reinstated; returned.

BUILDING YOUR LEGAL TRANSCRIPTION SKILL

Latin Abbreviations

e.g. (**exempli gratia** *ix em' plē grad' ē a*) For example.

et seq. (**et sequens** or **et sequentes** *et se quen'tās*) And the following (as pages 50 et seq.)

N.B. (**nota bene** *no'ta ben'ā*) Take notice, note well.

BUILDING YOUR LEGAL DICTATION PROFICIENCY

Preview

commission 

endeavor 

entitled 

formulated 

inapplicable 

lessor 

petitionee 

presiding 

schedule 

sublease 

Reading and Writing Practice

186. COMMONWEALTH OF MASSACHUSETTS ESSEX, SS. SEPTEMBER TERM 19__ SUPERIOR COURT BALDWIN'S, INC., V. GARDINER SHOPPING CENTER, INC., STETSON STORES, INC., LOVETT SHOE COMPANY, INC. PETITIONER'S REPLICATION TO THE ANSWER OF THE PETITIONEE, STETSON STORES, INC.

NOW COMES Baldwin's, Inc., Petitioner in the above action, and for its reply to the answer of[1] Stetson Stores, Inc., says as follows:

1. That it neither admits nor denies the allegations contained[2] in the

first paragraph of the affirmative matter pleaded in the said answer.

2. That it neither admits[3] nor denies the allegations contained in the second paragraph of the affirmative matter pleaded[4] in the said answer.

3. That it denies that the alleged receivers are necessary parties and denies that[5] the operation of the business of Stetson Stores, Inc., is under the direct supervision[6] of the alleged receivers, for the reason that said receivers were relieved of all supervision and control[7] over the affairs of Stetson Stores, Inc.; and their duties were terminated by the Order[8] Confirming Arrangement issued by the Honorable Edgar Higgins, Referee in Bankruptcy, United States District[9] Court, District of Massachusetts, dated July 26, 19—, which order revested[10] in Stetson Stores, Inc., possession of all its property.

4. That even if the alleged receivers[11] remain in control of the affairs of Stetson Stores, Inc., they are not necessary parties[12] to this proceeding.

WHEREFORE, the Petitioner prays that the relief prayed for in its petition be granted,[13] and that the relief prayed for in the answer be denied.

Baldwin's, Inc.
Maine, Carlson, Galey, Gene &[14] Bonn

By:______________________________Its Attorneys

September 3, 19—

I hereby certify that[15] a copy of the foregoing Replication was mailed on September 3, 19—, to Davis,[16] Miller, Starr & Best and Greenberg, O'Brien, Mason & McCann, counsel for the Petitionees. (337)

187. FREDERICK G. FRANKLIN, ESQ., HARRIS AND DONAVON, 160 STATE STREET, BOSTON, MA 02109

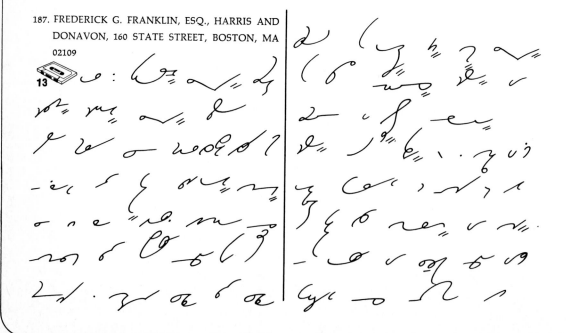

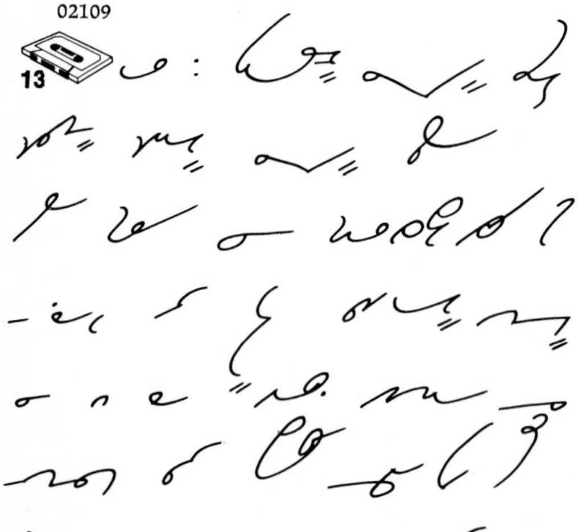

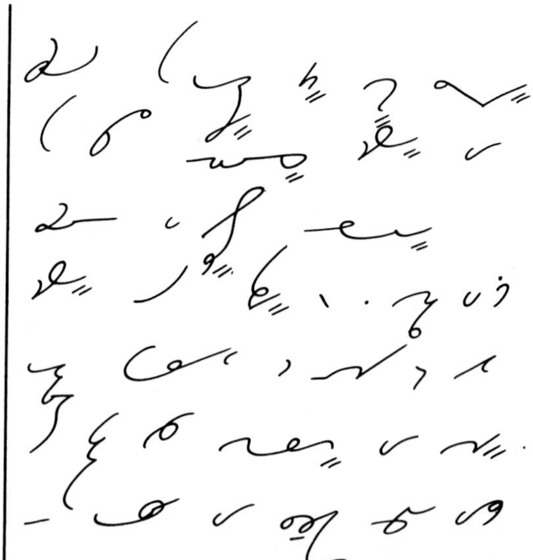

188. NORMA H. STARR, ESQ., DAVIS, MILLER, STARR & BEST, 16 FEDERAL STREET, BOSTON, MA 02109

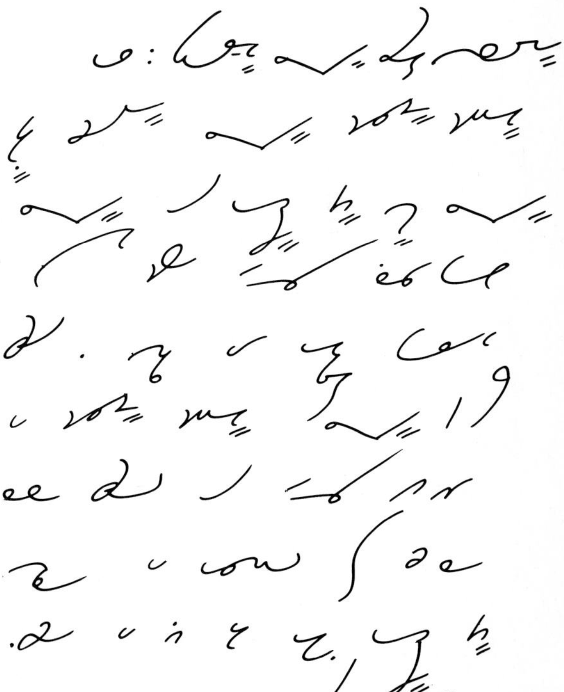

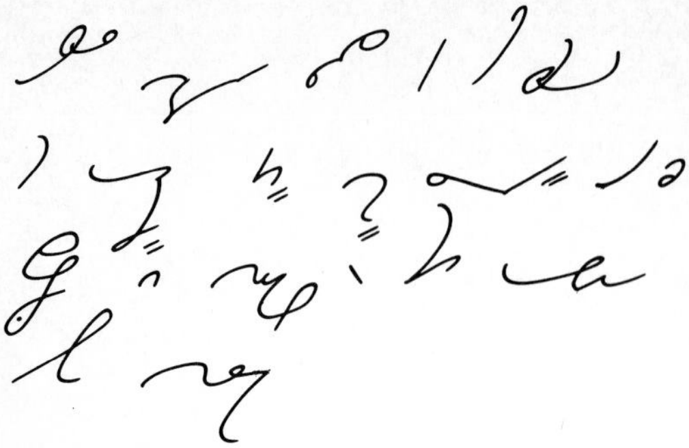

189. JOHN H. NICHOLS, ESQ., WILLIS, NORRIS, SUTHERLAND, NICHOLS & POLK, 96 DEVONSHIRE STREET, BOSTON, MA 02109

190. FREDERICK G. FRANKLIN, ESQ., HARRIS AND DONAVON, 160 STATE STREET, BOSTON, MA 02109

191. NORMA H. STARR, ESQ., DAVIS, MILLER, STARR & BEST, 16 FEDERAL STREET, BOSTON, MA 02109

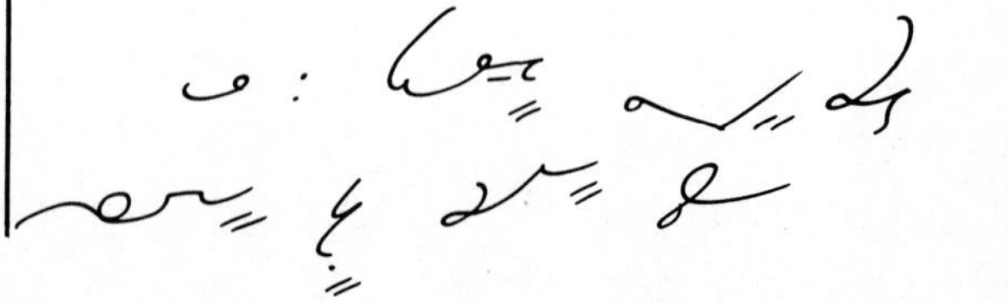

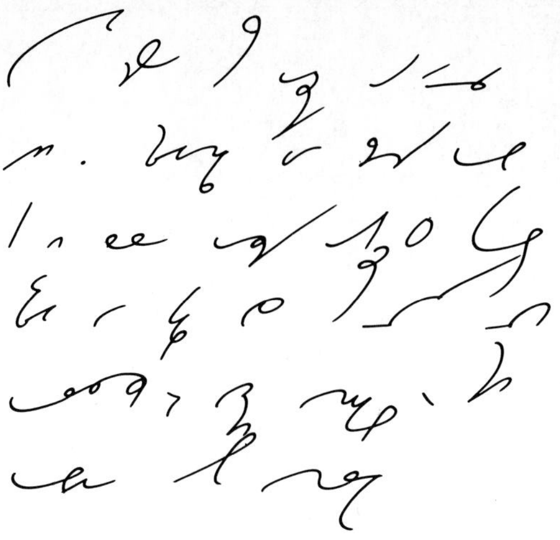

192. G. PETER GARY, ESQ., MAINE, CARLSON, GALEY, GENE & BONN, 45 CONGRESS STREET, BOSTON, MA 02109

Lesson 66

BUILDING YOUR LEGAL VOCABULARY

Disjoined Word Endings

-ulate is expressed by  ; *-ulation* is expressed by  .

stipulations 

consulate 

manipulate 

manipulator 

stimulated 

formulation 

Word Study

abated Reduced in value, deducted, omitted.

nonjoinder The omission of a necessary party, plaintiff, or defendant to a suit at law.

parol Word of mouth, oral.

BUILDING YOUR LEGAL TRANSCRIPTION SKILL

Legal Collocations

legal tender Currency which the law authorizes as payment when offered by a debtor.

statute of limitations Any law limiting the time within which an action must be brought after the right of action has arisen.

these presents A term used to refer to the specific instrument or document in which the expression appears.

KNOW ALL MEN BY THESE PRESENTS

temporary injunction A writ or order by the court requiring a person or a corporation to do or to refrain from doing something that threatens or causes injury during the time of litigation of the case. It may be dissolved or made permanent when the rights of the parties are determined by court.

restrictive covenant A provision in a written agreement that limits or restricts the performance of some action by one of the parties, as when the seller of a business agrees not to engage in the same business within a certain number of years.

BUILDING YOUR LEGAL DICTATION PROFICIENCY

Preview

docketed 

fundamental 

heroically 

interrogations 

multiple 

negotiated 

reconcile 

respective 

Reading and Writing Practice

193. FREDERICK G. FRANKLIN, ESQ., HARRIS AND DONAVON, 160 STATE STREET, BOSTON, MA 02109

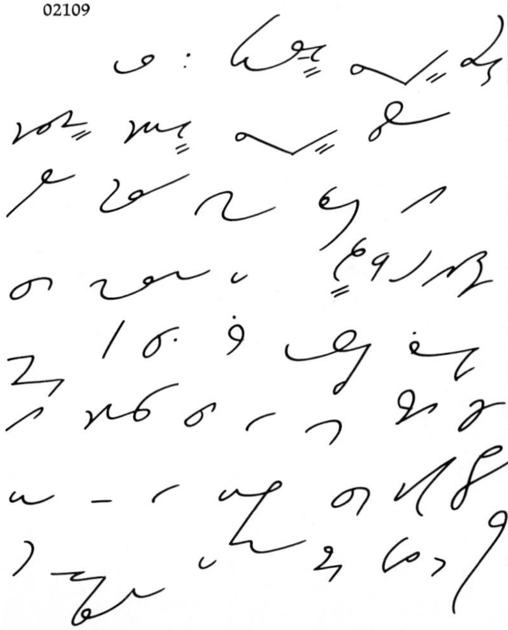

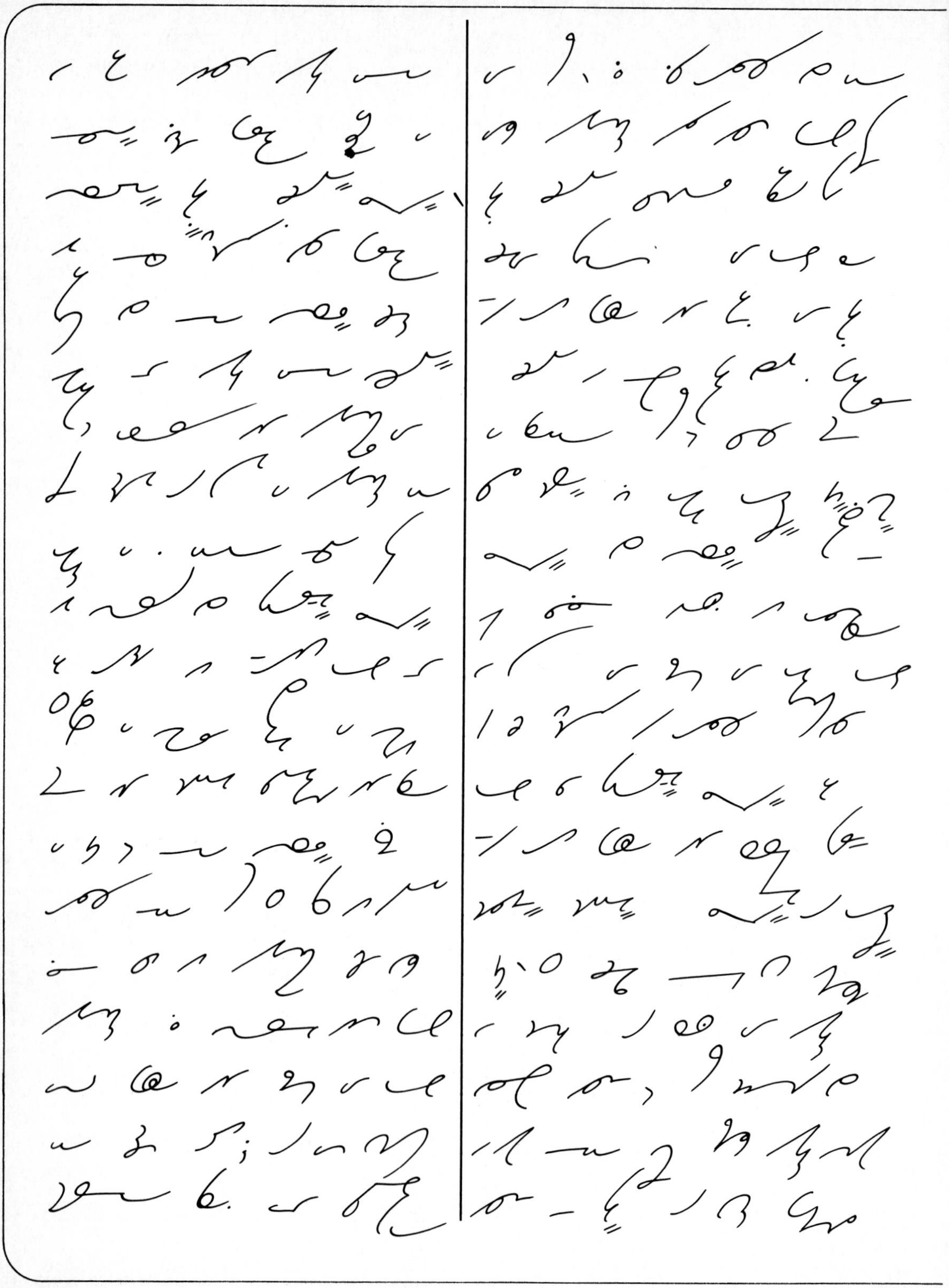

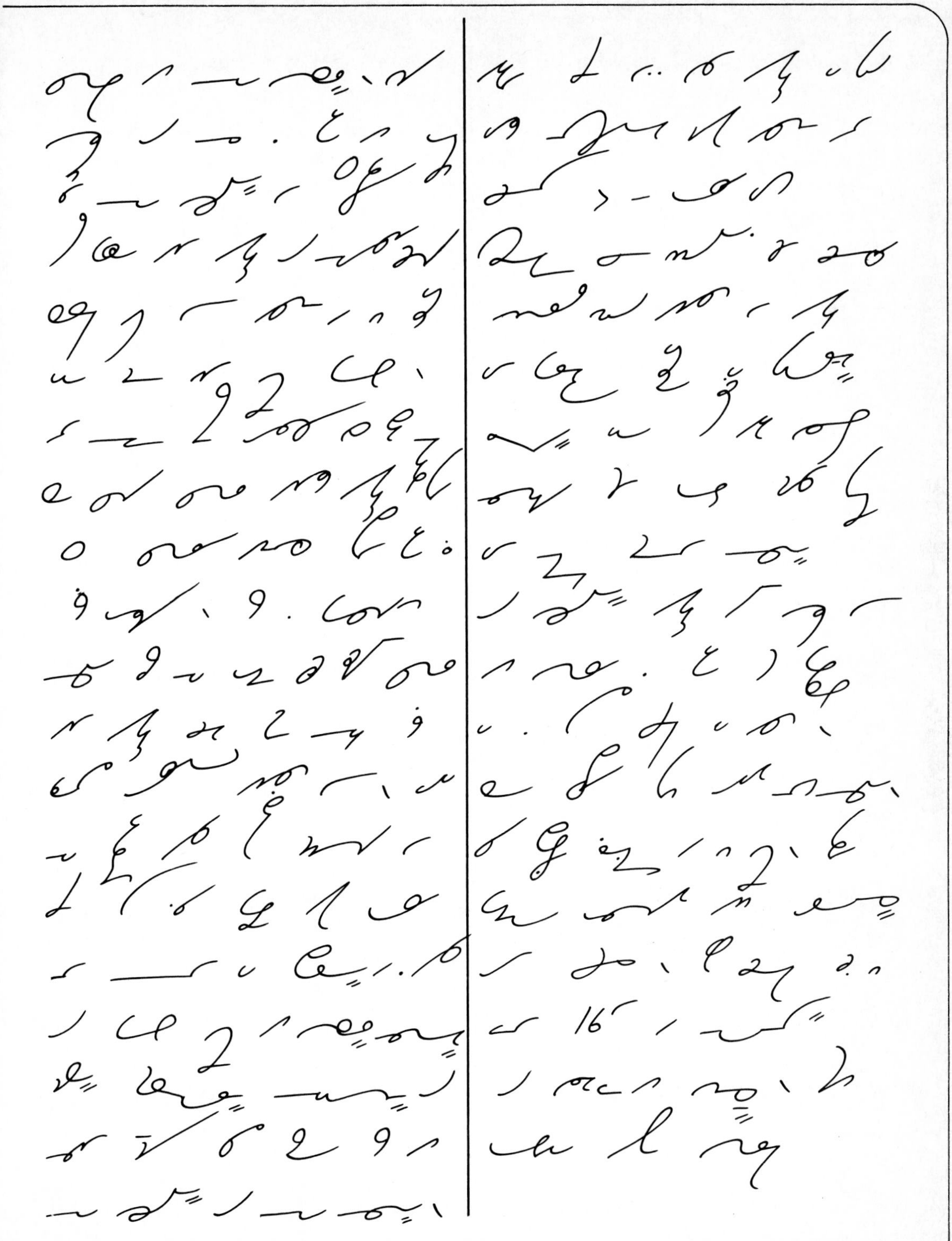

194. G. PETER GARY, ESQ., MAINE, CARLSON, GALEY, GENE & BONN, 45 CONGRESS STREET, BOSTON, MA 02109

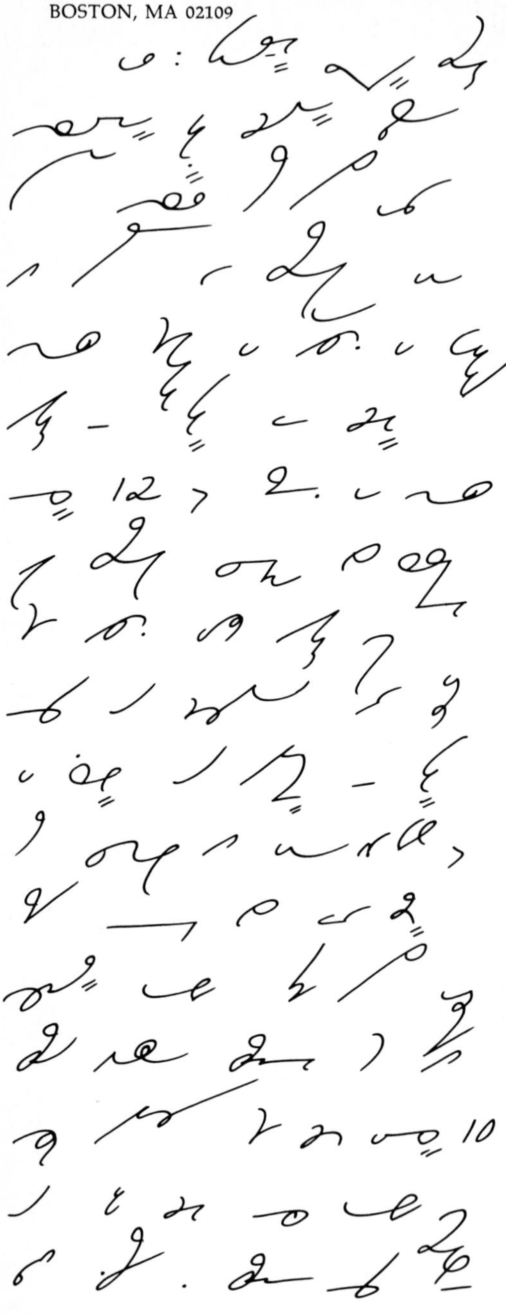

195. FREDERICK G. FRANKLIN, ESQ., HARRIS AND DONAVON, 160 STATE STREET, BOSTON, MA 02109

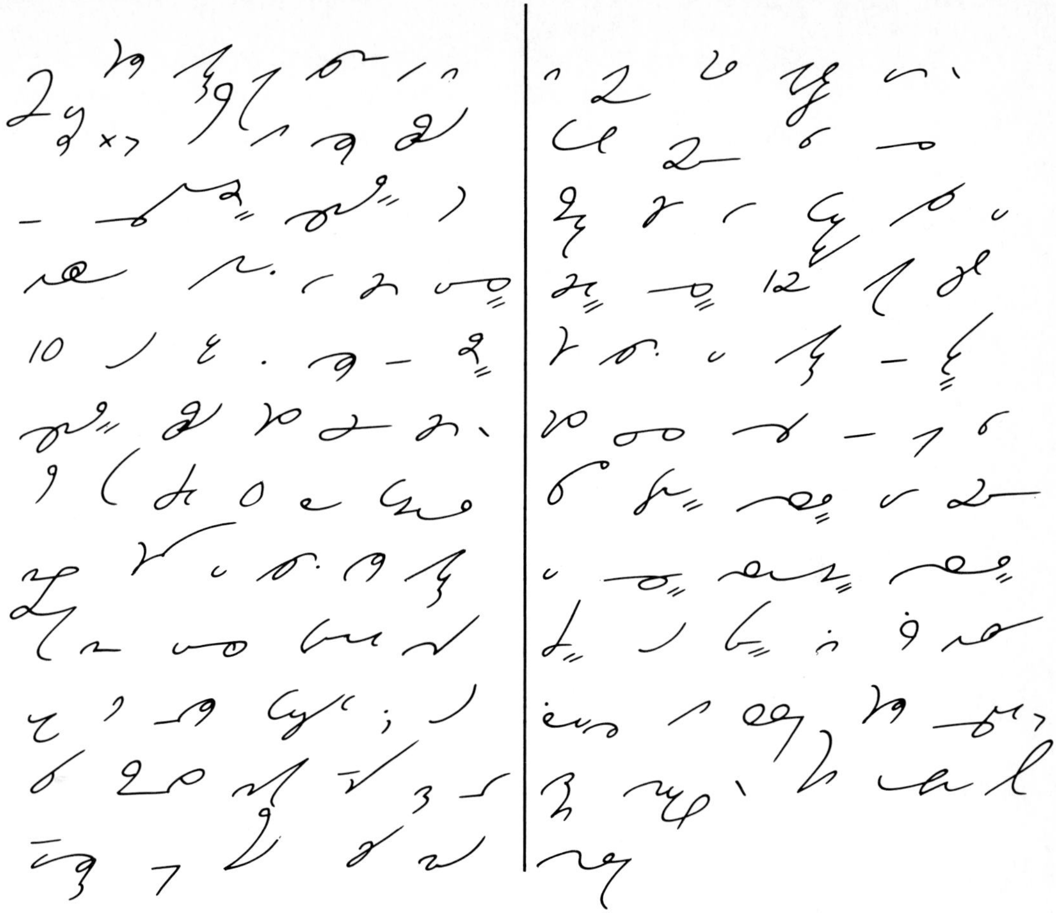

Lesson 67

BUILDING YOUR LEGAL VOCABULARY

Disjoined Word Endings *-ing* is expressed by ; *-ings* by ; and *-ingly* by .

ratifying 

rulings 

holdings

pleadings

willingly

unceasingly

Word Study

breach of contract Nonperformance of an agreement.

breach of warranty Failure to live up to the written or implied guarantee of the excellence of a product or service.

claimant A party making claims that ask the court to order the other party to do or not do something.

declarant A person making a formal declaration of fact.

BUILDING YOUR LEGAL TRANSCRIPTION SKILL

Latin Abbreviations

id. (**idem** *ī′dem*) The same; the same as above.

i.e. (**id est** *id est*) That is to say.

L.S. (**locus sigilli** *lō′kus si jil′lī*) The place of the seal. The word *seal* or *L.S.* is typed in solid capitals at the end of the signature line or lines on instruments that must be sealed.

BUILDING YOUR LEGAL DICTATION PROFICIENCY

Preview

assured

diminished

diminishment

insulate

notation

therefor

Reading and Writing Practice

14

196. COMMONWEALTH OF MASSACHUSETTS ESSEX, SS. SEPTEMBER TERM, 19__ SUPERIOR COURT BALDWIN'S, INC.,V. GARDINER SHOPPING CENTER, INC., STETSON STORES, INC., LOVETT SHOE COMPANY, INC. MOTION TO AMEND PETITION

NOW COMES Baldwin's, Inc., Petitioner in the above-entitled action, and moves that its Petition[1] be amended as follows:

1. That the name "Gardener Shopping Center, Inc.," be deleted[2] wherever it appears in the Petition and that there be substituted therefor the name "Gardiner Shopping[3] Center, Inc."

2. That there be added to the Petition a paragraph 15 as follows:[4] "15. That the operation of the shoe and handbag department by Lovett Shoe Company, Inc.,[5] on premises leased to Stetson Stores, Inc., referred to in paragraph 9 above has[6] diminished the value of the Petitioner's lease referred to in paragraph 2 above."

3. That paragraph (b)[7] of the Prayer for Relief be deleted and that the following paragraph be substituted therefor:[8]

"(b) That Gardiner Shopping Center, Inc., and Stetson Stores, Inc.,[9] be ordered to pay to Baldwin's, Inc., as compensation for its loss of profits, and as compensation[10] for the diminishment in the value of its lease, the sum of $29,000."

Respectfully[11] submitted, Baldwin's, Inc.
By its attorneys, Maine, Carlson, Galey, Gene & Bonn.

By:______________________________
G. Peter[12] Gary

I hereby certify that a copy of the foregoing motion was mailed on September 23,[13] 19__, to Davis, Miller, Starr & Best; Willis, Norris, Sutherland, Nichols & Polk; and Greenberg,[14] O'Brien, Mason & McCann, counsel for the Petitionees. (293)

197. G. PETER GARY, ESQ., MAINE, CARLSON, GALEY, GENE & BONN, 45 CONGRESS STREET, BOSTON, MA 02109

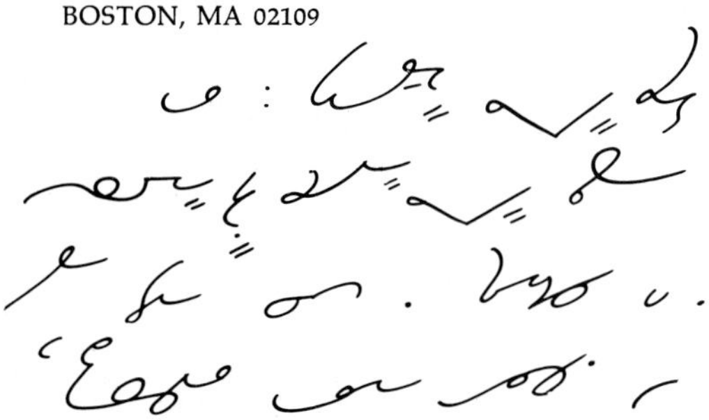

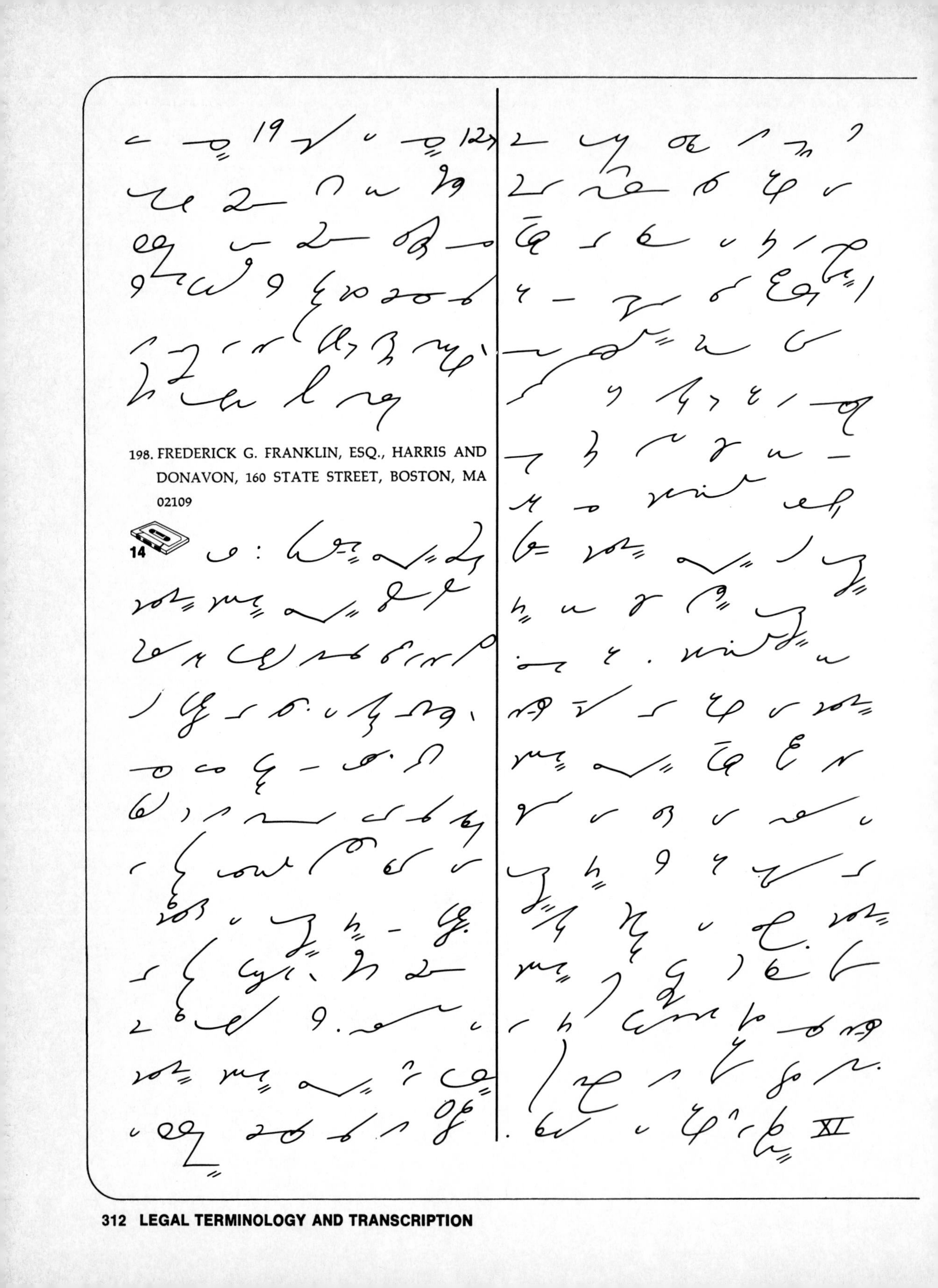

198. FREDERICK G. FRANKLIN, ESQ., HARRIS AND DONAVON, 160 STATE STREET, BOSTON, MA 02109

14

199. G. PETER GARY, ESQ., MAINE, CARLSON, GALEY, GENE & BONN, 45 CONGRESS STREET, BOSTON, MA 02109

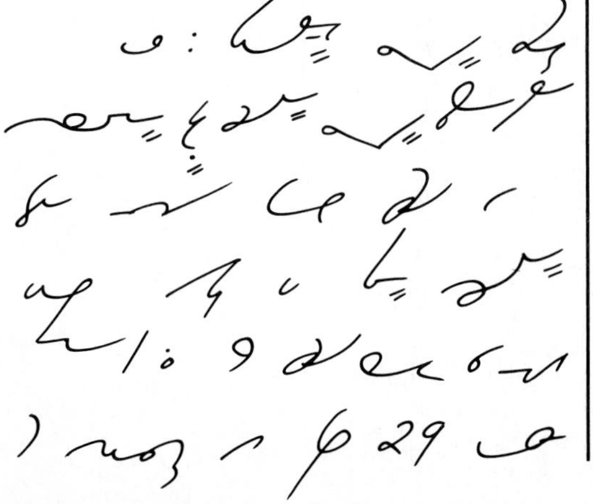

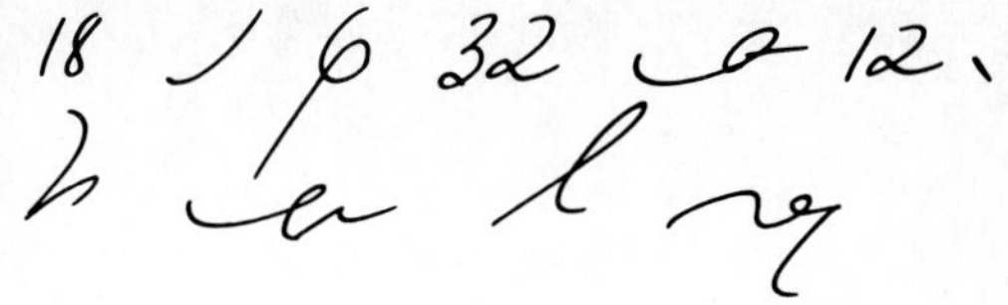

200. FREDERICK G. FRANKLIN, ESQ., HARRIS AND DONAVON, 160 STATE STREET, BOSTON, MA 02109

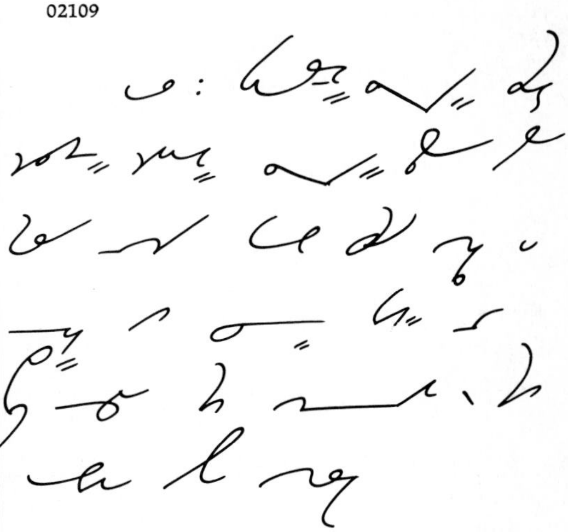

201. FREDERICK G. FRANKLIN, ESQ., HARRIS AND DONAVON, 160 STATE STREET, BOSTON, MA 02109

Lesson 68

BUILDING YOUR LEGAL VOCABULARY

Disjoined Word Endings

-lity and *-lty* are expressed by .

penalty 

admiralty 

cruelty 

legality 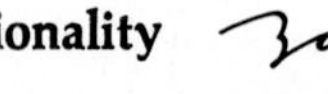

liabilities 

constitutionality

Word Study

ascertain To learn; find out.

assigns Those entitled to receive property; heirs.

enjoin To forbid or command by court order, usually an injunction.

rescind To cancel; withdraw; take back.

BUILDING YOUR LEGAL TRANSCRIPTION SKILL

Legal Collocations

negotiable instrument Written securities that may be transferred and negotiated, such as checks, promissory notes, and so on.

without recourse A phrase used in endorsing negotiable instruments which relieves the endorser from liability if the maker fails to pay the instrument when due.

pretrial conference A conference held prior to the trial at which the Court and the attorneys seek to simplify the issues in controversy and to eliminate matters not in dispute.

triplicate original A term used when the original and two carbon copies are signed and all treated as originals.

nominal damages Token damages or compensation for injury or loss for which the amount has not been proven.

BUILDING YOUR LEGAL DICTATION PROFICIENCY

Preview

conscientious	preclude
disbursements	prevails
docketed	pro rata
enforceable	sublessee
foreseeable	transmit

Reading and Writing Practice

202. COMMONWEALTH OF MASSACHUSETTS ESSEX, SS. APRIL TERM, 19—
SUPERIOR COURT EQUITY NO. 16205 BALDWIN'S, INC., V. GARDINER SHOPPING CENTER, INC., STETSON STORES, INC., LOVETT SHOE COMPANY, INC.

It is hereby stipulated and agreed by the parties that the following points of agreement may be entered in the record:[1]

1. That the petition of Baldwin's, Inc., is dismissed with prejudice.
2. That no damages[2] are awarded to any party.
3. That Lovett Shoe Company, Inc., shall terminate its arrangement[3] with Stetson Stores, Inc., on or before October 1, 19—.
4. Commencing[4] upon October 1, 19—, or at such earlier date as the arrangement between Lovett[5] Shoe Company, Inc., and Stetson Stores, Inc., is terminated, for the duration[6] of the term of the lease between Baldwin's, Inc., and Gardiner Shopping Center, Inc.,[7] dated January 12, 19—, and any renewals thereof, the minimum rental[8] payable by Baldwin's, Inc., shall be reduced at the rate of One Hundred Dollars ($100)[9] per month or a total of Twelve Hundred Dollars ($1200) per annum.
5. Article[10] VII. Section 1 of the lease between Gardiner Shopping Center, Inc., and Baldwin's, Inc.,[11] dated January 12, 19—, shall not be applicable to, or enforceable[12] against, Stetson Stores, Inc., its successors, or its assigns, with respect to any present or future retail[13] sales of shoes or handbags at the premises leased by Stetson Stores, Inc., from Gardiner Shopping[14] Center, Inc.
6. On October 1, 19—, or upon earlier[15] termination of Lovett Shoe Company, Inc.'s arrangement with Stetson Stores, Inc., Stetson[16] Stores, Inc., shall pay to Gardiner Shopping Center, Inc., the sum of One Hundred Dollars[17] ($100) per month additional rental for the duration of the term of the lease[18] between Baldwin's, Inc., and Gardiner Shopping Center, Inc., dated January 12,[19] 19—, and any renewals thereof; provided, however, that if, in the event of any[20] overage under Article IV, Section (d) of the lease between Stetson Stores, Inc., and[21] Gardiner Shopping Center, Inc., dated August 25, 19—, the first[22] Six Hundred Dollars ($600) of such overage shall be credited against the said Twelve Hundred[23] Dollars ($1200) of additional rental due.
7. Gardiner Shopping Center,[24] Inc., shall consent to sublease by Stetson Stores, Inc., to any responsible sublessee[25] of its shoe and handbag department.
8. The lease between Gardiner Shopping Center, Inc., and[26] Baldwin's, Inc., dated January 12, 19—, and the short-form lease between these[27] parties, dated January 12, 19—, recorded Essex County Records, Volume 885,[28] page 285, on August 18, 19—, and the lease between Gardiner Shopping[29] Center, Inc., and Stetson Stores, Inc., dated August 25, 19—,[30]

and short-form lease between the same parties, dated August 25, 19—, recorded[31] Volume 885, page 440, on September 11, 19—, are reformed to[32] conform with the provisions of this decree, which may be recorded by any party.

9. Nothing in the agreement[33] is intended to preclude Stetson Stores, Inc., from making an agreement subsequently with Lovett[34] Shoe Company, Inc., if the parties desire.

Baldwin's, Inc., by its attorneys: Maine,[35] Carlson, Galey, Gene & Bonn

By: ____________________

G. Peter Gary

Gardiner Shopping Center, Inc., by its[36] attorneys:
Willis, Norris, Sutherland, Nichols & Polk

By: ____________________

John H. Nichols

Stetson Stores, Inc., by its[37] attorneys:
Greenberg, O'Brien, Mason & McCann

By: ____________________

Lester L. Greenberg

Lovett Shoe Company, Inc.,[38] by its attorneys: Davis, Miller, Starr & Best

By: ____________________

Norma H. Starr (774)

203. FREDERICK G. FRANKLIN, ESQ., HARRIS AND DONAVON, 160 STATE STREET, BOSTON, MA 02109

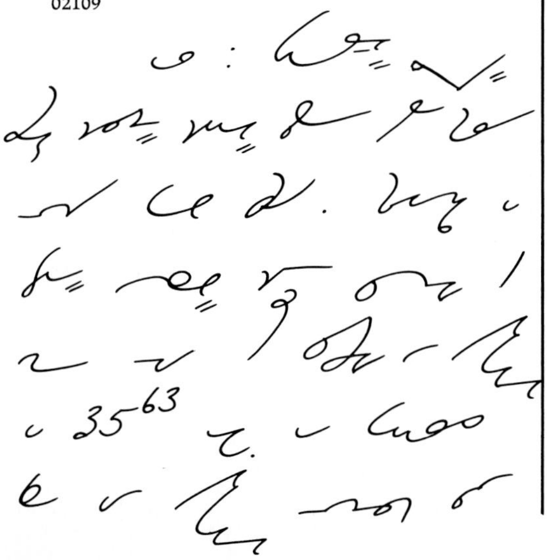

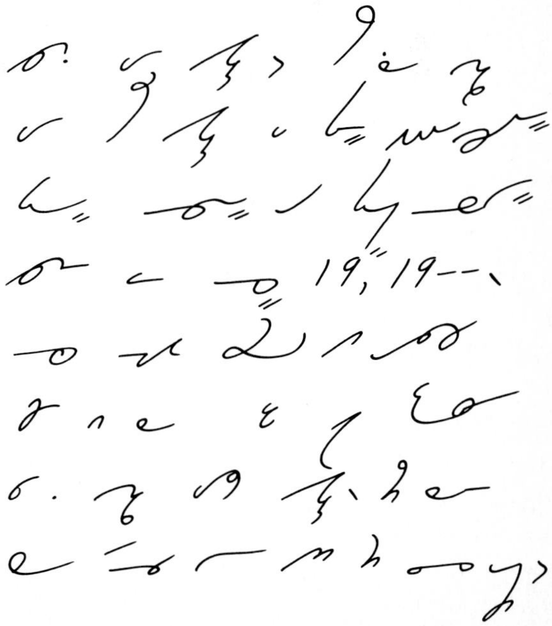

204. FREDERICK G. FRANKLIN, ESQ., HARRIS AND DONAVON, 160 STATE STREET, BOSTON, MA 02109

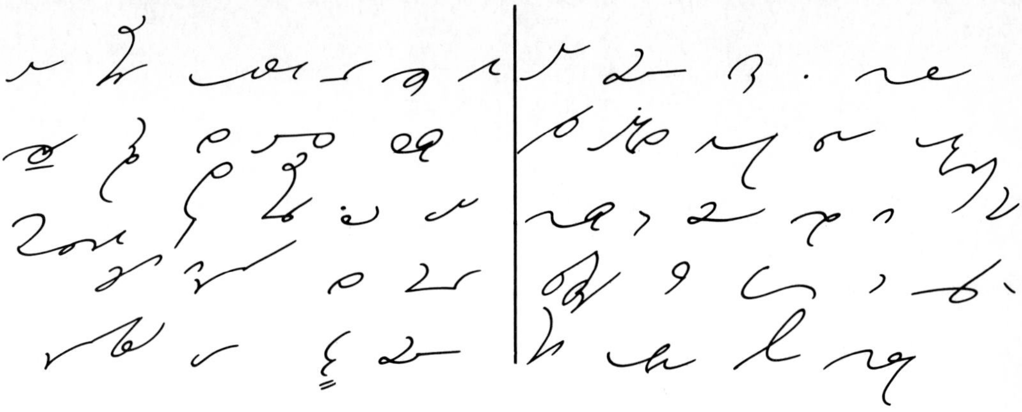

Lesson 69

BUILDING YOUR LEGAL VOCABULARY

Disjoined Word Endings

-rity is expressed by ◡ .

priorities

maturity

sureties

authorities

minority

securities

Word Study

monetary damages Relief in the form of money lost as a result of a breach of contract.

pecuniary damages Damages to be paid in money.

punitive damages Damages for more than the amount of the loss to punish the person who is to pay.

specific performance Fulfillment of an agreement according to the original terms instead of monetary damages.

BUILDING YOUR LEGAL TRANSCRIPTION SKILL

Latin Abbreviations

q.v. (**quod vide** *quod vī′ dē*) Which see.

ab init. (**ab initio** *ab in i′shē ō*) From the beginning.

viz. (**videlicet** *vi del′i set*) To wit; namely; that is to say.

BUILDING YOUR LEGAL DICTATION PROFICIENCY

Preview

accrued

engagement

expertise

forecast

integrated

renders

social security

withholding

Reading and Writing Practice

205. MEMORANDUM

14

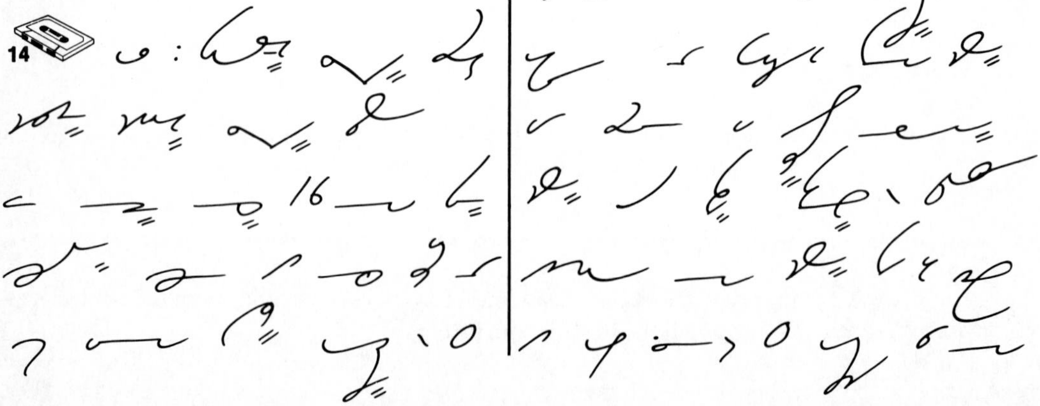

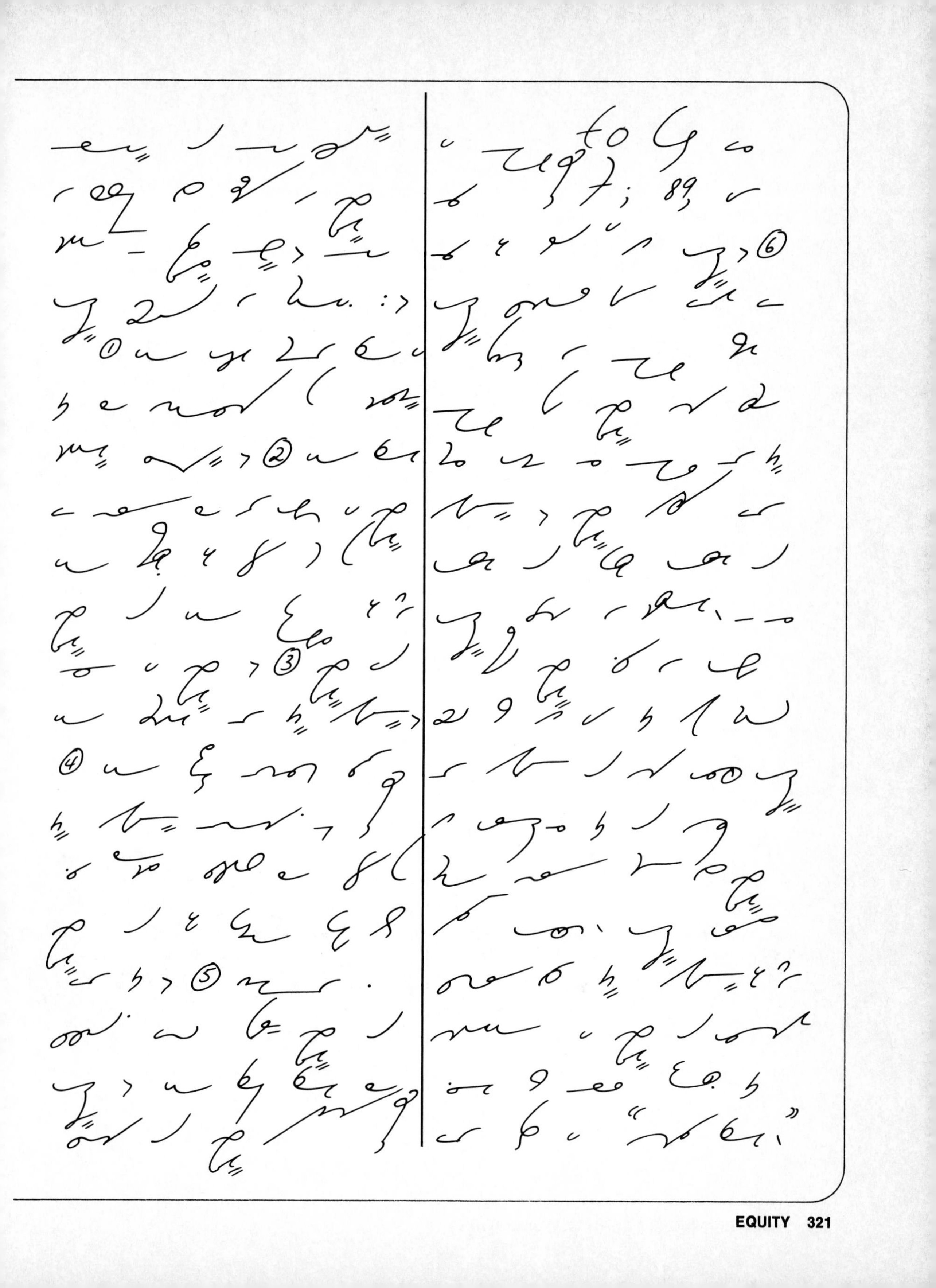

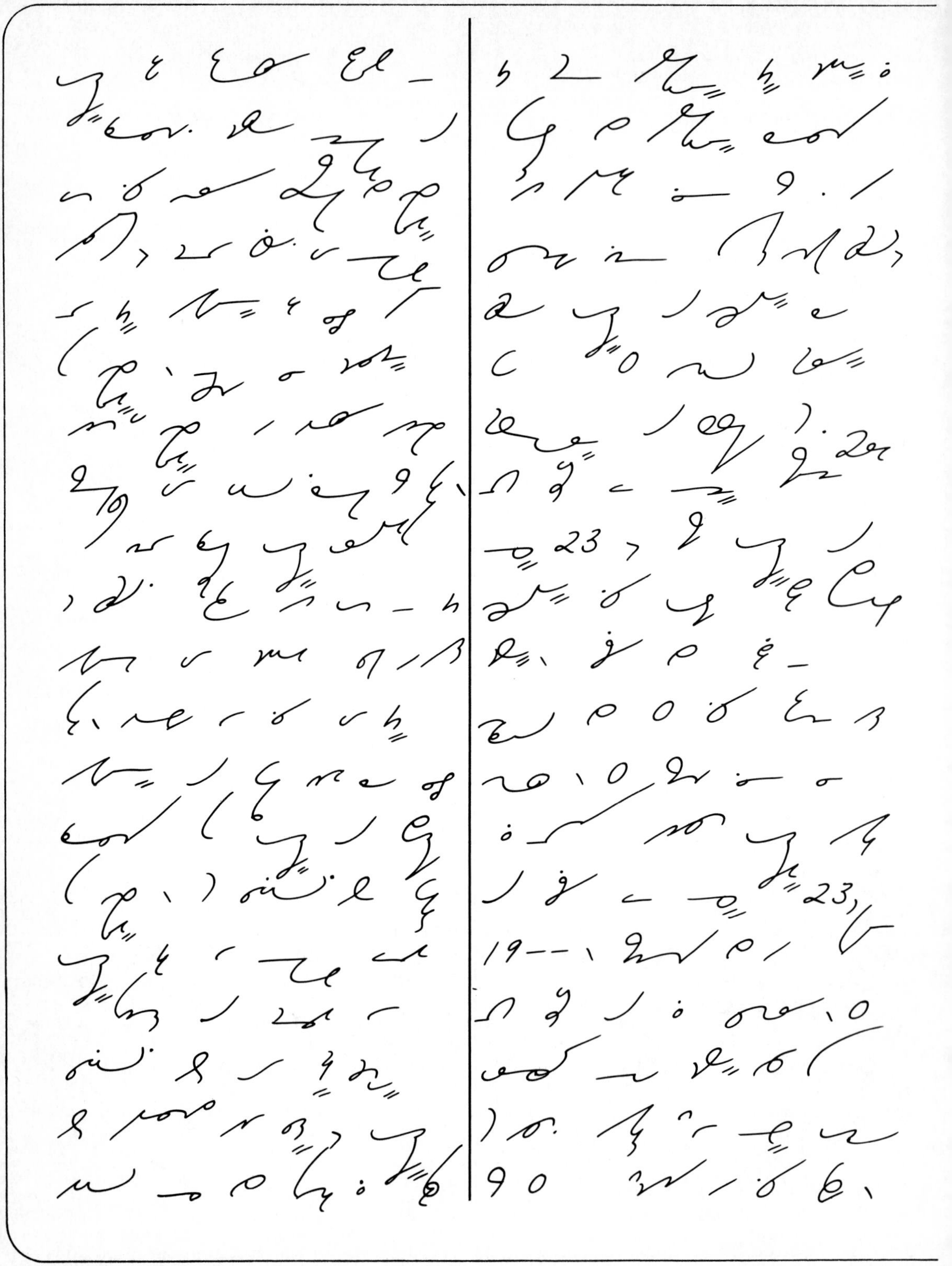

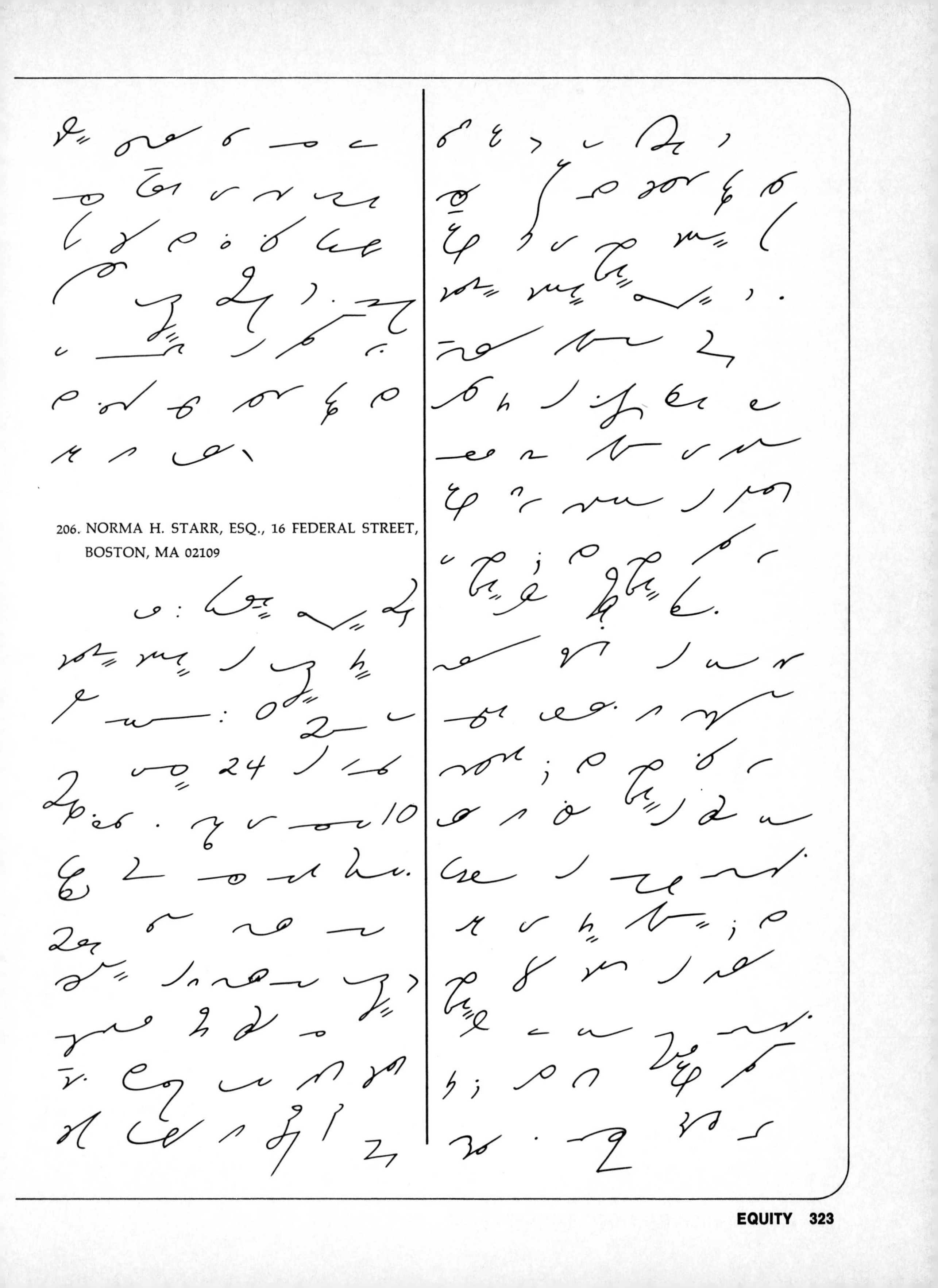

206. NORMA H. STARR, ESQ., 16 FEDERAL STREET, BOSTON, MA 02109

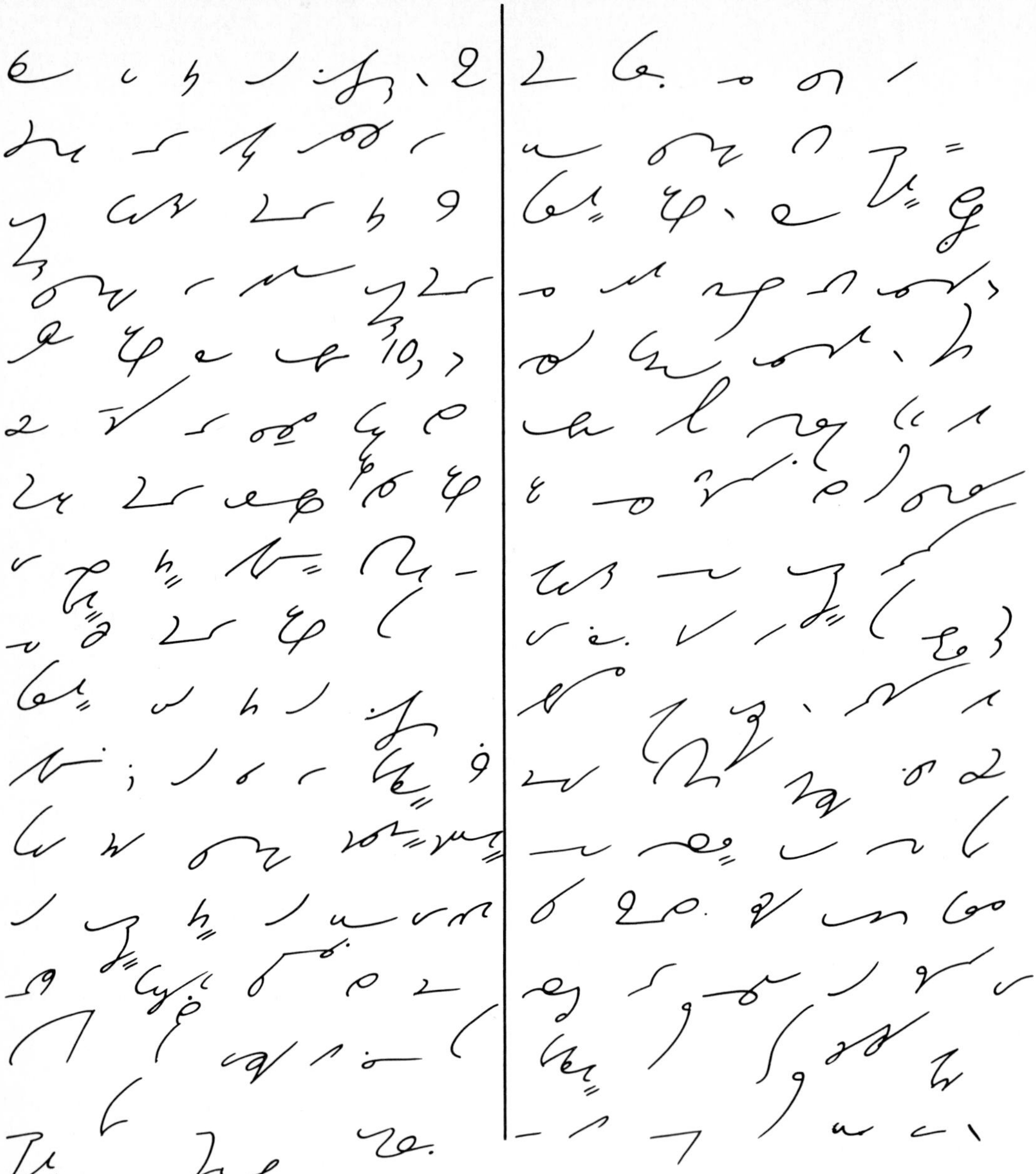

Lesson 70

BUILDING YOUR LEGAL VOCABULARY

Disjoined Word Endings *-ification* is expressed by .

diversification 

specifications 

ratification 

certification 

indemnification 

identification 

Word Study

 **chambers** Private office of the judge, usually just off the courtroom.

 **derogation** Annulment; disparagement.

 **moot** Unsettled; undecided, debatable, irrelevant.

BUILDING YOUR LEGAL TRANSCRIPTION SKILL

Typing Citations Legal Encyclopedias

When citing legal encyclopedias, list volume, topic, section, pages, and date.

7 Am. Jur. 2d, *Automobile Insurance* sec. 4691, p. 511, 1936

BUILDING YOUR LEGAL DICTATION PROFICIENCY

Preview

above-entitled 

elicited 

circumvent 

escalation 

prohibition 

purported 

sublessee 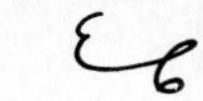

terminology 

Reading and Writing Practice

207. FREDERICK G. FRANKLIN, ESQ., HARRIS AND DONAVON, 160 STATE STREET, BOSTON, MA 02109

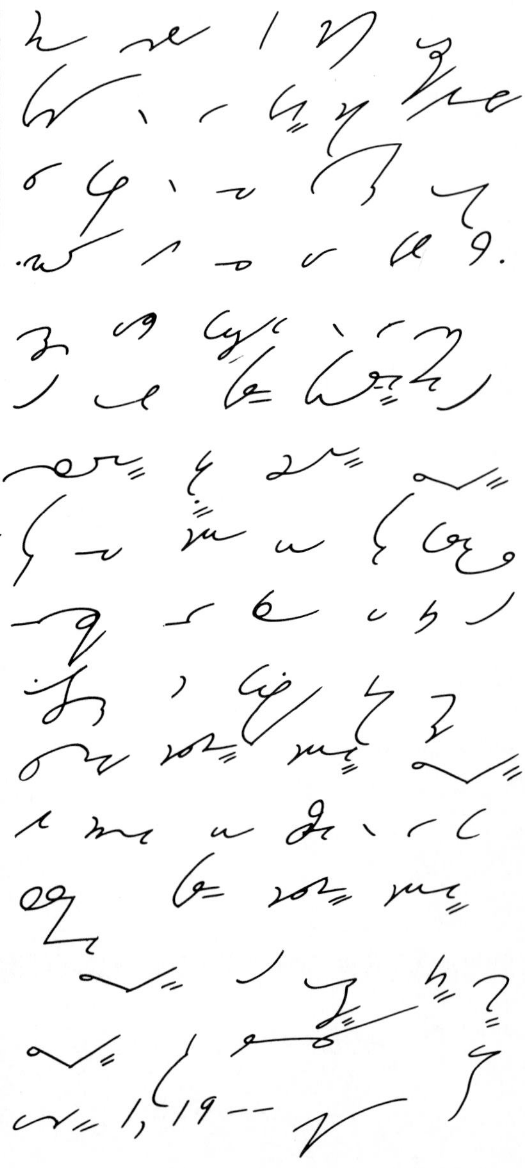

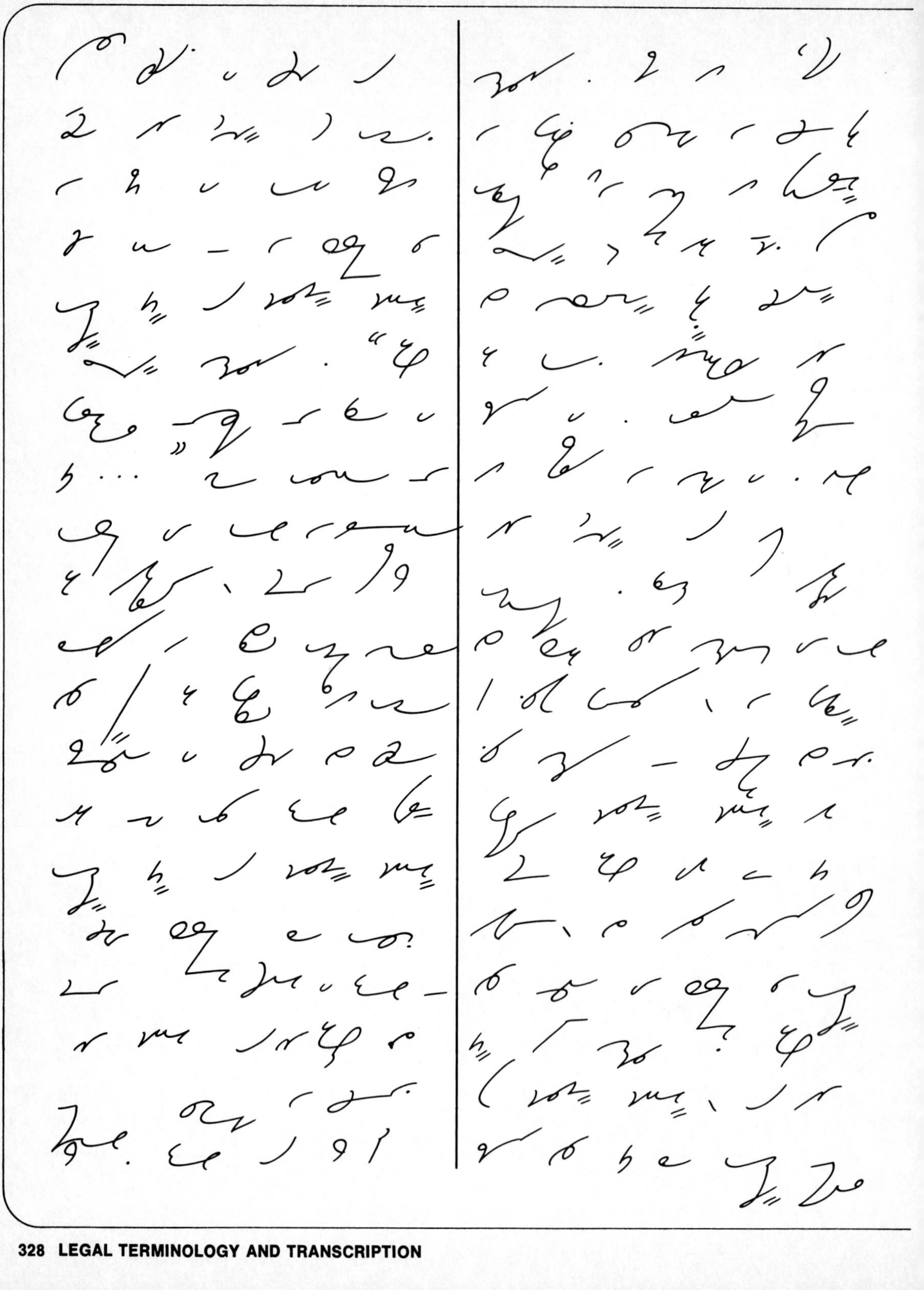

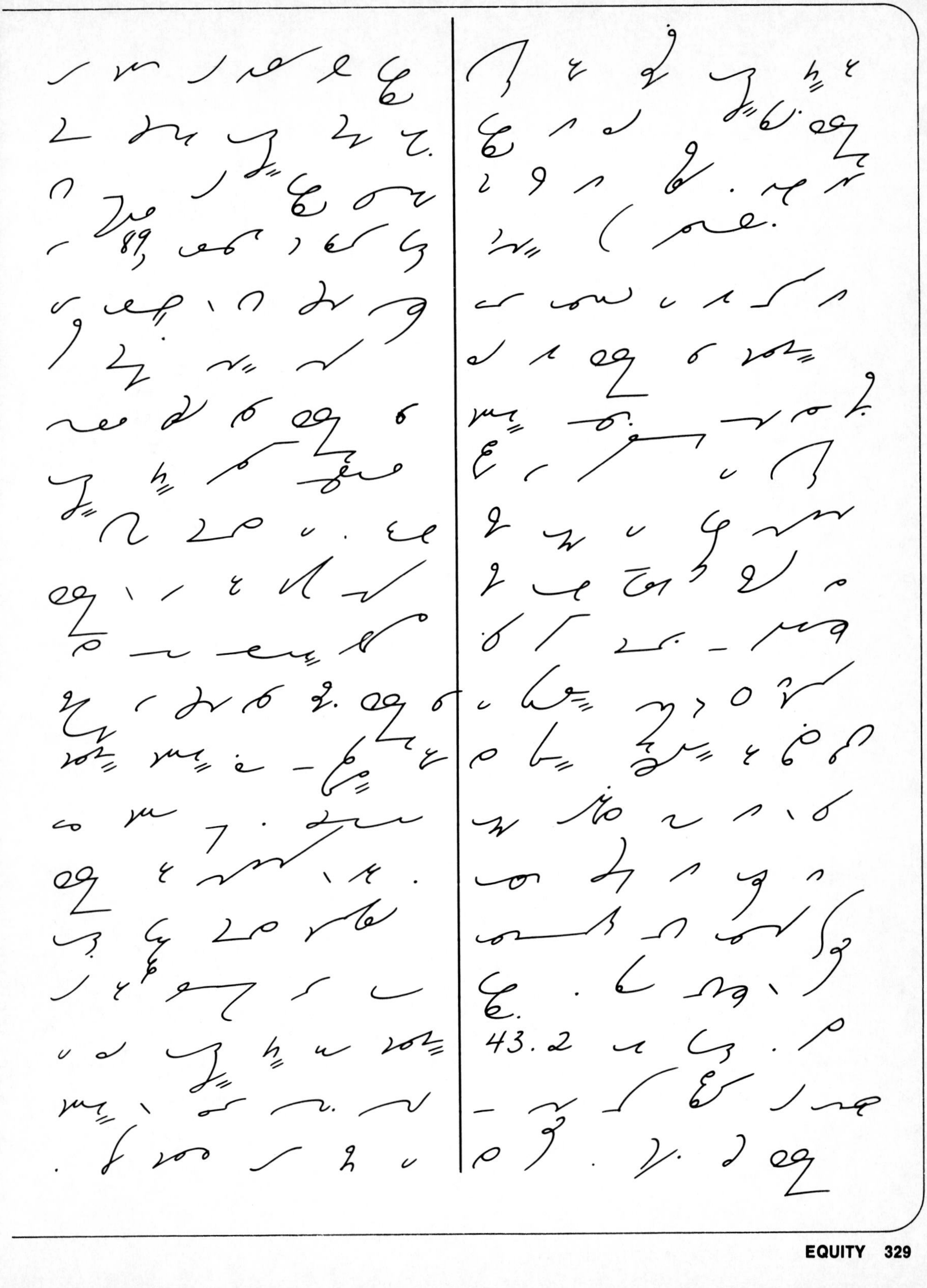

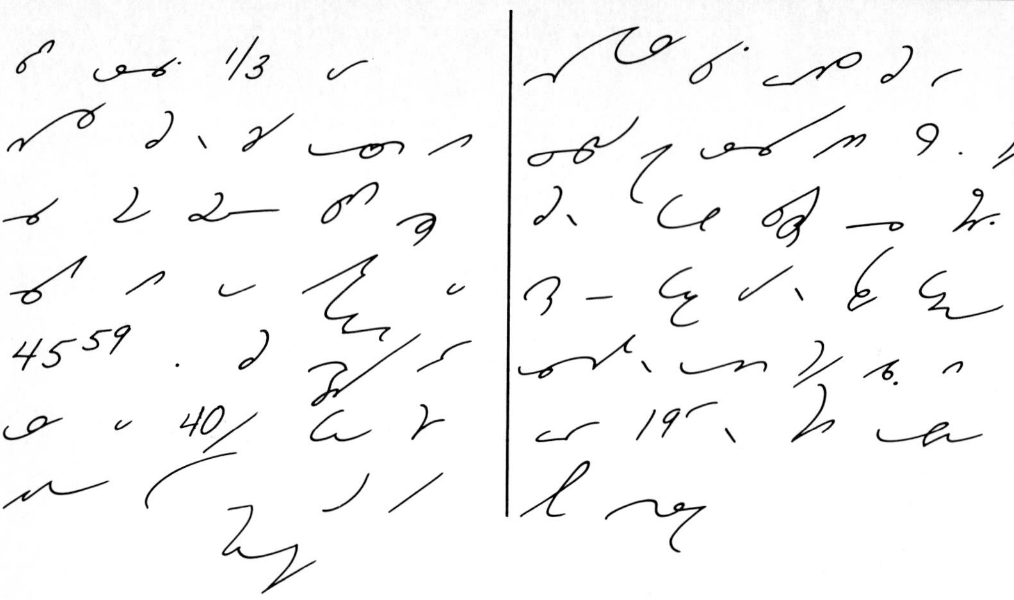

Index

Typing Citations

Transcription Aids

Complete Word List

(bold-face type indicates the lessons in which words are defined in the text.)